Table of Contents

Symbol Key / 2
Mercury Retrograde and Moon Void-of-Course /
How to Use the *Pocket Planner* / 5
World Map of Time Zones / 7
Time Zone Conversions / 8
Planetary Stations for 2018 / 9
2019 Week-at-a-Glance Calendar Pages / 10
2018–2020 Aspectarian and Ephemeris / 11

Mercury Retrograde 2019

	DATE	ET	PT			DATE	ET	PT
Mercury Retrograde	3/5	**1:19 pm**	10:19 am	—	Mercury Direct	3/28	**9:59 am**	6:59 am
Mercury Retrograde	7/7	**7:14 pm**	4:14 pm	—	Mercury Direct	7/31	**11:58 pm**	8:58 pm
Mercury Retrograde	10/31	**11:41 am**	8:41 am	—	Mercury Direct	11/20	**2:12 pm**	11:12 am

Moon Void-of-Course 2019

Times are listed in Eastern Time in this table only. All other information in the *Pocket Planner* is listed in both Eastern Time and Pacific Time. Refer to "Time Zone Conversions" on page 7 for changing to other time zones. Note: All times are corrected for daylight saving time.

Last Aspect		Moon Enters New Sign		
Date	Time	Date	Sign	Time
JANUARY				
1	5:26 pm	2	♐	3:58 am
4	12:41 pm	4	♑	1:55 pm
7	1:20 am	7	♒	1:46 am
9	11:53 am	9	♓	2:44 pm
11	9:25 am	12	♈	3:18 am
14	10:56 am	14	♉	1:31 pm
16	1:34 pm	16	♊	8:00 pm
18	8:32 pm	18	♋	10:44 pm
20	8:50 pm	20	♌	10:54 pm
22	8:19 pm	22	♍	10:22 pm
24	8:50 am	24	♎	11:02 pm
27	12:21 am	27	♏	2:31 am
28	5:39 pm	29	♐	9:33 am
31	5:33 pm	31	♑	7:47 pm

Last Aspect		Moon Enters New Sign		
Date	Time	Date	Sign	Time
FEBRUARY				
3	5:53 am	3	♒	8:03 am
5	6:59 pm	6	♓	9:02 pm
7	5:14 pm	8	♈	9:34 am
10	6:48 pm	10	♉	8:28 pm
12	5:26 pm	13	♊	4:32 am
15	7:48 am	15	♋	9:03 am
17	9:17 am	17	♌	10:21 am
19	8:51 am	19	♍	9:47 am
20	8:52 pm	21	♎	9:17 am
23	10:11 am	23	♏	10:56 am
25	7:14 am	25	♐	4:19 pm
28	1:17 am	28	♑	1:48 am

Last Aspect		Moon Enters New Sign		
Date	Time	Date	Sign	Time
MARCH				
2	1:47 pm	2	♒	2:06 pm
5	3:05 am	5	♓	3:11 am
7	2:08 pm	7	♈	3:27 pm
9	12:14 pm	10	♉	3:10 am
12	5:31 am	12	♊	11:48 am
14	8:30 am	14	♋	5:49 pm
16	2:03 pm	16	♌	8:57 pm
18	11:19 am	18	♍	9:41 pm
20	11:22 am	20	♎	9:28 pm
22	2:10 pm	22	♏	10:16 pm
24	10:24 pm	25	♐	2:06 am
26	10:37 pm	27	♑	10:07 am
29	8:05 pm	29	♒	9:46 pm
31	11:02 pm	4/1	♓	10:48 am

Moon Void-of-Course 2019 (cont.)

APRIL

Last Aspect		Moon Enters New Sign		
Date	Time	Date	Sign	Time
3/31	11:02 pm	1	♓	10:48 am
3	11:36 am	3	♈	10:56 pm
5	10:15 pm	6	♉	9:06 am
8	4:29 am	8	♊	5:15 pm
10	1:27 pm	10	♋	11:31 pm
12	7:33 pm	13	♌	3:50 am
14	9:38 pm	15	♍	6:14 am
17	12:29 am	17	♎	7:22 am
19	7:12 am	19	♏	8:41 am
21	12:00 am	21	♐	11:59 am
23	7:44 am	23	♑	6:50 pm
25	3:48 pm	26	♒	5:27 am
28	5:44 am	28	♓	6:11 pm
30	5:57 pm	5/1	♈	6:24 am

MAY

Last Aspect		Moon Enters New Sign		
Date	Time	Date	Sign	Time
4/30	5:57 pm	1	♈	6:24 am
3	4:47 am	3	♉	4:18 pm
5	11:10 am	5	♊	11:40 pm
7	7:50 pm	8	♋	5:06 am
9	10:06 pm	10	♌	9:14 am
12	8:24 am	12	♍	12:22 pm
14	1:19 pm	14	♎	2:51 pm
16	5:37 am	16	♏	5:26 pm
18	5:11 pm	18	♐	9:21 pm
20	1:05 pm	21	♑	3:56 am
22	11:58 pm	23	♒	1:49 pm
25	8:51 am	26	♓	2:08 am
28	12:21 am	28	♈	2:32 pm
30	11:08 am	31	♉	12:43 am

JUNE

Last Aspect		Moon Enters New Sign		
Date	Time	Date	Sign	Time
1	6:53 pm	2	♊	7:48 am
4	11:42 am	4	♋	12:17 pm
6	10:10 am	6	♌	3:16 pm
8	5:23 pm	8	♍	5:45 pm
10	8:01 am	10	♎	8:29 pm
12	11:15 am	13	♏	12:02 am
14	3:46 pm	15	♐	5:03 am
17	4:31 am	17	♑	12:13 pm
19	7:19 am	19	♒	10:01 pm
21	10:02 am	22	♓	10:01 am
24	7:10 pm	24	♈	10:38 pm
27	3:51 am	27	♉	9:32 am
29	2:38 pm	29	♊	5:09 pm

JULY

Last Aspect		Moon Enters New Sign		
Date	Time	Date	Sign	Time
1	5:48 pm	1	♋	9:24 pm
3	10:25 am	3	♌	11:19 pm
5	2:24 am	6	♍	12:25 am
7	12:50 pm	8	♎	2:07 am
9	3:36 pm	10	♏	5:29 am
11	8:28 pm	12	♐	11:05 am
13	9:30 pm	14	♑	7:05 pm
16	5:38 pm	17	♒	5:19 am
18	11:53 am	19	♓	5:19 pm
22	4:34 am	22	♈	6:02 am
24	10:48 am	24	♉	5:42 pm
27	12:28 am	27	♊	2:29 am
28	11:24 am	29	♋	7:31 am
30	11:32 pm	31	♌	9:18 am

AUGUST

Last Aspect		Moon Enters New Sign		
Date	Time	Date	Sign	Time
1	4:48 pm	2	♍	9:20 am
4	12:27 am	4	♎	9:30 am
6	3:36 am	6	♏	11:31 am
8	10:58 am	8	♐	4:35 pm
10	3:50 pm	11	♑	12:50 am
12	6:11 pm	13	♒	11:35 am
15	9:02 pm	15	♓	11:49 pm
17	6:35 pm	18	♈	12:33 pm
21	12:06 am	21	♉	12:37 am
22	5:33 pm	23	♊	10:34 am
25	2:58 am	25	♋	5:05 pm
27	4:55 am	27	♌	7:53 pm
28	8:07 pm	29	♍	7:57 pm
31	4:46 am	31	♎	7:08 pm

SEPTEMBER

Last Aspect		Moon Enters New Sign		
Date	Time	Date	Sign	Time
2	4:34 am	2	♏	7:35 pm
4	6:58 am	4	♐	11:08 pm
6	12:03 pm	7	♑	6:37 am
9	4:30 am	9	♒	5:24 pm
11	1:22 am	12	♓	5:52 am
14	12:33 am	14	♈	6:32 pm
16	12:03 pm	17	♉	6:31 am
19	9:57 am	19	♊	4:58 pm
21	10:41 pm	22	♋	12:50 am
23	6:05 pm	24	♌	5:19 am
25	12:14 pm	26	♍	6:37 am
27	11:58 pm	28	♎	6:03 am
29	10:06 pm	30	♏	5:42 am

OCTOBER

Last Aspect		Moon Enters New Sign		
Date	Time	Date	Sign	Time
2	5:46 am	2	♐	7:44 am
4	3:34 am	4	♑	1:43 pm
6	7:25 pm	6	♒	11:42 pm
8	2:27 pm	9	♓	12:05 pm
11	5:55 am	12	♈	12:46 am
13	5:59 pm	14	♉	12:24 pm
16	4:37 am	16	♊	10:30 pm
18	10:14 pm	19	♋	6:43 am
21	8:39 am	21	♌	12:29 pm
23	5:14 am	23	♍	3:29 pm
25	9:00 am	25	♎	4:20 pm
27	4:22 am	27	♏	4:29 pm
29	1:34 pm	29	♐	5:58 pm
31	10:30 am	31	♑	10:38 pm

NOVEMBER

Last Aspect		Moon Enters New Sign		
Date	Time	Date	Sign	Time
3	1:46 am	3	♒	6:19 am
5	9:37 am	5	♓	6:08 pm
7	8:13 pm	8	♈	6:49 am
10	9:00 am	10	♉	6:18 pm
12	10:48 am	13	♊	3:46 am
15	6:40 am	15	♋	11:15 am
17	3:14 pm	17	♌	4:57 pm
19	4:11 pm	19	♍	8:54 pm
21	10:31 pm	21	♎	11:20 pm
23	9:49 pm	24	♏	12:58 am
25	12:30 pm	26	♐	3:11 am
28	5:50 am	28	♑	7:33 am
29	10:57 pm	30	♒	3:13 pm

DECEMBER

Last Aspect		Moon Enters New Sign		
Date	Time	Date	Sign	Time
2	7:27 am	3	♓	2:11 am
5	3:15 am	5	♈	2:44 pm
7	10:01 am	8	♉	2:29 am
9	8:13 pm	10	♊	11:47 am
12	12:12 am	12	♋	6:23 pm
14	10:57 am	14	♌	10:56 pm
16	5:10 pm	17	♍	2:16 am
19	3:07 am	19	♎	5:04 am
21	6:45 am	21	♏	7:57 am
22	10:27 pm	23	♐	11:34 am
25	6:18 am	25	♑	4:45 pm
27	4:03 pm	28	♒	12:21 am
30	5:24 am	30	♓	10:41 am

How to Use the *Pocket Planner*

by Leslie Nielsen

This handy guide contains information that can be most valuable to you as you plan your daily activities. As you read through the first few pages, you can start to get a feel for how well organized this guide is.

Read the Symbol Key on the next page, which is rather like astrological shorthand. The characteristics of the planets can give you direction in planning your strategies. Much like traffic signs that signal "go," "stop," or even "caution," you can determine for yourself the most propitious time to get things done.

You'll find tables that show the dates when Mercury is retrograde (℞) or direct (D). Because Mercury deals with the exchange of information, a retrograde Mercury makes miscommunication more noticeable.

There's also a section dedicated to the times when the Moon is void-of-course (V/C). These are generally poor times to conduct business because activities begun during these times usually end badly or fail to get started. If you make an appointment during a void-of-course, you might save yourself a lot of aggravation by confirming the time and date later. The Moon is only void-of-course for 7 percent of the time when business is usually conducted during a normal workday (that is, 8:00 am to 5:00 pm). Sometimes, by waiting a matter of minutes or a few hours until the Moon has left the void-of-course phase, you have a much better chance to make action move more smoothly. Moon voids can also be used successfully to do routine activities or inner work, such as dream therapy or personal contemplation.

You'll find Moon phases, as well as each of the Moon's entries into a new sign. Times are expressed in Eastern time (in bold type) and Pacific time (in medium type). The New Moon time is generally best for beginning new activities, as the Moon is increasing in light and can offer the element of growth to our endeavors. When the Moon is Full, its illumination is greatest and we can see the results of our efforts. When it moves from the Full stage back to the New stage, it can best be used to reflect on our projects. If necessary, we can make corrections at the New Moon.

The section of "Planetary Stations" will give you the times when the planets are changing signs or direction, thereby affording us opportunities for new starts.

The ephemeris in the back of your *Pocket Planner* can be very helpful to you. As you start to work with the ephemeris, you may notice that not all planets seem to be comfortable in every sign. Think of the planets as actors, and the signs as the costumes they wear. Sometimes, costumes just itch. If you find this to be so for a certain time period, you may choose to delay your plans for a time or be more creative with the energies at hand.

As you turn to the daily pages, you'll find information about the Moon's sign, phase, and the time it changes phase. You'll find icons indicating the best days to plant and fish. Also, you will find times and dates when the planets and asteroids change sign and go either retrograde or direct, major holidays, a three-month calendar, and room to record your appointments.

This guide is a powerful tool. Make the most of it!

World Map of Time Zones

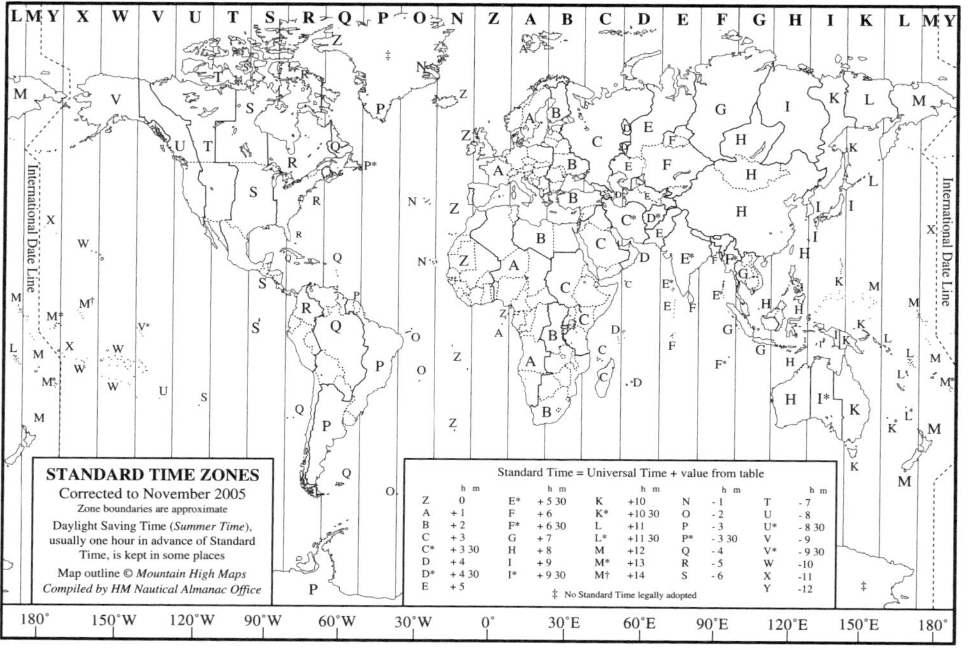
International Date Line
STANDARD TIME ZONES
Corrected to November 2005
Zone boundaries are approximate
Daylight Saving Time (Summer Time), usually one hour in advance of Standard Time, is kept in some places
Map outline © Mountain High Maps
Compiled by HM Nautical Almanac Office
Standard Time = Universal Time + value from table
Z 0, A +1, B +2, C +3, C* +3 30, D +4, D* +4 30, E +5
E* +5 30, F +6, F* +6 30, G +7, H +8, I +9, I* +9 30
K +10, K* +10 30, L +11, L* +11 30, M +12, M* +13, M† +14
N -1, O -2, P -3, P* -3 30, Q -4, R -5, S -6
T -7, U -8, U* -8 30, V -9, V* -9 30, W -10, X -11, Y -12
‡ No Standard Time legally adopted
180° 150°W 120°W 90°W 60°W 30°W 0° 30°E 60°E 90°E 120°E 150°E 180°

Time Zone Conversions

World Time Zones

Compared to Eastern Standard Time

( ) From Map
(S) CST/Subtract 1 hour
(R) EST
(Q) Add 1 hour
(P) Add 2 hours
(O) Add 3 hours
(N) Add 4 hours
(Z) Add 5 hours
(T) MST/Subtract 2 hours
(U) PST/Subtract 3 hours
(V) Subtract 4 hours
(W) Subtract 5 hours
(X) Subtract 6 hours
(Y) Subtract 7 hours
(A) Add 6 hours
(B) Add 7 hours
(C) Add 8 hours
(D) Add 9 hours
(E) Add 10 hours
(F) Add 11 hours
(G) Add 12 hours
(H) Add 13 hours
(I) Add 14 hours
(K) Add 15 hours
(L) Add 16 hours
(M) Add 17 hours
(C*) Add 8.5 hours
(D*) Add 9.5 hours
(E*) Add 10.5 hours
(F*) Add 11.5 hours
(I*) Add 14.5 hours
(K*) Add 15.5 hours
(L*) Add 16.5 hours
(M*) Add 18 hours
(P*) Add 2.5 hours
(U*) Subtract 3.5 hours
(V*) Subtract 4.5 hours

World Map of Time Zones is supplied by HM Nautical Almanac Office, © Center for the Central Laboratory of the Research Councils. Note: This is not an official map. Countries change their time zones as they wish.

Planetary Stations for 2019

	JAN	FEB	MAR	APR	MAY	JUN	JUL	AUG	SEP	OCT	NOV	DEC
☿			3/5–3/28				7/7–7/31				10/31–11/20	
♀												
♂												
♃						4/10–8/11						
♄							4/29–9/18					
♅	–1/6									8/11–1/10/20		
♆									6/21–11/27			
♇							4/24–10/3					
⚷									7/8–12/12			
⚳						4/9–7/17						
⚴				2/18–5/30								
⚵												
⚶											9/23–12/29	

31 Monday

4th ♏
♂ enters ♈ **9:20 pm** 6:20 pm

New Year's Eve

---

1 Tuesday

Butterfly
transformation } cocoon stage

4th ♏
☽ V/C **5:26 pm** 2:26 pm

New Year's Day • Kwanzaa ends

---

2 Wednesday

4th ♏
☽ enters ♐ **3:58 am** 12:58 am

---

3 Thursday

4th ♐

Eastern time in bold type
Pacific time in medium type

4 Friday

4th ♐
☽ V/C **12:41 pm** 9:41 am
☽ enters ♑ **1:55 pm** 10:55 am
☿ enters ♑ **10:40 pm** 7:40 pm

5 Saturday

4th ♑
New Moon **8:28 pm** 5:28 pm

6 Sunday

1st ♑
♅ D **3:27 pm** 12:27 pm
☽ V/C 10:20 pm
☽ enters ♒ 10:46 pm

December 2018

S	M	T	W	T	F	S
						1
2	3	4	5	6	7	8
9	10	11	12	13	14	15
16	17	18	19	20	21	22
23	24	25	26	27	28	29
30	31					

January 2019

S	M	T	W	T	F	S
		1	2	3	4	5
6	7	8	9	10	11	12
13	14	15	16	17	18	19
20	21	22	23	24	25	26
27	28	29	30	31		

February 2019

S	M	T	W	T	F	S
					1	2
3	4	5	6	7	8	9
10	11	12	13	14	15	16
17	18	19	20	21	22	23
24	25	26	27	28		

Eastern time in bold type
Pacific time in medium type

7 Monday
1st ♑
☽ V/C **1:20 am**
☽ enters ♒ **1:46 am**
♀ enters ♐ **6:18 am** 3:18 am

8 Tuesday
1st ♒

9 Wednesday
1st ♒
☽ V/C **11:53 am** 8:53 am
☽ enters ♓ **2:44 pm** 11:44 am

10 Thursday

1st ♓
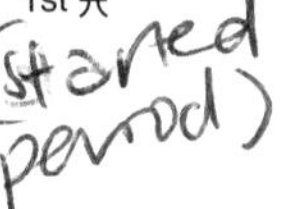

11 Friday

1st ♓

☽ V/C **9:25 am** 6:25 am

12 Saturday

1st ♓

☽ enters ♈ **3:18 am** 12:18 am

13 Sunday

1st ♈

2nd Quarter 10:46 pm

December 2018

S	M	T	W	T	F	S
						1
2	3	4	5	6	7	8
9	10	11	12	13	14	15
16	17	18	19	20	21	22
23	24	25	26	27	28	29
30	31					

January 2019

S	M	T	W	T	F	S
		1	2	3	4	5
6	7	8	9	10	11	12
13	14	15	16	17	18	19
20	21	22	23	24	25	26
27	28	29	30	31		

February 2019

S	M	T	W	T	F	S
					1	2
3	4	5	6	7	8	9
10	11	12	13	14	15	16
17	18	19	20	21	22	23
24	25	26	27	28		

Eastern time in bold type
Pacific time in medium type

14 Monday
1st ♈
2nd Quarter **1:46 am**
☽ V/C **10:56 am** 7:56 am
☽ enters ♉ **1:31 pm** 10:31 am

15 Tuesday

2nd ♉

16 Wednesday
2nd ♉
☽ V/C **1:34 pm** 10:34 am
☽ enters ♊ **8:00 pm** 5:00 pm

17 Thursday
2nd ♊

Eastern time in bold type
Pacific time in medium type

18 Friday
2nd ♊
☽ V/C **8:32 pm** 5:32 pm
☽ enters ♋ **10:44 pm** 7:44 pm

19 Saturday

2nd ♋

20 Sunday

2nd ♋
☉ enters ♒ **4:00 am** 1:00 am
☽ V/C **8:50 pm** 5:50 pm
☽ enters ♌ **10:54 pm** 7:54 pm
Full Moon 9:16 pm

December 2018

S	M	T	W	T	F	S
						1
2	3	4	5	6	7	8
9	10	11	12	13	14	15
16	17	18	19	20	21	22
23	24	25	26	27	28	29
30	31					

January 2019

S	M	T	W	T	F	S
		1	2	3	4	5
6	7	8	9	10	11	12
13	14	15	16	17	18	19
20	21	22	23	24	25	26
27	28	29	30	31		

February 2019

S	M	T	W	T	F	S
					1	2
3	4	5	6	7	8	9
10	11	12	13	14	15	16
17	18	19	20	21	22	23
24	25	26	27	28		

Eastern time in bold type
Pacific time in medium type

21 Monday
2nd ♌
Full Moon **12:16 am**

Martin Luther King Jr. Day

22 Tuesday
3rd ♌
☽ V/C **8:19 pm** 5:19 pm
☽ enters ♍ **10:22 pm** 7:22 pm

23 Wednesday
3rd ♍
☿ enters ♒ 9:49 pm

24 Thursday
3rd ♍
☿ enters ♒ **12:49 am**
☽ V/C **8:50 am** 5:50 am
☽ enters ♎ **11:02 pm** 8:02 pm

Eastern time in bold type
Pacific time in medium type

25 Friday

3rd ♎
⚳ enters ♐ **1:08 pm** 10:08 am

26 Saturday

3rd ♎
☽ V/C 9:21 pm
☽ enters ♏ 11:31 pm

27 Sunday

3rd ♎
☽ V/C **12:21 am**
☽ enters ♏ **2:31 am**
4th Quarter **4:10 pm** 1:10 pm

December 2018

S	M	T	W	T	F	S
						1
2	3	4	5	6	7	8
9	10	11	12	13	14	15
16	17	18	19	20	21	22
23	24	25	26	27	28	29
30	31					

January 2019

S	M	T	W	T	F	S
		1	2	3	4	5
6	7	8	9	10	11	12
13	14	15	16	17	18	19
20	21	22	23	24	25	26
27	28	29	30	31		

February 2019

S	M	T	W	T	F	S
					1	2
3	4	5	6	7	8	9
10	11	12	13	14	15	16
17	18	19	20	21	22	23
24	25	26	27	28		

Eastern time in bold type
Pacific time in medium type

28 Monday

4th ♏
☽ V/C **5:39 pm** 2:39 pm

29 Tuesday
4th ♏
☽ enters ♐ **9:33 am** 6:33 am

30 Wednesday
4th ♐

31 Thursday
4th ♐
☽ V/C **5:33 pm** 2:33 pm
☽ enters ♑ **7:47 pm** 4:47 pm

Eastern time in bold type
Pacific time in medium type

1 Friday

4th ♑

enters ♓ **6:04 am** 3:04 am

2 Saturday

4th ♑

Imbolc • Groundhog Day

3 Sunday

4th ♑

☽ V/C	**5:53 am**	2:53 am
☽ enters ♒	**8:03 am**	5:03 am
♀ enters ♑	**5:29 pm**	2:29 pm

January 2019

S	M	T	W	T	F	S
		1	2	3	4	5
6	7	8	9	10	11	12
13	14	15	16	17	18	19
20	21	22	23	24	25	26
27	28	29	30	31		

February 2019

S	M	T	W	T	F	S
					1	2
3	4	5	6	7	8	9
10	11	12	13	14	15	16
17	18	19	20	21	22	23
24	25	26	27	28		

March 2019

S	M	T	W	T	F	S
					1	2
3	4	5	6	7	8	9
10	11	12	13	14	15	16
17	18	19	20	21	22	23
24	25	26	27	28	29	30
31						

Eastern time in bold type
Pacific time in medium type

4 Monday
4th ♒
New Moon **4:04 pm** 1:04 pm

5 Tuesday
1st ♒
☽ V/C **6:59 pm** 3:59 pm
☽ enters ♓ **9:02 pm** 6:02 pm

Lunar New Year (Pig)

6 Wednesday
1st ♓

7 Thursday
1st ♓
☽ V/C **5:14 pm** 2:14 pm

Eastern time in bold type
Pacific time in medium type

8 Friday

1st ♓
☽ enters ♈ **9:34 am** 6:34 am

9 Saturday

1st ♈

10 Sunday

1st ♈
☿ enters ♓ **5:51 am** 2:51 am
☽ V/C **6:48 pm** 3:48 pm
☽ enters ♉ **8:28 pm** 5:28 pm
⚵ enters ♊ **11:21 pm** 8:21 pm

January 2019

S	M	T	W	T	F	S
		1	2	3	4	5
6	7	8	9	10	11	12
13	14	15	16	17	18	19
20	21	22	23	24	25	26
27	28	29	30	31		

February 2019

S	M	T	W	T	F	S
					1	2
3	4	5	6	7	8	9
10	11	12	13	14	15	16
17	18	19	20	21	22	23
24	25	26	27	28		

March 2019

S	M	T	W	T	F	S
					1	2
3	4	5	6	7	8	9
10	11	12	13	14	15	16
17	18	19	20	21	22	23
24	25	26	27	28	29	30
31						

11 Monday

1st ♉

12 Tuesday

1st ♉

☽ V/C	**5:26 pm**	2:26 pm
2nd Quarter	**5:26 pm**	2:26 pm

13 Wednesday

2nd ♉

☽ enters ♊	**4:32 am**	1:32 am

14 Thursday

2nd ♊

♂ enters ♉	**5:51 am**	2:51 am

Valentine's Day

Eastern time in bold type
Pacific time in medium type

15 Friday

2nd ♊
☽ V/C **7:48 am** 4:48 am
☽ enters ♋ **9:03 am** 6:03 am

16 Saturday

2nd ♋

17 Sunday

2nd ♋
☽ V/C **9:17 am** 6:17 am
☽ enters ♌ **10:21 am** 7:21 am

January 2019

S	M	T	W	T	F	S
		1	2	3	4	5
6	7	8	9	10	11	12
13	14	15	16	17	18	19
20	21	22	23	24	25	26
27	28	29	30	31		

February 2019

S	M	T	W	T	F	S
					1	2
3	4	5	6	7	8	9
10	11	12	13	14	15	16
17	18	19	20	21	22	23
24	25	26	27	28		

March 2019

S	M	T	W	T	F	S
					1	2
3	4	5	6	7	8	9
10	11	12	13	14	15	16
17	18	19	20	21	22	23
24	25	26	27	28	29	30
31						

Eastern time in bold type
Pacific time in medium type

18 Monday

2nd ♌
⚷ enters ♈ **4:10 am** 1:10 am
⚴ ℞ **11:40 am** 8:40 am
☉ enters ♓ **6:04 pm** 3:04 pm

Presidents' Day

19 Tuesday

2nd ♌
☽ V/C **8:51 am** 5:51 am
☽ enters ♍ **9:47 am** 6:47 am
Full Moon **10:54 am** 7:54 am

20 Wednesday

3rd ♍
 ☽ V/C **8:52 pm** 5:52 pm

21 Thursday

3rd ♍
☽ enters ♎ **9:17 am** 6:17 am

Eastern time in bold type
Pacific time in medium type

22 Friday
3rd ♎

23 Saturday

3rd ♎

☽ V/C **10:11 am** 7:11 am
☽ enters ♏ **10:56 am** 7:56 am

24 Sunday

3rd ♏

January 2019

S	M	T	W	T	F	S
		1	2	3	4	5
6	7	8	9	10	11	12
13	14	15	16	17	18	19
20	21	22	23	24	25	26
27	28	29	30	31		

February 2019

S	M	T	W	T	F	S
					1	2
3	4	5	6	7	8	9
10	11	12	13	14	15	16
17	18	19	20	21	22	23
24	25	26	27	28		

March 2019

S	M	T	W	T	F	S
					1	2
3	4	5	6	7	8	9
10	11	12	13	14	15	16
17	18	19	20	21	22	23
24	25	26	27	28	29	30
31						

25 Monday
3rd ♏
☽ V/C **7:14 am** 4:14 am
☽ enters ♐ **4:19 pm** 1:19 pm

26 Tuesday
3rd ♐
4th Quarter **6:28 am** 3:28 am

27 Wednesday
4th ♐
☽ V/C 10:17 pm
☽ enters ♑ 10:48 pm

28 Thursday

4th ♐
☽ V/C **1:17 am**
☽ enters ♑ **1:48 am**

Eastern time in bold type
Pacific time in medium type

1 Friday

4th ♑
♀ enters ♒ **11:45 am** 8:45 am

2 Saturday

4th ♑
☽ V/C **1:47 pm** 10:47 am
☽ enters ♒ **2:06 pm** 11:06 am

3 Sunday

4th ♒

February 2019

S	M	T	W	T	F	S
					1	2
3	4	5	6	7	8	9
10	11	12	13	14	15	16
17	18	19	20	21	22	23
24	25	26	27	28		

March 2019

S	M	T	W	T	F	S
					1	2
3	4	5	6	7	8	9
10	11	12	13	14	15	16
17	18	19	20	21	22	23
24	25	26	27	28	29	30
31						

April 2019

S	M	T	W	T	F	S
	1	2	3	4	5	6
7	8	9	10	11	12	13
14	15	16	17	18	19	20
21	22	23	24	25	26	27
28	29	30				

Eastern time in bold type
Pacific time in medium type

4 Monday
4th ♒

5 Tuesday

4th ♒

☽ V/C	**3:05 am**	12:05 am
☽ enters ♓	**3:11 am**	12:11 am
☿ ℞	**1:19 pm**	10:19 am

Mardi Gras (Fat Tuesday)

6 Wednesday
4th ♓

♅ enters ♉	**3:26 am**	12:26 am
New Moon	**11:04 am**	8:04 am

Ash Wednesday

7 Thursday

1st ♓

☽ V/C	**2:08 pm**	11:08 am
☽ enters ♈	**3:27 pm**	12:27 pm

Eastern time in bold type
Pacific time in medium type

8 Friday
1st ♈

9 Saturday
1st ♈

☽ V/C	**12:14 pm**	9:14 am
☽ enters ♉		11:10 pm

10 Sunday

1st ♈

☽ enters ♉ **3:10 am**

Daylight Saving Time begins at 2 am

February 2019

S	M	T	W	T	F	S
					1	2
3	4	5	6	7	8	9
10	11	12	13	14	15	16
17	18	19	20	21	22	23
24	25	26	27	28		

March 2019

S	M	T	W	T	F	S
					1	2
3	4	5	6	7	8	9
10	11	12	13	14	15	16
17	18	19	20	21	22	23
24	25	26	27	28	29	30
31						

April 2019

S	M	T	W	T	F	S
	1	2	3	4	5	6
7	8	9	10	11	12	13
14	15	16	17	18	19	20
21	22	23	24	25	26	27
28	29	30				

11 Monday

1st ♉

12 Tuesday

1st ♉

☽ V/C **5:31 am** 2:31 am

☽ enters ♊ **11:48 am** 8:48 am

13 Wednesday

1st ♊

14 Thursday

1st ♊

2nd Quarter **6:27 am** 3:27 am

☽ V/C **8:30 am** 5:30 am

☽ enters ♋ **5:49 pm** 2:49 pm

Eastern time in bold type

Pacific time in medium type

15 Friday
2nd ♋

16 Saturday
2nd ♋

☽ V/C **2:03 pm** 11:03 am
☽ enters ♌ **8:57 pm** 5:57 pm

17 Sunday
2nd ♌

St. Patrick's Day

February 2019

S	M	T	W	T	F	S
					1	2
3	4	5	6	7	8	9
10	11	12	13	14	15	16
17	18	19	20	21	22	23
24	25	26	27	28		

March 2019

S	M	T	W	T	F	S
					1	2
3	4	5	6	7	8	9
10	11	12	13	14	15	16
17	18	19	20	21	22	23
24	25	26	27	28	29	30
31						

April 2019

S	M	T	W	T	F	S
	1	2	3	4	5	6
7	8	9	10	11	12	13
14	15	16	17	18	19	20
21	22	23	24	25	26	27
28	29	30				

Eastern time in bold type
Pacific time in medium type

18 Monday
2nd ♌

☽ V/C	**11:19 am**	8:19 am
☽ enters ♍	**9:41 pm**	6:41 pm

19 Tuesday

2nd ♍

20 Wednesday
2nd ♍

☽ V/C	**11:22 am**	8:22 am
☉ enters ♈	**5:58 pm**	2:58 pm
☽ enters ♎	**9:28 pm**	6:28 pm
Full Moon	**9:43 pm**	6:43 pm

Ostara • Spring Equinox • Int'l Astrology Day

21 Thursday

3rd ♎

Eastern time in bold type
Pacific time in medium type

22 Friday
3rd ♎
☽ V/C **2:10 pm** 11:10 am
☽ enters ♏ **10:16 pm** 7:16 pm

23 Saturday
3rd ♏

24 Sunday
3rd ♏
☽ V/C **10:24 pm** 7:24 pm
☽ enters ♐ 11:06 pm

February 2019								March 2019								April 2019						
S	M	T	W	T	F	S		S	M	T	W	T	F	S		S	M	T	W	T	F	S
					1	2							1	2			1	2	3	4	5	6
3	4	5	6	7	8	9		3	4	5	6	7	8	9		7	8	9	10	11	12	13
10	11	12	13	14	15	16		10	11	12	13	14	15	16		14	15	16	17	18	19	20
17	18	19	20	21	22	23		17	18	19	20	21	22	23		21	22	23	24	25	26	27
24	25	26	27	28				24	25	26	27	28	29	30		28	29	30				
								31														

Eastern time in bold type
Pacific time in medium type

25 Monday

3rd ♏
☽ enters ♐ **2:06 am**

26 Tuesday

3rd ♐
♀ enters ♓ **3:43 pm** 12:43 pm
☽ V/C **10:37 pm** 7:37 pm

27 Wednesday

3rd ♐
☽ enters ♑ **10:07 am** 7:07 am
4th Quarter 9:10 pm

28 Thursday

3rd ♑
4th Quarter **12:10 am**
☿ D **9:59 am** 6:59 am

Eastern time in bold type
Pacific time in medium type

29 Friday

4th ♑

☽ V/C	**8:05 pm**	5:05 pm
☽ enters ♒	**9:46 pm**	6:46 pm

30 Saturday

4th ♒

♂ enters ♊		11:12 pm

31 Sunday

4th ♒

♂ enters ♊	**2:12 am**	
☽ V/C	**11:02 pm**	8:02 pm

February 2019

S	M	T	W	T	F	S
					1	2
3	4	5	6	7	8	9
10	11	12	13	14	15	16
17	18	19	20	21	22	23
24	25	26	27	28		

March 2019

S	M	T	W	T	F	S
					1	2
3	4	5	6	7	8	9
10	11	12	13	14	15	16
17	18	19	20	21	22	23
24	25	26	27	28	29	30
31						

April 2019

S	M	T	W	T	F	S
	1	2	3	4	5	6
7	8	9	10	11	12	13
14	15	16	17	18	19	20
21	22	23	24	25	26	27
28	29	30				

Eastern time in bold type
Pacific time in medium type

1 Monday

4th ♒
☽ enters ♓ **10:48 am** 7:48 am

Easter • April Fools' Day (All Fools' Day—Pagan)

2 Tuesday

4th ♓

3 Wednesday

4th ♓
⚶ enters ♈ **11:28 am** 8:28 am
☽ V/C **11:36 am** 8:36 am
☽ enters ♈ **10:56 pm** 7:56 pm

4 Thursday

4th ♈

Eastern time in bold type
Pacific time in medium type

5 Friday

4th ♈

New Moon **4:50 am** 1:50 am

☽ V/C **10:15 pm** 7:15 pm

6 Saturday

1st ♈

☽ enters ♉ **9:06 am** 6:06 am

7 Sunday

1st ♉

March 2019

S	M	T	W	T	F	S
					1	2
3	4	5	6	7	8	9
10	11	12	13	14	15	16
17	18	19	20	21	22	23
24	25	26	27	28	29	30
31						

April 2019

S	M	T	W	T	F	S
	1	2	3	4	5	6
7	8	9	10	11	12	13
14	15	16	17	18	19	20
21	22	23	24	25	26	27
28	29	30				

May 2019

S	M	T	W	T	F	S
			1	2	3	4
5	6	7	8	9	10	11
12	13	14	15	16	17	18
19	20	21	22	23	24	25
26	27	28	29	30	31	

Eastern time in bold type
Pacific time in medium type

8 Monday

1st ♉

☽ V/C	**4:29 am**	1:29 am
☽ enters ♊	**5:15 pm**	2:15 pm
⚳ ℞		9:35 pm

9 Tuesday

1st ♊

⚳ ℞	**12:35 am**	

10 Wednesday

1st ♊

♃ ℞	**1:01 pm**	10:01 am
☽ V/C	**1:27 pm**	10:27 am
☽ enters ♋	**11:31 pm**	8:31 pm

11 Thursday

1st ♋

Eastern time in bold type
Pacific time in medium type

12 Friday

1st ♋
2nd Quarter **3:06 pm** 12:06 pm
☽ V/C **7:33 pm** 4:33 pm

13 Saturday

2nd ♋
☽ enters ♌ **3:50 am** 12:50 am

14 Sunday

2nd ♌
☽ V/C **9:38 pm** 6:38 pm

Palm Sunday

March 2019

S	M	T	W	T	F	S
					1	2
3	4	5	6	7	8	9
10	11	12	13	14	15	16
17	18	19	20	21	22	23
24	25	26	27	28	29	30
31						

April 2019

S	M	T	W	T	F	S
	1	2	3	4	5	6
7	8	9	10	11	12	13
14	15	16	17	18	19	20
21	22	23	24	25	26	27
28	29	30				

May 2019

S	M	T	W	T	F	S
			1	2	3	4
5	6	7	8	9	10	11
12	13	14	15	16	17	18
19	20	21	22	23	24	25
26	27	28	29	30	31	

Eastern time in bold type
Pacific time in medium type

15 Monday
2nd ♌
☽ enters ♍ **6:14 am** 3:14 am

16 Tuesday
2nd ♍
☽ V/C 9:29 pm
☿ enters ♈ 11:01 pm

17 Wednesday
2nd ♍
☽ V/C **12:29 am**
☿ enters ♈ **2:01 am**
☽ enters ♎ **7:22 am** 4:22 am

18 Thursday

2nd ♎

Eastern time in bold type
Pacific time in medium type

19 Friday

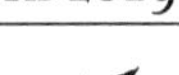

2nd ♎

☽ V/C	**7:12 am**	4:12 am
Full Moon	**7:12 am**	4:12 am
☽ enters ♏	**8:41 am**	5:41 am

Good Friday

20 Saturday

3rd ♏

☉ enters ♉	**4:55 am**	1:55 am
♀ enters ♈	**12:11 pm**	9:11 am
⚵ enters ♋	**12:38 pm**	9:38 am
☽ V/C		9:00 pm

Passover begins

21 Sunday

3rd ♏

☽ V/C	**12:00 am**	
☽ enters ♐	**11:59 am**	8:59 am

Easter

March 2019

S	M	T	W	T	F	S
					1	2
3	4	5	6	7	8	9
10	11	12	13	14	15	16
17	18	19	20	21	22	23
24	25	26	27	28	29	30
31						

April 2019

S	M	T	W	T	F	S
	1	2	3	4	5	6
7	8	9	10	11	12	13
14	15	16	17	18	19	20
21	22	23	24	25	26	27
28	29	30				

May 2019

S	M	T	W	T	F	S
			1	2	3	4
5	6	7	8	9	10	11
12	13	14	15	16	17	18
19	20	21	22	23	24	25
26	27	28	29	30	31	

Eastern time in bold type
Pacific time in medium type

22 Monday
3rd ♐

Earth Day

23 Tuesday
3rd ♐

☽ V/C	**7:44 am**	4:44 am
☽ enters ♑	**6:50 pm**	3:50 pm

24 Wednesday

3rd ♑

♇ ℞	**2:48 pm**	11:48 am

25 Thursday
3rd ♑

☽ V/C	**3:48 pm**	12:48 pm

Eastern time in bold type
Pacific time in medium type

26 Friday

3rd ♑
☽ enters ♒ **5:27 am** 2:27 am
4th Quarter **6:18 pm** 3:18 pm

Orthodox Good Friday

27 Saturday

4th ♒

Passover ends

28 Sunday

4th ♒
☽ V/C **5:44 am** 2:44 am
☽ enters ♓ **6:11 pm** 3:11 pm

Orthodox Easter

March 2019

S	M	T	W	T	F	S
					1	2
3	4	5	6	7	8	9
10	11	12	13	14	15	16
17	18	19	20	21	22	23
24	25	26	27	28	29	30
31						

April 2019

S	M	T	W	T	F	S
	1	2	3	4	5	6
7	8	9	10	11	12	13
14	15	16	17	18	19	20
21	22	23	24	25	26	27
28	29	30				

May 2019

S	M	T	W	T	F	S
			1	2	3	4
5	6	7	8	9	10	11
12	13	14	15	16	17	18
19	20	21	22	23	24	25
26	27	28	29	30	31	

29 Monday

4th ♓
♄ ℞ **8:54 pm** 5:54 pm

30 Tuesday

4th ♓
☽ V/C **5:57 pm** 2:57 pm

1 Wednesday

4th ♓
☽ enters ♈ **6:24 am** 3:24 am

Beltane

2 Thursday

4th ♈

Eastern time in bold type
Pacific time in medium type

3 Friday

4th ♈
☽ V/C **4:47 am** 1:47 am
☽ enters ♉ **4:18 pm** 1:18 pm

4 Saturday

4th ♉
New Moon **6:45 pm** 3:45 pm

5 Sunday

1st ♉
☽ V/C **11:10 am** 8:10 am
☽ enters ♊ **11:40 pm** 8:40 pm

Cinco de Mayo

April 2019

S	M	T	W	T	F	S
	1	2	3	4	5	6
7	8	9	10	11	12	13
14	15	16	17	18	19	20
21	22	23	24	25	26	27
28	29	30				

May 2019

S	M	T	W	T	F	S
			1	2	3	4
5	6	7	8	9	10	11
12	13	14	15	16	17	18
19	20	21	22	23	24	25
26	27	28	29	30	31	

June 2019

S	M	T	W	T	F	S
						1
2	3	4	5	6	7	8
9	10	11	12	13	14	15
16	17	18	19	20	21	22
23	24	25	26	27	28	29
30						

Eastern time in bold type
Pacific time in medium type

6 Monday
1st ♊
☿ enters ♉ **2:25 pm** 11:25 am

Ramadan begins

7 Tuesday
1st ♊
☽ V/C **7:50 pm** 4:50 pm

8 Wednesday
1st ♊
☽ enters ♋ **5:06 am** 2:06 am

9 Thursday
1st ♋
☽ V/C **10:06 pm** 7:06 pm

Eastern time in bold type
Pacific time in medium type

10 Friday

1st ♋
☽ enters ♌ **9:14 am** 6:14 am

11 Saturday

1st ♌
2nd Quarter **9:12 pm** 6:12 pm

12 Sunday

2nd ♌
☽ V/C **8:24 am** 5:24 am
☽ enters ♍ **12:22 pm** 9:22 am

Mother's Day

April 2019

S	M	T	W	T	F	S
	1	2	3	4	5	6
7	8	9	10	11	12	13
14	15	16	17	18	19	20
21	22	23	24	25	26	27
28	29	30				

May 2019

S	M	T	W	T	F	S
			1	2	3	4
5	6	7	8	9	10	11
12	13	14	15	16	17	18
19	20	21	22	23	24	25
26	27	28	29	30	31	

June 2019

S	M	T	W	T	F	S
						1
2	3	4	5	6	7	8
9	10	11	12	13	14	15
16	17	18	19	20	21	22
23	24	25	26	27	28	29
30						

Eastern time in bold type
Pacific time in medium type

13 Monday
2nd ♍

14 Tuesday
2nd ♍
☽ V/C **1:19 pm** 10:19 am
☽ enters ♎ **2:51 pm** 11:51 am

15 Wednesday
2nd ♎
♀ enters ♉ **5:46 am** 2:46 am
♂ enters ♋ **11:09 pm** 8:09 pm

16 Thursday
2nd ♎
☽ V/C **5:37 am** 2:37 am
☽ enters ♏ **5:26 pm** 2:26 pm

Eastern time in bold type
Pacific time in medium type

17 Friday

2nd ♏

18 Saturday

2nd ♏

☽ V/C **5:11 pm** 2:11 pm

Full Moon **5:11 pm** 2:11 pm

☽ enters ♐ **9:21 pm** 6:21 pm

19 Sunday

3rd ♐

April 2019

S	M	T	W	T	F	S
	1	2	3	4	5	6
7	8	9	10	11	12	13
14	15	16	17	18	19	20
21	22	23	24	25	26	27
28	29	30				

May 2019

S	M	T	W	T	F	S
			1	2	3	4
5	6	7	8	9	10	11
12	13	14	15	16	17	18
19	20	21	22	23	24	25
26	27	28	29	30	31	

June 2019

S	M	T	W	T	F	S
						1
2	3	4	5	6	7	8
9	10	11	12	13	14	15
16	17	18	19	20	21	22
23	24	25	26	27	28	29
30						

Eastern time in bold type
Pacific time in medium type

20 Monday
3rd ♐
☽ V/C **1:05 pm** 10:05 am

21 Tuesday
3rd ♐
☽ enters ♑ **3:56 am** 12:56 am
☉ enters ♊ **3:59 am** 12:59 am
☿ enters ♊ **6:52 am** 3:52 am

22 Wednesday

3rd ♑
☽ V/C **11:58 pm** 8:58 pm

23 Thursday
3rd ♑
☽ enters ♒ **1:49 pm** 10:49 am

Eastern time in bold type
Pacific time in medium type

24 Friday

3rd ≈

25 Saturday

3rd ≈

☽ V/C	**8:51 am**	5:51 am
☽ enters ♓		11:08 pm

26 Sunday

3rd ≈

☽ enters ♓	**2:08 am**	
4th Quarter	**12:34 pm**	9:34 am

April 2019

S	M	T	W	T	F	S
	1	2	3	4	5	6
7	8	9	10	11	12	13
14	15	16	17	18	19	20
21	22	23	24	25	26	27
28	29	30				

May 2019

S	M	T	W	T	F	S
			1	2	3	4
5	6	7	8	9	10	11
12	13	14	15	16	17	18
19	20	21	22	23	24	25
26	27	28	29	30	31	

June 2019

S	M	T	W	T	F	S
						1
2	3	4	5	6	7	8
9	10	11	12	13	14	15
16	17	18	19	20	21	22
23	24	25	26	27	28	29
30						

27 Monday

4th ♓
☽ V/C 9:21 pm

Memorial Day

28 Tuesday

4th ♓
☽ V/C **12:21 am**
☽ enters ♈ **2:32 pm** 11:32 am

29 Wednesday

4th ♈

30 Thursday

4th ♈
☽ V/C **11:08 am** 8:08 am
☿ D **10:52 pm** 7:52 pm
☽ enters ♉ 9:43 pm

Eastern time in bold type
Pacific time in medium type

31 Friday

4th ♈
☽ enters ♉ **12:43 am**

1 Saturday

4th ♉
☽ V/C **6:53 pm** 3:53 pm

2 Sunday

4th ♉
☽ enters ♊ **7:48 am** 4:48 am

May 2019

S	M	T	W	T	F	S
			1	2	3	4
5	6	7	8	9	10	11
12	13	14	15	16	17	18
19	20	21	22	23	24	25
26	27	28	29	30	31	

June 2019

S	M	T	W	T	F	S
						1
2	3	4	5	6	7	8
9	10	11	12	13	14	15
16	17	18	19	20	21	22
23	24	25	26	27	28	29
30						

July 2019

S	M	T	W	T	F	S
	1	2	3	4	5	6
7	8	9	10	11	12	13
14	15	16	17	18	19	20
21	22	23	24	25	26	27
28	29	30	31			

Eastern time in bold type
Pacific time in medium type

3 Monday
4th ♊
New Moon **6:02 am** 3:02 am

4 Tuesday
1st ♊
☽ V/C **11:42 am** 8:42 am
☽ enters ♋ **12:17 pm** 9:17 am
☿ enters ♋ **4:05 pm** 1:05 pm

Ramadan ends

5 Wednesday

1st ♋

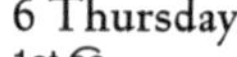

6 Thursday

1st ♋
☽ V/C **10:10 am** 7:10 am

☽ enters ♌ **3:16 pm** 12:16 pm

Eastern time in bold type
Pacific time in medium type

7 Friday

1st ♌

8 Saturday

1st ♌

☽ V/C	**5:23 pm**	2:23 pm
☽ enters ♍	**5:45 pm**	2:45 pm
♀ enters ♊	**9:37 pm**	6:37 pm

9 Sunday

1st ♍

⚵ enters ♉	**5:55 am**	2:55 am
2nd Quarter		10:59 am

May 2019

S	M	T	W	T	F	S
			1	2	3	4
5	6	7	8	9	10	11
12	13	14	15	16	17	18
19	20	21	22	23	24	25
26	27	28	29	30	31	

June 2019

S	M	T	W	T	F	S
						1
2	3	4	5	6	7	8
9	10	11	12	13	14	15
16	17	18	19	20	21	22
23	24	25	26	27	28	29
30						

July 2019

S	M	T	W	T	F	S
	1	2	3	4	5	6
7	8	9	10	11	12	13
14	15	16	17	18	19	20
21	22	23	24	25	26	27
28	29	30	31			

Eastern time in bold type
Pacific time in medium type

10 Monday

1st ♍
2nd Quarter **1:59 am**
☽ V/C **8:01 am** 5:01 am
☽ enters ♎ **8:29 pm** 5:29 pm

11 Tuesday

2nd ♎

12 Wednesday

2nd ♎
☽ V/C **11:15 am** 8:15 am
☽ enters ♏ 9:02 pm

13 Thursday

2nd ♎
☽ enters ♏ **12:02 am**

Eastern time in bold type
Pacific time in medium type

14 Friday

2nd ♏
☽ V/C **3:46 pm** 12:46 pm

Flag Day

15 Saturday

2nd ♏
☽ enters ♐ **5:03 am** 2:03 am

16 Sunday

2nd ♐

Father's Day

May 2019

S	M	T	W	T	F	S
			1	2	3	4
5	6	7	8	9	10	11
12	13	14	15	16	17	18
19	20	21	22	23	24	25
26	27	28	29	30	31	

June 2019

S	M	T	W	T	F	S
						1
2	3	4	5	6	7	8
9	10	11	12	13	14	15
16	17	18	19	20	21	22
23	24	25	26	27	28	29
30						

July 2019

S	M	T	W	T	F	S
	1	2	3	4	5	6
7	8	9	10	11	12	13
14	15	16	17	18	19	20
21	22	23	24	25	26	27
28	29	30	31			

Eastern time in bold type
Pacific time in medium type

17 Monday

2nd ♐

☽ V/C	**4:31 am**	1:31 am
Full Moon	**4:31 am**	1:31 am
☽ enters ♑	**12:13 pm**	9:13 am

18 Tuesday

3rd ♑

19 Wednesday

3rd ♑

☽ V/C	**7:19 am**	4:19 am
☽ enters ♒	**10:01 pm**	7:01 pm

20 Thursday

3rd ♒

⚵ enters ♌	**10:37 pm**	7:37 pm

Eastern time in bold type
Pacific time in medium type

21 Friday

3rd ≈

☽ V/C **10:02 am** 7:02 am

♆ ℞ **10:36 am** 7:36 am

☉ enters ♋ **11:54 am** 8:54 am

Litha • Summer Solstice

22 Saturday

3rd ≈

☽ enters ♓ **10:01 am** 7:01 am

23 Sunday

3rd ♓

May 2019

S	M	T	W	T	F	S
			1	2	3	4
5	6	7	8	9	10	11
12	13	14	15	16	17	18
19	20	21	22	23	24	25
26	27	28	29	30	31	

June 2019

S	M	T	W	T	F	S
						1
2	3	4	5	6	7	8
9	10	11	12	13	14	15
16	17	18	19	20	21	22
23	24	25	26	27	28	29
30						

July 2019

S	M	T	W	T	F	S
	1	2	3	4	5	6
7	8	9	10	11	12	13
14	15	16	17	18	19	20
21	22	23	24	25	26	27
28	29	30	31			

Eastern time in bold type
Pacific time in medium type

24 Monday

3rd ♓
☽ V/C **7:10 pm** 4:10 pm
☽ enters ♈ **10:38 pm** 7:38 pm

25 Tuesday

3rd ♈
4th Quarter **5:46 am** 2:46 am

26 Wednesday

4th ♈
☿ enters ♌ **8:19 pm** 5:19 pm

27 Thursday

4th ♈
☽ V/C **3:51 am** 12:51 am
☽ enters ♉ **9:32 am** 6:32 am

Eastern time in bold type
Pacific time in medium type

28 Friday

4th ♉

29 Saturday

4th ♉

☽ V/C	**2:38 pm**	11:38 am
☽ enters ♊	**5:09 pm**	2:09 pm

30 Sunday

4th ♊

May 2019

S	M	T	W	T	F	S
			1	2	3	4
5	6	7	8	9	10	11
12	13	14	15	16	17	18
19	20	21	22	23	24	25
26	27	28	29	30	31	

June 2019

S	M	T	W	T	F	S
						1
2	3	4	5	6	7	8
9	10	11	12	13	14	15
16	17	18	19	20	21	22
23	24	25	26	27	28	29
30						

July 2019

S	M	T	W	T	F	S
	1	2	3	4	5	6
7	8	9	10	11	12	13
14	15	16	17	18	19	20
21	22	23	24	25	26	27
28	29	30	31			

Eastern time in bold type
Pacific time in medium type

1 Monday

4th ♊
☽ V/C **5:48 pm** 2:48 pm
♂ enters ♌ **7:19 pm** 4:19 pm
☽ enters ♋ **9:24 pm** 6:24 pm

2 Tuesday

4th ♋
New Moon **3:16 pm** 12:16 pm

3 Wednesday

1st ♋
☽ V/C **10:25 am** 7:25 am
♀ enters ♋ **11:18 am** 8:18 am
☽ enters ♌ **11:19 pm** 8:19 pm

4 Thursday

1st ♌
☽ V/C 11:24 pm

Independence Day

Eastern time in bold type
Pacific time in medium type

5 Friday

1st ♌
☽ V/C **2:24 am**
☽ enters ♍ 9:25 pm

6 Saturday

1st ♌
☽ enters ♍ **12:25 am**

7 Sunday

1st ♍
☽ V/C **12:50 pm** 9:50 am
☿ ℞ **7:14 pm** 4:14 pm
☽ enters ♎ 11:07 pm

June 2019

S	M	T	W	T	F	S
						1
2	3	4	5	6	7	8
9	10	11	12	13	14	15
16	17	18	19	20	21	22
23	24	25	26	27	28	29
30						

July 2019

S	M	T	W	T	F	S
	1	2	3	4	5	6
7	8	9	10	11	12	13
14	15	16	17	18	19	20
21	22	23	24	25	26	27
28	29	30	31			

August 2019

S	M	T	W	T	F	S
				1	2	3
4	5	6	7	8	9	10
11	12	13	14	15	16	17
18	19	20	21	22	23	24
25	26	27	28	29	30	31

Eastern time in bold type
Pacific time in medium type

8 Monday

1st ♍

☽ enters ♎	**2:07 am**	
⚷ ℞	**7:40 pm**	4:40 pm

---

9 Tuesday

1st ♎

2nd Quarter	**6:55 am**	3:55 am
☽ V/C	**3:36 pm**	12:36 pm

---

10 Wednesday

2nd ♎

☽ enters ♏	**5:29 am**	2:29 am

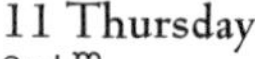

11 Thursday

2nd ♏

☽ V/C	**8:28 pm**	5:28 pm

Eastern time in bold type
Pacific time in medium type

12 Friday

2nd ♏
☽ enters ♐ **11:05 am** 8:05 am

13 Saturday

2nd ♐
☽ V/C **9:30 pm** 6:30 pm

14 Sunday

2nd ♐
☽ enters ♑ **7:05 pm** 4:05 pm

June 2019

S	M	T	W	T	F	S
						1
2	3	4	5	6	7	8
9	10	11	12	13	14	15
16	17	18	19	20	21	22
23	24	25	26	27	28	29
30						

July 2019

S	M	T	W	T	F	S
	1	2	3	4	5	6
7	8	9	10	11	12	13
14	15	16	17	18	19	20
21	22	23	24	25	26	27
28	29	30	31			

August 2019

S	M	T	W	T	F	S
				1	2	3
4	5	6	7	8	9	10
11	12	13	14	15	16	17
18	19	20	21	22	23	24
25	26	27	28	29	30	31

Eastern time in bold type
Pacific time in medium type

15 Monday

2nd ♑

16 Tuesday

2nd ♑

☽ V/C	**5:38 pm**	2:38 pm
Full Moon	**5:38 pm**	2:38 pm

17 Wednesday

3rd ♑

☽ enters ♒	**5:19 am**	2:19 am
⚳ D	**3:06 pm**	12:06 pm

18 Thursday

3rd ♒

☽ V/C	**11:53 am**	8:53 am

Eastern time in bold type
Pacific time in medium type

19 Friday

3rd ♒
☿ enters ♋ **3:06 am** 12:06 am
☽ enters ♓ **5:19 pm** 2:19 pm

20 Saturday

3rd ♓

21 Sunday

3rd ♓

June 2019

S	M	T	W	T	F	S
						1
2	3	4	5	6	7	8
9	10	11	12	13	14	15
16	17	18	19	20	21	22
23	24	25	26	27	28	29
30						

July 2019

S	M	T	W	T	F	S
	1	2	3	4	5	6
7	8	9	10	11	12	13
14	15	16	17	18	19	20
21	22	23	24	25	26	27
28	29	30	31			

August 2019

S	M	T	W	T	F	S
				1	2	3
4	5	6	7	8	9	10
11	12	13	14	15	16	17
18	19	20	21	22	23	24
25	26	27	28	29	30	31

22 Monday

3rd ♓

☽ V/C	**4:34 am**	1:34 am
☽ enters ♈	**6:02 am**	3:02 am
☉ enters ♌	**10:50 pm**	7:50 pm

23 Tuesday

3rd ♈

24 Wednesday

3rd ♈

☽ V/C	**10:48 am**	7:48 am
☽ enters ♉	**5:42 pm**	2:42 pm
4th Quarter	**9:18 pm**	6:18 pm

25 Thursday

4th ♉

Eastern time in bold type
Pacific time in medium type

26 Friday

4th ♉
☽ V/C 9:28 pm
☽ enters ♊ 11:29 pm

27 Saturday

4th ♉
☽ V/C **12:28 am**
☽ enters ♊ **2:29 am**
♀ enters ♌ **9:54 pm** 6:54 pm

28 Sunday

4th ♊
☽ V/C **11:24 am** 8:24 am

June 2019

S	M	T	W	T	F	S
						1
2	3	4	5	6	7	8
9	10	11	12	13	14	15
16	17	18	19	20	21	22
23	24	25	26	27	28	29
30						

July 2019

S	M	T	W	T	F	S
	1	2	3	4	5	6
7	8	9	10	11	12	13
14	15	16	17	18	19	20
21	22	23	24	25	26	27
28	29	30	31			

August 2019

S	M	T	W	T	F	S
				1	2	3
4	5	6	7	8	9	10
11	12	13	14	15	16	17
18	19	20	21	22	23	24
25	26	27	28	29	30	31

Eastern time in bold type
Pacific time in medium type

29 Monday

4th ♊

☽ enters ♋ **7:31 am** 4:31 am

30 Tuesday

4th ♋

☽ V/C **11:32 pm** 8:32 pm

31 Wednesday

4th ♋

☽ enters ♌ **9:18 am** 6:18 am

New Moon **11:12 pm** 8:12 pm

☿ D **11:58 pm** 8:58 pm

1 Thursday

1st ♌

☽ V/C **4:48 pm** 1:48 pm

Lammas

Eastern time in bold type
Pacific time in medium type

2 Friday
1st ♌
☽ enters ♍ **9:20 am** 6:20 am

3 Saturday
1st ♍
☽ V/C 9:27 pm

4 Sunday
1st ♍
☽ V/C **12:27 am**
☽ enters ♎ **9:30 am** 6:30 am

July 2019

S	M	T	W	T	F	S
	1	2	3	4	5	6
7	8	9	10	11	12	13
14	15	16	17	18	19	20
21	22	23	24	25	26	27
28	29	30	31			

August 2019

S	M	T	W	T	F	S
				1	2	3
4	5	6	7	8	9	10
11	12	13	14	15	16	17
18	19	20	21	22	23	24
25	26	27	28	29	30	31

September 2019

S	M	T	W	T	F	S
1	2	3	4	5	6	7
8	9	10	11	12	13	14
15	16	17	18	19	20	21
22	23	24	25	26	27	28
29	30					

Eastern time in bold type
Pacific time in medium type

5 Monday

1st ♎

6 Tuesday

1st ♎

☽ V/C **3:36 am** 12:36 am

☽ enters ♏ **11:31 am** 8:31 am

7 Wednesday

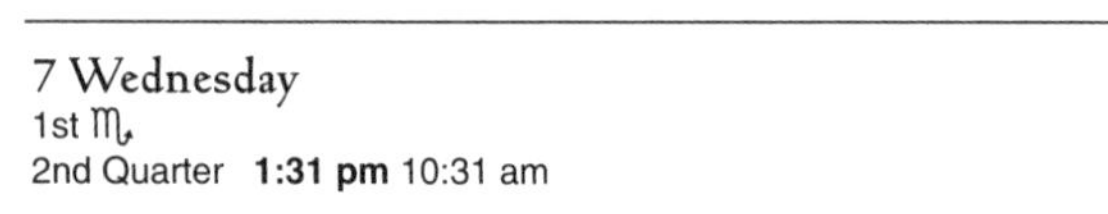

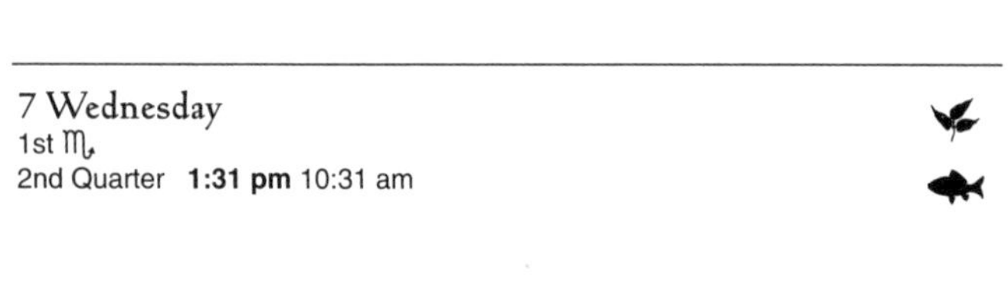

1st ♏

2nd Quarter **1:31 pm** 10:31 am

8 Thursday

2nd ♏

☽ V/C **10:58 am** 7:58 am

☽ enters ♐ **4:35 pm** 1:35 pm

Eastern time in bold type

Pacific time in medium type

9 Friday
2nd ♐

10 Saturday
2nd ♐

☽ V/C	**3:50 pm**	12:50 pm
☽ enters ♑		9:50 pm

11 Sunday
2nd ♐

☽ enters ♑	**12:50 am**	
♃ D	**9:37 am**	6:37 am
☿ enters ♌	**3:46 pm**	12:46 pm
♅ ℞	**10:27 pm**	7:27 pm

July 2019

S	M	T	W	T	F	S
	1	2	3	4	5	6
7	8	9	10	11	12	13
14	15	16	17	18	19	20
21	22	23	24	25	26	27
28	29	30	31			

August 2019

S	M	T	W	T	F	S
				1	2	3
4	5	6	7	8	9	10
11	12	13	14	15	16	17
18	19	20	21	22	23	24
25	26	27	28	29	30	31

September 2019

S	M	T	W	T	F	S
1	2	3	4	5	6	7
8	9	10	11	12	13	14
15	16	17	18	19	20	21
22	23	24	25	26	27	28
29	30					

12 Monday

2nd ♑

☽ V/C **6:11 pm** 3:11 pm

13 Tuesday

2nd ♑

☽ enters ♒ **11:35 am** 8:35 am

14 Wednesday

2nd ♒

15 Thursday

2nd ♒

Full Moon **8:29 am** 5:29 am

☽ V/C **9:02 pm** 6:02 pm

☽ enters ♓ **11:49 pm** 8:49 pm

Eastern time in bold type
Pacific time in medium type

16 Friday

3rd ♓

17 Saturday

3rd ♓

☽ V/C	**6:35 pm**	3:35 pm
♂ enters ♍		10:18 pm

18 Sunday

3rd ♓

♂ enters ♍	**1:18 am**	
☽ enters ♈	**12:33 pm**	9:33 am

July 2019

S	M	T	W	T	F	S
	1	2	3	4	5	6
7	8	9	10	11	12	13
14	15	16	17	18	19	20
21	22	23	24	25	26	27
28	29	30	31			

August 2019

S	M	T	W	T	F	S
				1	2	3
4	5	6	7	8	9	10
11	12	13	14	15	16	17
18	19	20	21	22	23	24
25	26	27	28	29	30	31

September 2019

S	M	T	W	T	F	S
1	2	3	4	5	6	7
8	9	10	11	12	13	14
15	16	17	18	19	20	21
22	23	24	25	26	27	28
29	30					

Eastern time in bold type
Pacific time in medium type

19 Monday
3rd ♈

20 Tuesday
3rd ♈

☽ V/C 9:06 pm

☽ enters ♉ 9:37 pm

21 Wednesday
3rd ♈

☽ V/C **12:06 am**

☽ enters ♉ **12:37 am**

♀ enters ♍ 5:06 am 2:06 am

22 Thursday

3rd ♉

☽ V/C **5:33 pm** 2:33 pm

Eastern time in bold type
Pacific time in medium type

23 Friday

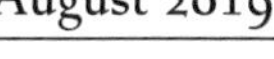

3rd ♉
☉ enters ♍ **6:02 am** 3:02 am
☽ enters ♊ **10:34 am** 7:34 am
4th Quarter **10:56 am** 7:56 am
⚵ enters ♍ **8:00 pm** 5:00 pm

24 Saturday

4th ♊
☽ V/C 11:58 pm

25 Sunday

4th ♊
☽ V/C **2:58 am**
☽ enters ♋ **5:05 pm** 2:05 pm

July 2019

S	M	T	W	T	F	S
	1	2	3	4	5	6
7	8	9	10	11	12	13
14	15	16	17	18	19	20
21	22	23	24	25	26	27
28	29	30	31			

August 2019

S	M	T	W	T	F	S
				1	2	3
4	5	6	7	8	9	10
11	12	13	14	15	16	17
18	19	20	21	22	23	24
25	26	27	28	29	30	31

September 2019

S	M	T	W	T	F	S
1	2	3	4	5	6	7
8	9	10	11	12	13	14
15	16	17	18	19	20	21
22	23	24	25	26	27	28
29	30					

Eastern time in bold type
Pacific time in medium type

26 Monday

4th ♋
♀ enters ♏ **4:56 am** 1:56 am

27 Tuesday

4th ♋
☽ V/C **4:55 am** 1:55 am
☽ enters ♌ **7:53 pm** 4:53 pm

28 Wednesday

4th ♌
☽ V/C **8:07 pm** 5:07 pm

29 Thursday

4th ♌
☿ enters ♍ **3:48 am** 12:48 am
☽ enters ♍ **7:57 pm** 4:57 pm

Eastern time in bold type
Pacific time in medium type

30 Friday

4th ♍

New Moon	**6:37 am**	3:37 am

31 Saturday

1st ♍

☽ V/C	**4:46 am**	1:46 am
☽ enters ♎	**7:08 pm**	4:08 pm

Islamic New Year

1 Sunday

1st ♎

August 2019

S	M	T	W	T	F	S
				1	2	3
4	5	6	7	8	9	10
11	12	13	14	15	16	17
18	19	20	21	22	23	24
25	26	27	28	29	30	31

September 2019

S	M	T	W	T	F	S
1	2	3	4	5	6	7
8	9	10	11	12	13	14
15	16	17	18	19	20	21
22	23	24	25	26	27	28
29	30					

October 2019

S	M	T	W	T	F	S
		1	2	3	4	5
6	7	8	9	10	11	12
13	14	15	16	17	18	19
20	21	22	23	24	25	26
27	28	29	30	31		

2 Monday

1st ♎
☽ V/C **4:34 am** 1:34 am
☽ enters ♏ **7:35 pm** 4:35 pm

Labor Day

---

3 Tuesday

1st ♏

---

4 Wednesday

1st ♏
☽ V/C **6:58 am** 3:58 am
☽ enters ♐ **11:08 pm** 8:08 pm

---

5 Thursday

1st ♐
2nd Quarter **11:10 pm** 8:10 pm

Eastern time in bold type
Pacific time in medium type

6 Friday

2nd ♐
☽ V/C **12:03 pm** 9:03 am

7 Saturday

2nd ♐
☽ enters ♑ **6:37 am** 3:37 am

8 Sunday

2nd ♑

August 2019

S	M	T	W	T	F	S
				1	2	3
4	5	6	7	8	9	10
11	12	13	14	15	16	17
18	19	20	21	22	23	24
25	26	27	28	29	30	31

September 2019

S	M	T	W	T	F	S
1	2	3	4	5	6	7
8	9	10	11	12	13	14
15	16	17	18	19	20	21
22	23	24	25	26	27	28
29	30					

October 2019

S	M	T	W	T	F	S
		1	2	3	4	5
6	7	8	9	10	11	12
13	14	15	16	17	18	19
20	21	22	23	24	25	26
27	28	29	30	31		

Eastern time in bold type
Pacific time in medium type

9 Monday

2nd ♑
☽ V/C **4:30 am** 1:30 am
☽ enters ♒ **5:24 pm** 2:24 pm

10 Tuesday

2nd ♒
☽ V/C 10:22 pm

11 Wednesday

2nd ♒
☽ V/C **1:22 am**

12 Thursday

2nd ♒
☽ enters ♓ **5:52 am** 2:52 am

Eastern time in bold type
Pacific time in medium type

13 Friday

2nd ♓

☽ V/C 9:33 pm

Full Moon 9:33 pm

14 Saturday

2nd ♓

☽ V/C **12:33 am**

Full Moon **12:33 am**

☿ enters ♎ **3:14 am** 12:14 am

♀ enters ♎ **9:43 am** 6:43 am

☽ enters ♈ **6:32 pm** 3:32 pm

15 Sunday

3rd ♈

August 2019

S	M	T	W	T	F	S
				1	2	3
4	5	6	7	8	9	10
11	12	13	14	15	16	17
18	19	20	21	22	23	24
25	26	27	28	29	30	31

September 2019

S	M	T	W	T	F	S
1	2	3	4	5	6	7
8	9	10	11	12	13	14
15	16	17	18	19	20	21
22	23	24	25	26	27	28
29	30					

October 2019

S	M	T	W	T	F	S
		1	2	3	4	5
6	7	8	9	10	11	12
13	14	15	16	17	18	19
20	21	22	23	24	25	26
27	28	29	30	31		

16 Monday

3rd ♈

☽ V/C **12:03 pm** 9:03 am

17 Tuesday

3rd ♈

☽ enters ♉ **6:31 am** 3:31 am

18 Wednesday

3rd ♉

♄ D **4:47 am** 1:47 am

19 Thursday

3rd ♉

☽ V/C **9:57 am** 6:57 am

☽ enters ♊ **4:58 pm** 1:58 pm

Eastern time in bold type
Pacific time in medium type

20 Friday
3rd ♊

21 Saturday
3rd ♊

☽ V/C	**10:41 pm**	7:41 pm
4th Quarter	**10:41 pm**	7:41 pm
☽ enters ♋		9:50 pm

UN International Day of Peace

22 Sunday

4th ♊

☽ enters ♋ **12:50 am**

August 2019

S	M	T	W	T	F	S
				1	2	3
4	5	6	7	8	9	10
11	12	13	14	15	16	17
18	19	20	21	22	23	24
25	26	27	28	29	30	31

September 2019

S	M	T	W	T	F	S
1	2	3	4	5	6	7
8	9	10	11	12	13	14
15	16	17	18	19	20	21
22	23	24	25	26	27	28
29	30					

October 2019

S	M	T	W	T	F	S
		1	2	3	4	5
6	7	8	9	10	11	12
13	14	15	16	17	18	19
20	21	22	23	24	25	26
27	28	29	30	31		

Eastern time in bold type
Pacific time in medium type

23 Monday

4th ♋
☉ enters ♎ **3:50 am** 12:50 am
☽ V/C **6:05 pm** 3:05 pm
⚶ R **11:43 pm** 8:43 pm

Mabon • Fall Equinox

24 Tuesday

4th ♋
☽ enters ♌ **5:19 am** 2:19 am

25 Wednesday

4th ♌
☽ V/C **12:14 pm** 9:14 am

26 Thursday

4th ♌
☽ enters ♍ **6:37 am** 3:37 am

Eastern time in bold type
Pacific time in medium type

27 Friday

4th ♍

☽ V/C **11:58 pm** 8:58 pm

28 Saturday

4th ♍

☽ enters ♎ **6:03 am** 3:03 am

New Moon **2:26 pm** 11:26 am

29 Sunday

1st ♎

☽ V/C **10:06 pm** 7:06 pm

August 2019

S	M	T	W	T	F	S
				1	2	3
4	5	6	7	8	9	10
11	12	13	14	15	16	17
18	19	20	21	22	23	24
25	26	27	28	29	30	31

September 2019

S	M	T	W	T	F	S
1	2	3	4	5	6	7
8	9	10	11	12	13	14
15	16	17	18	19	20	21
22	23	24	25	26	27	28
29	30					

October 2019

S	M	T	W	T	F	S
		1	2	3	4	5
6	7	8	9	10	11	12
13	14	15	16	17	18	19
20	21	22	23	24	25	26
27	28	29	30	31		

Eastern time in bold type
Pacific time in medium type

30 Monday

1st ♎
☽ enters ♏ **5:42 am** 2:42 am

Rosh Hashanah

1 Tuesday

1st ♏

2 Wednesday

1st ♏
☽ V/C **5:46 am** 2:46 am
☽ enters ♐ **7:44 am** 4:44 am
♇ D 11:39 pm

3 Thursday

1st ♐
♇ D **2:39 am**
☿ enters ♏ **4:14 am** 1:14 am
♂ enters ♎ 9:22 pm

Eastern time in bold type
Pacific time in medium type

4 Friday

1st ♐

♂ enters ♎ **12:22 am**

☽ V/C **3:34 am** 12:34 am

☽ enters ♑ **1:43 pm** 10:43 am

5 Saturday

1st ♑

2nd Quarter **12:47 pm** 9:47 am

6 Sunday

2nd ♑

☽ V/C **7:25 pm** 4:25 pm

☽ enters ♒ **11:42 pm** 8:42 pm

September 2019

S	M	T	W	T	F	S
1	2	3	4	5	6	7
8	9	10	11	12	13	14
15	16	17	18	19	20	21
22	23	24	25	26	27	28
29	30					

October 2019

S	M	T	W	T	F	S
		1	2	3	4	5
6	7	8	9	10	11	12
13	14	15	16	17	18	19
20	21	22	23	24	25	26
27	28	29	30	31		

November 2019

S	M	T	W	T	F	S
					1	2
3	4	5	6	7	8	9
10	11	12	13	14	15	16
17	18	19	20	21	22	23
24	25	26	27	28	29	30

7 Monday
2nd ♒

8 Tuesday
2nd ♒
♀ enters ♏ **1:06 pm** 10:06 am
☽ V/C **2:27 pm** 11:27 am

9 Wednesday
2nd ♒
☽ enters ♓ **12:05 pm** 9:05 am

Yom Kippur

10 Thursday
2nd ♓

Eastern time in bold type
Pacific time in medium type

11 Friday

2nd ♓

☽ V/C	**5:55 am**	2:55 am
☽ enters ♈		9:46 pm

12 Saturday

2nd ♓

☽ enters ♈ **12:46 am**

13 Sunday

2nd ♈

Full Moon	**5:08 pm**	2:08 pm
☽ V/C	**5:59 pm**	2:59 pm

September 2019

S	M	T	W	T	F	S
1	2	3	4	5	6	7
8	9	10	11	12	13	14
15	16	17	18	19	20	21
22	23	24	25	26	27	28
29	30					

October 2019

S	M	T	W	T	F	S
		1	2	3	4	5
6	7	8	9	10	11	12
13	14	15	16	17	18	19
20	21	22	23	24	25	26
27	28	29	30	31		

November 2019

S	M	T	W	T	F	S
					1	2
3	4	5	6	7	8	9
10	11	12	13	14	15	16
17	18	19	20	21	22	23
24	25	26	27	28	29	30

14 Monday

3rd ♈
☽ enters ♉ **12:24 pm** 9:24 am

Columbus Day • Indigenous Peoples' Day • Sukkot begins

15 Tuesday

3rd ♉

16 Wednesday

3rd ♉
☽ V/C **4:37 am** 1:37 am
☽ enters ♊ **10:30 pm** 7:30 pm

17 Thursday

3rd ♊

Eastern time in bold type
Pacific time in medium type

18 Friday
3rd ♊
☽ V/C **10:14 pm** 7:14 pm

19 Saturday

3rd ♊
☽ enters ♋ **6:43 am** 3:43 am

20 Sunday

3rd ♋

Sukkot ends

September 2019						
S	M	T	W	T	F	S
1	2	3	4	5	6	7
8	9	10	11	12	13	14
15	16	17	18	19	20	21
22	23	24	25	26	27	28
29	30					

October 2019						
S	M	T	W	T	F	S
		1	2	3	4	5
6	7	8	9	10	11	12
13	14	15	16	17	18	19
20	21	22	23	24	25	26
27	28	29	30	31		

November 2019						
S	M	T	W	T	F	S
					1	2
3	4	5	6	7	8	9
10	11	12	13	14	15	16
17	18	19	20	21	22	23
24	25	26	27	28	29	30

21 Monday

3rd ♋
☽ V/C **8:39 am** 5:39 am
4th Quarter **8:39 am** 5:39 am
☽ enters ♌ **12:29 pm** 9:29 am

22 Tuesday

4th ♌

23 Wednesday

4th ♌
☽ V/C **5:14 am** 2:14 am
☉ enters ♏ **1:20 pm** 10:20 am
☽ enters ♍ **3:29 pm** 12:29 pm

24 Thursday

4th

Eastern time in bold type
Pacific time in medium type

25 Friday

4th ♍
☽ V/C **9:00 am** 6:00 am
☽ enters ♎ **4:20 pm** 1:20 pm

26 Saturday

4th ♎

27 Sunday

4th ♎
☽ V/C **4:22 am** 1:22 am
☽ enters ♏ **4:29 pm** 1:29 pm
New Moon **11:39 pm** 8:39 pm

September 2019

S	M	T	W	T	F	S
1	2	3	4	5	6	7
8	9	10	11	12	13	14
15	16	17	18	19	20	21
22	23	24	25	26	27	28
29	30					

October 2019

S	M	T	W	T	F	S
		1	2	3	4	5
6	7	8	9	10	11	12
13	14	15	16	17	18	19
20	21	22	23	24	25	26
27	28	29	30	31		

November 2019

S	M	T	W	T	F	S
					1	2
3	4	5	6	7	8	9
10	11	12	13	14	15	16
17	18	19	20	21	22	23
24	25	26	27	28	29	30

28 Monday

1st ♏

29 Tuesday

1st ♏

☽ V/C	**1:34 pm**	10:34 am
☽ enters ♐	**5:58 pm**	2:58 pm

30 Wednesday

1st ♐

31 Thursday

1st ♐

☽ V/C	**10:30 am**	7:30 am
☿ ℞	**11:41 am**	8:41 am
☽ enters ♑	**10:38 pm**	7:38 pm

Halloween • Samhain

Eastern time in bold type
Pacific time in medium type

1 Friday

1st ♑
♀ enters ♐ **4:25 pm** 1:25 pm

All Saints' Day

2 Saturday

1st ♑
☽ V/C 10:46 pm

3 Sunday

1st ♑
☽ V/C **1:46 am**
☽ enters ♒ **6:19 am** 3:19 am
⚵ enters ♎ **9:28 pm** 6:28 pm

Daylight Saving Time ends at 2 am

October 2019

S	M	T	W	T	F	S
		1	2	3	4	5
6	7	8	9	10	11	12
13	14	15	16	17	18	19
20	21	22	23	24	25	26
27	28	29	30	31		

November 2019

S	M	T	W	T	F	S
					1	2
3	4	5	6	7	8	9
10	11	12	13	14	15	16
17	18	19	20	21	22	23
24	25	26	27	28	29	30

December 2019

S	M	T	W	T	F	S
1	2	3	4	5	6	7
8	9	10	11	12	13	14
15	16	17	18	19	20	21
22	23	24	25	26	27	28
29	30	31				

Eastern time in bold type
Pacific time in medium type

4 Monday

1st ≈
2nd Quarter **5:23 am** 2:23 am

5 Tuesday

2nd ≈
☽ V/C **9:37 am** 6:37 am
☽ enters ♓ **6:08 pm** 3:08 pm

Election Day (general)

6 Wednesday

2nd ♓

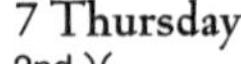

7 Thursday

2nd ♓
☽ V/C **8:13 pm** 5:13 pm

Eastern time in bold type
Pacific time in medium type

8 Friday

2nd ♓︎
♀ enters ♐︎ **5:18 am** 2:18 am
☽ enters ♈︎ **6:49 am** 3:49 am

9 Saturday

2nd ♈︎

10 Sunday

2nd ♈︎
☽ V/C **9:00 am** 6:00 am
☽ enters ♉︎ **6:18 pm** 3:18 pm

October 2019

S	M	T	W	T	F	S
		1	2	3	4	5
6	7	8	9	10	11	12
13	14	15	16	17	18	19
20	21	22	23	24	25	26
27	28	29	30	31		

November 2019

S	M	T	W	T	F	S
					1	2
3	4	5	6	7	8	9
10	11	12	13	14	15	16
17	18	19	20	21	22	23
24	25	26	27	28	29	30

December 2019

S	M	T	W	T	F	S
1	2	3	4	5	6	7
8	9	10	11	12	13	14
15	16	17	18	19	20	21
22	23	24	25	26	27	28
29	30	31				

11 Monday

2nd ♉

Veterans Day

12 Tuesday

2nd ♉

Full Moon	**8:34 am**	5:34 am
☽ V/C	**10:48 am**	7:48 am

13 Wednesday

3rd ♉

☽ enters ♊	**3:46 am**	12:46 am

14 Thursday

3rd ♊

Eastern time in bold type
Pacific time in medium type

15 Friday

3rd ♊

☽ V/C	**6:40 am**	3:40 am
☽ enters ♋	**11:15 am**	8:15 am
⚳ enters ♑	**11:36 pm**	8:36 pm

16 Saturday

3rd ♋

17 Sunday

3rd ♋

☽ V/C	**3:14 pm**	12:14 pm
☽ enters ♌	**4:57 pm**	1:57 pm

October 2019

S	M	T	W	T	F	S
		1	2	3	4	5
6	7	8	9	10	11	12
13	14	15	16	17	18	19
20	21	22	23	24	25	26
27	28	29	30	31		

November 2019

S	M	T	W	T	F	S
					1	2
3	4	5	6	7	8	9
10	11	12	13	14	15	16
17	18	19	20	21	22	23
24	25	26	27	28	29	30

December 2019

S	M	T	W	T	F	S
1	2	3	4	5	6	7
8	9	10	11	12	13	14
15	16	17	18	19	20	21
22	23	24	25	26	27	28
29	30	31				

Eastern time in bold type
Pacific time in medium type

18 Monday

3rd ♌
♂ enters ♏ 11:40 pm

19 Tuesday

3rd ♌
♂ enters ♏ **2:40 am**
☽ V/C **4:11 pm** 1:11 pm
4th Quarter **4:11 pm** 1:11 pm
☽ enters ♍ **8:54 pm** 5:54 pm

20 Wednesday

4th ♍
☿ D **2:12 pm** 11:12 am

21 Thursday

4th ♍
☽ V/C **10:31 pm** 7:31 pm
☽ enters ♎ **11:20 pm** 8:20 pm

Eastern time in bold type
Pacific time in medium type

22 Friday

4th ♎
☉ enters ♐ **9:59 am** 6:59 am

23 Saturday

4th ♎
☽ V/C **9:49 pm** 6:49 pm
☽ enters ♏ 9:58 pm

24 Sunday

4th ♎
☽ enters ♏ **12:58 am**

October 2019						
S	M	T	W	T	F	S
		1	2	3	4	5
6	7	8	9	10	11	12
13	14	15	16	17	18	19
20	21	22	23	24	25	26
27	28	29	30	31		

November 2019						
S	M	T	W	T	F	S
					1	2
3	4	5	6	7	8	9
10	11	12	13	14	15	16
17	18	19	20	21	22	23
24	25	26	27	28	29	30

December 2019						
S	M	T	W	T	F	S
1	2	3	4	5	6	7
8	9	10	11	12	13	14
15	16	17	18	19	20	21
22	23	24	25	26	27	28
29	30	31				

25 Monday

4th ♏
☽ V/C **12:30 pm** 9:30 am
♀ enters ♑ **7:28 pm** 4:28 pm

26 Tuesday

4th ♏
☽ enters ♐ **3:11 am** 12:11 am
New Moon **10:06 am** 7:06 am

27 Wednesday

1st ♐
♆ D **7:32 am** 4:32 am

28 Thursday

1st ♐
☽ V/C **5:50 am** 2:50 am
☽ enters ♑ **7:33 am** 4:33 am

Thanksgiving Day

Eastern time in bold type
Pacific time in medium type

29 Friday
1st ♑
☽ V/C **10:57 pm** 7:57 pm

30 Saturday
1st ♑
☽ enters ♒ **3:13 pm** 12:13 pm

1 Sunday
1st ♒

November 2019

S	M	T	W	T	F	S
					1	2
3	4	5	6	7	8	9
10	11	12	13	14	15	16
17	18	19	20	21	22	23
24	25	26	27	28	29	30

December 2019

S	M	T	W	T	F	S
1	2	3	4	5	6	7
8	9	10	11	12	13	14
15	16	17	18	19	20	21
22	23	24	25	26	27	28
29	30	31				

January 2020

S	M	T	W	T	F	S
			1	2	3	4
5	6	7	8	9	10	11
12	13	14	15	16	17	18
19	20	21	22	23	24	25
26	27	28	29	30	31	

Eastern time in bold type
Pacific time in medium type

2 Monday

1st ♒
☽ V/C **7:27 am** 4:27 am
♃ enters ♑ **1:20 pm** 10:20 am
☽ enters ♓ 11:11 pm

3 Tuesday

1st ♒
☽ enters ♓ **2:11 am**
2nd Quarter 10:58 pm

4 Wednesday

1st ♓
2nd Quarter **1:58 am**

5 Thursday

2nd ♓
☽ V/C **3:15 am** 12:15 am
☽ enters ♈ **2:44 pm** 11:44 am

Eastern time in bold type
Pacific time in medium type

6 Friday
2nd ♈

7 Saturday
2nd ♈

☽ V/C **10:01 am** 7:01 am

☽ enters ♉ 11:29 pm

8 Sunday

2nd ♈

☽ enters ♉ **2:29 am**

November 2019

S	M	T	W	T	F	S
					1	2
3	4	5	6	7	8	9
10	11	12	13	14	15	16
17	18	19	20	21	22	23
24	25	26	27	28	29	30

December 2019

S	M	T	W	T	F	S
1	2	3	4	5	6	7
8	9	10	11	12	13	14
15	16	17	18	19	20	21
22	23	24	25	26	27	28
29	30	31				

January 2020

S	M	T	W	T	F	S
			1	2	3	4
5	6	7	8	9	10	11
12	13	14	15	16	17	18
19	20	21	22	23	24	25
26	27	28	29	30	31	

9 Monday

2nd ♉

☿ enters ♐	**4:42 am**	1:42 am
☽ V/C	**8:13 pm**	5:13 pm

10 Tuesday

2nd ♉

☽ enters ♊	**11:47 am**	8:47 am

11 Wednesday

2nd ♊

☽ V/C		9:12 pm
Full Moon		9:12 pm

12 Thursday

2nd ♊

☽ V/C	**12:12 am**	
Full Moon	**12:12 am**	
☽ enters ♋	**6:23 pm**	3:23 pm
⚷ D	**10:48 pm**	7:48 pm

Eastern time in bold type
Pacific time in medium type

13 Friday

3rd ♋

14 Saturday

3rd ♋

☽ V/C **10:57 am** 7:57 am

☽ enters ♌ **10:56 pm** 7:56 pm

15 Sunday

3rd ♌

November 2019

S	M	T	W	T	F	S
					1	2
3	4	5	6	7	8	9
10	11	12	13	14	15	16
17	18	19	20	21	22	23
24	25	26	27	28	29	30

December 2019

S	M	T	W	T	F	S
1	2	3	4	5	6	7
8	9	10	11	12	13	14
15	16	17	18	19	20	21
22	23	24	25	26	27	28
29	30	31				

January 2020

S	M	T	W	T	F	S
			1	2	3	4
5	6	7	8	9	10	11
12	13	14	15	16	17	18
19	20	21	22	23	24	25
26	27	28	29	30	31	

16 Monday

3rd ♌
☽ V/C **5:10 pm** 2:10 pm
☽ enters ♍ 11:16 pm

17 Tuesday

3rd ♌
☽ enters ♍ **2:16 am**

18 Wednesday

3rd ♍
4th Quarter **11:57 pm** 8:57 pm

19 Thursday

4th ♍
☽ V/C **3:07 am** 12:07 am
☽ enters ♎ **5:04 am** 2:04 am
♀ enters ♒ 10:42 pm

Eastern time in bold type
Pacific time in medium type

20 Friday
4th ♎
♀ enters ♒ **1:42 am**

21 Saturday
4th ♎
☽ V/C **6:45 am** 3:45 am
☽ enters ♏ **7:57 am** 4:57 am
☉ enters ♑ **11:19 pm** 8:19 pm

Yule • Winter Solstice

22 Sunday

4th ♏
☽ V/C **10:27 pm** 7:27 pm

November 2019

S	M	T	W	T	F	S
					1	2
3	4	5	6	7	8	9
10	11	12	13	14	15	16
17	18	19	20	21	22	23
24	25	26	27	28	29	30

December 2019

S	M	T	W	T	F	S
1	2	3	4	5	6	7
8	9	10	11	12	13	14
15	16	17	18	19	20	21
22	23	24	25	26	27	28
29	30	31				

January 2020

S	M	T	W	T	F	S
			1	2	3	4
5	6	7	8	9	10	11
12	13	14	15	16	17	18
19	20	21	22	23	24	25
26	27	28	29	30	31	

23 Monday

4th ♏
☽ enters ♐ **11:34 am** 8:34 am

Hanukkah begins

24 Tuesday

4th ♐

Christmas Eve

25 Wednesday

4th ♐
☽ V/C **6:18 am** 3:18 am
☽ enters ♑ **4:45 pm** 1:45 pm
New Moon 9:13 pm

Christmas Day

26 Thursday

4th ♑
New Moon **12:13 am**

Kwanzaa begins

27 Friday

1st ♑
☽ V/C **4:03 pm** 1:03 pm
☽ enters ♒ 9:21 pm

28 Saturday

1st ♑
☽ enters ♒ **12:21 am**
☿ enters ♑ **11:55 pm** 8:55 pm

29 Sunday

1st ♒
⚴ D **5:40 pm** 2:40 pm

November 2019

S	M	T	W	T	F	S
					1	2
3	4	5	6	7	8	9
10	11	12	13	14	15	16
17	18	19	20	21	22	23
24	25	26	27	28	29	30

December 2019

S	M	T	W	T	F	S
1	2	3	4	5	6	7
8	9	10	11	12	13	14
15	16	17	18	19	20	21
22	23	24	25	26	27	28
29	30	31				

January 2020

S	M	T	W	T	F	S
			1	2	3	4
5	6	7	8	9	10	11
12	13	14	15	16	17	18
19	20	21	22	23	24	25
26	27	28	29	30	31	

30 Monday
1st ♒
☽ V/C **5:24 am** 2:24 am
☽ enters ♓ **10:41 am** 7:41 am

Hanukkah ends

31 Tuesday

1st ♓

New Year's Eve

1 Wednesday
1st ♓
☽ V/C **9:14 pm** 6:14 pm

☽ enters ♈ **11:00 pm** 8:00 pm

Kwanzaa ends • New Year's Day

2 Thursday

1st ♈
2nd Quarter **11:45 pm** 8:45 pm

Eastern time in bold type
Pacific time in medium type

The Year 2020

January

S	M	T	W	T	F	S
			1	2	3	4
5	6	7	8	9	10	11
12	13	14	15	16	17	18
19	20	21	22	23	24	25
26	27	28	29	30	31	

February

S	M	T	W	T	F	S
						1
2	3	4	5	6	7	8
9	10	11	12	13	14	15
16	17	18	19	20	21	22
23	24	25	26	27	28	29

March

S	M	T	W	T	F	S
1	2	3	4	5	6	7
8	9	10	11	12	13	14
15	16	17	18	19	20	21
22	23	24	25	26	27	28
29	30	31				

April

S	M	T	W	T	F	S
			1	2	3	4
5	6	7	8	9	10	11
12	13	14	15	16	17	18
19	20	21	22	23	24	25
26	27	28	29	30		

May

S	M	T	W	T	F	S
					1	2
3	4	5	6	7	8	9
10	11	12	13	14	15	16
17	18	19	20	21	22	23
24	25	26	27	28	29	30
31						

June

S	M	T	W	T	F	S
	1	2	3	4	5	6
7	8	9	10	11	12	13
14	15	16	17	18	19	20
21	22	23	24	25	26	27
28	29	30				

July

S	M	T	W	T	F	S
			1	2	3	4
5	6	7	8	9	10	11
12	13	14	15	16	17	18
19	20	21	22	23	24	25
26	27	28	29	30	31	

August

S	M	T	W	T	F	S
						1
2	3	4	5	6	7	8
9	10	11	12	13	14	15
16	17	18	19	20	21	22
23	24	25	26	27	28	29
30	31					

September

S	M	T	W	T	F	S
		1	2	3	4	5
6	7	8	9	10	11	12
13	14	15	16	17	18	19
20	21	22	23	24	25	26
27	28	29	30			

October

S	M	T	W	T	F	S
				1	2	3
4	5	6	7	8	9	10
11	12	13	14	15	16	17
18	19	20	21	22	23	24
25	26	27	28	29	30	31

November

S	M	T	W	T	F	S
1	2	3	4	5	6	7
8	9	10	11	12	13	14
15	16	17	18	19	20	21
22	23	24	25	26	27	28
29	30					

December

S	M	T	W	T	F	S
		1	2	3	4	5
6	7	8	9	10	11	12
13	14	15	16	17	18	19
20	21	22	23	24	25	26
27	28	29	30	31		

JANUARY 2018

☽ Last Aspect day	ET / hr:mn / PT	asp	☽ Ingress sign day	ET / hr:mn / PT
12/31	**6:38 pm** 3:38 pm	⚹ ♅	♋ 1	**3:10 am** 12:10 am
2	**5:46 pm** 2:46 pm	□ ♅	♌ 2	11:23 pm
2	**5:46 pm** 2:46 pm	□ ♅	♌ 3	**2:23 am**
4	**6:10 pm** 3:10 pm	△ ♅	♍ 5	**3:12 am** 12:12 am
6	**9:51 pm** 6:51 pm	□ ☿	♎ 7	**7:15 am** 4:15 am
9	**11:13 am** 8:13 am	⚹ ☿	♏ 9	**3:05 pm** 12:05 pm
11	**9:53 am** 6:53 am	⚹ ♀	♐ 11	11:04 pm
11	**9:53 am** 6:53 am	⚹ ♀	♐ 12	**2:04 am**
14	**3:48 am** 12:48 am	△ ♅	♑ 14	**2:42 pm** 11:42 am
16	10:30 pm	☌ ♀	♒ 17	**3:32 am** 12:32 am
17	**1:30 am**	☌ ♀	♒ 17	**3:32 am** 12:32 am
19	**6:52 am** 3:52 am	□ ♂	♓ 19	**3:26 pm** 12:26 pm
21	**8:13 pm** 5:13 pm	△ ♂	♈ 21	10:27 pm
21	**8:13 pm** 5:13 pm	△ ♂	♈ 22	**1:27 am**
23	**11:16 pm** 8:16 pm	☌ ♅	♉ 24	**8:39 am** 5:39 am
25	**10:17 pm** 7:17 pm	△ ☿	♊ 26	**12:40 pm** 9:40 am
28	**5:39 am** 2:39 am	⚹ ♅	♋ 28	**1:57 pm** 10:57 am
30	**11:40 am** 8:40 am	☍ ☿	♌ 30	**1:53 pm** 10:53 am

☽ Phases & Eclipses phase	day	ET / hr:mn / PT
Full Moon	1	**9:24 pm** 6:24 pm
4th Quarter	8	**5:25 pm** 2:25 pm
New Moon	16	**9:17 pm** 6:17 pm
2nd Quarter	24	**5:20 pm** 2:20 pm
Full Moon	31	**8:27 am** 5:27 am
(eclipse)	31	11° ♌ 37'

Planet Ingress	day	ET / hr:mn / PT
☿ ♑	10	9:09 pm
☿ ♑	11	**12:09 pm**
⚵ ♐	14	**11:45 pm** 8:45 pm
♀ ♒	17	**8:44 pm** 5:44 pm
♀ ♉	19	**9:35 pm** 6:35 pm
☉ ♒	19	**10:09 pm** 7:09 pm
♂ ♐	26	**7:56 am** 4:56 am
☿ ♒	31	**8:39 am** 5:39 am

Planetary Motion	day	ET / hr:mn / PT
♅ D	2	**9:13 am** 6:13 am

1 MONDAY
☽ ☍ ♄ **5:26 am** 2:26 am
☿ ⚺ ♇ **3:51 pm** 12:51 pm
☽ ☍ ♀ **6:28 pm** 3:28 pm
☽ ☍ ☉ **9:24 pm** 6:24 pm
☽ △ ♆ **9:52 pm** 6:52 pm
☽ △ ♂ 11:41 pm

2 TUESDAY
☽ △ ♂ **2:41 am**
☉ ⚹ ♆ **4:37 am** 1:37 am
☽ △ ♃ **6:07 am** 3:07 am
☽ ☍ ♇ **8:43 am** 5:43 am
☽ ⚻ ☿ **9:54 am** 6:54 am
☽ □ ♅ **5:46 pm** 2:46 pm

3 WEDNESDAY
☽ ⚻ ♄ **5:02 am** 2:02 am
♀ ⚹ ♆ **12:38 pm** 9:38 am
☽ ⚻ ♆ **9:34 pm** 6:34 pm
☽ ⚻ ♀ **10:23 pm** 7:23 pm
☽ ⚻ ☉ 9:31 pm

4 THURSDAY
☽ ⚻ ☉ **12:31 am**
☽ □ ♂ **4:34 am** 1:34 am
☽ □ ♃ **6:34 am** 3:34 am
☽ ⚻ ♇ **8:50 am** 5:50 am
☽ △ ☿ **1:52 pm** 10:52 am
☽ △ ♅ **6:10 pm** 3:10 pm

5 FRIDAY
☽ △ ♄ **6:25 am** 3:25 am
☽ ☍ ♆ **11:37 pm** 8:37 pm

6 SATURDAY
☽ △ ♀ **5:23 am** 2:23 am
☽ △ ☉ **6:40 am** 3:40 am
☽ ⚹ ♂ **9:22 am** 6:22 am
☽ ⚹ ♃ **9:43 am** 6:43 am
☽ △ ♇ **11:41 am** 8:41 am
☿ △ ♅ **6:39 pm** 3:39 pm
♂ ☌ ♃ **7:39 pm** 4:39 pm
☽ ⚻ ♅ **9:33 pm** 6:33 pm
☽ □ ☿ **9:51 pm** 6:51 pm

7 SUNDAY
☽ □ ♄ **11:09 am** 8:09 am

8 MONDAY
☽ ⚻ ♆ **5:17 am** 2:17 am
☉ ⚹ ♃ **7:07 am** 4:07 am
♀ ⚹ ♃ **11:13 am** 8:13 am
♂ ⚹ ♇ **2:59 pm** 11:59 am
☽ ⚺ ♃ **4:43 pm** 1:43 pm
☽ □ ♀ **5:15 pm** 2:15 pm
☽ □ ☉ **5:25 pm** 2:25 pm
☽ □ ♇ **6:17 pm** 3:17 pm
☽ ⚺ ♂ **6:26 pm** 3:26 pm
☉ ☌ ♀ 11:02 pm

9 TUESDAY
☉ ☌ ♀ **2:02 am**
♀ ☌ ♇ **4:03 am** 1:03 am
☉ ☌ ♇ **4:33 am** 1:33 am
☽ ☍ ♅ **4:45 am** 1:45 am
☽ ⚹ ☿ **11:13 am** 8:13 am
♀ ⚹ ♂ **4:08 pm** 1:08 pm
☽ ⚹ ♄ **7:47 pm** 4:47 pm
☉ ⚹ ♂ 9:36 pm

10 WEDNESDAY
☉ ⚹ ♂ **12:36 am**
☽ △ ♆ **2:39 pm** 11:39 am

11 THURSDAY
☽ ☌ ♃ **3:21 am** 12:21 am
☽ ⚹ ♇ **4:26 am** 1:26 am
☽ ☌ ♂ **7:34 am** 4:34 am
☽ ⚹ ☉ **8:41 am** 5:41 am
☽ ⚹ ♀ **9:53 am** 6:53 am
☽ ⚻ ♅ **3:18 pm** 12:18 pm

12 FRIDAY
☽ ⚺ ☿ **5:21 am** 2:21 am
☽ ⚺ ♄ **7:32 am** 4:32 am
☿ ☌ ♄ 11:03 pm
☽ □ ♆ 11:38 pm

13 SATURDAY
☿ ☌ ♄ **2:03 am**
☽ □ ♆ **2:38 am**
♀ □ ♅ **2:09 pm** 11:09 am
☽ ⚺ ♃ **4:19 pm** 1:19 pm
☽ ⚺ ♇ **4:49 pm** 1:49 pm
☽ ⚺ ♂ **11:12 pm** 8:12 pm
☽ ⚺ ☉ 11:41 pm

14 SUNDAY
☽ ⚺ ☉ **2:41 am**
☽ △ ♅ **3:48 am** 12:48 am
☽ ⚺ ♀ **5:25 am** 2:25 am
☉ □ ♅ **3:45 pm** 12:45 pm
☽ ☌ ♄ **8:49 pm** 5:49 pm
☽ ☌ ☿ 11:03 pm

15 MONDAY
☽ ☌ ☿ **2:03 am**
☽ ⚹ ♆ **3:39 pm** 12:39 pm
♃ ⚹ ♇ **11:13 pm** 8:13 pm

16 TUESDAY
☽ ☌ ♇ **5:54 am** 2:54 am
☽ ⚹ ♃ **5:58 am** 2:58 am
☽ ⚹ ♂ **3:27 pm** 12:27 pm
☽ □ ♅ **4:44 pm** 1:44 pm
☽ ☌ ☉ **9:17 pm** 6:17 pm
☽ ☌ ♀ 10:30 pm

17 WEDNESDAY
☽ ☌ ♀ **1:30 am**
☽ ⚺ ♄ **10:11 am** 7:11 am
♂ ⚻ ♅ **4:37 pm** 1:37 pm
☽ ⚺ ☿ **10:59 pm** 7:59 pm

18 THURSDAY
☽ ⚺ ♆ **4:22 am** 1:22 am
☽ ⚺ ♇ **6:25 pm** 3:25 pm
☽ □ ♃ **7:00 pm** 4:00 pm

19 FRIDAY
☽ ⚹ ♅ **4:57 am** 1:57 am
☽ □ ♂ **6:52 am** 3:52 am
☽ ⚺ ☉ **2:50 pm** 11:50 am
☿ ⚹ ♆ **8:08 pm** 5:08 pm
☽ ⚺ ♀ **8:21 pm** 5:21 pm
☽ ⚹ ♄ **10:28 pm** 7:28 pm

20 SATURDAY
☽ ☌ ♆ **3:45 pm** 12:45 pm
☽ ⚹ ☿ **6:20 pm** 3:20 pm
♀ ⚺ ♄ **6:45 pm** 3:45 pm

21 SUNDAY
☽ ⚹ ♇ **5:22 am** 2:22 am
☽ △ ♃ **6:25 am** 3:25 am
☽ ⚺ ♅ **3:27 pm** 12:27 pm
☽ △ ♂ **8:13 pm** 5:13 pm

22 MONDAY
☽ ⚹ ☉ **5:55 am** 2:55 am
☽ □ ♄ **8:41 am** 5:41 am
☽ ⚹ ♀ **12:28 pm** 9:28 am
☽ ⚺ ♆ 9:50 pm

23 TUESDAY
☽ ⚺ ♆ **12:50 am**
☽ □ ☿ **10:29 am** 7:29 am
☽ □ ♇ **1:47 pm** 10:47 am
☽ ⚻ ♃ **3:11 pm** 12:11 pm
☉ ⚺ ♄ **8:31 pm** 5:31 pm
☽ ☌ ♅ **11:16 pm** 8:16 pm

24 WEDNESDAY
☽ ⚻ ♂ **6:23 am** 3:23 am
☿ ☌ ♇ **3:50 pm** 12:50 pm
☽ △ ♄ **3:56 pm** 12:56 pm
☽ □ ☉ **5:20 pm** 2:20 pm
☽ □ ♀ 9:35 pm

25 THURSDAY
☽ □ ♀ **12:35 am**
☿ ⚹ ♃ **6:28 am** 3:28 am
☽ ⚹ ♆ **6:49 am** 3:49 am
☽ △ ♇ **7:02 pm** 4:02 pm
☽ ☍ ♃ **8:40 pm** 5:40 pm
☽ △ ☿ **10:17 pm** 7:17 pm

26 FRIDAY
☽ ⚺ ♅ **3:53 am** 12:53 am
☽ ☍ ♂ **12:52 pm** 9:52 am
☽ ⚻ ♄ **7:54 pm** 4:54 pm
☽ △ ☉ 9:45 pm

27 SATURDAY
☽ △ ☉ **12:45 am**
☽ △ ♀ **8:31 am** 5:31 am
☽ □ ♆ **9:41 am** 6:41 am
☽ ⚻ ♇ **9:15 pm** 6:15 pm
♀ ⚺ ♆ **10:22 pm** 7:22 pm
☽ ⚻ ♃ **11:07 pm** 8:07 pm
☿ □ ♅ 11:08 pm

28 SUNDAY
☿ □ ♅ **2:08 am**
☽ ⚹ ♅ **5:39 am** 2:39 am
☽ ⚻ ☿ **6:03 am** 3:03 am
☽ ⚻ ♂ **4:17 pm** 1:17 pm
☽ ☍ ♄ **9:15 pm** 6:15 pm

29 MONDAY
☽ ⚻ ☉ **5:07 am** 2:07 am
☽ △ ♆ **10:19 am** 7:19 am
☽ ⚻ ♀ **1:30 pm** 10:30 am
☽ ☍ ♇ **9:34 pm** 6:34 pm
☽ △ ♃ **11:38 pm** 8:38 pm

30 TUESDAY
☽ □ ♅ **5:46 am** 2:46 am
☽ ☍ ☿ **11:40 am** 8:40 am
☽ △ ♂ **6:13 pm** 3:13 pm
☽ ⚻ ♄ **9:27 pm** 6:27 pm

31 WEDNESDAY
☽ ☍ ☉ **8:27 am** 5:27 am
☽ ⚻ ♆ **10:17 am** 7:17 am
☽ ☍ ♀ **5:48 pm** 2:48 pm
☽ ⚻ ♇ **9:39 pm** 6:39 pm
☽ □ ♃ 9:00 pm

Eastern time in bold type
Pacific time in medium type

JANUARY 2018

DATE	SID.TIME	SUN	MOON	NODE	MERCURY	VENUS	MARS	JUPITER	SATURN	URANUS	NEPTUNE	PLUTO	CERES	PALLAS	JUNO	VESTA	CHIRON
1 M	6 42 23	10♑30 29	24♊48	15♌21℞	17♐57	8♑31	14♏10	16♏56	1♑23	24♈34℞	11♓54	18♑47	17♌23℞	26♈02	6♒11	23♏08	24♓39
2 T	6 46 20	11 31 37	10♋06	15 16	18 56	9 47	14 47	17 06	1 30	24 34D	11 56	18 49	17 16	26 10	6 36	23 37	24 40
3 W	6 50 16	12 32 44	25 21	15 13	19 59	11 02	15 25	17 16	1 37	24 34	11 57	18 51	17 09	26 19	7 01	24 07	24 42
4 Th	6 54 13	13 33 52	10♌23	15 12 D	21 05	12 18	16 02	17 26	1 44	24 34	11 58	18 53	17 02	26 28	7 26	24 36	24 43
5 F	6 58 9	14 35 00	25 05	15 12	22 13	13 33	16 40	17 36	1 51	24 34	12 00	18 55	16 54	26 38	7 51	25 05	24 45
6 Sa	7 2 6	15 36 08	9♍20	15 14	23 23	14 49	17 17	17 46	1 58	24 35	12 01	18 57	16 45	26 48	8 17	25 34	24 46
7 Su	7 6 2	16 37 17	23 08	15 15	24 36	16 04	17 54	17 55	2 05	24 35	12 03	18 59	16 37	26 59	8 42	26 04	24 48
8 M	7 9 59	17 38 25	6♎29	15 17℞	25 50	17 20	18 32	18 05	2 12	24 35	12 04	19 01	16 28	27 10	9 07	26 33	24 50
9 T	7 13 55	18 39 34	19 26	15 17	27 06	18 35	19 09	18 14	2 19	24 35	12 06	19 03	16 18	27 21	9 33	27 02	24 52
10 W	7 17 52	19 40 42	2♏02	15 16	28 24	19 51	19 46	18 23	2 26	24 36	12 07	19 05	16 09	27 33	9 58	27 31	24 54
11 Th	7 21 49	20 41 51	14 21	15 14	29 43	21 06	20 24	18 32	2 33	24 36	12 09	19 07	15 58	27 46	10 24	27 59	24 55
12 F	7 25 45	21 43 00	26 28	15 11	1♑03	22 22	21 01	18 41	2 40	24 37	12 10	19 09	15 48	27 59	10 50	28 28	24 57
13 Sa	7 29 42	22 44 08	8♐25	15 08	2 24	23 37	21 38	18 50	2 47	24 37	12 12	19 11	15 37	28 12	11 16	28 57	24 59
14 Su	7 33 38	23 45 17	20 18	15 04	3 47	24 53	22 15	18 59	2 53	24 38	12 14	19 13	15 26	28 26	11 41	29 26	25 02
15 M	7 37 35	24 46 25	2♑07	15 00	5 10	26 08	22 53	19 08	3 00	24 38	12 15	19 15	15 15	28 40	12 07	29 54	25 04
16 T	7 41 31	25 47 33	13 56	14 57	6 35	27 24	23 30	19 16	3 07	24 39	12 17	19 17	15 03	28 55	12 33	0♐23	25 06
17 W	7 45 28	26 48 40	25 47	14 55	8 00	28 39	24 07	19 25	3 14	24 40	12 19	19 19	14 51	29 10	12 59	0 51	25 08
18 Th	7 49 25	27 49 47	7♒41	14 54 D	9 26	29 55	24 44	19 33	3 20	24 40	12 20	19 21	14 39	29 26	13 25	1 20	25 10
19 F	7 53 21	28 50 53	19 41	14 54	10 52	1♒10	25 21	19 41	3 27	24 41	12 22	19 23	14 26	29 42	13 52	1 48	25 12
20 Sa	7 57 18	29 51 59	1♓48	14 55	12 20	2 25	25 58	19 49	3 34	24 42	12 24	19 25	14 14	29 58	14 18	2 16	25 15
21 Su	8 1 14	0♒53 04	14 06	14 56	13 48	3 41	26 35	19 57	3 40	24 43	12 26	19 27	14 01	0♉15	14 44	2 44	25 17
22 M	8 5 11	1 54 08	26 36	14 57	15 17	4 56	27 12	20 05	3 47	24 44	12 27	19 30	13 47	0 32	15 10	3 12	25 20
23 T	8 9 7	2 55 11	9♈21	14 58	16 46	6 12	27 49	20 13	3 53	24 45	12 29	19 32	13 34	0 50	15 37	3 40	25 22
24 W	8 13 4	3 56 13	22 25	14 59℞	18 16	7 27	28 26	20 20	4 00	24 46	12 31	19 34	13 21	1 08	16 03	4 08	25 24
25 Th	8 17 0	4 57 14	5♉49	14 59	19 47	8 42	29 03	20 27	4 06	24 47	12 33	19 35	13 07	1 26	16 30	4 36	25 27
26 F	8 20 57	5 58 14	19 37	14 59	21 19	9 58	29 40	20 35	4 12	24 48	12 35	19 37	12 53	1 45	16 56	5 04	25 29
27 Sa	8 24 53	6 59 13	3♊47	14 58	22 51	11 13	0♐17	20 42	4 19	24 50	12 37	19 39	12 39	2 04	17 23	5 31	25 32
28 Su	8 28 50	8 00 10	18 19	14 58	24 24	12 29	0 54	20 49	4 25	24 51	12 39	19 41	12 25	2 23	17 49	5 59	25 35
29 M	8 32 47	9 01 07	3♋08	14 57	25 57	13 44	1 31	20 56	4 31	24 52	12 41	19 43	12 11	2 43	18 16	6 26	25 37
30 T	8 36 43	10 02 03	18 09	14 56	27 31	14 59	2 08	21 02	4 38	24 54	12 43	19 45	11 57	3 03	18 43	6 53	25 40
31 W	8 40 40	11 02 57	3♌13	14 56 D	29 06	16 14	2 44	21 09	4 44	24 55	12 45	19 47	11 43	3 23	19 09	7 21	25 43

EPHEMERIS CALCULATED FOR 12 MIDNIGHT GREENWICH MEAN TIME. ALL OTHER DATA AND FACING ASPECTARIAN PAGE IN **EASTERN TIME (BOLD)** AND PACIFIC TIME (REGULAR).

FEBRUARY 2018

☽ Last Aspect day	ET / hr:mn / PT	asp	☽ Ingress sign	day	ET / hr:mn / PT
1	**5:59 am** 2:59 am	△ ♅	♍	1	**2:13 pm** 11:13 am
2	11:07 pm	⚹ ♃	♎	3	**4:47 pm** 1:47 pm
3	**2:07 am**	⚹ ♃	♎	3	**4:47 pm** 1:47 pm
5	**1:46 pm** 10:46 am	☍ ♅	♏	5	**10:56 pm** 7:56 pm
7	11:16 pm	□ ♀	♐	8	**8:53 am** 5:53 am
8	**2:16 am**	□ ♀	♐	8	**8:53 am** 5:53 am
10	**11:38 am** 8:38 am	△ ♅	♑	10	**9:21 pm** 6:21 pm
12	9:43 pm	□ ♅	♒	13	**10:11 am** 7:11 am
13	**12:43 am**	□ ♅	♒	13	**10:11 am** 7:11 am
15	**4:05 pm** 1:05 pm	☌ ☉	♓	15	**9:42 pm** 6:42 pm
17	**5:14 pm** 2:14 pm	△ ♃	♈	18	**7:05 am** 4:05 am
20	**6:11 am** 3:11 am	☌ ♅	♉	20	**2:12 pm** 11:12 am
22	**6:46 am** 3:46 am	☍ ♃	♊	22	**7:07 pm** 4:07 pm
24	**2:58 pm** 11:58 am	⚹ ♅	♋	24	**10:06 pm** 7:06 pm
26	**4:51 pm** 1:51 pm	□ ♅	♌	26	**11:42 pm** 8:42 pm
28	**6:13 pm** 3:13 pm	△ ♅	♍	28	9:57 pm
28	**6:13 pm** 3:13 pm	△ ♅	♍	3/1	**12:57 am**

☽ Phases & Eclipses phase	day	ET / hr:mn / PT
4th Quarter	7	**10:54 am** 7:54 am
New Moon	15	**4:05 pm** 1:05 pm
●	15	27° ♒ 08'
2nd Quarter	23	**3:09 am** 12:09 am

Planet Ingress	day	ET / hr:mn / PT
♀ ♓	10	**6:20 pm** 3:20 pm
☿ ♓	17	**11:28 pm** 8:28 pm
☉ ♓	18	**12:18 pm** 9:18 am
⚵ ♓	23	**3:10 pm** 12:10 pm

Planetary Motion	day	ET / hr:mn / PT

1 THURSDAY
☽ □ ♃ **12:00 am**
☽ △ ♅ **5:59 am** 2:59 am
☉ ⚺ ♆ **12:30 pm** 9:30 am
☽ ⚻ ☿ **5:51 pm** 2:51 pm
☽ □ ♂ **8:48 pm** 5:48 pm
☽ △ ♄ **10:22 pm** 7:22 pm

2 FRIDAY
☽ ☍ ♆ **11:29 am** 8:29 am
☽ ⚻ ☉ **1:11 pm** 10:11 am
♀ ⚺ ♇ **4:36 pm** 1:36 pm
☽ △ ♇ **11:24 pm** 8:24 pm
☽ ⚻ ♀ 9:02 pm
☽ ⚹ ♃ 11:07 pm

3 SATURDAY
☽ ⚻ ♀ **12:02 am**
☽ ⚹ ♃ **2:07 am**
☽ ⚻ ♅ **8:09 am** 5:09 am
☿ ⚹ ♂ **10:57 am** 7:57 am
☿ ⚺ ♄ **12:51 pm** 9:51 am
♂ ⚺ ♄ **4:36 pm** 1:36 pm
♀ □ ♃ 10:07 pm
☽ □ ♄ 10:50 pm
☽ ⚹ ♂ 11:11 pm

4 SUNDAY
♀ □ ♃ **1:07 am**
☽ □ ♄ **1:50 am**
☽ ⚹ ♂ **2:11 am**
☽ △ ☿ **3:29 am** 12:29 am
☽ ⚻ ♆ **3:36 pm** 12:36 pm
☽ △ ☉ **9:35 pm** 6:35 pm

5 MONDAY
☽ □ ♇ **4:22 am** 1:22 am
☽ ⚺ ♃ **7:34 am** 4:34 am
☽ △ ♀ **10:33 am** 7:33 am
☽ ☍ ♅ **1:46 pm** 10:46 am

6 TUESDAY
☽ ⚹ ♄ **9:05 am** 6:05 am
☽ ⚺ ♂ **11:50 am** 8:50 am
☽ □ ☿ **6:45 pm** 3:45 pm
♀ ⚹ ♅ **8:37 pm** 5:37 pm
☽ △ ♆ **11:37 pm** 8:37 pm

7 WEDNESDAY
☽ □ ☉ **10:54 am** 7:54 am
☽ ⚹ ♇ **1:16 pm** 10:16 am
☽ ☌ ♃ **4:57 pm** 1:57 pm
☽ ⚻ ♅ **11:17 pm** 8:17 pm
☽ □ ♀ 11:16 pm

8 THURSDAY
☽ □ ♀ **2:16 am**
☿ ⚺ ♆ **7:37 am** 4:37 am
☉ ⚺ ♇ **4:29 pm** 1:29 pm
☽ ⚺ ♄ **8:06 pm** 5:06 pm
☽ ☌ ♂ 10:40 pm

9 FRIDAY
☽ ☌ ♂ **1:40 am**
☽ □ ♆ **11:04 am** 8:04 am
☽ ⚹ ☿ **3:32 pm** 12:32 pm
☽ ⚺ ♇ 10:16 pm

10 SATURDAY
☽ ⚺ ♇ **1:16 am**
☽ ⚹ ☉ **4:14 am** 1:14 am
☽ ⚺ ♃ **5:21 am** 2:21 am
☽ △ ♅ **11:38 am** 8:38 am
☉ □ ♃ **6:21 pm** 3:21 pm
☽ ⚹ ♀ **9:43 pm** 6:43 pm

11 SUNDAY
☽ ☌ ♄ **9:17 am** 6:17 am
☽ ⚺ ♂ **5:44 pm** 2:44 pm
☽ ⚹ ♆ 9:08 pm

12 MONDAY
☽ ⚹ ♆ **12:08 am**
☿ ⚺ ♇ **11:24 am** 8:24 am
☽ ☌ ♇ **2:22 pm** 11:22 am
☽ ⚺ ☿ **2:52 pm** 11:52 am
☽ ⚹ ♃ **6:42 pm** 3:42 pm
☽ ⚺ ☉ **10:52 pm** 7:52 pm
☽ □ ♅ 9:43 pm

13 TUESDAY
☽ □ ♅ **12:43 am**
☿ □ ♃ **5:39 pm** 2:39 pm
☽ ⚺ ♀ **5:40 pm** 2:40 pm
☉ ⚹ ♅ **9:23 pm** 6:23 pm
☽ ⚺ ♄ **10:26 pm** 7:26 pm

14 WEDNESDAY
☽ ⚹ ♂ **9:29 am** 6:29 am
☽ ⚺ ♆ **12:44 pm** 9:44 am
☽ ⚺ ♇ 11:35 pm

15 THURSDAY
☽ ⚺ ♇ **2:35 am**
☽ □ ♃ **7:00 am** 4:00 am
☿ ⚹ ♅ **10:07 am** 7:07 am
☽ ⚹ ♅ **12:41 pm** 9:41 am
☽ ☌ ☿ **1:06 pm** 10:06 am
☽ ☌ ☉ **4:05 pm** 1:05 pm
♀ ⚹ ♄ **6:19 pm** 3:19 pm

16 FRIDAY
☽ ⚹ ♄ **9:58 am** 6:58 am
☽ ☌ ♀ **11:36 am** 8:36 am
☽ □ ♂ **11:11 pm** 8:11 pm
☽ ☌ ♆ **11:31 pm** 8:31 pm

17 SATURDAY
♂ □ ♆ **6:20 am** 3:20 am
☉ ☌ ☿ **7:27 am** 4:27 am
☽ ⚹ ♇ **12:49 pm** 9:49 am
☽ △ ♃ **5:14 pm** 2:14 pm
☽ ⚺ ♅ **10:34 pm** 7:34 pm

18 SUNDAY
☽ ⚺ ☉ **6:38 am** 3:38 am
☽ ⚺ ☿ **8:20 am** 5:20 am
☽ □ ♄ **7:15 pm** 4:15 pm
☽ ⚺ ♀ 11:31 pm

19 MONDAY
☽ ⚺ ♀ **2:31 am**
☽ ⚺ ♆ **8:03 am** 5:03 am
☽ △ ♂ **10:18 am** 7:18 am
☽ □ ♇ **8:47 pm** 5:47 pm
☽ ⚻ ♃ 10:08 pm

20 TUESDAY
☽ ⚻ ♃ **1:08 am**
☽ ☌ ♅ **6:11 am** 3:11 am
☽ ⚹ ☉ **6:16 pm** 3:16 pm
☽ ⚹ ☿ 9:12 pm
☽ △ ♄ 11:14 pm

21 WEDNESDAY
☽ ⚹ ☿ **12:12 am**
☽ △ ♄ **2:14 am**
♀ ☌ ♆ **1:42 pm** 10:42 am
☽ ⚹ ♆ **2:19 pm** 11:19 am
☽ ⚹ ♀ **2:23 pm** 11:23 am
☿ ⚹ ♄ **3:23 pm** 12:23 pm
☽ ⚻ ♂ **6:49 pm** 3:49 pm
☽ △ ♇ 11:30 pm

22 THURSDAY
☽ △ ♇ **2:30 am**
☽ ☍ ♃ **6:46 am** 3:46 am
☽ ⚺ ♅ **11:35 am** 8:35 am

23 FRIDAY
☽ □ ☉ **3:09 am** 12:09 am
☽ ⚻ ♄ **7:00 am** 4:00 am
☽ □ ☿ **12:51 pm** 9:51 am
☽ □ ♆ **6:28 pm** 3:28 pm
☽ □ ♀ **11:26 pm** 8:26 pm
☽ ☍ ♂ 9:57 pm

24 SATURDAY
☽ ☍ ♂ **12:57 am**
☽ ⚻ ♇ **6:09 am** 3:09 am
☽ ⚻ ♃ **10:19 am** 7:19 am
☽ ⚹ ♅ **2:58 pm** 11:58 am

25 SUNDAY
♀ □ ♂ **7:01 am** 4:01 am
☿ ☌ ♆ **7:26 am** 4:26 am
☽ △ ☉ **9:40 am** 6:40 am
☽ ☍ ♄ **9:52 am** 6:52 am
☉ ⚹ ♄ **12:46 pm** 9:46 am
☽ △ ♆ **8:51 pm** 5:51 pm
☽ △ ☿ **10:49 pm** 7:49 pm

26 MONDAY
☽ ⚻ ♂ **5:09 am** 2:09 am
☽ △ ♀ **6:14 am** 3:14 am
☽ ☍ ♇ **8:11 am** 5:11 am
☽ △ ♃ **12:17 pm** 9:17 am
☽ □ ♅ **4:51 pm** 1:51 pm

27 TUESDAY
♀ ⚹ ♇ **5:20 am** 2:20 am
☽ ⚻ ♄ **11:32 am** 8:32 am
☽ ⚻ ☉ **2:43 pm** 11:43 am
☽ ⚻ ♆ **10:15 pm** 7:15 pm

28 WEDNESDAY
☽ ⚻ ☿ **7:25 am** 4:25 am
☽ △ ♂ **8:29 am** 5:29 am
☽ ⚻ ♇ **9:30 am** 6:30 am
☽ ⚻ ♀ **12:04 pm** 9:04 am
☽ □ ♃ **1:36 pm** 10:36 am
☽ △ ♅ **6:13 pm** 3:13 pm
☿ □ ♂ **6:56 pm** 3:56 pm
☿ ⚹ ♇ **11:42 pm** 8:42 pm

Eastern time in bold type
Pacific time in medium type

FEBRUARY 2018

DATE	SID.TIME	SUN	MOON	NODE	MERCURY	VENUS	MARS	JUPITER	SATURN	URANUS	NEPTUNE	PLUTO	CERES	PALLAS	JUNO	VESTA	CHIRON
1 Th	8 44 36	12♒03 50	18♌11	14♌56	0♒41	17♒30	3♐21	21♏15	4♑50	24♈57	12♓47	19♑49	11♌29 R	3♉44	19♒36	7♐48	25♓46
2 F	8 48 33	13 04 42	2♍55	14 56	2 17	18 45	3 58	21 21	4 56	24 58	12 49	19 51	11 15	4 05	20 03	8 15	25 48
3 Sa	8 52 29	14 05 34	17 18	14 56 R	3 54	20 00	4 35	21 27	5 02	25 00	12 51	19 53	11 01	4 26	20 30	8 42	25 51
4 Su	8 56 26	15 06 24	1♎16	14 56	5 32	21 16	5 11	21 33	5 08	25 01	12 53	19 55	10 46	4 48	20 57	9 08	25 54
5 M	9 0 22	16 07 13	14 48	14 56	7 10	22 31	5 48	21 39	5 14	25 03	12 55	19 57	10 32	5 10	21 24	9 35	25 57
6 T	9 4 19	17 08 02	27 53	14 56	8 49	23 46	6 24	21 45	5 20	25 05	12 57	19 59	10 18	5 32	21 51	10 01	26 00
7 W	9 8 16	18 08 50	10♏35	14 56 D	10 29	25 01	7 01	21 50	5 26	25 06	12 59	20 01	10 04	5 54	22 18	10 28	26 03
8 Th	9 12 12	19 09 36	22 58	14 56	12 09	26 17	7 38	21 55	5 32	25 08	13 01	20 02	9 51	6 17	22 45	10 54	26 06
9 F	9 16 9	20 10 22	5♐05	14 56	13 51	27 32	8 14	22 01	5 37	25 10	13 03	20 04	9 37	6 40	23 12	11 20	26 09
10 Sa	9 20 5	21 11 07	17 01	14 56	15 33	28 47	8 51	22 06	5 43	25 12	13 06	20 06	9 23	7 04	23 40	11 46	26 12
11 Su	9 24 2	22 11 51	28 51	14 57	17 16	0♓02	9 27	22 10	5 49	25 14	13 08	20 08	9 10	7 27	24 07	12 12	26 15
12 M	9 27 58	23 12 33	10♑39	14 58	18 59	1 17	10 03	22 15	5 54	25 16	13 10	20 10	8 57	7 51	24 34	12 38	26 18
13 T	9 31 55	24 13 15	22 28	14 59	20 44	2 32	10 40	22 19	6 00	25 18	13 12	20 11	8 44	8 16	25 01	13 04	26 21
14 W	9 35 51	25 13 55	4♒23	15 00 R	22 29	3 48	11 16	22 24	6 05	25 20	13 14	20 13	8 31	8 40	25 29	13 29	26 24
15 Th	9 39 48	26 14 34	16 25	15 00	24 16	5 03	11 52	22 28	6 11	25 22	13 16	20 15	8 19	9 05	25 56	13 55	26 28
16 F	9 43 45	27 15 11	28 37	14 59	26 03	6 18	12 29	22 32	6 16	25 24	13 19	20 17	8 06	9 30	26 24	14 20	26 31
17 Sa	9 47 41	28 15 47	11♓00	14 58	27 51	7 33	13 05	22 36	6 21	25 26	13 21	20 18	7 54	9 55	26 51	14 45	26 34
18 Su	9 51 38	29 16 21	23 35	14 57	29 40	8 48	13 41	22 39	6 26	25 28	13 23	20 20	7 42	10 21	27 19	15 10	26 37
19 M	9 55 34	0♓16 54	6♈23	14 54	1♓29	10 03	14 17	22 43	6 31	25 31	13 25	20 22	7 31	10 46	27 46	15 35	26 41
20 T	9 59 31	1 17 25	19 25	14 52	3 20	11 18	14 53	22 46	6 36	25 33	13 27	20 23	7 20	11 12	28 14	16 00	26 44
21 W	10 3 27	2 17 54	2♉40	14 50	5 11	12 33	15 29	22 49	6 41	25 35	13 30	20 25	7 09	11 38	28 41	16 24	26 47
22 Th	10 7 24	3 18 21	16 11	14 48	7 03	13 48	16 05	22 52	6 46	25 38	13 32	20 26	6 58	12 05	29 09	16 48	26 51
23 F	10 11 20	4 18 47	29 56	14 47 D	8 55	15 03	16 41	22 55	6 51	25 40	13 34	20 28	6 48	12 32	29 37	17 13	26 54
24 Sa	10 15 17	5 19 11	13♊55	14 47	10 48	16 18	17 17	22 57	6 56	25 42	13 36	20 30	6 38	12 58	0♓04	17 37	26 57
25 Su	10 19 14	6 19 32	28 09	14 48	12 41	17 33	17 52	22 59	7 01	25 45	13 39	20 31	6 29	13 26	0 32	18 01	27 01
26 M	10 23 10	7 19 52	12♋34	14 50	14 35	18 48	18 28	23 02	7 05	25 47	13 41	20 33	6 20	13 53	1 00	18 24	27 04
27 T	10 27 7	8 20 10	27 08	14 51	16 28	20 03	19 04	23 04	7 10	25 50	13 43	20 34	6 11	14 20	1 28	18 48	27 08
28 W	10 31 3	9 20 25	11♌47	14 52 R	18 22	21 18	19 40	23 05	7 14	25 53	13 46	20 36	6 03	14 48	1 56	19 11	27 11

EPHEMERIS CALCULATED FOR 12 MIDNIGHT GREENWICH MEAN TIME. ALL OTHER DATA AND FACING ASPECTARIAN PAGE IN **EASTERN TIME (BOLD)** AND PACIFIC TIME (REGULAR).

MARCH 2018

☽ Last Aspect				☽ Ingress			
day	ET / hr:mn / PT		asp	sign	day	ET / hr:mn / PT	
2/28	**6:13 pm**	3:13 pm	△♅	♍	1	**12:57 am**	
2	**6:50 pm**	3:50 pm	☍♀	♎	3	**3:20 am**	12:20 am
4		10:19 pm	☍♅	♏	5	**8:23 am**	5:23 am
5	**1:19 am**		☍♅	♏	5	**8:23 am**	5:23 am
7	**3:55 am**	12:55 am	☌♃	♐	7	**5:03 pm**	2:03 pm
9	**9:27 pm**	6:27 pm	△♅	♑	10	**4:52 am**	1:52 am
12	**11:36 am**	8:36 am	□♅	♒	12	**6:44 pm**	3:44 pm
15	**3:32 am**	12:32 am	✶♂	♓	15	**6:12 am**	3:12 am
17	**9:12 am**	6:12 am	☌☉	♈	17	**2:57 pm**	11:57 am
19	**3:29 pm**	12:29 pm	☌♅	♉	19	**9:07 pm**	6:07 pm
21	**1:21 pm**	10:21 am	☍♃	♊	21		10:30 pm
21	**1:21 pm**	10:21 am	☍♃	♊	22	**1:30 am**	
23	**11:52 pm**	8:52 pm	✶♅	♋	24	**4:53 am**	1:53 am
25		11:58 pm	□♅	♌	26	**7:45 am**	4:45 am
26	**2:58 am**		□♅	♌	26	**7:45 am**	4:45 am
28	**5:54 am**	2:54 am	△♅	♍	28	**10:30 am**	7:30 am
29		9:59 pm	✶♃	♎	30	**1:52 pm**	10:52 am
30	**12:59 am**		✶♃	♎	30	**1:52 pm**	10:52 am

☽ Phases & Eclipses			
phase	day	ET / hr:mn / PT	
Full Moon	1	**7:51 pm**	4:51 pm
4th Quarter	9	**6:20 am**	3:20 am
New Moon	17	**9:12 am**	6:12 am
2nd Quarter	24	**11:35 am**	8:35 am
Full Moon	31	**8:37 am**	5:37 am

Planet Ingress			
	day	ET / hr:mn / PT	
☿ ♈	5		11:34 pm
☿ ♈	6	**2:34 am**	
♀ ♈	6	**6:45 pm**	3:45 pm
♂ ♑	17	**12:40 pm**	9:40 am
☉ ♈	20	**12:15 pm**	9:15 am
♀ ♊	29	**9:34 pm**	6:34 pm
♀ ♉	30		9:54 pm
♀ ♉	31	**12:54 am**	

Planetary Motion			
	day	ET / hr:mn / PT	
♃ R	8	**11:45 pm**	8:45 pm
⚳ D	18		9:12 pm
⚳ D	19	**12:12 am**	
☿ R	22	**8:19 pm**	5:19 pm

1 THURSDAY
♀△♃ **6:22 am** 3:22 am
♂⚺♇ **10:32 am** 7:32 am
☽△♄ **1:10 pm** 10:10 am
☽☍☉ **7:51 pm** 4:51 pm
☽☍♆ **11:58 pm** 8:58 pm

2 FRIDAY
☿△♃ **8:05 am** 5:05 am
☽△♇ **11:26 am** 8:26 am
☽□♂ **12:29 pm** 9:29 am
☽✶♃ **3:40 pm** 12:40 pm
☽☍☿ **4:48 pm** 1:48 pm
☽☍♀ **6:50 pm** 3:50 pm
☽⚻♅ **8:31 pm** 5:31 pm

3 SATURDAY
♀⚺♅ **2:31 pm** 11:31 am
☽□♄ **4:20 pm** 1:20 pm
☿⚺♅ **9:49 pm** 6:49 pm

4 SUNDAY
☽⚻☉ **3:08 am** 12:08 am
☽⚻♆ **3:33 am** 12:33 am
☉☌♆ **8:54 am** 5:54 am
☿☌♀ **1:05 pm** 10:05 am
☽□♇ **3:36 pm** 12:36 pm
☽✶♂ **7:01 pm** 4:01 pm
☽⚺♃ **8:03 pm** 5:03 pm
☽☍♅ 10:19 pm

5 MONDAY
☽☍♅ **1:19 am**
☽⚻♀ **4:48 am** 1:48 am
☽⚻☿ **5:34 am** 2:34 am
♂⚺♃ **7:07 pm** 4:07 pm
☽✶♄ **10:31 pm** 7:31 pm

6 TUESDAY
☽△♆ **10:23 am** 7:23 am
☽△☉ **2:27 pm** 11:27 am
☽✶♇ **11:12 pm** 8:12 pm

7 WEDNESDAY
☽☌♃ **3:55 am** 12:55 am
☽⚺♂ **5:31 am** 2:31 am
☽⚻♅ **9:42 am** 6:42 am
☽△♀ **7:33 pm** 4:33 pm
☽△☿ **11:15 pm** 8:15 pm

8 THURSDAY
☽⚺♄ **8:25 am** 5:25 am
☽□♆ **8:52 pm** 5:52 pm

9 FRIDAY
☽□☉ **6:20 am** 3:20 am
☽⚺♇ **10:19 am** 7:19 am
☽⚺♃ **3:10 pm** 12:10 pm
☽☌♂ **7:54 pm** 4:54 pm
☽△♅ **9:27 pm** 6:27 pm

10 SATURDAY
☽□♀ **2:31 pm** 11:31 am
☽□☿ **8:25 pm** 5:25 pm
☽☌♄ **9:05 pm** 6:05 pm
☿□♄ 11:00 pm

11 SUNDAY
☿□♄ **2:00 am**
♂△♅ **7:23 am** 4:23 am
☉✶♇ **7:56 am** 4:56 am
☽✶♆ **10:43 am** 7:43 am
☽☌♇ 9:15 pm
☽✶☉ 10:44 pm

12 MONDAY
☽☌♇ **12:15 am**
☽✶☉ **1:44 am**
☽✶♃ **5:00 am** 2:00 am
☽□♅ **11:36 am** 8:36 am
☽⚺♂ **12:56 pm** 9:56 am

13 TUESDAY
♀□♄ **8:39 am** 5:39 am
☽⚺♄ **11:05 am** 8:05 am
☽✶♀ **11:21 am** 8:21 am
☉△♃ **4:06 pm** 1:06 pm
☽✶☿ **5:36 pm** 2:36 pm
☽⚺♆ **11:22 pm** 8:22 pm

14 WEDNESDAY
☽⚺♇ **12:27 pm** 9:27 am
☽□♃ **4:53 pm** 1:53 pm
☽⚺☉ **7:07 pm** 4:07 pm
☽✶♅ **11:34 pm** 8:34 pm

15 THURSDAY
☽✶♂ **3:32 am** 12:32 am
☽✶♄ **10:07 pm** 7:07 pm

16 FRIDAY
☽⚺♀ **4:33 am** 1:33 am
☽⚺☿ **9:14 am** 6:14 am
☽☌♆ **9:46 am** 6:46 am
☿⚺♆ **5:44 pm** 2:44 pm
☽✶♇ **10:09 pm** 7:09 pm
☽△♃ 11:11 pm

17 SATURDAY
☽△♃ **2:11 am**
☉⚺♅ **4:41 am** 1:41 am
☽⚺♅ **8:52 am** 5:52 am
☽☌☉ **9:12 am** 6:12 am
☽□♂ **3:03 pm** 12:03 pm

18 SUNDAY
☽□♄ **6:19 am** 3:19 am
♀⚺♆ **11:13 am** 8:13 am
☽⚺♆ **5:21 pm** 2:21 pm
☽☌♀ **5:58 pm** 2:58 pm
☽☌☿ **7:47 pm** 4:47 pm

19 MONDAY
☽□♇ **5:05 am** 2:05 am
☽⚻♃ **8:46 am** 5:46 am
☽☌♅ **3:29 pm** 12:29 pm
☽⚺☉ **7:55 pm** 4:55 pm
☽△♂ **11:36 pm** 8:36 pm
☿☌♀ 9:03 pm

20 TUESDAY
☿☌♀ **12:03 am**
☽△♄ **12:05 pm** 9:05 am
☽✶♆ **10:42 pm** 7:42 pm
☽⚺☿ 11:27 pm

21 WEDNESDAY
☽⚺☿ **2:27 am**
☽⚺♀ **4:24 am** 1:24 am
☽△♇ **9:58 am** 6:58 am
☽☍♃ **1:21 pm** 10:21 am
☽⚺♅ **8:13 pm** 5:13 pm

22 THURSDAY
☽✶☉ **4:22 am** 1:22 am
☽⚻♂ **6:09 am** 3:09 am
☽⚻♄ **4:17 pm** 1:17 pm
☽□♆ 11:39 pm

23 FRIDAY
☽□♆ **2:39 am**
☽✶☿ **6:31 am** 3:31 am
☽✶♀ **1:07 pm** 10:07 am
☽⚻♇ **1:39 pm** 10:39 am
☽⚻♃ **4:45 pm** 1:45 pm
♀□♇ **7:17 pm** 4:17 pm
☽✶♅ **11:52 pm** 8:52 pm

24 SATURDAY
☽□☉ **11:35 am** 8:35 am
☽☍♂ **11:36 am** 8:36 am
☉□♂ **12:08 pm** 9:08 am
☽☍♄ **7:37 pm** 4:37 pm

25 SUNDAY
♀⚻♃ **5:08 am** 2:08 am
☽△♆ **5:52 am** 2:52 am
☽□☿ **8:54 am** 5:54 am
☽☍♇ **4:41 pm** 1:41 pm
☽△♃ **7:32 pm** 4:32 pm
☽□♀ **8:58 pm** 5:58 pm
☽□♅ 11:58 pm

26 MONDAY
☽□♅ **2:58 am**
☽⚻♂ **4:31 pm** 1:31 pm
☽△☉ **6:13 pm** 3:13 pm
☽⚻♄ **10:33 pm** 7:33 pm

27 TUESDAY
☽⚻♆ **8:45 am** 5:45 am
☽△☿ **10:09 am** 7:09 am
☽⚻♇ **7:28 pm** 4:28 pm
☽□♃ **10:05 pm** 7:05 pm

28 WEDNESDAY
☽△♀ **4:33 am** 1:33 am
☽△♅ **5:54 am** 2:54 am
☿⚺♆ **6:01 pm** 3:01 pm
♀☌♅ **8:47 pm** 5:47 pm
☽△♂ **9:24 pm** 6:24 pm
☽⚻☉ 9:52 pm
☽△♄ 10:30 pm

29 THURSDAY
☽⚻☉ **12:52 am**
☽△♄ **1:30 am**
☉□♄ **10:16 am** 7:16 am
☽⚻☿ **10:57 am** 7:57 am
☽☍♆ **11:49 am** 8:49 am
☽△♇ **10:35 pm** 7:35 pm
☽✶♃ 9:59 pm

30 FRIDAY
☽✶♃ **12:59 am**
☽⚻♅ **9:23 am** 6:23 am
☽⚻♀ **12:47 pm** 9:47 am

31 SATURDAY
☽□♂ **3:12 am** 12:12 am
☽□♄ **5:22 am** 2:22 am
☽☍☉ **8:37 am** 5:37 am
☽☍☿ **12:16 pm** 9:16 am
☽⚻♆ **4:01 pm** 1:01 pm

Eastern time in bold type
Pacific time in medium type

MARCH 2018

DATE	SID.TIME	SUN	MOON	NODE	MERCURY	VENUS	MARS	JUPITER	SATURN	URANUS	NEPTUNE	PLUTO	CERES	PALLAS	JUNO	VESTA	CHIRON
1 Th	10 35 0	10♓20 39	26♌23	14♌52℞	20♓15	22♓32	20♐15	23♏07	7♑19	25♈55	13♓48	20♑37	5♌55℞	15♉16	2♓23	19♐34	27♓14
2 F	10 38 56	11 20 51	10♍52	14 50	22 08	23 47	20 51	23 09	7 23	25 58	13 50	20 39	5 47	15 44	2 51	19 57	27 18
3 Sa	10 42 53	12 21 01	25 07	14 47	24 00	25 02	21 26	23 10	7 28	26 00	13 52	20 40	5 40	16 12	3 19	20 20	27 21
4 Su	10 46 49	13 21 09	9♎03	14 43	25 51	26 17	22 02	23 11	7 32	26 03	13 55	20 41	5 33	16 41	3 47	20 43	27 25
5 M	10 50 46	14 21 16	22 37	14 38	27 40	27 31	22 37	23 12	7 36	26 06	13 57	20 43	5 27	17 10	4 15	21 05	27 28
6 T	10 54 43	15 21 21	5♏47	14 33	29 27	28 46	23 12	23 12	7 40	26 09	13 59	20 44	5 21	17 38	4 43	21 27	27 32
7 W	10 58 39	16 21 25	18 34	14 29	1♈11	0♈01	23 47	23 13	7 44	26 11	14 01	20 46	5 16	18 07	5 11	21 49	27 35
8 Th	11 2 36	17 21 27	1♐00	14 26	2 53	1 15	24 23	23 13	7 48	26 14	14 04	20 47	5 11	18 37	5 39	22 11	27 39
9 F	11 6 32	18 21 27	13 10	14 25 D	4 31	2 30	24 58	23 13℞	7 51	26 17	14 06	20 48	5 06	19 06	6 07	22 33	27 42
10 Sa	11 10 29	19 21 26	25 07	14 25	6 05	3 45	25 33	23 13	7 55	26 20	14 08	20 49	5 02	19 36	6 35	22 54	27 46
11 Su	11 14 25	20 21 23	6♑58	14 26	7 35	4 59	26 08	23 13	7 59	26 23	14 11	20 51	4 58	20 05	7 03	23 16	27 50
12 M	11 18 22	21 21 18	18 46	14 28	8 59	6 14	26 43	23 13	8 02	26 26	14 13	20 52	4 55	20 35	7 32	23 37	27 53
13 T	11 22 18	22 21 12	0♒37	14 29	10 18	7 28	27 18	23 12	8 06	26 29	14 15	20 53	4 52	21 05	8 00	23 57	27 57
14 W	11 26 15	23 21 04	12 36	14 30℞	11 31	8 43	27 52	23 11	8 09	26 32	14 17	20 54	4 49	21 35	8 28	24 18	28 00
15 Th	11 30 12	24 20 54	24 46	14 30	12 37	9 57	28 27	23 10	8 13	26 35	14 20	20 55	4 47	22 06	8 56	24 38	28 04
16 F	11 34 8	25 20 42	7♓09	14 27	13 36	11 12	29 02	23 09	8 16	26 38	14 22	20 56	4 45	22 36	9 24	24 58	28 07
17 Sa	11 38 5	26 20 29	19 49	14 23	14 29	12 26	29 36	23 08	8 19	26 41	14 24	20 57	4 44	23 07	9 53	25 18	28 11
18 Su	11 42 1	27 20 13	2♈45	14 17	15 13	13 41	0♑11	23 06	8 22	26 44	14 26	20 58	4 44	23 38	10 21	25 38	28 15
19 M	11 45 58	28 19 56	15 56	14 09	15 49	14 55	0 45	23 04	8 25	26 47	14 29	21 00	4 43 D	24 09	10 49	25 57	28 18
20 T	11 49 54	29 19 36	29 22	14 01	16 18	16 09	1 19	23 02	8 28	26 50	14 31	21 00	4 43	24 40	11 18	26 16	28 22
21 W	11 53 51	0♈19 14	13♉01	13 54	16 38	17 24	1 53	23 00	8 30	26 53	14 33	21 01	4 44	25 11	11 46	26 35	28 25
22 Th	11 57 47	1 18 50	26 49	13 48	16 50	18 38	2 27	22 58	8 33	26 57	14 35	21 02	4 45	25 42	12 14	26 53	28 29
23 F	12 1 44	2 18 24	10♊45	13 44	16 54℞	19 52	3 01	22 55	8 36	27 00	14 37	21 03	4 46	26 14	12 43	27 12	28 32
24 Sa	12 5 40	3 17 56	24 47	13 42 D	16 51	21 06	3 35	22 53	8 38	27 03	14 40	21 04	4 48	26 46	13 11	27 30	28 36
25 Su	12 9 37	4 17 25	8♋54	13 41	16 39	22 21	4 09	22 50	8 40	27 06	14 42	21 05	4 51	27 17	13 39	27 47	28 40
26 M	12 13 34	5 16 52	23 03	13 42	16 21	23 35	4 43	22 47	8 43	27 09	14 44	21 06	4 53	27 49	14 08	28 05	28 43
27 T	12 17 30	6 16 16	7♌15	13 43℞	15 55	24 49	5 16	22 44	8 45	27 13	14 46	21 07	4 56	28 21	14 36	28 22	28 47
28 W	12 21 27	7 15 39	21 26	13 43	15 24	26 03	5 50	22 40	8 47	27 16	14 48	21 07	5 00	28 53	15 05	28 39	28 50
29 Th	12 25 23	8 14 58	5♍35	13 41	14 47	27 17	6 23	22 37	8 49	27 19	14 50	21 08	5 04	29 26	15 33	28 55	28 54
30 F	12 29 20	9 14 16	19 39	13 37	14 06	28 31	6 56	22 33	8 51	27 23	14 53	21 09	5 08	29 58	16 01	29 12	28 57
31 Sa	12 33 16	10 13 32	3♎32	13 30	13 21	29 45	7 30	22 29	8 53	27 26	14 55	21 10	5 13	0♊30	16 30	29 28	29 01

EPHEMERIS CALCULATED FOR 12 MIDNIGHT GREENWICH MEAN TIME. ALL OTHER DATA AND FACING ASPECTARIAN PAGE IN **EASTERN TIME (BOLD)** AND PACIFIC TIME (REGULAR).

☽ Last Aspect day	ET / hr:mn / PT	asp	☽ Ingress sign	day	ET / hr:mn / PT
1	**2:29 pm** 11:29 am	☍ ♅	♏	1	**6:57 pm** 3:57 pm
3	**12:06 pm** 9:06 am	☌ ♃	♐	3	11:55 pm
3	**12:06 pm** 9:06 am	☌ ♃	♐	4	**2:55 am**
6	**9:36 am** 6:36 am	△ ♅	♑	6	**2:01 pm** 11:01 am
8	**10:40 pm** 7:40 pm	☐ ♅	♒	8	11:50 pm
8	**10:40 pm** 7:40 pm	☐ ♅	♒	9	**2:50 am**
11	**10:55 am** 7:55 am	⚹ ♅	♓	11	**2:40 pm** 11:40 am
13	**7:27 am** 4:27 am	△ ♃	♈	13	**11:25 pm** 8:25 pm
15	10:59 pm	☌ ♅	♉	16	**4:51 am** 1:51 am
16	**1:59 am**	☌ ♅	♉	16	**4:51 am** 1:51 am
17	**6:05 pm** 3:05 pm	☌ ♀	♊	18	**8:02 am** 5:02 am
20	**8:05 am** 5:05 am	⚹ ♅	♋	20	**10:26 am** 7:26 am
22	**10:58 am** 7:58 am	☐ ♅	♌	22	**1:09 pm** 10:09 am
24	**2:40 pm** 11:40 am	△ ♅	♍	24	**4:40 pm** 1:40 pm
26	**5:49 am** 2:49 am	△ ♇	♎	26	**9:13 pm** 6:13 pm
28	10:32 pm	☍ ♅	♏	29	**3:11 am** 12:11 am
29	**1:32 am**	☍ ♅	♏	29	**3:11 am** 12:11 am
30	**10:56 pm** 7:56 pm	⚹ ♂	♐	5/1	**11:20 am** 8:20 am

☽ Phases & Eclipses phase	day	ET / hr:mn / PT
4th Quarter	8	**3:18 am** 12:18 am
New Moon	15	**9:57 pm** 6:57 pm
2nd Quarter	22	**5:46 pm** 2:46 pm
Full Moon	29	**8:58 pm** 5:58 pm

Planet Ingress		day	ET / hr:mn / PT
⚶	♑	1	**9:54 pm** 6:54 pm
⚷	♈	17	**4:12 am** 1:12 am
☉	♉	19	**11:13 pm** 8:13 pm
♀	♊	24	**12:40 pm** 9:40 am
⚵	♈	28	**3:44 am** 12:44 am

Planetary Motion		day	ET / hr:mn / PT
☿	D	15	**5:21 am** 2:21 am
♄	℞	17	**9:47 pm** 6:47 pm
♇	℞	22	**11:26 am** 8:26 am

1 SUNDAY
- ☽ ☐ ♇ **3:05 am** 12:05 am
- ☽ ⚺ ♃ **5:16 am** 2:16 am
- ☉ ☌ ☿ **1:53 pm** 10:53 am
- ☽ ☍ ♅ **2:29 pm** 11:29 am
- ☽ ☍ ♀ **11:17 pm** 8:17 pm

2 MONDAY
- ☽ ⚹ ♂ **11:18 am** 8:18 am
- ☽ ⚹ ♄ **11:19 am** 8:19 am
- ♂ ☌ ♄ **11:44 am** 8:44 am
- ☽ ⚻ ☿ **3:14 pm** 12:14 pm
- ☽ ⚻ ☉ **7:05 pm** 4:05 pm
- ☽ △ ♆ **10:34 pm** 7:34 pm

3 TUESDAY
- ☽ ⚹ ♇ **10:09 am** 7:09 am
- ☽ ☌ ♃ **12:06 pm** 9:06 am
- ☽ ⚻ ♅ **10:26 pm** 7:26 pm

4 WEDNESDAY
- ☿ ☐ ♂ **3:05 am** 12:05 am
- ☽ ⚻ ♀ **1:41 pm** 10:41 am
- ☉ ⚺ ♆ **6:10 pm** 3:10 pm
- ☽ ⚺ ♄ **8:22 pm** 5:22 pm
- ☽ △ ☿ **8:51 pm** 5:51 pm
- ☽ ⚺ ♂ **10:53 pm** 7:53 pm

5 THURSDAY
- ☿ ☐ ♄ **4:22 am** 1:22 am
- ☽ ☐ ♆ **8:19 am** 5:19 am

- ☽ △ ☉ **9:31 am** 6:31 am
- ☽ ⚺ ♇ **8:27 pm** 5:27 pm
- ☽ ⚺ ♃ **10:04 pm** 7:04 pm

6 FRIDAY
- ☽ △ ♅ **9:36 am** 6:36 am
- ☿ ⚺ ♀ **1:05 pm** 10:05 am

7 SATURDAY
- ☽ ☐ ☿ **5:15 am** 2:15 am
- ☽ △ ♀ **8:10 am** 5:10 am
- ☽ ☌ ♄ **8:19 am** 5:19 am
- ♀ △ ♄ **9:37 am** 6:37 am
- ☽ ☌ ♂ **1:41 pm** 10:41 am
- ☽ ⚹ ♆ **8:45 pm** 5:45 pm

8 SUNDAY
- ☽ ☐ ☉ **3:18 am** 12:18 am
- ☽ ☌ ♇ **9:03 am** 6:03 am
- ☽ ⚹ ♃ **10:14 am** 7:14 am
- ☽ ☐ ♅ **10:40 pm** 7:40 pm

9 MONDAY
- ☽ ⚹ ☿ **3:16 pm** 12:16 pm
- ☽ ⚺ ♄ **9:12 pm** 6:12 pm

10 TUESDAY
- ☽ ☐ ♀ **3:56 am** 12:56 am
- ☽ ⚺ ♂ **5:17 am** 2:17 am
- ☽ ⚺ ♆ **9:34 am** 6:34 am
- ☽ ⚹ ☉ **9:11 pm** 6:11 pm
- ☽ ⚺ ♇ **9:29 pm** 6:29 pm

- ☽ ☐ ♃ **10:09 pm** 7:09 pm
- ☉ ☐ ♇ 9:54 pm
- ♀ △ ♂ 11:03 pm

11 WEDNESDAY
- ☉ ☐ ♇ **12:54 am**
- ♀ △ ♂ **2:03 am**
- ☉ ⚻ ♃ **8:15 am** 5:15 am
- ☽ ⚹ ♅ **10:55 am** 7:55 am
- ☽ ⚺ ☿ 9:48 pm

12 THURSDAY
- ☽ ⚺ ☿ **12:48 am**
- ☽ ⚹ ♄ **8:18 am** 5:18 am
- ♀ ⚹ ♆ **12:26 pm** 9:26 am
- ☽ ⚹ ♂ **6:29 pm** 3:29 pm
- ☽ ☌ ♆ **8:09 pm** 5:09 pm
- ☽ ⚹ ♀ **8:57 pm** 5:57 pm

13 FRIDAY
- ☽ ⚹ ♇ **7:16 am** 4:16 am
- ☽ △ ♃ **7:27 am** 4:27 am
- ☽ ⚺ ☉ **11:43 am** 8:43 am
- ☽ ⚺ ♅ **8:10 pm** 5:10 pm

14 SATURDAY
- ♃ ⚹ ♇ **5:58 am** 2:58 am
- ☽ ☌ ☿ **8:12 am** 5:12 am
- ♂ ⚹ ♆ **1:27 pm** 10:27 am
- ☽ ☐ ♄ **4:01 pm** 1:01 pm

15 SUNDAY
- ☽ ⚺ ♆ **3:15 am** 12:15 am
- ☽ ☐ ♂ **3:46 am** 12:46 am
- ☽ ⚺ ♀ **9:20 am** 6:20 am

- ☽ ⚻ ♃ **1:22 pm** 10:22 am
- ☽ ☐ ♇ **1:36 pm** 10:36 am
- ☽ ☌ ☉ **9:57 pm** 6:57 pm
- ☽ ☌ ♅ 10:59 pm

16 MONDAY
- ☽ ☌ ♅ **1:59 am**
- ☽ ⚺ ☿ **1:15 pm** 10:15 am
- ☽ △ ♄ **8:38 pm** 5:38 pm

17 TUESDAY
- ♀ ☍ ♃ **3:00 am** 12:00 am
- ☽ ⚹ ♆ **7:27 am** 4:27 am
- ♀ △ ♇ **9:04 am** 6:04 am
- ☽ △ ♂ **9:48 am** 6:48 am
- ☽ ☍ ♃ **4:40 pm** 1:40 pm
- ☽ △ ♇ **5:18 pm** 2:18 pm
- ☽ ☌ ♀ **6:05 pm** 3:05 pm

18 WEDNESDAY
- ☽ ⚺ ☉ **5:09 am** 2:09 am
- ☽ ⚺ ♅ **5:28 am** 2:28 am
- ☉ ☌ ♅ **10:00 am** 7:00 am
- ☽ ⚹ ☿ **4:57 pm** 1:57 pm
- ☽ ⚻ ♄ **11:26 pm** 8:26 pm

19 THURSDAY
- ☽ ☐ ♆ **10:10 am** 7:10 am
- ☽ ⚻ ♂ **2:15 pm** 11:15 am
- ☽ ⚻ ♃ **6:47 pm** 3:47 pm
- ☽ ⚻ ♇ **7:48 pm** 4:48 pm
- ☽ ⚺ ♀ 10:17 pm

20 FRIDAY
- ☽ ⚺ ♀ **1:17 am**
- ☽ ⚹ ♅ **8:05 am** 5:05 am
- ☽ ⚹ ☉ **11:16 am** 8:16 am
- ☽ ☐ ☿ **8:42 pm** 5:42 pm
- ☽ ☍ ♄ 10:49 pm

21 SATURDAY
- ☽ ☍ ♄ **1:49 am**
- ☽ △ ♆ **12:44 pm** 9:44 am
- ☽ ☍ ♂ **6:36 pm** 3:36 pm
- ☽ △ ♃ **8:56 pm** 5:56 pm
- ☽ ☍ ♇ **10:21 pm** 7:21 pm

22 SUNDAY
- ☽ ⚹ ♀ **8:40 am** 5:40 am
- ☽ ☐ ♅ **10:58 am** 7:58 am
- ☽ ☐ ☉ **5:46 pm** 2:46 pm
- ☽ △ ☿ 10:32 pm

23 MONDAY
- ☽ △ ☿ **1:32 am**
- ☽ ⚻ ♄ **4:44 am** 1:44 am
- ♀ ⚺ ♅ **12:34 pm** 9:34 am
- ☽ ⚻ ♆ **3:56 pm** 12:56 pm
- ☽ ⚻ ♂ **11:40 pm** 8:40 pm
- ☽ ☐ ♃ **11:44 pm** 8:44 pm
- ♂ ⚹ ♃ 10:13 pm
- ☽ ⚻ ♇ 10:37 pm

24 TUESDAY
- ♂ ⚹ ♃ **1:13 am**
- ☽ ⚻ ♇ **1:37 am**

- ☽ △ ♅ **2:40 pm** 11:40 am
- ☽ ☐ ♀ **5:03 pm** 2:03 pm
- ☽ △ ☉ 10:17 pm

25 WEDNESDAY
- ☽ △ ☉ **1:17 am**
- ☽ ⚻ ☿ **7:58 am** 4:58 am
- ☽ △ ♄ **8:30 am** 5:30 am
- ☿ ☐ ♄ **5:28 pm** 2:28 pm
- ☽ ☍ ♆ **8:04 pm** 5:04 pm

26 THURSDAY
- ☽ ⚹ ♃ **3:28 am** 12:28 am
- ☽ △ ♂ **5:47 am** 2:47 am
- ☽ △ ♇ **5:49 am** 2:49 am
- ♂ ☌ ♇ **7:00 am** 4:00 am
- ☽ ⚻ ♅ **7:23 pm** 4:23 pm
- ☽ △ ♀ 11:48 pm

27 FRIDAY
- ☽ △ ♀ **2:48 am**
- ☽ ⚻ ☉ **10:08 am** 7:08 am
- ☽ ☐ ♄ **1:21 pm** 10:21 am
- ☽ ☍ ☿ **4:17 pm** 1:17 pm
- ☽ ⚻ ♆ 10:24 pm

28 SATURDAY
- ☽ ⚻ ♆ **1:24 am**
- ☽ ⚺ ♃ **8:25 am** 5:25 am
- ☽ ☐ ♇ **11:19 am** 8:19 am
- ☽ ☐ ♂ **1:17 pm** 10:17 am
- ☽ ☍ ♅ 10:32 pm

29 SUNDAY
- ☽ ☍ ♅ **1:32 am**
- ☉ △ ♄ **6:04 am** 3:04 am
- ☽ ⚻ ♀ **2:32 pm** 11:32 am
- ☽ ⚹ ♄ **7:50 pm** 4:50 pm
- ☽ ☍ ☉ **8:58 pm** 5:58 pm

30 MONDAY
- ☽ ⚻ ☿ **3:15 am** 12:15 am
- ☽ △ ♆ **8:31 am** 5:31 am
- ☽ ☌ ♃ **3:11 pm** 12:11 pm
- ☽ ⚹ ♇ **6:43 pm** 3:43 pm
- ☽ ⚹ ♂ **10:56 pm** 7:56 pm

Eastern time in bold type
Pacific time in medium type

APRIL 2018

DATE	SID.TIME	SUN	MOON	NODE	MERCURY	VENUS	MARS	JUPITER	SATURN	URANUS	NEPTUNE	PLUTO	CERES	PALLAS	JUNO	VESTA	CHIRON
1 Su	12 37 13	11 ♈ 12 45	17 ♎ 12	13 ♌ 21 R	12 ♈ 33 R	0 ♉ 59	8 ♑ 03	22 ♏ 25 R	8 ♑ 55	27 ♈ 29	14 ♓ 57	21 ♑ 10	5 ♌ 18	1 ♊ 03	16 ♓ 58	29 ♐ 43	29 ♓ 04
2 M	12 41 9	12 11 56	0 ♏ 35	13 10	11 44	2 13	8 36	22 21	8 56	27 33	14 59	21 11	5 23	1 36	17 27	29 59	29 08
3 T	12 45 6	13 11 06	13 39	13 00	10 55	3 27	9 08	22 17	8 58	27 36	15 01	21 11	5 29	2 08	17 55	0 ♑ 14	29 11
4 W	12 49 3	14 10 14	26 23	12 51	10 05	4 40	9 41	22 12	8 59	27 39	15 03	21 12	5 36	2 41	18 24	0 29	29 15
5 Th	12 52 59	15 09 19	8 ♐ 49	12 43	9 17	5 54	10 14	22 07	9 00	27 43	15 05	21 13	5 42	3 14	18 53	0 43	29 18
6 F	12 56 56	16 08 23	21 00	12 37	8 31	7 08	10 46	22 03	9 02	27 46	15 07	21 13	5 49	3 47	19 21	0 57	29 22
7 Sa	13 0 52	17 07 26	2 ♑ 58	12 34	7 48	8 22	11 19	21 58	9 03	27 49	15 09	21 14	5 57	4 20	19 50	1 11	29 25
8 Su	13 4 49	18 06 26	14 49	12 33D	7 09	9 35	11 51	21 52	9 04	27 53	15 11	21 14	6 04	4 54	20 18	1 24	29 29
9 M	13 8 45	19 05 25	26 38	12 33	6 34	10 49	12 23	21 47	9 05	27 56	15 13	21 14	6 12	5 27	20 47	1 37	29 32
10 T	13 12 42	20 04 22	8 ♒ 30	12 34 R	6 03	12 03	12 55	21 42	9 06	28 00	15 15	21 15	6 21	6 00	21 15	1 50	29 36
11 W	13 16 38	21 03 17	20 30	12 33	5 38	13 16	13 27	21 36	9 06	28 03	15 17	21 15	6 29	6 34	21 44	2 02	29 39
12 Th	13 20 35	22 02 10	2 ♓ 45	12 31	5 17	14 30	13 58	21 31	9 07	28 06	15 19	21 16	6 39	7 07	22 13	2 14	29 42
13 F	13 24 32	23 01 02	15 16	12 27	5 02	15 43	14 30	21 25	9 08	28 10	15 21	21 16	6 48	7 41	22 41	2 25	29 46
14 Sa	13 28 28	23 59 52	28 08	12 20	4 52	16 57	15 01	21 19	9 08	28 13	15 23	21 16	6 58	8 15	23 10	2 37	29 49
15 Su	13 32 25	24 58 40	11 ♈ 21	12 11	4 47 D	18 10	15 32	21 13	9 08	28 17	15 24	21 16	7 08	8 49	23 38	2 47	29 52
16 M	13 36 21	25 57 26	24 55	12 00	4 48	19 24	16 03	21 06	9 09	28 20	15 26	21 17	7 18	9 23	24 07	2 58	29 56
17 T	13 40 18	26 56 10	8 ♉ 47	11 48	4 53	20 37	16 34	21 00	9 09	28 24	15 28	21 17	7 29	9 57	24 36	3 08	29 59
18 W	13 44 14	27 54 52	22 52	11 37	5 04	21 50	17 05	20 54	9 09 R	28 27	15 30	21 17	7 40	10 31	25 04	3 17	0 ♈ 02
19 Th	13 48 11	28 53 32	7 ♊ 06	11 27	5 20	23 04	17 35	20 47	9 09	28 31	15 32	21 17	7 51	11 05	25 33	3 26	0 05
20 F	13 52 7	29 52 10	21 24	11 20	5 40	24 17	18 06	20 41	9 09	28 34	15 34	21 17	8 03	11 39	26 02	3 35	0 09
21 Sa	13 56 4	0 ♉ 50 46	5 ♋ 41	11 16	6 05	25 30	18 36	20 34	9 09	28 37	15 35	21 17	8 15	12 13	26 30	3 43	0 12
22 Su	14 0 1	1 49 19	19 54	11 14 D	6 34	26 43	19 06	20 27	9 08	28 41	15 37	21 17 R	8 27	12 47	26 59	3 51	0 15
23 M	14 3 57	2 47 51	4 ♌ 01	11 14 R	7 08	27 56	19 36	20 20	9 08	28 44	15 39	21 17	8 40	13 22	27 28	3 58	0 18
24 T	14 7 54	3 46 20	18 02	11 14	7 45	29 09	20 05	20 13	9 07	28 48	15 40	21 17	8 53	13 56	27 56	4 05	0 21
25 W	14 11 50	4 44 47	1 ♍ 55	11 13	8 26	0 ♊ 22	20 35	20 06	9 07	28 51	15 42	21 17	9 06	14 31	28 25	4 12	0 24
26 Th	14 15 47	5 43 11	15 41	11 10	9 11	1 35	21 04	19 59	9 06	28 55	15 44	21 17	9 19	15 05	28 53	4 18	0 27
27 F	14 19 43	6 41 34	29 19	11 04	9 59	2 48	21 33	19 52	9 05	28 58	15 45	21 17	9 33	15 40	29 22	4 24	0 30
28 Sa	14 23 40	7 39 55	12 ♎ 47	10 55	10 51	4 01	22 01	19 44	9 04	29 01	15 47	21 17	9 47	16 14	29 51	4 29	0 33
29 Su	14 27 36	8 38 13	26 04	10 43	11 46	5 14	22 30	19 37	9 03	29 05	15 48	21 17	10 01	16 49	0 ♈ 19	4 34	0 36
30 M	14 31 33	9 36 30	9 ♏ 07	10 31	12 43	6 27	22 58	19 30	9 02	29 08	15 50	21 16	10 15	17 24	0 48	4 38	0 39

EPHEMERIS CALCULATED FOR 12 MIDNIGHT GREENWICH MEAN TIME. ALL OTHER DATA AND FACING ASPECTARIAN PAGE IN **EASTERN TIME (BOLD)** AND PACIFIC TIME (REGULAR).

MAY 2018

☽ Last Aspect day	ET / hr:mn / PT		asp	☽ Ingress sign	day	ET / hr:mn / PT	
4/30	**10:56 pm**	7:56 pm	⚹♂	♐	1	**11:20 am**	8:20 am
3	**8:50 pm**	5:50 pm	△♅	♑	3	**10:06 pm**	7:06 pm
6	**9:48 am**	6:48 am	□♅	♒	6	**10:48 am**	7:48 am
8	**10:29 pm**	7:29 pm	⚹♅	♓	8	**11:11 pm**	8:11 pm
11	**5:02 am**	2:02 am	⚹♂	♈	11	**8:40 am**	5:40 am
13	**2:05 pm**	11:05 am	☌♅	♉	13	**2:15 pm**	11:15 am
15	**4:30 pm**	1:30 pm	△♂	♊	15	**4:43 pm**	1:43 pm
17	**2:18 pm**	11:18 am	☌♀	♋	17	**5:47 pm**	2:47 pm
19	**5:14 pm**	2:14 pm	⚹☉	♌	19	**7:11 pm**	4:11 pm
20	**11:30 pm**	8:30 pm	□♃	♍	21	**10:03 pm**	7:03 pm
23	**10:55 am**	7:55 am	△♇	♎	23		11:52 pm
23	**10:55 am**	7:55 am	△♇	♎	24	**2:52 am**	
25	**5:04 pm**	2:04 pm	□♇	♏	26	**9:39 am**	6:39 am
28	**1:25 pm**	10:25 am	☍☿	♐	28	**6:29 pm**	3:29 pm
29		11:26 pm	□♆	♑	31	**5:27 am**	2:27 am
30	**2:26 am**		□♆	♑	31	**5:27 am**	2:27 am

☽ Phases & Eclipses phase	day	ET / hr:mn / PT	
4th Quarter	7	**10:09 pm**	7:09 pm
New Moon	15	**7:48 am**	4:48 am
2nd Quarter	21	**11:49 pm**	8:49 pm
Full Moon	29	**10:20 am**	7:20 am

Planet Ingress		day	ET / hr:mn / PT	
☿	♉	13	**8:40 am**	5:40 am
♅	♉	15	**11:16 am**	8:16 am
♂	♒	15		9:55 pm
♂	♒	16	**12:55 am**	
♀	♋	19	**9:11 am**	6:11 am
☉	♊	20	**10:15 pm**	7:15 pm
♀	♋	21	**9:09 am**	6:09 am
☿	♊	29	**7:49 pm**	4:49 pm

Planetary Motion		day	ET / hr:mn / PT	
♇	℞	8	**3:48 am**	12:48 am

1 TUESDAY
☽ ⚻ ♅ **9:51 am** 6:51 am
♀ ⚻ ♄ **10:24 pm** 7:24 pm

2 WEDNESDAY
☽ ⚺ ♄ **4:39 am** 1:39 am
☽ ☍ ♀ **5:21 am** 2:21 am
☽ ⚻ ☉ **10:49 am** 7:49 am
☽ △ ☿ **5:58 pm** 2:58 pm
☽ □ ♆ **6:10 pm** 3:10 pm
☿ ⚺ ♆ **8:03 pm** 5:03 pm
☽ ⚺ ♃ 9:27 pm

3 THURSDAY
☽ ⚺ ♃ **12:27 am**
☽ ⚺ ♇ **4:43 am** 1:43 am
☽ ⚺ ♂ **11:27 am** 8:27 am
☽ △ ♅ **8:50 pm** 5:50 pm

4 FRIDAY
☽ ☌ ♄ **4:02 pm** 1:02 pm
☽ ⚻ ♀ **11:38 pm** 8:38 pm

5 SATURDAY
☽ △ ☉ **3:52 am** 12:52 am
☽ ⚹ ♆ **6:17 am** 3:17 am
☿ ⚻ ♃ **7:05 am** 4:05 am
☽ ⚹ ♃ **12:00 pm** 9:00 am
☽ □ ☿ **12:38 pm** 9:38 am
☽ ☌ ♇ **5:00 pm** 2:00 pm
☽ ☌ ♂ 11:20 pm

6 SUNDAY
☽ ☌ ♂ **2:20 am**
☽ □ ♅ **9:48 am** 6:48 am
☉ ⚹ ♆ **9:56 am** 6:56 am

7 MONDAY
☽ ⚺ ♄ **4:47 am** 1:47 am
☿ □ ♇ **4:52 am** 1:52 am
♀ □ ♆ **5:58 pm** 2:58 pm
☽ ⚺ ♆ **7:16 pm** 4:16 pm
☽ △ ♀ **7:25 pm** 4:25 pm
☽ □ ☉ **10:09 pm** 7:09 pm
☽ □ ♃ 9:11 pm

8 TUESDAY
☽ □ ♃ **12:11 am**
☽ ⚺ ♇ **5:43 am** 2:43 am
☽ ⚹ ☿ **8:50 am** 5:50 am
☽ ⚺ ♂ **5:12 pm** 2:12 pm
☉ ☍ ♃ **8:39 pm** 5:39 pm
☽ ⚹ ♅ **10:29 pm** 7:29 pm

9 WEDNESDAY
♀ ⚻ ♃ **2:36 pm** 11:36 am
☽ ⚹ ♄ **4:22 pm** 1:22 pm

10 THURSDAY
☽ ☌ ♆ **6:27 am** 3:27 am
☽ △ ♃ **10:26 am** 7:26 am
☽ □ ♀ **12:44 pm** 9:44 am
☽ ⚹ ☉ **1:58 pm** 10:58 am
☽ ⚹ ♇ **4:13 pm** 1:13 pm
☽ ⚺ ☿ 11:23 pm

11 FRIDAY
☽ ⚺ ☿ **2:23 am**
☽ ⚹ ♂ **5:02 am** 2:02 am
☽ ⚺ ♅ **8:15 am** 5:15 am
☉ △ ♇ **7:10 pm** 4:10 pm
☽ □ ♄ 9:35 pm
♀ ⚻ ♇ 10:05 pm

12 SATURDAY
☽ □ ♄ **12:35 am**
♀ ⚻ ♇ **1:05 am**
☿ □ ♂ **9:30 am** 6:30 am
☽ ⚺ ♆ **1:56 pm** 10:56 am
☽ ⚻ ♃ **5:02 pm** 2:02 pm
☽ □ ♇ **10:54 pm** 7:54 pm
☽ ⚹ ♀ 10:01 pm
☽ ⚺ ☉ 10:02 pm
☉ ⚺ ♀ 10:25 pm

13 SUNDAY
☽ ⚹ ♀ **1:01 am**
☽ ⚺ ☉ **1:02 am**
☉ ⚺ ♀ **1:25 am**
☿ ☌ ♅ **6:50 am** 3:50 am
☽ □ ♂ **12:31 pm** 9:31 am
☽ ☌ ♅ **2:05 pm** 11:05 am
☽ ☌ ☿ **2:57 pm** 11:57 am

14 MONDAY
☽ △ ♄ **4:58 am** 1:58 am
☽ ⚹ ♆ **5:44 pm** 2:44 pm
☽ ☍ ♃ **8:08 pm** 5:08 pm
☽ △ ♇ 11:05 pm

15 TUESDAY
☽ △ ♇ **2:05 am**
☽ ☌ ☉ **7:48 am** 4:48 am
☽ ⚺ ♀ **8:46 am** 5:46 am
☽ △ ♂ **4:30 pm** 1:30 pm
☽ ⚺ ♅ **4:44 pm** 1:44 pm
☽ ⚺ ☿ **11:32 pm** 8:32 pm

16 WEDNESDAY
♂ □ ♅ **3:04 am** 12:04 am
☽ ⚻ ♄ **6:42 am** 3:42 am
☽ □ ♆ **7:16 pm** 4:16 pm
☽ ⚻ ♃ **9:08 pm** 6:08 pm

17 THURSDAY
☽ ⚻ ♇ **3:20 am** 12:20 am
☽ ⚺ ☉ **12:26 pm** 9:26 am
☽ ☌ ♀ **2:18 pm** 11:18 am
☽ ⚹ ♅ **5:59 pm** 2:59 pm
☽ ⚻ ♂ **6:54 pm** 3:54 pm

18 FRIDAY
☽ ⚹ ☿ **6:51 am** 3:51 am
☽ ☍ ♄ **7:34 am** 4:34 am
☿ △ ♄ **12:49 pm** 9:49 am
☽ △ ♆ **8:23 pm** 5:23 pm
☽ △ ♃ **9:47 pm** 6:47 pm

19 SATURDAY
☽ ☍ ♇ **4:26 am** 1:26 am
♀ ⚹ ♅ **1:30 pm** 10:30 am
☽ ⚹ ☉ **5:14 pm** 2:14 pm
☽ □ ♅ **7:33 pm** 4:33 pm
☽ ⚺ ♀ **8:05 pm** 5:05 pm
☽ ☍ ♂ **9:37 pm** 6:37 pm

20 SUNDAY
☽ ⚻ ♄ **9:07 am** 6:07 am
☽ □ ☿ **3:31 pm** 12:31 pm
♀ ⚻ ♂ **10:06 pm** 7:06 pm
☽ ⚻ ♆ **10:32 pm** 7:32 pm
☽ □ ♃ **11:30 pm** 8:30 pm

21 MONDAY
☉ ⚺ ♅ **5:47 am** 2:47 am
☽ ⚻ ♇ **6:45 am** 3:45 am
☽ △ ♅ **10:38 pm** 7:38 pm
☽ □ ☉ **11:49 pm** 8:49 pm
☽ ⚻ ♂ 10:57 pm

22 TUESDAY
☽ ⚻ ♂ **1:57 am**
☽ ⚹ ♀ **3:47 am** 12:47 am
☽ △ ♄ **12:19 pm** 9:19 am
☿ ⚹ ♆ **10:13 pm** 7:13 pm
☿ ☍ ♃ 10:54 pm
☽ ☍ ♆ 11:30 pm
☽ ⚹ ♃ 11:59 pm

23 WEDNESDAY
☿ ☍ ♃ **1:54 am**
☽ ☍ ♆ **2:30 am**
☽ ⚹ ♃ **2:59 am**
☽ △ ☿ **3:10 am** 12:10 am
☽ △ ♇ **10:55 am** 7:55 am
☉ △ ♂ **10:39 pm** 7:39 pm

24 THURSDAY
☽ ⚻ ♅ **3:40 am** 12:40 am
☽ △ ♂ **8:19 am** 5:19 am
☽ △ ☉ **8:48 am** 5:48 am
☽ □ ♀ **2:03 pm** 11:03 am
☽ □ ♄ **5:28 pm** 2:28 pm

25 FRIDAY
♃ △ ♆ **5:52 am** 2:52 am
☽ ⚺ ♃ **8:25 am** 5:25 am
☽ ⚻ ♆ **8:27 am** 5:27 am
☿ △ ♇ **9:38 am** 6:38 am
☽ □ ♇ **5:04 pm** 2:04 pm
☽ ⚻ ☿ **6:23 pm** 3:23 pm
♀ ☍ ♄ 11:40 pm

26 SATURDAY
♀ ☍ ♄ **2:40 am**
☽ ☍ ♅ **10:43 am** 7:43 am
☽ □ ♂ **4:46 pm** 1:46 pm
☽ ⚻ ☉ **8:16 pm** 5:16 pm
☽ ⚹ ♄ 9:34 pm
☽ △ ♀ 11:55 pm

27 SUNDAY
☽ ⚹ ♄ **12:34 am**
☽ △ ♀ **2:55 am**
☽ ☌ ♃ **3:48 pm** 12:48 pm
☽ △ ♆ **4:23 pm** 1:23 pm
☽ ⚹ ♇ 10:12 pm

28 MONDAY
☽ ⚹ ♇ **1:12 am**
☽ ☍ ☿ **1:25 pm** 10:25 am
☽ ⚻ ♅ **7:48 pm** 4:48 pm
☉ ⚻ ♄ 11:36 pm

29 TUESDAY
☉ ⚻ ♄ **2:36 am**
☽ ⚹ ♂ **3:20 am** 12:20 am
☽ ⚺ ♄ **9:42 am** 6:42 am
☽ ☍ ☉ **10:20 am** 7:20 am
☽ ⚻ ♀ **6:33 pm** 3:33 pm
☽ ⚺ ♃ 10:15 pm
☽ □ ♆ 11:26 pm

30 WEDNESDAY
☽ ⚺ ♃ **1:15 am**
☽ □ ♆ **2:26 am**
☿ ⚺ ♅ **4:22 am** 1:22 am
☽ ⚺ ♇ **11:27 am** 8:27 am

31 THURSDAY
☽ △ ♅ **7:02 am** 4:02 am
☽ ⚻ ☿ **12:39 pm** 9:39 am
☽ ⚺ ♂ **4:06 pm** 1:06 pm
☽ ☌ ♄ **8:53 pm** 5:53 pm

Pacific time in medium type

DATE	SID.TIME	SUN	MOON	NODE	MERCURY	VENUS	MARS	JUPITER	SATURN	URANUS	NEPTUNE	PLUTO	CERES	PALLAS	JUNO	VESTA	CHIRON
1 T	14 35 29	10 ♉ 34 45	21 ♏ 57	10 ♌ 18 ℞	13 ♈ 44	7 ♊ 39	23 ♑ 26	19 ♏ 22 ℞	9 ♑ 01 ℞	29 ♈ 12	15 ♓ 51	21 ♑ 16 ℞	10 ♌ 30	17 ♊ 59	1 ♈ 17	4 ♑ 42	0 ♈ 42
2 W	14 39 26	11 32 59	4 ♐ 31	10 05	14 48	8 52	23 54	19 15	9 00	29 15	15 53	21 16	10 45	18 33	1 45	4 45	0 45
3 Th	14 43 23	12 31 11	16 50	9 55	15 54	10 05	24 22	19 07	8 58	29 18	15 54	21 16	11 00	19 08	2 14	4 48	0 48
4 F	14 47 19	13 29 21	28 57	9 47	17 03	11 17	24 49	19 00	8 57	29 22	15 56	21 15	11 16	19 43	2 43	4 50	0 51
5 Sa	14 51 16	14 27 29	10 ♑ 53	9 42	18 15	12 30	25 16	18 52	8 55	29 25	15 57	21 15	11 31	20 18	3 11	4 52	0 54
6 Su	14 55 12	15 25 37	22 43	9 39	19 29	13 42	25 43	18 45	8 53	29 28	15 59	21 15	11 47	20 53	3 40	4 53	0 56
7 M	14 59 9	16 23 43	4 ♒ 31	9 38 D	20 45	14 55	26 10	18 37	8 52	29 32	16 00	21 14	12 03	21 28	4 08	4 54	0 59
8 T	15 3 5	17 21 47	16 23	9 38 ℞	22 04	16 07	26 36	18 29	8 50	29 35	16 01	21 14	12 19	22 03	4 37	4 55 ℞	1 02
9 W	15 7 2	18 19 50	28 24	9 38	23 25	17 20	27 02	18 22	8 48	29 38	16 03	21 13	12 36	22 38	5 06	4 55	1 05
10 Th	15 10 58	19 17 51	10 ♓ 39	9 37	24 48	18 32	27 28	18 14	8 46	29 42	16 04	21 13	12 53	23 13	5 34	4 54	1 07
11 F	15 14 55	20 15 52	23 13	9 33	26 14	19 44	27 53	18 06	8 44	29 45	16 05	21 12	13 10	23 48	6 03	4 53	1 10
12 Sa	15 18 52	21 13 50	6 ♈ 10	9 27	27 42	20 56	28 18	17 59	8 42	29 48	16 06	21 12	13 27	24 23	6 31	4 51	1 12
13 Su	15 22 48	22 11 48	19 33	9 18	29 12	22 09	28 43	17 51	8 39	29 52	16 07	21 11	13 44	24 59	7 00	4 49	1 15
14 M	15 26 45	23 09 44	3 ♉ 20	9 08	0 ♉ 44	23 21	29 07	17 43	8 37	29 55	16 09	21 11	14 02	25 34	7 29	4 47	1 17
15 T	15 30 41	24 07 39	17 31	8 56	2 18	24 33	29 31	17 36	8 35	29 58	16 10	21 10	14 19	26 09	7 57	4 44	1 20
16 W	15 34 38	25 05 32	1 ♊ 59	8 46	3 54	25 45	29 55	17 28	8 32	0 ♉ 01	16 11	21 09	14 37	26 44	8 26	4 40	1 22
17 Th	15 38 34	26 03 24	16 39	8 36	5 33	26 57	0 ♒ 19	17 21	8 29	0 04	16 12	21 09	14 56	27 19	8 54	4 36	1 25
18 F	15 42 31	27 01 15	1 ♋ 21	8 30	7 13	28 09	0 42	17 13	8 27	0 08	16 13	21 08	15 14	27 55	9 23	4 31	1 27
19 Sa	15 46 27	27 59 04	16 00	8 25	8 56	29 21	1 04	17 06	8 24	0 11	16 14	21 07	15 32	28 30	9 51	4 26	1 29
20 Su	15 50 24	28 56 51	0 ♌ 30	8 24 D	10 41	0 ♋ 32	1 27	16 58	8 21	0 14	16 15	21 07	15 51	29 05	10 20	4 21	1 31
21 M	15 54 21	29 54 36	14 46	8 24	12 27	1 44	1 48	16 51	8 18	0 17	16 16	21 06	16 10	29 41	10 48	4 15	1 34
22 T	15 58 17	0 ♊ 52 20	28 49	8 24 ℞	14 16	2 56	2 10	16 44	8 15	0 20	16 17	21 05	16 29	0 ♋ 16	11 17	4 08	1 36
23 W	16 2 14	1 50 02	12 ♍ 36	8 24	16 07	4 07	2 31	16 37	8 12	0 23	16 18	21 04	16 48	0 51	11 45	4 01	1 38
24 Th	16 6 10	2 47 42	26 10	8 21	18 00	5 19	2 52	16 30	8 09	0 26	16 19	21 03	17 08	1 27	12 13	3 54	1 40
25 F	16 10 7	3 45 21	9 ♎ 30	8 17	19 56	6 30	3 12	16 23	8 06	0 29	16 19	21 03	17 27	2 02	12 42	3 46	1 42
26 Sa	16 14 3	4 42 59	22 37	8 10	21 53	7 42	3 32	16 16	8 03	0 32	16 20	21 02	17 47	2 37	13 10	3 38	1 44
27 Su	16 18 0	5 40 35	5 ♏ 33	8 00	23 52	8 53	3 51	16 09	7 59	0 35	16 21	21 01	18 07	3 13	13 38	3 29	1 46
28 M	16 21 56	6 38 09	18 16	7 50	25 53	10 05	4 10	16 02	7 56	0 38	16 22	21 00	18 27	3 48	14 07	3 20	1 48
29 T	16 25 53	7 35 43	0 ♐ 47	7 39	27 56	11 16	4 29	15 55	7 53	0 41	16 22	20 59	18 47	4 23	14 35	3 11	1 50
30 W	16 29 50	8 33 15	13 07	7 29	0 ♊ 01	12 27	4 47	15 49	7 49	0 44	16 23	20 58	19 07	4 59	15 03	3 01	1 52
31 Th	16 33 46	9 30 47	25 16	7 20	2 07	13 38	5 05	15 42	7 45	0 47	16 24	20 57	19 28	5 34	15 32	2 50	1 54

EPHEMERIS CALCULATED FOR 12 MIDNIGHT GREENWICH MEAN TIME. ALL OTHER DATA AND FACING ASPECTARIAN PAGE IN **EASTERN TIME (BOLD)** AND PACIFIC TIME (REGULAR).

JUNE 2018

☽ Last Aspect day	ET / hr:mn / PT	asp	☽ Ingress sign	day	ET / hr:mn / PT
1	**11:37 pm** 8:37 pm	☌ ♇	♒	2	**6:06 pm** 3:06 pm
3	10:10 pm	□ ♃	♓	5	**6:53 am** 3:53 am
4	**1:10 am**	□ ♃	♓	5	**6:53 am** 3:53 am
6	11:35 pm	△ ♀	♈	7	**5:26 pm** 2:26 pm
7	**2:35 am**	△ ♀	♈	7	**5:26 pm** 2:26 pm
9	**3:37 pm** 12:37 pm	□ ♀	♉	9	9:04 pm
9	**3:37 pm** 12:37 pm	□ ♀	♉	10	**12:04 am**
11	**11:29 pm** 8:29 pm	⚹ ♀	♊	11	11:53 pm
11	**11:29 pm** 8:29 pm	⚹ ♀	♊	12	**2:53 am**
13	**3:43 pm** 12:43 pm	☌ ☉	♋	14	**3:20 am** 12:20 am
15	**12:18 pm** 9:18 am	☍ ♇	♌	16	**3:21 am** 12:21 am
17	**11:26 pm** 8:26 pm	⚹ ☉	♍	18	**4:41 am** 1:41 am
20	**6:51 am** 3:51 am	□ ☉	♎	20	**8:29 am** 5:29 am
21	**9:34 pm** 6:34 pm	□ ♇	♏	22	**3:11 pm** 12:11 pm
24	**10:00 am** 7:00 am	△ ☿	♐	24	9:29 pm
24	**10:00 am** 7:00 am	△ ☿	♐	25	**12:29 am**
26	**8:53 am** 5:53 am	□ ♆	♑	27	**11:52 am** 8:52 am
29	**4:58 am** 1:58 am	☌ ♇	♒	29	9:37 pm
29	**4:58 am** 1:58 am	☌ ♇	♒	30	**12:37 am**

☽ Phases & Eclipses phase	day	ET / hr:mn / PT
4th Quarter	6	**2:32 pm** 11:32 am
New Moon	13	**3:43 pm** 12:43 pm
2nd Quarter	20	**6:51 am** 3:51 am
Full Moon	27	9:53 pm
Full Moon	28	**12:53 am**

Planet Ingress	day	ET / hr:mn / PT
☿ ♋	12	**4:00 pm** 1:00 pm
⚶ ♐	13	**9:15 am** 6:15 am
♀ ♌	13	**5:54 pm** 2:54 pm
☉ ♋	21	**6:07 am** 3:07 am
⚳ ♍	28	**5:04 am** 2:04 am
☿ ♌	28	10:16 pm
☿ ♌	29	**1:16 am**

Planetary Motion	day	ET / hr:mn / PT
♆ ℞	18	**7:26 pm** 4:26 pm
♂ ℞	26	**5:04 pm** 2:04 pm

1 FRIDAY
☽ ⚻ ☉ **3:03 am** 12:03 am
☿ △ ♂ **10:13 am** 7:13 am
♀ △ ♃ **10:29 am** 7:29 am
☽ ⚹ ♃ **12:41 pm** 9:41 am
☽ ☍ ♀ **12:57 pm** 9:57 am
☽ ⚹ ♆ **2:29 pm** 11:29 am
☽ ☌ ♇ **11:37 pm** 8:37 pm

2 SATURDAY
♀ △ ♆ **4:26 am** 1:26 am
☿ ⚻ ♄ **9:16 am** 6:16 am
☽ □ ♅ **7:58 pm** 4:58 pm

3 SUNDAY
☽ ☌ ♂ **6:22 am** 3:22 am
☽ ⚺ ♄ **9:27 am** 6:27 am
☽ △ ☿ **3:06 pm** 12:06 pm
☽ △ ☉ **9:23 pm** 6:23 pm
☽ □ ♃ 10:10 pm

4 MONDAY
☽ □ ♃ **1:10 am**
☽ ⚺ ♆ **3:32 am** 12:32 am
☽ ⚻ ♀ **8:43 am** 5:43 am
☽ ⚺ ♇ **12:31 pm** 9:31 am

5 TUESDAY
☽ ⚹ ♅ **8:58 am** 5:58 am
☉ ⚻ ♃ **4:10 pm** 1:10 pm
☿ ⚻ ♃ **7:21 pm** 4:21 pm
☽ ⚺ ♂ **8:09 pm** 5:09 pm
☽ ⚹ ♄ **9:35 pm** 6:35 pm
☉ ☌ ☿ **10:02 pm** 7:02 pm
♀ ☍ ♇ **10:25 pm** 7:25 pm

6 WEDNESDAY
☿ □ ♆ **10:07 am** 7:07 am
☽ △ ♃ **12:38 pm** 9:38 am
☽ □ ☉ **2:32 pm** 11:32 am
☽ ☌ ♆ **3:25 pm** 12:25 pm
☽ □ ☿ **4:34 pm** 1:34 pm
☽ ⚹ ♇ **11:53 pm** 8:53 pm
☉ □ ♆ 10:58 pm
☽ △ ♀ 11:35 pm

7 THURSDAY
☉ □ ♆ **1:58 am**
☽ △ ♀ **2:35 am**
☽ ⚺ ♅ **7:35 pm** 4:35 pm

8 FRIDAY
☽ ⚹ ♂ **6:56 am** 3:56 am
☽ □ ♄ **6:57 am** 3:57 am
♂ ⚺ ♄ **8:22 am** 5:22 am
☿ ⚻ ♇ **9:32 am** 6:32 am
☽ ⚻ ♃ **8:55 pm** 5:55 pm
☽ ⚺ ♆ **11:56 pm** 8:56 pm

9 SATURDAY
☽ ⚹ ☉ **3:29 am** 12:29 am
☽ □ ♇ **7:42 am** 4:42 am
☽ ⚹ ☿ **12:03 pm** 9:03 am
☽ □ ♀ **3:37 pm** 12:37 pm
☽ ☌ ♅ 11:14 pm

10 SUNDAY
☽ ☌ ♅ **2:14 am**
☽ △ ♄ **12:20 pm** 9:20 am
☽ □ ♂ **1:21 pm** 10:21 am
☽ ☍ ♃ 10:14 pm

11 MONDAY
☽ ☍ ♃ **1:14 am**
☽ ⚹ ♆ **4:22 am** 1:22 am
☿ ⚺ ♀ **8:23 am** 5:23 am
☽ ⚺ ☉ **11:23 am** 8:23 am
☽ △ ♇ **11:31 am** 8:31 am
☉ ⚻ ♇ **1:14 pm** 10:14 am
☽ ⚹ ♀ **11:29 pm** 8:29 pm
☽ ⚺ ☿ 9:39 pm

12 TUESDAY
☽ ⚺ ☿ **12:39 am**
☽ ⚺ ♅ **5:04 am** 2:04 am
☽ ⚻ ♄ **2:12 pm** 11:12 am
☽ △ ♂ **4:00 pm** 1:00 pm
☽ ⚻ ♃ 11:24 pm

13 WEDNESDAY
☽ ⚻ ♃ **2:24 am**
☽ □ ♆ **5:40 am** 2:40 am
☿ ⚹ ♅ **7:41 am** 4:41 am
☽ ⚻ ♇ **12:26 pm** 9:26 am
☽ ☌ ☉ **3:43 pm** 12:43 pm

14 THURSDAY
☽ ⚺ ♀ **4:07 am** 1:07 am
☽ ⚹ ♅ **5:35 am** 2:35 am
☽ ☌ ☿ **9:02 am** 6:02 am
☽ ☍ ♄ **2:09 pm** 11:09 am
☽ ⚻ ♂ **4:39 pm** 1:39 pm
♀ □ ♅ **11:33 pm** 8:33 pm
☽ △ ♃ 11:10 pm

15 FRIDAY
☽ △ ♃ **2:10 am**
☽ △ ♆ **5:39 am** 2:39 am
☽ ☍ ♇ **12:18 pm** 9:18 am
☽ ⚺ ☉ **6:56 pm** 3:56 pm
☿ ☍ ♄ **9:47 pm** 6:47 pm

16 SATURDAY
☽ □ ♅ **5:45 am** 2:45 am
☽ ☌ ♀ **8:14 am** 5:14 am
☽ ⚻ ♄ **2:06 pm** 11:06 am
☽ ⚺ ☿ **4:45 pm** 1:45 pm
☽ ☍ ♂ **5:18 pm** 2:18 pm
☿ ⚻ ♂ **9:03 pm** 6:03 pm
☽ □ ♃ 11:23 pm

17 SUNDAY
☽ □ ♃ **2:23 am**
☽ ⚻ ♆ **6:12 am** 3:12 am
☽ ⚻ ♇ **1:00 pm** 10:00 am
☽ ⚹ ☉ **11:26 pm** 8:26 pm

18 MONDAY
☽ △ ♅ **7:19 am** 4:19 am
☽ ⚺ ♀ **2:12 pm** 11:12 am
☽ △ ♄ **3:39 pm** 12:39 pm
☽ ⚻ ♂ **7:39 pm** 4:39 pm
☽ ⚹ ☿ 11:44 pm

19 TUESDAY
☽ ⚹ ☿ **2:44 am**
☽ ⚹ ♃ **4:33 am** 1:33 am
♀ ⚻ ♄ **6:54 am** 3:54 am
☽ ☍ ♆ **8:49 am** 5:49 am
☿ △ ♃ **3:43 pm** 12:43 pm
☽ △ ♇ **3:52 pm** 12:52 pm

20 WEDNESDAY
☽ □ ☉ **6:51 am** 3:51 am
☽ ⚻ ♅ **11:25 am** 8:25 am
☽ □ ♄ **7:48 pm** 4:48 pm
☽ ⚹ ♀ **11:32 pm** 8:32 pm
☿ △ ♆ **11:58 pm** 8:58 pm
☽ △ ♂ 9:38 pm

21 THURSDAY
☽ △ ♂ **12:38 am**
☽ ⚺ ♃ **9:28 am** 6:28 am
♀ ☍ ♂ **12:54 pm** 9:54 am
☽ ⚻ ♆ **2:12 pm** 11:12 am
☽ □ ☿ **4:29 pm** 1:29 pm
☽ □ ♇ **9:34 pm** 6:34 pm

22 FRIDAY
☽ △ ☉ **5:50 pm** 2:50 pm
☽ ☍ ♅ **6:25 pm** 3:25 pm
☉ ⚹ ♅ 10:58 pm
☽ ⚹ ♄ 11:46 pm

23 SATURDAY
☉ ⚹ ♅ **1:58 am**
☽ ⚹ ♄ **2:46 am**
☿ ☍ ♇ **5:26 am** 2:26 am
☽ □ ♂ **8:24 am** 5:24 am
☽ □ ♀ **12:34 pm** 9:34 am
☽ ☌ ♃ **5:11 pm** 2:11 pm
☽ △ ♆ **10:23 pm** 7:23 pm

24 SUNDAY
☽ ⚹ ♇ **6:00 am** 3:00 am
☽ △ ☿ **10:00 am** 7:00 am

25 MONDAY
☽ ⚻ ♅ **4:01 am** 1:01 am
☽ ⚻ ☉ **8:05 am** 5:05 am
☽ ⚺ ♄ **12:12 pm** 9:12 am
♀ □ ♃ **1:19 pm** 10:19 am
☽ ⚹ ♂ **6:32 pm** 3:32 pm

26 TUESDAY
☽ ⚺ ♃ **3:18 am** 12:18 am
☽ △ ♀ **4:49 am** 1:49 am
☽ □ ♆ **8:53 am** 5:53 am
☽ ⚺ ♇ **4:40 pm** 1:40 pm

27 WEDNESDAY
☽ ⚻ ☿ **6:17 am** 3:17 am
☉ ☍ ♄ **9:28 am** 6:28 am
☽ △ ♅ **3:41 pm** 12:41 pm
☽ ☌ ♄ **11:34 pm** 8:34 pm
♀ ⚻ ♆ **11:41 pm** 8:41 pm
☽ ☍ ☉ 9:53 pm

28 THURSDAY
☽ ☍ ☉ **12:53 am**
☽ ⚺ ♂ **6:24 am** 3:24 am
☽ ⚹ ♃ **3:13 pm** 12:13 pm
☽ ⚹ ♆ **9:06 pm** 6:06 pm
☽ ⚻ ♀ **11:24 pm** 8:24 pm

29 FRIDAY
☽ ☌ ♇ **4:58 am** 1:58 am

30 SATURDAY
☽ ☍ ☿ **4:01 am** 1:01 am
☽ □ ♅ **4:38 am** 1:38 am
☿ □ ♅ **9:01 am** 6:01 am
☽ ⚺ ♄ **12:04 pm** 9:04 am
☽ ⚻ ☉ **7:08 pm** 4:08 pm
☽ ☌ ♂ **7:10 pm** 4:10 pm
☉ ⚻ ♂ **7:29 pm** 4:29 pm

Eastern time in bold type
Pacific time in medium type

JUNE 2018

DATE	SID.TIME	SUN	MOON	NODE	MERCURY	VENUS	MARS	JUPITER	SATURN	URANUS	NEPTUNE	PLUTO	CERES	PALLAS	JUNO	VESTA	CHIRON
1 F	16 37 43	10♊28 17	7♑15	7♌14℞	4♊15	14♋49	5♒22	15♏36℞	7♑42℞	0♉50	16♓24	20♑56℞	19♌48	6♋09	16♈00	2♑40℞	1♈55
2 Sa	16 41 39	11 25 46	19 08	7 10	6 24	16 00	5 38	15 29	7 38	0 52	16 25	20 55	20 09	6 45	16 28	2 29	1 57
3 Su	16 45 36	12 23 15	0♒56	7 08D	8 34	17 11	5 54	15 23	7 34	0 55	16 25	20 54	20 30	7 20	16 56	2 17	1 59
4 M	16 49 32	13 20 42	12 43	7 08	10 46	18 22	6 10	15 17	7 31	0 58	16 26	20 53	20 51	7 55	17 24	2 06	2 00
5 T	16 53 29	14 18 09	24 35	7 09	12 57	19 33	6 25	15 11	7 27	1 01	16 26	20 52	21 12	8 31	17 53	1 54	2 02
6 W	16 57 25	15 15 35	6♓35	7 10℞	15 09	20 43	6 39	15 06	7 23	1 03	16 27	20 50	21 34	9 06	18 21	1 41	2 03
7 Th	17 1 22	16 13 01	18 49	7 10	17 21	21 54	6 53	15 00	7 19	1 06	16 27	20 49	21 55	9 41	18 49	1 29	2 05
8 F	17 5 19	17 10 26	1♈22	7 09	19 33	23 04	7 06	14 54	7 15	1 09	16 28	20 48	22 16	10 17	19 17	1 16	2 06
9 Sa	17 9 15	18 07 50	14 18	7 06	21 45	24 15	7 19	14 49	7 11	1 11	16 28	20 47	22 38	10 52	19 45	1 02	2 08
10 Su	17 13 12	19 05 13	27 41	7 02	23 56	25 25	7 31	14 44	7 07	1 14	16 28	20 46	23 00	11 27	20 13	0 49	2 09
11 M	17 17 8	20 02 37	11♉32	6 55	26 05	26 36	7 43	14 38	7 03	1 16	16 28	20 45	23 22	12 02	20 41	0 36	2 10
12 T	17 21 5	20 59 59	25 50	6 48	28 14	27 46	7 53	14 33	6 59	1 19	16 29	20 43	23 44	12 38	21 09	0 22	2 11
13 W	17 25 1	21 57 21	10♊30	6 41	0♋21	28 56	8 03	14 29	6 55	1 21	16 29	20 42	24 06	13 13	21 36	0 08	2 13
14 Th	17 28 58	22 54 43	25 25	6 36	2 27	0♌06	8 13	14 24	6 50	1 24	16 29	20 41	24 28	13 48	22 04	29♐54	2 14
15 F	17 32 55	23 52 04	10♋27	6 32	4 31	1 16	8 22	14 19	6 46	1 26	16 29	20 40	24 51	14 23	22 32	29 39	2 15
16 Sa	17 36 51	24 49 24	25 26	6 29D	6 33	2 26	8 30	14 15	6 42	1 28	16 29	20 38	25 13	14 58	23 00	29 25	2 16
17 Su	17 40 48	25 46 43	10♌16	6 29	8 33	3 36	8 37	14 11	6 38	1 31	16 29	20 37	25 36	15 34	23 28	29 11	2 17
18 M	17 44 44	26 44 01	24 49	6 30	10 30	4 46	8 44	14 07	6 33	1 33	16 30℞	20 36	25 59	16 09	23 55	28 56	2 18
19 T	17 48 41	27 41 19	9♍03	6 31	12 26	5 55	8 50	14 03	6 29	1 35	16 30	20 35	26 21	16 44	24 23	28 42	2 18
20 W	17 52 37	28 38 35	22 55	6 32℞	14 20	7 05	8 56	13 59	6 25	1 38	16 30	20 33	26 44	17 19	24 50	28 27	2 19
21 Th	17 56 34	29 35 51	6♎27	6 32	16 11	8 14	9 00	13 55	6 20	1 40	16 29	20 32	27 07	17 54	25 18	28 13	2 20
22 F	18 0 30	0♋33 06	19 39	6 30	18 00	9 24	9 04	13 52	6 16	1 42	16 29	20 31	27 30	18 29	25 45	27 58	2 21
23 Sa	18 4 27	1 30 21	2♏35	6 27	19 47	10 33	9 08	13 49	6 11	1 44	16 29	20 29	27 54	19 04	26 13	27 44	2 21
24 Su	18 8 24	2 27 35	15 15	6 23	21 32	11 42	9 10	13 46	6 07	1 46	16 29	20 28	28 17	19 39	26 40	27 30	2 22
25 M	18 12 20	3 24 48	27 42	6 18	23 14	12 51	9 12	13 43	6 03	1 48	16 29	20 26	28 40	20 14	27 07	27 15	2 23
26 T	18 16 17	4 22 01	9♐58	6 12	24 54	14 00	9 13℞	13 40	5 58	1 50	16 29	20 25	29 04	20 49	27 35	27 01	2 23
27 W	18 20 13	5 19 13	22 04	6 07	26 32	15 09	9 13	13 38	5 54	1 52	16 29	20 24	29 27	21 24	28 02	26 47	2 24
28 Th	18 24 10	6 16 25	4♑03	6 03	28 07	16 18	9 13	13 35	5 49	1 54	16 28	20 22	29 51	21 59	28 29	26 34	2 24
29 F	18 28 6	7 13 37	15 55	6 00	29 40	17 26	9 11	13 33	5 45	1 56	16 28	20 21	0♍15	22 34	28 56	26 20	2 24
30 Sa	18 32 3	8 10 49	27 44	5 58D	1♌11	18 35	9 09	13 31	5 41	1 58	16 28	20 19	0 39	23 08	29 23	26 07	2 25

EPHEMERIS CALCULATED FOR 12 MIDNIGHT GREENWICH MEAN TIME. ALL OTHER DATA AND FACING ASPECTARIAN PAGE IN **EASTERN TIME (BOLD)** AND PACIFIC TIME (REGULAR).

JULY 2018

☽ Last Aspect day	ET / hr:mn	PT	asp	☽ Ingress sign	day	ET / hr:mn	PT
1	**6:56 pm**	3:56 pm	☍♀	♓	2	**1:31 pm**	10:31 am
4	**5:47 am**	2:47 am	⚹♇	♈	4		9:50 pm
4	**5:47 am**	2:47 am	⚹♇	♈	5	**12:50 am**	
7	**3:09 am**	12:09 am	△♀	♉	7	**8:51 am**	5:51 am
9	**12:09 pm**	9:09 am	□♀	♊	9	**12:58 pm**	9:58 am
10	**4:00 pm**	1:00 pm	□♆	♋	11	**1:59 pm**	10:59 am
12	**10:48 pm**	7:48 pm	☌☉	♌	13	**1:31 pm**	10:31 am
14	**7:12 pm**	4:12 pm	☌☿	♍	15	**1:31 pm**	10:31 am
17	**6:50 am**	3:50 am	⚹☉	♎	17	**3:42 pm**	12:42 pm
19	**3:52 pm**	12:52 pm	□☉	♏	19	**9:13 pm**	6:13 pm
22	**5:18 am**	2:18 am	△☉	♐	22	**6:12 am**	3:12 am
24	**4:22 am**	1:22 am	△☿	♑	24	**5:49 pm**	2:49 pm
26	**9:41 am**	6:41 am	☌♇	♒	27	**6:41 am**	3:41 am
29	**5:25 am**	2:25 am	☍☿	♓	29	**7:28 pm**	4:28 pm
31	**6:42 pm**	3:42 pm	☍♀	♈	8/1	**6:54 am**	3:54 am

☽ Phases & Eclipses phase	day	ET / hr:mn	PT
4th Quarter	6	**3:51 am**	12:51 am
New Moon	12	**10:48 pm**	7:48 pm
●	12	20° ♋ 41′	
2nd Quarter	19	**3:52 pm**	12:52 pm
Full Moon	27	**4:20 pm**	1:20 pm
●●	27	4° ♒ 45′	

Planet Ingress		day	ET / hr:mn	PT
⚵	♉	1	**4:46 am**	1:46 am
♀	♍	9	**10:32 pm**	7:32 pm
♀	♌	11	**5:47 pm**	2:47 pm
☉	♌	22	**5:00 pm**	2:00 pm

Planetary Motion		day	ET / hr:mn	PT
⚷	℞	4		9:46 pm
⚷	℞	5	**12:46 am**	
♃	D	10	**1:02 pm**	10:02 am
☿	℞	25		10:02 pm
☿	℞	26	**1:02 am**	

1 SUNDAY
- ☽□♃ **4:03 am** 1:03 am
- ♀⚻♇ **7:59 am** 4:59 am
- ☽⚺♆ **10:05 am** 7:05 am
- ☽⚺♇ **5:52 pm** 2:52 pm
- ☽☍♀ **6:56 pm** 3:56 pm

2 MONDAY
- ☽⚹♅ **5:38 pm** 2:38 pm
- ☿⚻♄ **7:49 pm** 4:49 pm
- ☽⚹♄ 9:27 pm
- ☽⚻☿ 10:05 pm

3 TUESDAY
- ☽⚹♄ **12:27 am**
- ☽⚻☿ **1:05 am**
- ☽⚺♂ **7:27 am** 4:27 am
- ☽△☉ **12:58 pm** 9:58 am
- ☽△♃ **4:21 pm** 1:21 pm
- ☽☌♆ **10:19 pm** 7:19 pm

4 WEDNESDAY
- ☽⚹♇ **5:47 am** 2:47 am
- ☽⚻♀ **1:03 pm** 10:03 am

5 THURSDAY
- ☽⚺♅ **4:54 am** 1:54 am
- ☉△♃ **7:04 am** 4:04 am
- ☿☍♂ **7:48 am** 4:48 am
- ☽□♄ **10:56 am** 7:56 am
- ☽⚹♂ **5:29 pm** 2:29 pm
- ☽△☿ **6:38 pm** 3:38 pm
- ☽⚻♃ 11:17 pm

6 FRIDAY
- ☽⚻♃ **2:17 am**
- ☽□☉ **3:51 am** 12:51 am
- ☽⚺♆ **7:57 am** 4:57 am
- ☽□♇ **2:54 pm** 11:54 am

7 SATURDAY
- ☽△♀ **3:09 am** 12:09 am
- ☽☌♅ **12:45 pm** 9:45 am
- ☽△♄ **5:59 pm** 2:59 pm
- ☽□♂ **11:52 pm** 8:52 pm

8 SUNDAY
- ☽□☿ **6:40 am** 3:40 am
- ☽☍♃ **8:30 am** 5:30 am
- ☉△♆ **10:42 am** 7:42 am
- ☽⚹♆ **1:47 pm** 10:47 am
- ☽⚹☉ **2:01 pm** 11:01 am
- ☽△♇ **8:11 pm** 5:11 pm

9 MONDAY
- ☿□♃ **5:14 am** 2:14 am
- ☽□♀ **12:09 pm** 9:09 am
- ☽⚺♅ **4:42 pm** 1:42 pm
- ☽⚻♄ **9:14 pm** 6:14 pm
- ☽△♂ 11:27 pm

10 TUESDAY
- ☽△♂ **2:27 am**
- ☽⚻♃ **11:04 am** 8:04 am
- ☽⚹☿ **1:24 pm** 10:24 am
- ☽□♆ **4:00 pm** 1:00 pm
- ☽⚺☉ **7:43 pm** 4:43 pm
- ☽⚻♇ **9:59 pm** 6:59 pm

11 WEDNESDAY
- ☽⚹♀ **5:09 pm** 2:09 pm
- ☽⚹♅ **5:36 pm** 2:36 pm
- ☽☍♄ **9:38 pm** 6:38 pm
- ♀△♅ **11:26 pm** 8:26 pm
- ☽⚻♂ 11:19 pm

12 THURSDAY
- ☽⚻♂ **2:19 am**
- ☿⚻♆ **3:52 am** 12:52 am
- ☉☍♇ **6:04 am** 3:04 am
- ☽△♃ **11:12 am** 8:12 am
- ☽△♆ **3:56 pm** 12:56 pm
- ☽⚺☿ **4:44 pm** 1:44 pm
- ☽☍♇ **9:43 pm** 6:43 pm
- ☽☌☉ **10:48 pm** 7:48 pm

13 FRIDAY
- ☽□♅ **5:10 pm** 2:10 pm
- ☽⚺♀ **8:25 pm** 5:25 pm
- ☽⚻♄ **8:54 pm** 5:54 pm
- ☽☍♂ 10:12 pm
- ♀△♄ 11:44 pm

14 SATURDAY
- ☽☍♂ **1:12 am**
- ♀△♄ **2:44 am**
- ☽□♃ **10:44 am** 7:44 am
- ☽⚻♆ **3:27 pm** 12:27 pm
- ☽☌☿ **7:12 pm** 4:12 pm
- ☽⚻♇ **9:17 pm** 6:17 pm
- ☽⚺☉ 10:43 pm

15 SUNDAY
- ☽⚺☉ **1:43 am**
- ☽△♅ **5:21 pm** 2:21 pm
- ☽△♄ **8:55 pm** 5:55 pm
- ☽☌♀ 9:35 pm
- ☽⚻♂ 9:53 pm

16 MONDAY
- ☽☌♀ **12:35 am**
- ☽⚻♂ **12:53 am**
- ♀⚻♂ **3:56 am** 12:56 am
- ☿⚻♇ **11:24 am** 8:24 am
- ☽⚹♃ **11:34 am** 8:34 am
- ☽☍♆ **4:24 pm** 1:24 pm
- ☽△♇ **10:29 pm** 7:29 pm
- ☽⚺☿ **11:04 pm** 8:04 pm

17 TUESDAY
- ☽⚹☉ **6:50 am** 3:50 am
- ☽⚻♅ **7:50 pm** 4:50 pm
- ☽□♄ **11:19 pm** 8:19 pm
- ☽△♂ 11:56 pm

18 WEDNESDAY
- ☽△♂ **2:56 am**
- ☽⚺♀ **7:55 am** 4:55 am
- ☽⚺♃ **3:14 pm** 12:14 pm
- ☽⚻♆ **8:15 pm** 5:15 pm
- ☽□♇ 11:43 pm

19 THURSDAY
- ☽□♇ **2:43 am**
- ☽⚹☿ **5:54 am** 2:54 am
- ☽□☉ **3:52 pm** 12:52 pm
- ☽☍♅ 10:42 pm

20 FRIDAY
- ☽☍♅ **1:42 am**
- ☽⚹♄ **5:05 am** 2:05 am
- ☽□♂ **8:13 am** 5:13 am
- ☽⚹♀ **7:40 pm** 4:40 pm
- ☽☌♃ **10:29 pm** 7:29 pm

21 SATURDAY
- ☽△♆ **3:38 am** 12:38 am
- ☽⚹♇ **10:28 am** 7:28 am
- ☽□☿ **4:00 pm** 1:00 pm

22 SUNDAY
- ☽△☉ **5:18 am** 2:18 am
- ♀⚹♃ **5:21 am** 2:21 am
- ☽⚻♅ **11:00 am** 8:00 am
- ☽⚺♄ **2:13 pm** 11:13 am
- ☽⚹♂ **4:37 pm** 1:37 pm

23 MONDAY
- ☽⚺♃ **8:58 am** 5:58 am
- ☽□♀ **11:35 am** 8:35 am
- ☽□♆ **2:07 pm** 11:07 am
- ☽⚺♇ **9:13 pm** 6:13 pm

24 TUESDAY
- ☽△☿ **4:22 am** 1:22 am
- ♀☍♆ **3:22 pm** 12:22 pm
- ☽⚻☉ **10:04 pm** 7:04 pm
- ☽△♅ **10:49 pm** 7:49 pm
- ☽☌♄ 10:46 pm

25 WEDNESDAY
- ☽☌♄ **1:46 am**
- ☽⚺♂ **3:14 am** 12:14 am
- ☉□♅ **7:36 am** 4:36 am
- ☽⚹♃ **9:32 pm** 6:32 pm
- ☽⚹♆ 11:29 pm

26 THURSDAY
- ☽⚹♆ **2:29 am**
- ☽△♀ **6:03 am** 3:03 am
- ☽☌♇ **9:41 am** 6:41 am
- ☽⚻☿ **5:20 pm** 2:20 pm
- ☉⚻♄ **5:40 pm** 2:40 pm
- ☉☍♂ 10:13 pm

27 FRIDAY
- ☉☍♂ **1:13 am**
- ☽□♅ **11:47 am** 8:47 am
- ☽⚺♄ **2:24 pm** 11:24 am
- ☽☌♂ **2:48 pm** 11:48 am
- ☽☍☉ **4:20 pm** 1:20 pm
- ♀△♇ **9:26 pm** 6:26 pm

28 SATURDAY
- ☽□♃ **10:47 am** 7:47 am
- ♂⚺♄ **12:40 pm** 9:40 am
- ☽⚺♆ **3:22 pm** 12:22 pm
- ☽⚺♇ **10:31 pm** 7:31 pm
- ☽⚻♀ 10:03 pm

29 SUNDAY
- ☽⚻♀ **1:03 am**
- ☽☍☿ **5:25 am** 2:25 am
- ☽⚹♅ 9:33 pm
- ☽⚺♂ 11:07 pm
- ☽⚹♄ 11:48 pm

30 MONDAY
- ☽⚹♅ **12:33 am**
- ☽⚺♂ **2:07 am**
- ☽⚹♄ **2:48 am**
- ☽⚻☉ **10:15 am** 7:15 am
- ☿⚺♀ **3:35 pm** 12:35 pm
- ☽△♃ **11:23 pm** 8:23 pm

31 TUESDAY
- ☽☌♆ **3:29 am** 12:29 am
- ☽⚹♇ **10:27 am** 7:27 am
- ☽⚻☿ **3:32 pm** 12:32 pm
- ☽☍♀ **6:42 pm** 3:42 pm

Eastern time in bold type
Pacific time in medium type

JULY 2018

DATE	SID.TIME	SUN	MOON	NODE	MERCURY	VENUS	MARS	JUPITER	SATURN	URANUS	NEPTUNE	PLUTO	CERES	PALLAS	JUNO	VESTA	CHIRON
1 Su	18 35 59	9♋08 00	9♒31	5♌58	2♌39	19♌43	9♒07℞	13♏29℞	5♑36℞	2♉00	16♓27℞	20♑18℞	1♍03	23♋43	29♈50	25♐53℞	2♈25
2 M	18 39 56	10 05 12	21 20	5 59	4 05	20 51	9 03	13 28	5 32	2 01	16 27	20 17	1 27	24 18	0♉17	25 40	2 25
3 T	18 43 53	11 02 23	3♓13	6 00	5 28	22 00	8 59	13 26	5 27	2 03	16 26	20 15	1 51	24 52	0 44	25 28	2 25
4 W	18 47 49	11 59 35	15 15	6 02	6 49	23 08	8 54	13 25	5 23	2 05	16 26	20 14	2 15	25 27	1 11	25 15	2 25
5 Th	18 51 46	12 56 47	27 30	6 03	8 07	24 15	8 48	13 24	5 19	2 06	16 25	20 12	2 39	26 02	1 37	25 03	2 25℞
6 F	18 55 42	13 53 59	10♈02	6 04℞	9 23	25 23	8 42	13 23	5 14	2 08	16 25	20 11	3 03	26 36	2 04	24 51	2 25
7 Sa	18 59 39	14 51 11	22 56	6 04	10 37	26 31	8 35	13 22	5 10	2 09	16 24	20 09	3 28	27 11	2 31	24 40	2 25
8 Su	19 3 35	15 48 24	6♉14	6 03	11 47	27 38	8 27	13 21	5 06	2 11	16 24	20 08	3 52	27 45	2 57	24 29	2 25
9 M	19 7 32	16 45 37	20 00	6 01	12 55	28 46	8 18	13 21	5 01	2 12	16 23	20 06	4 17	28 20	3 24	24 18	2 25
10 T	19 11 28	17 42 51	4♊12	5 59	14 01	29 53	8 09	13 21D	4 57	2 14	16 23	20 05	4 41	28 54	3 50	24 07	2 25
11 W	19 15 25	18 40 05	18 50	5 56	15 03	1♍00	7 59	13 21	4 53	2 15	16 22	20 03	5 06	29 29	4 16	23 57	2 24
12 Th	19 19 22	19 37 19	3♋47	5 55	16 02	2 07	7 48	13 21	4 49	2 16	16 21	20 02	5 31	0♌03	4 42	23 48	2 24
13 F	19 23 18	20 34 34	18 55	5 53	16 58	3 14	7 37	13 21	4 44	2 18	16 20	20 00	5 55	0 38	5 09	23 38	2 24
14 Sa	19 27 15	21 31 49	4♌06	5 53D	17 51	4 20	7 25	13 22	4 40	2 19	16 20	19 59	6 20	1 12	5 35	23 29	2 23
15 Su	19 31 11	22 29 04	19 10	5 53	18 41	5 27	7 12	13 22	4 36	2 20	16 19	19 58	6 45	1 46	6 00	23 21	2 23
16 M	19 35 8	23 26 19	3♍58	5 54	19 27	6 33	7 00	13 23	4 32	2 21	16 18	19 56	7 10	2 20	6 26	23 13	2 22
17 T	19 39 4	24 23 34	18 26	5 55	20 10	7 39	6 46	13 24	4 28	2 22	16 17	19 55	7 35	2 54	6 52	23 05	2 22
18 W	19 43 1	25 20 49	2♎29	5 56	20 49	8 45	6 32	13 25	4 24	2 23	16 16	19 53	8 01	3 29	7 18	22 58	2 21
19 Th	19 46 57	26 18 05	16 07	5 56℞	21 24	9 51	6 18	13 27	4 20	2 24	16 15	19 52	8 26	4 03	7 43	22 52	2 20
20 F	19 50 54	27 15 20	29 20	5 56	21 55	10 57	6 03	13 28	4 16	2 25	16 15	19 50	8 51	4 37	8 09	22 45	2 20
21 Sa	19 54 51	28 12 36	12♏12	5 56	22 22	12 02	5 48	13 30	4 12	2 26	16 14	19 49	9 16	5 11	8 34	22 40	2 19
22 Su	19 58 47	29 09 52	24 45	5 56	22 44	13 08	5 33	13 32	4 09	2 27	16 13	19 47	9 42	5 45	8 59	22 34	2 18
23 M	20 2 44	0♌07 09	7♐02	5 55	23 02	14 13	5 17	13 34	4 05	2 28	16 12	19 46	10 07	6 18	9 24	22 30	2 17
24 T	20 6 40	1 04 26	19 08	5 54	23 15	15 18	5 01	13 37	4 01	2 28	16 11	19 44	10 33	6 52	9 49	22 25	2 16
25 W	20 10 37	2 01 43	1♑05	5 54	23 24	16 22	4 45	13 39	3 58	2 29	16 10	19 43	10 58	7 26	10 14	22 22	2 15
26 Th	20 14 33	2 59 01	12 57	5 53	23 27℞	17 27	4 29	13 42	3 54	2 30	16 09	19 42	11 24	8 00	10 39	22 18	2 14
27 F	20 18 30	3 56 19	24 45	5 53D	23 26	18 31	4 12	13 45	3 50	2 30	16 07	19 40	11 49	8 33	11 04	22 15	2 13
28 Sa	20 22 26	4 53 38	6♒33	5 53	23 19	19 35	3 56	13 47	3 47	2 31	16 06	19 39	12 15	9 07	11 28	22 13	2 12
29 Su	20 26 23	5 50 57	18 22	5 53℞	23 08	20 39	3 40	13 51	3 44	2 31	16 05	19 37	12 41	9 41	11 52	22 11	2 11
30 M	20 30 20	6 48 18	0♓16	5 53	22 51	21 42	3 23	13 54	3 40	2 32	16 04	19 36	13 06	10 14	12 17	22 10	2 10
31 T	20 34 16	7 45 39	12 16	5 53	22 30	22 46	3 07	13 57	3 37	2 32	16 03	19 35	13 32	10 48	12 41	22 09	2 08

EPHEMERIS CALCULATED FOR 12 MIDNIGHT GREENWICH MEAN TIME. ALL OTHER DATA AND FACING ASPECTARIAN PAGE IN **EASTERN TIME (BOLD)** AND PACIFIC TIME (REGULAR).

AUGUST 2018

☽ Last Aspect day	ET / hr:mn / PT	asp	☽ Ingress sign	day	ET / hr:mn / PT
7/31	**6:42 pm** 3:42 pm	☍♀	♈	1	**6:54 am** 3:54 am
2	**10:52 pm** 7:52 pm	△☿	♉	3	**3:51 pm** 12:51 pm
5	**7:46 pm** 4:46 pm	△♀	♊	5	**9:32 pm** 6:32 pm
7	**3:54 am** 12:54 am	✶☿	♋	7	9:01 pm
7	**3:54 am** 12:54 am	✶☿	♋	8	**12:01 am**
9	**7:21 am** 4:21 am	☍♇	♌	9	9:18 pm
9	**7:21 am** 4:21 am	☍♇	♌	10	**12:18 am**
11	**5:58 am** 2:58 am	☌☉	♍	11	**11:59 pm** 8:59 pm
13	9:37 pm	△♂	♎	13	9:57 pm
14	**12:37 am**	△♂	♎	14	**12:57 am**
16	**3:56 am** 12:56 am	□♂	♏	16	**4:54 am** 1:54 am
18	**11:07 am** 8:07 am	✶♂	♐	18	**12:45 pm** 9:45 am
20	**7:47 pm** 4:47 pm	△☉	♑	20	9:00 pm
20	**7:47 pm** 4:47 pm	△☉	♑	21	**12:00 am**
23	**10:19 am** 7:19 am	☌♂	♒	23	**12:56 pm** 9:56 am
24	9:39 pm	△♀	♓	25	10:32 pm
25	**12:39 am**	△♀	♓	26	**1:32 am**
28	**9:54 am** 6:54 am	✶♂	♈	28	**12:35 pm** 9:35 am
30	**7:04 pm** 4:04 pm	□♂	♉	30	**9:30 pm** 6:30 pm

☽ Phases & Eclipses phase	day	ET / hr:mn / PT
4th Quarter	4	**2:18 pm** 11:18 am
New Moon	11	**5:58 am** 2:58 am
●	11	18° ♌ 42'
2nd Quarter	18	**3:49 am** 12:49 am
Full Moon	26	**7:56 am** 4:56 am

Planet Ingress		day	ET / hr:mn / PT
♀	♎	6	**7:27 pm** 4:27 pm
♂	♑	12	**10:14 pm** 7:14 pm
☉	♍	22	9:09 pm
☉	♍	23	**12:09 am**

Planetary Motion		day	ET / hr:mn / PT
♇	D	1	**6:39 am** 3:39 am
♅	R	7	**12:48 pm** 9:48 am
☿	D	18	9:25 pm
☿	D	19	**12:25 am**
♂	D	27	**10:05 am** 7:05 am

1 WEDNESDAY
☽ ⚺ ♅ **11:51 am** 8:51 am
☽ ✶ ♂ **12:05 pm** 9:05 am
☽ □ ♄ **1:45 pm** 10:45 am
♂ □ ♅ **10:39 pm** 7:39 pm
☽ △ ☉ 11:03 pm

2 THURSDAY
☽ △ ☉ **2:03 am**
☽ ⚻ ♃ **10:05 am** 7:05 am
☽ ⚺ ♆ **1:38 pm** 10:38 am
☽ □ ♇ **8:17 pm** 5:17 pm
☽ △ ☿ **10:52 pm** 7:52 pm

3 FRIDAY
☽ ⚻ ♀ **9:19 am** 6:19 am
☽ □ ♂ **7:38 pm** 4:38 pm
☽ ☌ ♅ **8:33 pm** 5:33 pm
☽ △ ♄ **10:07 pm** 7:07 pm

4 SATURDAY
☽ □ ☉ **2:18 pm** 11:18 am
☽ ☍ ♃ **5:50 pm** 2:50 pm
☽ ✶ ♆ **8:48 pm** 5:48 pm
☿ ⚻ ♇ 10:15 pm
☽ □ ☿ 11:58 pm

5 SUNDAY
☿ ⚻ ♇ **1:15 am**
☽ □ ☿ **2:58 am**
☽ △ ♇ **3:03 am** 12:03 am
☽ △ ♀ **7:46 pm** 4:46 pm
☽ △ ♂ 9:08 pm
☽ ⚺ ♅ 10:57 pm

6 MONDAY
☽ △ ♂ **12:08 am**
☽ ⚺ ♅ **1:57 am**
☽ ⚻ ♄ **3:13 am** 12:13 am
☉ □ ♃ **7:27 pm** 4:27 pm
☽ ⚻ ♃ **10:12 pm** 7:12 pm
☽ ✶ ☉ **10:23 pm** 7:23 pm
☽ □ ♆ 9:38 pm

7 TUESDAY
☽ □ ♆ **12:38 am**
☽ ✶ ☿ **3:54 am** 12:54 am
☽ ⚻ ♇ **6:31 am** 3:31 am
♀ △ ♂ **8:33 pm** 5:33 pm
☽ ⚻ ♂ 10:41 pm
☽ □ ♀ 11:09 pm

8 WEDNESDAY
☽ ⚻ ♂ **1:41 am**
☽ □ ♀ **2:09 am**
☽ ✶ ♅ **4:12 am** 1:12 am
☽ ☍ ♄ **5:15 am** 2:15 am
☉ ⚻ ♆ **7:10 am** 4:10 am
☉ ☌ ☿ **10:06 pm** 7:06 pm
☽ △ ♃ **11:43 pm** 8:43 pm
☽ △ ♆ 10:42 pm
☽ ⚺ ☿ 11:27 pm

9 THURSDAY
☽ △ ♆ **1:42 am**
☽ ⚺ ☿ **2:27 am**
☽ ⚺ ☉ **3:00 am** 12:00 am
☽ ☍ ♇ **7:21 am** 4:21 am
♀ ⚻ ♅ **7:57 am** 4:57 am
☿ ⚻ ♆ **5:29 pm** 2:29 pm
♀ □ ♄ **9:34 pm** 6:34 pm
☽ ☍ ♂ 10:12 pm

10 FRIDAY
☽ ☍ ♂ **1:12 am**
☽ □ ♅ **4:21 am** 1:21 am
☽ ⚻ ♄ **5:15 am** 2:15 am
☽ ✶ ♀ **5:49 am** 2:49 am
☽ □ ♃ **11:46 pm** 8:46 pm
☽ ☌ ☿ **11:54 pm** 8:54 pm
☽ ⚻ ♆ 10:22 pm
☿ □ ♃ 11:31 pm

11 SATURDAY
☽ ⚻ ♆ **1:22 am**
☿ □ ♃ **2:31 am**
☽ ☌ ☉ **5:58 am** 2:58 am
☽ ⚻ ♇ **6:58 am** 3:58 am
☉ ⚻ ♇ **9:28 pm** 6:28 pm
☽ ⚻ ♂ 9:16 pm

12 SUNDAY
☽ ⚻ ♂ **12:16 am**
☽ △ ♅ **4:04 am** 1:04 am
☽ △ ♄ **4:51 am** 1:51 am
☽ ⚺ ♀ **8:59 am** 5:59 am
☽ ⚺ ☿ **9:53 pm** 6:53 pm
☽ ✶ ♃ 9:09 pm
☽ ☍ ♆ 10:25 pm

13 MONDAY
☽ ✶ ♃ **12:09 am**
☽ ☍ ♆ **1:25 am**
☽ △ ♇ **7:12 am** 4:12 am
☽ ⚺ ☉ **9:38 am** 6:38 am
☽ △ ♂ 9:37 pm

14 TUESDAY
☽ △ ♂ **12:37 am**
☽ ⚻ ♅ **5:13 am** 2:13 am
☽ □ ♄ **5:56 am** 2:56 am
☽ ☌ ♀ **2:06 pm** 11:06 am
☽ ✶ ☿ **10:09 pm** 7:09 pm
☽ ⚺ ♃ 11:47 pm

15 WEDNESDAY
☽ ⚺ ♃ **2:47 am**
☽ ⚻ ♆ **3:41 am** 12:41 am
☽ □ ♇ **9:51 am** 6:51 am
☽ ✶ ☉ **4:22 pm** 1:22 pm

16 THURSDAY
☽ □ ♂ **3:56 am** 12:56 am
☽ ☍ ♅ **9:27 am** 6:27 am
☽ ✶ ♄ **10:06 am** 7:06 am
☽ ⚺ ♀ **11:15 pm** 8:15 pm
☽ □ ☿ 11:18 pm

17 FRIDAY
☽ □ ☿ **2:18 am**
☽ ☌ ♃ **9:06 am** 6:06 am
☽ △ ♆ **9:32 am** 6:32 am
☽ ✶ ♇ **4:12 pm** 1:12 pm

18 SATURDAY
☽ □ ☉ **3:49 am** 12:49 am
☽ ✶ ♂ **11:07 am** 8:07 am
☿ ✶ ♀ **11:35 am** 8:35 am
☽ ⚻ ♅ **5:36 pm** 2:36 pm
☽ ⚺ ♄ **6:11 pm** 3:11 pm

19 SUNDAY
♃ △ ♆ **3:44 am** 12:44 am
☽ △ ☿ **11:13 am** 8:13 am
☽ ✶ ♀ **1:14 pm** 10:14 am
☽ □ ♆ **7:12 pm** 4:12 pm
☽ ⚺ ♃ **7:22 pm** 4:22 pm
☽ ⚺ ♇ 11:17 pm

20 MONDAY
☽ ⚺ ♇ **2:17 am**
☽ △ ☉ **7:47 pm** 4:47 pm
☽ ⚺ ♂ **9:47 pm** 6:47 pm

21 TUESDAY
☽ △ ♅ **5:01 am** 2:01 am
☽ ☌ ♄ **5:33 am** 2:33 am
☉ ⚻ ♂ **6:52 pm** 3:52 pm
☽ ⚻ ☿ 9:29 pm

22 WEDNESDAY
☽ ⚻ ☿ **12:29 am**
☽ □ ♀ **6:36 am** 3:36 am
☽ ✶ ♆ **7:27 am** 4:27 am
☽ ✶ ♃ **8:21 am** 5:21 am
☽ ☌ ♇ **2:46 pm** 11:46 am
♀ ⚻ ♆ **5:10 pm** 2:10 pm

23 THURSDAY
♀ ⚺ ♃ **8:04 am** 5:04 am
☽ ☌ ♂ **10:19 am** 7:19 am
☽ ⚻ ☉ **2:04 pm** 11:04 am
☽ □ ♅ **5:55 pm** 2:55 pm
☽ ⚺ ♄ **6:24 pm** 3:24 pm

24 FRIDAY
☽ ☍ ☿ **4:27 pm** 1:27 pm
☽ ⚺ ♆ **8:17 pm** 5:17 pm
☽ □ ♃ **9:56 pm** 6:56 pm
☽ △ ♀ 9:39 pm

25 SATURDAY
☽ △ ♀ **12:39 am**
☽ ⚺ ♇ **3:35 am** 12:35 am
☉ △ ♅ **12:38 pm** 9:38 am
☉ △ ♄ **6:07 pm** 3:07 pm
☽ ⚺ ♂ **10:47 pm** 7:47 pm

26 SUNDAY
☽ ✶ ♅ **6:22 am** 3:22 am
☽ ✶ ♄ **6:49 am** 3:49 am
☽ ☍ ☉ **7:56 am** 4:56 am
♀ □ ♇ **3:21 pm** 12:21 pm
☿ ⚻ ♆ **8:29 pm** 5:29 pm

27 MONDAY
☽ ☌ ♆ **8:04 am** 5:04 am
☽ ⚻ ☿ **9:08 am** 6:08 am
☽ △ ♃ **10:25 am** 7:25 am
☽ ✶ ♇ **3:14 pm** 12:14 pm
☽ ⚻ ♀ **5:06 pm** 2:06 pm
☿ □ ♃ 10:32 pm

28 TUESDAY
☿ □ ♃ **1:32 am**
☽ ✶ ♂ **9:54 am** 6:54 am
☽ ⚺ ♅ **5:11 pm** 2:11 pm
☽ □ ♄ **5:37 pm** 2:37 pm
☽ ⚻ ☉ **11:42 pm** 8:42 pm

29 WEDNESDAY
☽ ⚺ ♆ **5:56 pm** 2:56 pm
☽ ⚻ ♃ **8:56 pm** 5:56 pm
☿ ⚻ ♇ **11:40 pm** 8:40 pm
☽ □ ♇ 9:54 pm
☽ △ ☿ 10:02 pm

30 THURSDAY
☽ □ ♇ **12:54 am**
☽ △ ☿ **1:02 am**
☽ ☍ ♀ **6:56 am** 3:56 am
☽ □ ♂ **7:04 pm** 4:04 pm
☽ ☌ ♅ 10:50 pm
☽ △ ♄ 11:17 pm

31 FRIDAY
☽ ☌ ♅ **1:50 am**
☽ △ ♄ **2:17 am**
☽ △ ☉ **12:42 pm** 9:42 am
☽ ✶ ♆ 10:33 pm

Eastern time in bold type
Pacific time in medium type

AUGUST 2018

DATE	SID.TIME	SUN	MOON	NODE	MERCURY	VENUS	MARS	JUPITER	SATURN	URANUS	NEPTUNE	PLUTO	CERES	PALLAS	JUNO	VESTA	CHIRON
1 W	20 38 13	8♌43 01	24♓25	5♌53℞	22♌03℞	23♍49	2♒51℞	14♏01	3♑34℞	2♉33	16♓02℞	19♑33℞	13♍58	11♌21	13♉05	22♐08 D	2♈07℞
2 Th	20 42 9	9 40 24	6♈46	5 52	21 32	24 51	2 35	14 05	3 31	2 33	16 00	19 32	14 24	11 55	13 29	22 08	2 06
3 F	20 46 6	10 37 48	19 22	5 52	20 58	25 54	2 19	14 09	3 27	2 33	15 59	19 31	14 50	12 28	13 52	22 09	2 04
4 Sa	20 50 2	11 35 14	2♉15	5 51 D	20 19	26 56	2 03	14 13	3 24	2 33	15 58	19 29	15 16	13 01	14 16	22 10	2 03
5 Su	20 53 59	12 32 40	15 30	5 51	19 37	27 58	1 48	14 17	3 22	2 33	15 57	19 28	15 42	13 34	14 40	22 11	2 01
6 M	20 57 55	13 30 08	29 07	5 52	18 53	29 00	1 33	14 22	3 19	2 34	15 55	19 27	16 08	14 08	15 03	22 13	2 00
7 T	21 1 52	14 27 38	13♊09	5 52	18 07	0♎01	1 18	14 26	3 16	2 34℞	15 54	19 25	16 34	14 41	15 26	22 16	1 58
8 W	21 5 49	15 25 08	27 33	5 53	17 19	1 03	1 04	14 31	3 13	2 34	15 53	19 24	17 00	15 14	15 49	22 18	1 56
9 Th	21 9 45	16 22 40	12♋18	5 54	16 32	2 03	0 51	14 36	3 11	2 34	15 51	19 23	17 27	15 47	16 12	22 22	1 55
10 F	21 13 42	17 20 13	27 18	5 54℞	15 45	3 04	0 37	14 41	3 08	2 34	15 50	19 21	17 53	16 20	16 34	22 26	1 53
11 Sa	21 17 38	18 17 48	12♌25	5 54	15 00	4 04	0 25	14 47	3 06	2 33	15 48	19 20	18 19	16 53	16 57	22 30	1 51
12 Su	21 21 35	19 15 23	27 31	5 54	14 17	5 04	0 13	14 52	3 03	2 33	15 47	19 19	18 45	17 26	17 19	22 34	1 49
13 M	21 25 31	20 13 00	12♍25	5 52	13 38	6 04	0 01	14 57	3 01	2 33	15 46	19 18	19 12	17 59	17 41	22 40	1 48
14 T	21 29 28	21 10 37	27 02	5 51	13 03	7 03	29♑50	15 03	2 59	2 33	15 44	19 17	19 38	18 31	18 03	22 45	1 46
15 W	21 33 24	22 08 16	11♎15	5 49	12 32	8 02	29 40	15 09	2 57	2 32	15 43	19 15	20 05	19 04	18 25	22 51	1 44
16 Th	21 37 21	23 05 55	25 01	5 47	12 07	9 00	29 31	15 15	2 54	2 32	15 41	19 14	20 31	19 37	18 46	22 58	1 42
17 F	21 41 18	24 03 36	8♏19	5 45	11 49	9 58	29 22	15 21	2 53	2 32	15 40	19 13	20 58	20 09	19 07	23 05	1 40
18 Sa	21 45 14	25 01 17	21 13	5 45 D	11 37	10 56	29 14	15 28	2 51	2 31	15 38	19 12	21 24	20 42	19 29	23 12	1 38
19 Su	21 49 11	25 59 00	3♐45	5 45	11 32 D	11 53	29 06	15 34	2 49	2 30	15 37	19 11	21 51	21 14	19 49	23 20	1 36
20 M	21 53 7	26 56 43	15 59	5 46	11 34	12 50	29 00	15 41	2 47	2 30	15 35	19 10	22 17	21 47	20 10	23 28	1 34
21 T	21 57 4	27 54 28	28 01	5 47	11 44	13 46	28 54	15 47	2 46	2 29	15 33	19 09	22 44	22 19	20 31	23 36	1 32
22 W	22 1 0	28 52 14	9♑53	5 49	12 02	14 42	28 49	15 54	2 44	2 29	15 32	19 08	23 10	22 51	20 51	23 45	1 29
23 Th	22 4 57	29 50 01	21 41	5 50	12 27	15 37	28 45	16 01	2 43	2 28	15 30	19 07	23 37	23 24	21 11	23 54	1 27
24 F	22 8 53	0♍47 50	3♒29	5 51℞	13 00	16 32	28 42	16 08	2 41	2 27	15 29	19 06	24 04	23 56	21 31	24 04	1 25
25 Sa	22 12 50	1 45 40	15 19	5 51	13 40	17 26	28 39	16 16	2 40	2 26	15 27	19 05	24 30	24 28	21 50	24 14	1 23
26 Su	22 16 47	2 43 31	27 14	5 49	14 28	18 20	28 38	16 23	2 39	2 25	15 26	19 04	24 57	25 00	22 09	24 25	1 20
27 M	22 20 43	3 41 23	9♓17	5 46	15 23	19 13	28 37 D	16 30	2 38	2 25	15 24	19 03	25 24	25 32	22 28	24 36	1 18
28 T	22 24 40	4 39 17	21 28	5 42	16 25	20 06	28 37	16 38	2 37	2 24	15 22	19 02	25 51	26 04	22 47	24 47	1 16
29 W	22 28 36	5 37 13	3♈50	5 37	17 33	20 58	28 37	16 46	2 36	2 23	15 21	19 01	26 18	26 36	23 06	24 58	1 13
30 Th	22 32 33	6 35 10	16 24	5 32	18 48	21 49	28 39	16 54	2 35	2 22	15 19	19 00	26 44	27 08	23 24	25 10	1 11
31 F	22 36 29	7 33 10	29 11	5 27	20 08	22 40	28 41	17 02	2 35	2 21	15 18	18 59	27 11	27 39	23 42	25 23	1 09

EPHEMERIS CALCULATED FOR 12 MIDNIGHT GREENWICH MEAN TIME. ALL OTHER DATA AND FACING ASPECTARIAN PAGE IN **EASTERN TIME (BOLD)** AND PACIFIC TIME (REGULAR).

SEPTEMBER 2018

☽ Last Aspect day	ET / hr:mn / PT		asp	☽ Ingress sign	day	ET / hr:mn / PT	
1		10:56 pm	△♂	♊	2	**4:02 am**	1:02 am
2	**1:56 am**		△♂	♊	2	**4:02 am**	1:02 am
3		11:37 pm	⚹☿	♋	4	**8:03 am**	5:03 am
4	**2:37 am**		⚹☿	♋	4	**8:03 am**	5:03 am
6	**8:43 am**	5:43 am	☍♂	♌	6	**9:54 am**	6:54 am
8	**9:31 am**	6:31 am	⚹♀	♍	8	**10:29 am**	7:29 am
10	**11:12 am**	8:12 am	△♂	♎	10	**11:20 am**	8:20 am
11	**6:58 pm**	3:58 pm	□♇	♏	12	**2:15 pm**	11:15 am
14	**4:54 am**	1:54 am	⚹☉	♐	14	**8:45 pm**	5:45 pm
16	**7:15 pm**	4:15 pm	□☉	♑	17	**7:07 am**	4:07 am
19	**1:10 pm**	10:10 am	△☉	♒	19	**7:52 pm**	4:52 pm
21	**1:13 pm**	10:13 am	□♃	♓	22	**8:27 am**	5:27 am
23		10:26 pm	△♃	♈	24	**7:04 pm**	4:04 pm
24	**1:26 am**		△♃	♈	24	**7:04 pm**	4:04 pm
26	**6:28 am**	3:28 am	□♇	♉	27	**3:16 am**	12:16 am
28	**6:36 pm**	3:36 pm	☍♃	♊	29	**9:26 am**	6:26 am
30	**11:38 am**	8:38 am	△☿	♋	10/1	**2:00 pm**	11:00 am

☽ Phases & Eclipses phase	day	ET / hr:mn / PT	
4th Quarter	2	**10:37 pm**	7:37 pm
New Moon	9	**2:01 pm**	11:01 am
2nd Quarter	16	**7:15 pm**	4:15 pm
Full Moon	24	**10:52 pm**	7:52 pm

Planet Ingress	day	ET / hr:mn / PT	
♀ ♍	4	**6:52 am**	3:52 am
☿ ♍	5	**10:39 pm**	7:39 pm
⚳ ♎	5		11:26 pm
⚳ ♎	6	**2:26 am**	
♀ ♏	9	**5:25 am**	2:25 am
♂ ♒	10	**8:56 pm**	5:56 pm
⚶ ♑	17		9:02 pm
⚶ ♑	18	**12:02 am**	
☿ ♎	21	**11:39 pm**	8:39 pm
☉ ♎	22	**9:54 pm**	6:54 pm
⚷ ♓	25	**8:09 pm**	5:09 pm
⚵ ♊	29	**7:39 pm**	4:39 pm

Planetary Motion	day	ET / hr:mn / PT	
♄ D	6	**7:09 am**	4:09 am
♇ D	30	**10:03 pm**	7:03 pm

1 SATURDAY
☽ ⚹ ♆ **1:33 am**
☽ ☍ ♃ **5:06 am** 2:06 am
☽ △ ♇ **8:16 am** 5:16 am
☽ □ ☿ **3:07 pm** 12:07 pm
☽ ⚻ ♀ **5:46 pm** 2:46 pm
☽ △ ♂ 10:56 pm

2 SUNDAY
☽ △ ♂ **1:56 am**
☽ ⚺ ♅ **8:05 am** 5:05 am
☽ ⚻ ♄ **8:33 am** 5:33 am
☽ □ ☉ **10:37 pm** 7:37 pm

3 MONDAY
☽ □ ♆ **6:41 am** 3:41 am
☿ ⚹ ♀ **8:58 am** 5:58 am
☽ ⚻ ♃ **10:44 am** 7:44 am
☽ ⚻ ♇ **1:09 pm** 10:09 am
☽ △ ♀ 10:27 pm
☽ ⚹ ☿ 11:37 pm

4 TUESDAY
☽ △ ♀ **1:27 am**
☽ ⚹ ☿ **2:37 am**
☽ ⚻ ♂ **6:24 am** 3:24 am
☽ ⚹ ♅ **11:52 am** 8:52 am
☽ ☍ ♄ **12:22 pm** 9:22 am

5 WEDNESDAY
☽ ⚹ ☉ **5:31 am** 2:31 am
☽ △ ♆ **9:27 am** 6:27 am
☿ ⚻ ♂ **11:18 am** 8:18 am
☽ △ ♃ **1:55 pm** 10:55 am
☽ ☍ ♇ **3:41 pm** 12:41 pm

6 THURSDAY
☽ □ ♀ **6:20 am** 3:20 am
☽ ☍ ♂ **8:43 am** 5:43 am
☽ ⚺ ☿ **11:28 am** 8:28 am
☽ □ ♅ **1:30 pm** 10:30 am
☽ ⚻ ♄ **2:03 pm** 11:03 am

7 FRIDAY
☿ △ ♅ **3:41 am** 12:41 am
☿ △ ♄ **8:20 am** 5:20 am
☽ ⚺ ☉ **10:07 am** 7:07 am
☽ ⚻ ♆ **10:24 am** 7:24 am
☉ ☍ ♆ **2:27 pm** 11:27 am
☽ □ ♃ **3:21 pm** 12:21 pm
☽ ⚻ ♇ **4:33 pm** 1:33 pm

8 SATURDAY
☽ ⚹ ♀ **9:31 am** 6:31 am
☽ ⚻ ♂ **9:48 am** 6:48 am
☽ △ ♅ **1:58 pm** 10:58 am
☽ △ ♄ **2:36 pm** 11:36 am
♀ □ ♂ **4:38 pm** 1:38 pm
☽ ☌ ☿ **6:54 pm** 3:54 pm

9 SUNDAY
☽ ☍ ♆ **10:49 am** 7:49 am
☽ ☌ ☉ **2:01 pm** 11:01 am
☽ ⚹ ♃ **4:23 pm** 1:23 pm
☽ △ ♇ **5:03 pm** 2:03 pm

10 MONDAY
☽ △ ♂ **11:12 am** 8:12 am
☽ ⚺ ♀ **12:51 pm** 9:51 am
☽ ⚻ ♅ **2:49 pm** 11:49 am
☽ □ ♄ **3:34 pm** 12:34 pm

11 TUESDAY
☽ ⚺ ☿ **3:25 am** 12:25 am
☉ ⚹ ♃ **8:10 am** 5:10 am
☉ △ ♇ **11:31 am** 8:31 am
☽ ⚻ ♆ **12:22 pm** 9:22 am
☽ ⚺ ♃ **6:51 pm** 3:51 pm
☽ □ ♇ **6:58 pm** 3:58 pm
☽ ⚺ ☉ **7:31 pm** 4:31 pm

12 WEDNESDAY
♃ ⚹ ♇ **3:55 am** 12:55 am
♀ ☍ ♅ **5:02 am** 2:02 am
☽ □ ♂ **2:52 pm** 11:52 am
☽ ☍ ♅ **5:51 pm** 2:51 pm
☽ ☌ ♀ **6:31 pm** 3:31 pm
☽ ⚹ ♄ **6:47 pm** 3:47 pm
♀ ⚹ ♄ **11:58 pm** 8:58 pm

13 THURSDAY
☽ ⚹ ☿ **4:02 pm** 1:02 pm
☽ △ ♆ **4:50 pm** 1:50 pm
☿ ☍ ♆ **9:31 pm** 6:31 pm
☽ ⚹ ♇ **11:59 pm** 8:59 pm
☽ ☌ ♃ 9:33 pm

14 FRIDAY
☽ ☌ ♃ **12:33 am**
☽ ⚹ ☉ **4:54 am** 1:54 am
☽ ⚹ ♂ **10:23 pm** 7:23 pm
☽ ⚻ ♅ 9:30 pm
☽ ⚺ ♄ 10:41 pm

15 SATURDAY
☽ ⚻ ♅ **12:30 am**
☽ ⚺ ♄ **1:41 am**
☽ ⚺ ♀ **4:14 am** 1:14 am
☿ △ ♇ **10:54 pm** 7:54 pm
☽ □ ♆ 10:12 pm

16 SUNDAY
☽ □ ♆ **1:12 am**
☿ ⚹ ♃ **7:51 am** 4:51 am
☽ ⚺ ♇ **8:57 am** 5:57 am
☽ ⚺ ♃ **10:23 am** 7:23 am
☽ □ ☿ **10:48 am** 7:48 am
☽ □ ☉ **7:15 pm** 4:15 pm

17 MONDAY
☽ ⚺ ♂ **10:07 am** 7:07 am
☽ △ ♅ **10:57 am** 7:57 am
☽ ☌ ♄ **12:25 pm** 9:25 am
☽ ⚹ ♀ **6:03 pm** 3:03 pm

18 TUESDAY
☽ ⚹ ♆ **12:54 pm** 9:54 am
♂ □ ♅ **7:01 pm** 4:01 pm
☽ ☌ ♇ **9:03 pm** 6:03 pm
☽ ⚹ ♃ **11:25 pm** 8:25 pm

19 WEDNESDAY
☽ △ ☿ **10:20 am** 7:20 am
☽ △ ☉ **1:10 pm** 10:10 am
☽ □ ♅ **11:36 pm** 8:36 pm
☽ ☌ ♂ 9:23 pm
☽ ⚺ ♄ 10:21 pm

20 THURSDAY
☽ ☌ ♂ **12:23 am**
☽ ⚺ ♄ **1:21 am**
☽ □ ♀ **9:46 am** 6:46 am
☉ ☌ ☿ **9:52 pm** 6:52 pm
☽ ⚺ ♆ 10:44 pm

21 FRIDAY
☽ ⚺ ♆ **1:44 am**
☽ ⚺ ♇ **9:57 am** 6:57 am
☽ □ ♃ **1:13 pm** 10:13 am
♂ ⚺ ♄ **5:20 pm** 2:20 pm

22 SATURDAY
☽ ⚻ ☉ **7:15 am** 4:15 am
☽ ⚻ ☿ **10:00 am** 7:00 am
☽ ⚹ ♅ **11:56 am** 8:56 am
☽ ⚹ ♄ **1:56 pm** 10:56 am
☽ ⚺ ♂ **2:26 pm** 11:26 am
☿ ⚻ ♅ **10:46 pm** 7:46 pm
☽ △ ♀ 9:22 pm

23 SUNDAY
☽ △ ♀ **12:22 am**
☿ □ ♄ **12:46 pm** 9:46 am
☽ ☌ ♆ **1:22 pm** 10:22 am
☽ ⚹ ♇ **9:24 pm** 6:24 pm
☿ △ ♂ **9:30 pm** 6:30 pm
☽ △ ♃ 10:26 pm

24 MONDAY
☽ △ ♃ **1:26 am**
☉ ⚻ ♅ **3:09 pm** 12:09 pm
☽ ⚺ ♅ **10:15 pm** 7:15 pm
☽ ☍ ☉ **10:52 pm** 7:52 pm
☽ □ ♄ 9:27 pm
☽ ⚹ ♂ 11:23 pm

25 TUESDAY
☽ □ ♄ **12:27 am**
☽ ⚹ ♂ **2:23 am**
☽ ☍ ☿ **6:12 am** 3:12 am
☽ ⚻ ♀ **12:08 pm** 9:08 am
☉ □ ♄ **7:50 pm** 4:50 pm
☽ ⚺ ♆ **10:40 pm** 7:40 pm

26 WEDNESDAY
☽ □ ♇ **6:28 am** 3:28 am
☽ ⚻ ♃ **11:08 am** 8:08 am

27 THURSDAY
☽ ☌ ♅ **6:11 am** 3:11 am
☽ △ ♄ **8:35 am** 5:35 am
☿ ⚺ ♀ **9:48 am** 6:48 am
☽ ⚻ ☉ **11:27 am** 8:27 am
☽ □ ♂ **11:50 am** 8:50 am
☉ △ ♂ **7:34 pm** 4:34 pm
☽ ☍ ♀ **9:02 pm** 6:02 pm
☽ ⚻ ☿ **10:26 pm** 7:26 pm

28 FRIDAY
☽ ⚹ ♆ **5:43 am** 2:43 am
☽ △ ♇ **1:20 pm** 10:20 am
☽ ☍ ♃ **6:36 pm** 3:36 pm

29 SATURDAY
☽ ⚺ ♅ **12:07 pm** 9:07 am
☽ ⚻ ♄ **2:44 pm** 11:44 am
☽ △ ♂ **7:16 pm** 4:16 pm
☽ △ ☉ **9:34 pm** 6:34 pm

30 SUNDAY
☽ ⚻ ♀ **3:37 am** 12:37 am
☿ ⚻ ♆ **6:22 am** 3:22 am
☽ □ ♆ **10:58 am** 7:58 am
☽ △ ☿ **11:38 am** 8:38 am
☽ ⚻ ♇ **6:28 pm** 3:28 pm
☽ ⚻ ♃ 9:19 pm

Eastern time in bold type
Pacific time in medium type

SEPTEMBER 2018

DATE	SID.TIME	SUN	MOON	NODE	MERCURY	VENUS	MARS	JUPITER	SATURN	URANUS	NEPTUNE	PLUTO	CERES	PALLAS	JUNO	VESTA	CHIRON
1 Sa	22 40 26	8♍31 11	12♉13	5♌23℞	21♌34	23♎30	28♑44	17♏10	2♑34℞	2♉19℞	15♓16℞	18♑58℞	27♍38	28♌11	24♉00	25♐35	1♈06℞
2 Su	22 44 22	9 29 14	25 30	5 21	23 05	24 19	28 48	17 18	2 34	2 18	15 14	18 57	28 05	28 43	24 17	25 48	1 04
3 M	22 48 19	10 27 18	9♊04	5 20D	24 41	25 08	28 53	17 27	2 33	2 17	15 13	18 57	28 32	29 14	24 34	26 01	1 01
4 T	22 52 15	11 25 25	22 55	5 21	26 20	25 56	28 59	17 35	2 33	2 16	15 11	18 56	28 59	29 46	24 51	26 15	0 59
5 W	22 56 12	12 23 34	7♋05	5 22	28 03	26 43	29 05	17 44	2 33	2 14	15 09	18 55	29 26	0♍17	25 08	26 29	0 56
6 Th	23 0 9	13 21 45	21 31	5 23℞	29 48	27 29	29 12	17 53	2 33D	2 13	15 08	18 54	29 53	0 49	25 24	26 43	0 54
7 F	23 4 5	14 19 58	6♌12	5 24	1♍36	28 15	29 20	18 01	2 33	2 12	15 06	18 54	0♎20	1 20	25 40	26 58	0 51
8 Sa	23 8 2	15 18 13	21 01	5 23	3 26	28 59	29 29	18 10	2 33	2 10	15 04	18 53	0 47	1 51	25 55	27 13	0 48
9 Su	23 11 58	16 16 30	5♍53	5 20	5 18	29 43	29 38	18 19	2 33	2 09	15 03	18 52	1 14	2 22	26 10	27 28	0 46
10 M	23 15 55	17 14 48	20 40	5 15	7 11	0♏26	29 49	18 29	2 33	2 07	15 01	18 52	1 41	2 54	26 25	27 43	0 43
11 T	23 19 51	18 13 08	5♎14	5 09	9 04	1 08	0♒00	18 38	2 34	2 06	14 59	18 51	2 08	3 25	26 40	27 59	0 41
12 W	23 23 48	19 11 30	19 27	5 02	10 58	1 49	0 11	18 47	2 34	2 04	14 58	18 51	2 35	3 56	26 54	28 15	0 38
13 Th	23 27 44	20 09 54	3♏16	4 55	12 53	2 28	0 24	18 57	2 35	2 03	14 56	18 50	3 02	4 27	27 08	28 31	0 35
14 F	23 31 41	21 08 19	16 39	4 49	14 47	3 07	0 37	19 07	2 35	2 01	14 54	18 50	3 29	4 57	27 21	28 48	0 33
15 Sa	23 35 38	22 06 46	29 36	4 45	16 41	3 44	0 51	19 16	2 36	1 59	14 53	18 49	3 56	5 28	27 34	29 05	0 30
16 Su	23 39 34	23 05 15	12♐10	4 42 D	18 35	4 21	1 05	19 26	2 37	1 58	14 51	18 49	4 23	5 59	27 47	29 22	0 27
17 M	23 43 31	24 03 45	24 25	4 42	20 28	4 56	1 20	19 36	2 38	1 56	14 50	18 48	4 50	6 30	27 59	29 39	0 24
18 T	23 47 27	25 02 17	6♑25	4 42	22 21	5 30	1 36	19 46	2 39	1 54	14 48	18 48	5 18	7 00	28 11	29 57	0 22
19 W	23 51 24	26 00 50	18 17	4 44	24 13	6 02	1 53	19 56	2 40	1 52	14 46	18 48	5 45	7 31	28 22	0♑15	0 19
20 Th	23 55 20	26 59 25	0♒04	4 44℞	26 04	6 33	2 10	20 06	2 42	1 50	14 45	18 47	6 12	8 01	28 34	0 33	0 16
21 F	23 59 17	27 58 02	11 53	4 44	27 54	7 02	2 28	20 17	2 43	1 48	14 43	18 47	6 39	8 32	28 44	0 52	0 14
22 Sa	0 3 13	28 56 41	23 47	4 42	29 43	7 30	2 46	20 27	2 44	1 46	14 42	18 47	7 06	9 02	28 54	1 10	0 11
23 Su	0 7 10	29 55 21	5♓49	4 38	1♎32	7 57	3 05	20 38	2 46	1 45	14 40	18 46	7 33	9 32	29 04	1 29	0 08
24 M	0 11 7	0♎54 03	18 03	4 31	3 19	8 22	3 25	20 48	2 48	1 43	14 38	18 46	8 00	10 02	29 14	1 48	0 05
25 T	0 15 3	1 52 47	0♈30	4 22	5 06	8 45	3 45	20 59	2 49	1 41	14 37	18 46	8 28	10 32	29 22	2 07	0 03
26 W	0 19 0	2 51 33	13 10	4 12	6 52	9 06	4 06	21 10	2 51	1 38	14 35	18 46	8 55	11 02	29 31	2 27	0 00
27 Th	0 22 56	3 50 21	26 03	4 02	8 36	9 26	4 27	21 20	2 53	1 36	14 34	18 46	9 22	11 32	29 39	2 47	29♓57
28 F	0 26 53	4 49 11	9♉10	3 52	10 20	9 43	4 49	21 31	2 55	1 34	14 32	18 46	9 49	12 02	29 46	3 07	29 55
29 Sa	0 30 49	5 48 04	22 28	3 43	12 03	9 59	5 11	21 42	2 57	1 32	14 31	18 45	10 16	12 32	29 54	3 27	29 52
30 Su	0 34 46	6 46 58	5♊58	3 37	13 45	10 13	5 34	21 53	3 00	1 30	14 29	18 45	10 44	13 02	0♊00	3 47	29 49

EPHEMERIS CALCULATED FOR 12 MIDNIGHT GREENWICH MEAN TIME. ALL OTHER DATA AND FACING ASPECTARIAN PAGE IN **EASTERN TIME (BOLD)** AND PACIFIC TIME (REGULAR).

OCTOBER 2018

☽ Last Aspect day	ET / hr:mn / PT	asp	☽ Ingress sign	day	ET / hr:mn / PT
9/30	**11:38 am** 8:38 am	△☿	♋	1	**2:00 pm** 11:00 am
3	**4:33 am** 1:33 am	△♃	♌	3	**5:12 pm** 2:12 pm
5	**7:34 am** 4:34 am	□♃	♍	5	**7:19 pm** 4:19 pm
7	**10:03 am** 7:03 am	✶♃	♎	7	**9:10 pm** 6:10 pm
9	**4:50 am** 1:50 am	□♇	♏	9	9:09 pm
9	**4:50 am** 1:50 am	□♇	♏	10	**12:09 am**
11	**7:12 pm** 4:12 pm	☌♃	♐	12	**5:53 am** 2:53 am
13	**8:58 pm** 5:58 pm	✶⊙	♑	14	**3:17 pm** 12:17 pm
16	**5:49 pm** 2:49 pm	✶♃	♒	17	**3:36 am** 12:36 am
19	**8:27 am** 5:27 am	△⊙	♓	19	**4:20 pm** 1:20 pm
21	**7:47 pm** 4:47 pm	△♃	♈	21	11:58 pm
21	**7:47 pm** 4:47 pm	△♃	♈	22	**2:58 am**
23	**2:18 pm** 11:18 am	□♇	♉	24	**10:33 am** 7:33 am
26	**10:49 am** 7:49 am	☍♃	♊	26	**3:41 pm** 12:41 pm
27	9:37 pm	△♂	♋	28	**7:27 pm** 4:27 pm
28	**12:37 am**	△♂	♋	28	**7:27 pm** 4:27 pm
30	**10:31 pm** 7:31 pm	△☿	♌	30	**10:42 pm** 7:42 pm

☽ Phases & Eclipses phase	day	ET / hr:mn / PT
4th Quarter	2	**5:45 am** 2:45 am
New Moon	8	**11:47 pm** 8:47 pm
2nd Quarter	16	**2:02 pm** 11:02 am
Full Moon	24	**12:45 pm** 9:45 am
4th Quarter	31	**12:40 pm** 9:40 am

Planet Ingress	day	ET / hr:mn / PT
☿ ♏	9	**8:40 pm** 5:40 pm
⊙ ♏	23	**7:22 am** 4:22 am
⚵ ♉	24	**3:56 am** 12:56 am
☿ ♐	30	9:38 pm
☿ ♐	31	**12:38 am**
♀ ♎	31	**3:42 pm** 12:42 pm

Planetary Motion	day	ET / hr:mn / PT
♀ ℞	5	**3:04 pm** 12:04 pm
⚵ ℞	11	9:05 pm
⚵ ℞	12	**12:05 am**

1 MONDAY
☽ ⚻ ♃ **12:19 am**
☽ ✶ ♅ **4:29 pm** 1:29 pm
☽ ☍ ♄ **7:18 pm** 4:18 pm
☽ ⚻ ♂ 10:05 pm

2 TUESDAY
☽ ⚻ ♂ **1:05 am**
☽ □ ⊙ **5:45 am** 2:45 am
☽ △ ♀ **8:18 am** 5:18 am
☽ △ ♆ **2:46 pm** 11:46 am
☿ □ ♇ **8:03 pm** 5:03 pm
☽ ☍ ♇ **10:10 pm** 7:10 pm
☽ □ ☿ **10:27 pm** 7:27 pm

3 WEDNESDAY
☽ △ ♃ **4:33 am** 1:33 am
☽ □ ♅ **7:29 pm** 4:29 pm
⊙ ⚺ ♀ **9:36 pm** 6:36 pm
☽ ⚻ ♄ **10:31 pm** 7:31 pm

4 THURSDAY
☽ ☍ ♂ **5:31 am** 2:31 am
☽ □ ♀ **11:22 am** 8:22 am
☽ ✶ ⊙ **12:19 pm** 9:19 am
☽ ⚻ ♆ **5:18 pm** 2:18 pm
☽ ⚻ ♇ 9:38 pm

5 FRIDAY
☽ ⚻ ♇ **12:38 am**
☽ ✶ ☿ **7:20 am** 4:20 am
☽ □ ♃ **7:34 am** 4:34 am
☿ ⚺ ♃ **9:39 am** 6:39 am
☽ △ ♅ **9:26 pm** 6:26 pm
☽ △ ♄ 9:43 pm

6 SATURDAY
☽ △ ♄ **12:43 am**
☽ ⚻ ♂ **8:59 am** 5:59 am
☽ ✶ ♀ **1:16 pm** 10:16 am
☽ ⚺ ⊙ **5:51 pm** 2:51 pm
☽ ☍ ♆ **7:04 pm** 4:04 pm
☽ △ ♇ 11:27 pm

7 SUNDAY
☽ △ ♇ **2:27 am**
☽ ✶ ♃ **10:03 am** 7:03 am
⊙ ⚻ ♆ **11:17 am** 8:17 am
☽ ⚺ ☿ **3:21 pm** 12:21 pm
☽ ⚻ ♅ **11:10 pm** 8:10 pm
☽ □ ♄ 11:47 pm

8 MONDAY
☽ □ ♄ **2:47 am**
☽ △ ♂ **12:35 pm** 9:35 am
☽ ⚺ ♀ **3:04 pm** 12:04 pm
☽ ⚻ ♆ **9:11 pm** 6:11 pm
☽ ☌ ⊙ **11:47 pm** 8:47 pm

9 TUESDAY
☽ □ ♇ **4:50 am** 1:50 am
☽ ⚺ ♃ **1:21 pm** 10:21 am
☽ ☌ ☿ 9:36 pm
☽ ☍ ♅ 11:05 pm

10 WEDNESDAY
☽ ☌ ☿ **12:36 am**
☽ ☍ ♅ **2:05 am**
☽ ✶ ♄ **6:12 am** 3:12 am
☿ ☍ ♅ **1:36 pm** 10:36 am
☽ □ ♂ **6:02 pm** 3:02 pm
☽ ☌ ♀ **6:15 pm** 3:15 pm
♀ □ ♂ **10:29 pm** 7:29 pm
☽ △ ♆ 10:12 pm

11 THURSDAY
☽ △ ♆ **1:12 am**
☽ ⚺ ⊙ **8:12 am** 5:12 am
☽ ✶ ♇ **9:23 am** 6:23 am
☽ ☌ ♃ **7:12 pm** 4:12 pm
⊙ □ ♇ 9:11 pm

12 FRIDAY
⊙ □ ♇ **12:11 am**
☿ ✶ ♄ **4:20 am** 1:20 am
☽ ⚻ ♅ **7:47 am** 4:47 am
☽ ⚺ ♄ **12:34 pm** 9:34 am
☽ ⚺ ☿ **1:38 pm** 10:38 am
☽ ⚺ ♀ 9:09 pm

13 SATURDAY
☽ ⚺ ♀ **12:09 am**
☽ ✶ ♂ **3:06 am** 12:06 am
☽ □ ♆ **8:32 am** 5:32 am
☽ ⚺ ♇ **5:25 pm** 2:25 pm
☽ ✶ ⊙ **8:58 pm** 5:58 pm

14 SUNDAY
☽ ⚺ ♃ **4:50 am** 1:50 am
☽ △ ♅ **5:07 pm** 2:07 pm
☽ ☌ ♄ **10:40 pm** 7:40 pm

15 MONDAY
☽ ✶ ☿ **7:48 am** 4:48 am
☽ ✶ ♀ **9:05 am** 6:05 am
☽ ⚺ ♂ **4:17 pm** 1:17 pm
☿ ☌ ♀ **4:21 pm** 1:21 pm
☽ ✶ ♆ **7:26 pm** 4:26 pm

16 TUESDAY
☽ ☌ ♇ **4:54 am** 1:54 am
☽ □ ⊙ **2:02 pm** 11:02 am
☽ ✶ ♃ **5:49 pm** 2:49 pm

17 WEDNESDAY
☽ □ ♅ **5:17 am** 2:17 am
☽ ⚺ ♄ **11:31 am** 8:31 am
☽ □ ♀ **7:44 pm** 4:44 pm

18 THURSDAY
☽ □ ☿ **5:10 am** 2:10 am
☽ ☌ ♂ **7:50 am** 4:50 am
☽ ⚺ ♆ **8:13 am** 5:13 am
♂ ⚺ ♆ **4:30 pm** 1:30 pm
☽ ⚺ ♇ **5:52 pm** 2:52 pm
⊙ ⚺ ♃ **10:01 pm** 7:01 pm

19 FRIDAY
☿ △ ♆ **5:47 am** 2:47 am
☽ □ ♃ **7:45 am** 4:45 am
☽ △ ⊙ **8:27 am** 5:27 am
☿ □ ♂ **1:23 pm** 10:23 am
☽ ✶ ♅ **5:47 pm** 2:47 pm
☽ ✶ ♄ 9:26 pm

20 SATURDAY
☽ ✶ ♄ **12:26 am**
☽ △ ♀ **5:44 am** 2:44 am
☽ ☌ ♆ **8:07 pm** 5:07 pm
☽ ⚺ ♂ **10:28 pm** 7:28 pm
☽ △ ☿ 10:14 pm

21 SUNDAY
☽ △ ☿ **1:14 am**
☽ ✶ ♇ **5:33 am** 2:33 am
☽ △ ♃ **7:47 pm** 4:47 pm
☽ ⚻ ⊙ 9:32 pm

22 MONDAY
☽ ⚻ ⊙ **12:32 am**
☽ ⚺ ♅ **4:10 am** 1:10 am
☽ □ ♄ **10:59 am** 7:59 am
☽ ⚻ ♀ **1:16 pm** 10:16 am
☿ ✶ ♇ **3:14 pm** 12:14 pm

23 TUESDAY
☽ ⚺ ♆ **5:15 am** 2:15 am
☽ ✶ ♂ **9:58 am** 6:58 am
☽ □ ♇ **2:18 pm** 11:18 am
☽ ⚻ ☿ **5:01 pm** 2:01 pm
⊙ ☍ ♅ **8:47 pm** 5:47 pm

24 WEDNESDAY
☽ ⚻ ♃ **4:39 am** 1:39 am
♀ ✶ ♄ **8:52 am** 5:52 am
☽ ☌ ♅ **11:31 am** 8:31 am
☽ ☍ ⊙ **12:45 pm** 9:45 am
☽ ☍ ♀ **6:00 pm** 3:00 pm
☽ △ ♄ **6:27 pm** 3:27 pm

25 THURSDAY
☽ ✶ ♆ **11:30 am** 8:30 am
☽ □ ♂ **6:18 pm** 3:18 pm
☽ △ ♇ **8:15 pm** 5:15 pm

26 FRIDAY
☽ ☍ ☿ **4:46 am** 1:46 am
⊙ ☌ ♀ **10:16 am** 7:16 am
☽ ☍ ♃ **10:49 am** 7:49 am
☽ ⚺ ♅ **4:27 pm** 1:27 pm
☽ ⚻ ♀ **8:38 pm** 5:38 pm
☽ ⚻ ⊙ **9:56 pm** 6:56 pm
☽ ⚻ ♄ **11:36 pm** 8:36 pm

27 SATURDAY
☽ □ ♆ **3:48 pm** 12:48 pm
♂ ⚺ ♇ **8:19 pm** 5:19 pm
⊙ ✶ ♄ **10:52 pm** 7:52 pm
☽ ⚻ ♇ 9:27 pm
☽ △ ♂ 9:37 pm

28 SUNDAY
☽ ⚻ ♇ **12:27 am**
☽ △ ♂ **12:37 am**
☽ ⚻ ☿ **2:09 pm** 11:09 am
☽ ⚻ ♃ **3:28 pm** 12:28 pm
☽ ✶ ♅ **8:03 pm** 5:03 pm
☽ △ ♀ **10:10 pm** 7:10 pm

29 MONDAY
☽ ☍ ♄ **3:32 am** 12:32 am
☽ △ ⊙ **5:34 am** 2:34 am
☿ ☌ ♃ **7:05 am** 4:05 am
☽ △ ♆ **7:12 pm** 4:12 pm

30 TUESDAY
☽ ☍ ♇ **3:53 am** 12:53 am
☽ ⚻ ♂ **6:07 am** 3:07 am
☽ △ ♃ **7:32 pm** 4:32 pm
☽ △ ☿ **10:31 pm** 7:31 pm
☽ □ ♅ **11:09 pm** 8:09 pm
☽ □ ♀ **11:21 pm** 8:21 pm

31 WEDNESDAY
♀ ☍ ♅ **4:45 am** 1:45 am
☿ ⚺ ♀ **5:21 am** 2:21 am
☿ ⚻ ♅ **5:36 am** 2:36 am
☽ ⚻ ♄ **7:02 am** 4:02 am
☽ □ ⊙ **12:40 pm** 9:40 am
☽ ⚻ ♆ **10:18 pm** 7:18 pm

Eastern time in bold type
Pacific time in medium type

OCTOBER 2018

DATE	SID.TIME	SUN	MOON	NODE	MERCURY	VENUS	MARS	JUPITER	SATURN	URANUS	NEPTUNE	PLUTO	CERES	PALLAS	JUNO	VESTA	CHIRON
1 M	0 38 42	7 ♎ 45 55	19 ♊ 38	3 ♌ 33 ℞	15 ♎ 26	10 ♏ 24	5 ♒ 57	22 ♏ 04	3 ♑ 02	1 ♉ 28 ℞	14 ♓ 28 ℞	18 ♑ 45 D	11 ♎ 11	13 ♍ 32	0 ♊ 06	4 ♑ 08	29 ♓ 46 ℞
2 T	0 42 39	8 44 55	3 ♋ 28	3 32 D	17 06	10 34	6 20	22 16	3 04	1 26	14 26	18 45	11 38	14 01	0 12	4 29	29 44
3 W	0 46 36	9 43 56	17 29	3 32	18 45	10 41	6 45	22 27	3 07	1 23	14 25	18 45	12 05	14 31	0 17	4 50	29 41
4 Th	0 50 32	10 43 00	1 ♌ 40	3 32 ℞	20 24	10 47	7 09	22 38	3 09	1 21	14 23	18 46	12 32	15 00	0 21	5 11	29 38
5 F	0 54 29	11 42 07	15 59	3 32	22 01	10 50 ℞	7 34	22 50	3 12	1 19	14 22	18 46	12 59	15 30	0 26	5 32	29 36
6 Sa	0 58 25	12 41 15	0 ♍ 25	3 29	23 38	10 50	8 00	23 01	3 15	1 17	14 20	18 46	13 27	15 59	0 29	5 54	29 33
7 Su	1 2 22	13 40 26	14 53	3 24	25 14	10 49	8 26	23 13	3 18	1 14	14 19	18 46	13 54	16 28	0 32	6 16	29 31
8 M	1 6 18	14 39 39	29 18	3 16	26 49	10 45	8 52	23 25	3 21	1 12	14 18	18 46	14 21	16 57	0 35	6 38	29 28
9 T	1 10 15	15 38 54	13 ♎ 35	3 06	28 24	10 38	9 19	23 36	3 24	1 10	14 16	18 46	14 48	17 26	0 37	7 00	29 25
10 W	1 14 11	16 38 11	27 36	2 54	29 57	10 29	9 46	23 48	3 27	1 07	14 15	18 47	15 15	17 55	0 38	7 22	29 23
11 Th	1 18 8	17 37 30	11 ♏ 18	2 42	1 ♏ 30	10 18	10 14	24 00	3 30	1 05	14 14	18 47	15 42	18 24	0 39	7 45	29 20
12 F	1 22 4	18 36 51	24 38	2 32	3 03	10 05	10 42	24 12	3 33	1 03	14 12	18 47	16 10	18 53	0 39 ℞	8 07	29 18
13 Sa	1 26 1	19 36 14	7 ♐ 34	2 23	4 34	9 49	11 11	24 24	3 37	1 00	14 11	18 47	16 37	19 22	0 39	8 30	29 15
14 Su	1 29 58	20 35 39	20 08	2 17	6 05	9 30	11 39	24 36	3 40	0 58	14 10	18 48	17 04	19 50	0 38	8 53	29 13
15 M	1 33 54	21 35 06	2 ♑ 23	2 13	7 35	9 10	12 08	24 48	3 44	0 55	14 09	18 48	17 31	20 19	0 37	9 16	29 10
16 T	1 37 51	22 34 34	14 24	2 12 D	9 04	8 47	12 38	25 00	3 47	0 53	14 07	18 49	17 58	20 47	0 35	9 39	29 08
17 W	1 41 47	23 34 04	26 16	2 12 ℞	10 33	8 22	13 08	25 13	3 51	0 51	14 06	18 49	18 25	21 16	0 33	10 03	29 05
18 Th	1 45 44	24 33 36	8 ♒ 04	2 12	12 01	7 55	13 38	25 25	3 55	0 48	14 05	18 50	18 52	21 44	0 30	10 26	29 03
19 F	1 49 40	25 33 10	19 53	2 11	13 28	7 27	14 08	25 37	3 59	0 46	14 04	18 50	19 19	22 12	0 27	10 50	29 01
20 Sa	1 53 37	26 32 46	1 ♓ 50	2 08	14 54	6 56	14 39	25 50	4 03	0 43	14 03	18 51	19 46	22 41	0 23	11 14	28 58
21 Su	1 57 33	27 32 23	13 58	2 02	16 20	6 24	15 10	26 02	4 07	0 41	14 02	18 51	20 13	23 09	0 18	11 38	28 56
22 M	2 1 30	28 32 02	26 21	1 54	17 45	5 51	15 42	26 14	4 11	0 38	14 01	18 52	20 40	23 37	0 14	12 02	28 54
23 T	2 5 27	29 31 42	9 ♈ 01	1 43	19 09	5 16	16 13	26 27	4 15	0 36	14 00	18 53	21 07	24 04	0 08	12 26	28 51
24 W	2 9 23	0 ♏ 31 25	22 00	1 30	20 32	4 41	16 45	26 40	4 19	0 33	13 58	18 53	21 34	24 32	0 02	12 51	28 49
25 Th	2 13 20	1 31 10	5 ♉ 15	1 17	21 55	4 05	17 18	26 52	4 24	0 31	13 57	18 54	22 01	25 00	29 ♉ 56	13 15	28 47
26 F	2 17 16	2 30 57	18 46	1 04	23 16	3 28	17 50	27 05	4 28	0 29	13 57	18 55	22 28	25 28	29 49	13 40	28 45
27 Sa	2 21 13	3 30 45	2 ♊ 29	0 54	24 36	2 52	18 23	27 18	4 33	0 26	13 56	18 55	22 55	25 55	29 41	14 05	28 43
28 Su	2 25 9	4 30 36	16 21	0 46	25 55	2 15	18 56	27 30	4 37	0 24	13 55	18 56	23 22	26 22	29 33	14 30	28 41
29 M	2 29 6	5 30 29	0 ♋ 19	0 40	27 13	1 39	19 29	27 43	4 42	0 21	13 54	18 57	23 49	26 50	29 25	14 55	28 39
30 T	2 33 2	6 30 25	14 21	0 38	28 30	1 03	20 02	27 56	4 47	0 19	13 53	18 58	24 16	27 17	29 16	15 20	28 37
31 W	2 36 59	7 30 22	28 25	0 37	29 46	0 28	20 36	28 09	4 51	0 16	13 52	18 59	24 43	27 44	29 07	15 45	28 35

EPHEMERIS CALCULATED FOR 12 MIDNIGHT GREENWICH MEAN TIME. ALL OTHER DATA AND FACING ASPECTARIAN PAGE IN **EASTERN TIME (BOLD)** AND PACIFIC TIME (REGULAR).

NOVEMBER 2018

☽ Last Aspect day	ET / hr:mn / PT		asp	☽ Ingress sign	day	ET / hr:mn / PT	
1		9:32 pm	⚹ ♀	♍	1		10:48 pm
2	**12:32 am**		⚹ ♀	♍	2	**1:48 am**	
4	**2:26 am**	12:26 am	⚹ ♃	♎	4	**4:01 am**	1:01 am
6	**3:19 am**	12:19 am	☌ ♀	♏	6	**8:02 am**	5:02 am
8	**5:42 am**	2:42 am	□ ♂	♐	8	**1:59 pm**	10:59 am
10	**10:35 pm**	7:35 pm	△ ♅	♑	10	**10:55 pm**	7:55 pm
13	**10:13 am**	7:13 am	□ ♅	♒	13	**10:45 am**	7:45 am
15	**10:58 pm**	7:58 pm	⚹ ♅	♓	15	**11:41 pm**	8:41 pm
18	**3:04 am**	12:04 am	△ ☉	♈	18	**10:56 am**	7:56 am
20	**5:46 pm**	2:46 pm	☌ ♅	♉	20	**6:43 pm**	3:43 pm
22	**4:59 am**	1:59 am	△ ♇	♊	22	**11:10 pm**	8:10 pm
24		9:31 pm	⚹ ♅	♋	24		10:38 pm
25	**12:31 am**		⚹ ♅	♋	25	**1:38 am**	
26		11:22 pm	□ ♅	♌	27	**3:35 am**	12:35 am
27	**2:22 am**		□ ♅	♌	27	**3:35 am**	12:35 am
29	**4:47 am**	1:47 am	△ ♅	♍	29	**6:08 am**	3:08 am

☽ Phases & Eclipses phase	day	ET / hr:mn / PT	
New Moon	7	**11:02 am**	8:02 am
2nd Quarter	15	**9:54 am**	6:54 am
Full Moon	22		9:39 pm
Full Moon	23	**12:39 am**	
4th Quarter	29	**7:19 pm**	4:19 pm

Planet Ingress		day	ET / hr:mn / PT	
♀	♎	4	**8:30 pm**	5:30 pm
♅	♈	6	**2:00 pm**	11:00 am
♃	♐	8	**7:38 am**	4:38 am
⚳	♏	11	**4:37 pm**	1:37 pm
♂	♓	15	**5:21 pm**	2:21 pm
☉	♐	22	**4:01 am**	1:01 am

Planetary Motion		day	ET / hr:mn / PT	
♀	D	16	**5:51 am**	2:51 am
☿	℞	16	**8:33 pm**	5:33 pm
♆	D	24	**8:08 pm**	5:08 pm

1 THURSDAY
☽ ⚻ ♇ **7:04 am** 4:04 am
☽ ☍ ♂ **11:22 am** 8:22 am
☽ □ ♃ **11:25 pm** 8:25 pm
☽ ⚹ ♀ 9:32 pm
☽ △ ♅ 11:06 pm

2 FRIDAY
☽ ⚹ ♀ **12:32 am**
☽ △ ♅ **2:06 am**
☽ □ ☿ **6:24 am** 3:24 am
☽ △ ♄ **10:26 am** 7:26 am
☽ ⚹ ☉ **7:40 pm** 4:40 pm
♀ ⚺ ♃ **9:22 pm** 6:22 pm
☽ ☍ ♆ 10:21 pm

3 SATURDAY
☽ ☍ ♆ **1:21 am**
☽ △ ♇ **10:15 am** 7:15 am
☽ ⚻ ♂ **4:41 pm** 1:41 pm
☽ ⚺ ♀ 10:58 pm

4 SUNDAY
☽ ⚺ ♀ **1:58 am**
☽ ⚹ ♃ **2:26 am** 12:26 am
☽ ⚻ ♅ **4:11 am** 1:11 am
☿ ⚺ ♄ **11:01 am** 8:01 am
☽ □ ♄ **1:02 pm** 10:02 am
☽ ⚹ ☿ **1:12 pm** 10:12 am
☽ ⚺ ☉ 11:04 pm

5 MONDAY
☽ ⚺ ☉ **2:04 am**
☽ ⚻ ♆ **3:47 am** 12:47 am
☽ □ ♇ **12:56 pm** 9:56 am
☽ △ ♂ **9:43 pm** 6:43 pm
☉ △ ♆ 10:40 pm

6 TUESDAY
☉ △ ♆ **1:40 am**
☽ ☌ ♀ **3:19 am** 12:19 am
☽ ⚺ ♃ **7:16 am** 4:16 am
☽ ☍ ♅ **8:03 am** 5:03 am
☽ ⚹ ♄ **5:39 pm** 2:39 pm
☽ ⚺ ☿ **9:48 pm** 6:48 pm

7 WEDNESDAY
☽ △ ♆ **8:30 am** 5:30 am
☽ ☌ ☉ **11:02 am** 8:02 am
☽ ⚹ ♇ **6:06 pm** 3:06 pm
♃ ⚻ ♅ 10:20 pm

8 THURSDAY
♃ ⚻ ♅ **1:20 am**
☽ □ ♂ **5:42 am** 2:42 am
☽ ⚺ ♀ **7:36 am** 4:36 am
☽ ⚻ ♅ **1:51 pm** 10:51 am
☽ ☌ ♃ **2:06 pm** 11:06 am
☽ ⚺ ♄ 9:27 pm

9 FRIDAY
☽ ⚺ ♄ **12:27 am**
☽ ☌ ☿ **8:37 am** 5:37 am
♀ △ ♂ **10:12 am** 7:12 am
☽ □ ♆ **3:42 pm** 12:42 pm
☽ ⚺ ☉ **11:11 pm** 8:11 pm
☽ ⚺ ♇ 10:57 pm

10 SATURDAY
☽ ⚺ ♇ **1:57 am**
☽ ⚹ ♀ **2:55 pm** 11:55 am
☽ ⚹ ♂ **4:59 pm** 1:59 pm
☽ △ ♅ **10:35 pm** 7:35 pm
☽ ⚺ ♃ 9:04 pm

11 SUNDAY
☽ ⚺ ♃ **12:04 am**
☉ ⚹ ♇ **10:22 am** 7:22 am
☽ ☌ ♄ **10:25 am** 7:25 am
☽ ⚺ ☿ **10:17 pm** 7:17 pm
☽ ⚹ ♆ 11:01 pm

12 MONDAY
☽ ⚹ ♆ **2:01 am**
☽ ☌ ♇ **12:57 pm** 9:57 am
☽ ⚹ ☉ **3:21 pm** 12:21 pm
☽ □ ♀ 10:32 pm

13 TUESDAY
☽ □ ♀ **1:32 am**
☽ ⚺ ♂ **7:47 am** 4:47 am
☽ □ ♅ **10:13 am** 7:13 am
☽ ⚹ ♃ **1:05 pm** 10:05 am
☽ ⚺ ♄ **11:09 pm** 8:09 pm

14 WEDNESDAY
☽ ⚹ ☿ **1:25 pm** 10:25 am
☽ ⚺ ♆ **2:40 pm** 11:40 am
☽ ⚺ ♇ 10:55 pm

15 THURSDAY
☽ ⚺ ♇ **1:55 am**
♂ ⚹ ♅ **4:31 am** 1:31 am
☽ □ ☉ **9:54 am** 6:54 am
☽ △ ♀ **2:05 pm** 11:05 am
☽ ⚹ ♅ **10:58 pm** 7:58 pm
☽ ☌ ♂ 9:02 pm

16 FRIDAY
☽ ☌ ♂ **12:02 am**
☽ □ ♃ **3:10 am** 12:10 am
☽ ⚹ ♄ **12:27 pm** 9:27 am
☽ □ ☿ 11:41 pm

17 SATURDAY
☽ □ ☿ **2:41 am**
☽ ☌ ♆ **3:07 am** 12:07 am
☉ ⚺ ♀ **11:35 am** 8:35 am
☽ ⚹ ♇ **2:10 pm** 11:10 am
☽ ⚻ ♀ 10:52 pm

18 SUNDAY
☽ ⚻ ♀ **1:52 am**
☽ △ ☉ **3:04 am** 12:04 am
☽ ⚺ ♅ **10:05 am** 7:05 am
☽ ⚺ ♂ **2:20 pm** 11:20 am
☽ △ ♃ **3:18 pm** 12:18 pm
☽ □ ♄ **11:30 pm** 8:30 pm

19 MONDAY
☽ △ ☿ **11:26 am** 8:26 am
☽ ⚺ ♆ **12:52 pm** 9:52 am
♂ □ ♃ **8:30 pm** 5:30 pm
☽ □ ♇ **11:22 pm** 8:22 pm

20 TUESDAY
☽ ☍ ♀ **10:45 am** 7:45 am
☽ ⚻ ☉ **3:59 pm** 12:59 pm
☽ ☌ ♅ **5:46 pm** 2:46 pm
☽ ⚻ ♃ **11:45 pm** 8:45 pm
☽ ⚹ ♂ 9:36 pm

21 WEDNESDAY
☽ ⚹ ♂ **12:36 am**
☽ △ ♄ **6:54 am** 3:54 am
☉ ⚻ ♅ **2:51 pm** 11:51 am
☽ ⚻ ☿ **3:18 pm** 12:18 pm
☽ ⚹ ♆ **7:01 pm** 4:01 pm

22 THURSDAY
☽ △ ♇ **4:59 am** 1:59 am
☽ ⚻ ♀ **4:25 pm** 1:25 pm
☽ ⚺ ♅ **10:09 pm** 7:09 pm
☽ ☍ ☉ 9:39 pm

23 FRIDAY
☽ ☍ ☉ **12:39 am**
☽ ☍ ♃ **4:47 am** 1:47 am
☽ □ ♂ **7:11 am** 4:11 am
☽ ⚻ ♄ **11:09 am** 8:09 am
☽ ☍ ☿ **3:30 pm** 12:30 pm
☽ □ ♆ **10:21 pm** 7:21 pm

24 SATURDAY
☽ ⚻ ♇ **8:03 am** 5:03 am
☽ △ ♀ **8:03 pm** 5:03 pm
☽ ⚹ ♅ 9:31 pm

25 SUNDAY
☽ ⚹ ♅ **12:31 am**
☽ ⚻ ☉ **6:53 am** 3:53 am
☽ ⚻ ♃ **7:55 am** 4:55 am
☽ △ ♂ **11:46 am** 8:46 am
☿ ⚺ ♄ **1:22 pm** 10:22 am
☽ ⚻ ☿ **1:41 pm** 10:41 am
☽ ☍ ♄ **1:43 pm** 10:43 am
☽ △ ♆ 9:25 pm
☉ ☌ ♃ 10:33 pm

26 MONDAY
☽ △ ♆ **12:25 am**
☉ ☌ ♃ **1:33 am**
☿ □ ♂ **3:06 am** 12:06 am
☽ ☍ ♇ **10:07 am** 7:07 am
☽ □ ♀ **11:16 pm** 8:16 pm
☽ □ ♅ 11:22 pm

27 TUESDAY
☽ □ ♅ **2:22 am**
☉ ☌ ☿ **4:15 am** 1:15 am
☽ △ ♃ **10:41 am** 7:41 am
☽ △ ☿ **11:22 am** 8:22 am
☽ △ ☉ **12:39 pm** 9:39 am
☽ ⚻ ♂ **4:06 pm** 1:06 pm
☽ ⚻ ♄ **4:07 pm** 1:07 pm
♂ ⚹ ♄ **4:31 pm** 1:31 pm
☿ ☌ ♃ **5:27 pm** 2:27 pm
☽ ⚻ ♆ 11:33 pm

28 WEDNESDAY
☽ ⚻ ♆ **2:33 am**
☽ ⚻ ♇ **12:27 pm** 9:27 am

29 THURSDAY
☽ ⚹ ♀ **3:17 am** 12:17 am
☽ △ ♅ **4:47 am** 1:47 am
☽ □ ☿ **9:42 am** 6:42 am
☽ □ ♃ **2:11 pm** 11:11 am
☉ ⚺ ♄ **7:03 pm** 4:03 pm
☽ △ ♄ **7:18 pm** 4:18 pm
☽ □ ☉ **7:19 pm** 4:19 pm
☽ ☍ ♂ **9:19 pm** 6:19 pm

30 FRIDAY
☽ ☍ ♆ **5:34 am** 2:34 am
☽ △ ♇ **3:48 pm** 12:48 pm
♀ ☍ ♅ **9:13 pm** 6:13 pm

Eastern time in bold type
Pacific time in medium type

NOVEMBER 2018

DATE	SID.TIME	SUN	MOON	NODE	MERCURY	VENUS	MARS	JUPITER	SATURN	URANUS	NEPTUNE	PLUTO	CERES	PALLAS	JUNO	VESTA	CHIRON
1 Th	2 40 56	8 ♏ 30 22	12 ♌ 30	0 ♌ 37 ℞	0 ♐ 59	29 ♎ 54 ℞	21 ♒ 10	28 ♏ 22	4 ♑ 56	0 ♉ 14 ℞	13 ♓ 51 ℞	19 ♑ 00	25 ♎ 09	28 ♍ 11	28 ♉ 57 ℞	16 ♑ 10	28 ♓ 33 ℞
2 F	2 44 52	9 30 24	26 36	0 37	2 12	29 21	21 44	28 35	5 01	0 11	13 51	19 01	25 36	28 38	28 47	16 36	28 31
3 Sa	2 48 49	10 30 28	10 ♍ 41	0 34	3 22	28 50	22 18	28 48	5 06	0 09	13 50	19 01	26 03	29 05	28 37	17 01	28 29
4 Su	2 52 45	11 30 34	24 44	0 28	4 30	28 21	22 53	29 01	5 11	0 07	13 49	19 02	26 30	29 32	28 26	17 27	28 27
5 M	2 56 42	12 30 42	8 ♎ 43	0 20	5 36	27 53	23 28	29 14	5 16	0 04	13 48	19 03	26 56	29 58	28 15	17 53	28 25
6 T	3 0 38	13 30 52	22 33	0 09	6 40	27 27	24 03	29 27	5 21	0 02	13 48	19 04	27 23	0 ♎ 25	28 03	18 19	28 24
7 W	3 4 35	14 31 04	6 ♏ 12	29 ♋ 57	7 40	27 03	24 38	29 40	5 27	0 00	13 47	19 06	27 50	0 51	27 51	18 45	28 22
8 Th	3 8 31	15 31 18	19 36	29 44	8 38	26 42	25 13	29 53	5 32	29 ♈ 57	13 47	19 07	28 16	1 18	27 39	19 11	28 20
9 F	3 12 28	16 31 34	2 ♐ 43	29 32	9 32	26 22	25 49	0 ♐ 06	5 37	29 55	13 46	19 08	28 43	1 44	27 27	19 37	28 19
10 Sa	3 16 25	17 31 51	15 30	29 23	10 21	26 05	26 25	0 19	5 43	29 53	13 45	19 09	29 10	2 10	27 14	20 04	28 17
11 Su	3 20 21	18 32 10	28 00	29 16	11 07	25 51	27 00	0 33	5 48	29 50	13 45	19 10	29 36	2 36	27 01	20 30	28 16
12 M	3 24 18	19 32 31	10 ♑ 13	29 12	11 47	25 39	27 37	0 46	5 54	29 48	13 45	19 11	0 ♏ 03	3 02	26 48	20 57	28 14
13 T	3 28 14	20 32 53	22 12	29 10 D	12 21	25 29	28 13	0 59	6 00	29 46	13 44	19 12	0 29	3 28	26 35	21 23	28 13
14 W	3 32 11	21 33 17	4 ♒ 04	29 10	12 50	25 22	28 49	1 12	6 05	29 43	13 44	19 14	0 56	3 53	26 22	21 50	28 11
15 Th	3 36 7	22 33 42	15 51	29 10 ℞	13 11	25 17	29 26	1 26	6 11	29 41	13 43	19 15	1 22	4 19	26 08	22 17	28 10
16 F	3 40 4	23 34 08	27 41	29 10	13 24	25 15 D	0 ♓ 03	1 39	6 17	29 39	13 43	19 16	1 48	4 44	25 55	22 44	28 09
17 Sa	3 44 0	24 34 36	9 ♓ 37	29 09	13 29 ℞	25 15	0 39	1 52	6 23	29 37	13 43	19 18	2 15	5 09	25 41	23 11	28 08
18 Su	3 47 57	25 35 04	21 47	29 06	13 25	25 17	1 16	2 06	6 28	29 35	13 42	19 19	2 41	5 35	25 28	23 38	28 06
19 M	3 51 54	26 35 35	4 ♈ 13	29 00	13 11	25 22	1 54	2 19	6 34	29 33	13 42	19 20	3 07	6 00	25 14	24 05	28 05
20 T	3 55 50	27 36 06	17 00	28 52	12 47	25 29	2 31	2 32	6 40	29 31	13 42	19 22	3 33	6 25	25 01	24 32	28 04
21 W	3 59 47	28 36 39	0 ♉ 10	28 42	12 13	25 39	3 08	2 46	6 46	29 28	13 42	19 23	3 59	6 49	24 47	24 59	28 03
22 Th	4 3 43	29 37 13	13 41	28 31	11 27	25 51	3 46	2 59	6 53	29 26	13 42	19 24	4 25	7 14	24 34	25 27	28 02
23 F	4 7 40	0 ♐ 37 49	27 34	28 21	10 32	26 05	4 23	3 12	6 59	29 24	13 42	19 26	4 52	7 39	24 21	25 54	28 01
24 Sa	4 11 36	1 38 26	11 ♊ 42	28 13	9 27	26 21	5 01	3 26	7 05	29 22	13 42	19 27	5 18	8 03	24 07	26 21	28 00
25 Su	4 15 33	2 39 04	26 01	28 06	8 15	26 39	5 39	3 39	7 11	29 20	13 42 D	19 29	5 44	8 27	23 54	26 49	28 00
26 M	4 19 29	3 39 45	10 ♋ 26	28 03	6 57	26 59	6 17	3 53	7 17	29 19	13 42	19 30	6 09	8 51	23 42	27 17	27 59
27 T	4 23 26	4 40 26	24 51	28 01 D	5 36	27 21	6 55	4 06	7 24	29 17	13 42	19 32	6 35	9 15	23 29	27 44	27 58
28 W	4 27 23	5 41 10	9 ♌ 12	28 02	4 13	27 44	7 33	4 19	7 30	29 15	13 42	19 33	7 01	9 39	23 17	28 12	27 57
29 Th	4 31 19	6 41 54	23 27	28 03	2 53	28 10	8 12	4 33	7 36	29 13	13 42	19 35	7 27	10 03	23 05	28 40	27 57
30 F	4 35 16	7 42 41	7 ♍ 32	28 03 ℞	1 38	28 38	8 50	4 46	7 43	29 11	13 42	19 37	7 53	10 27	22 53	29 08	27 56

EPHEMERIS CALCULATED FOR 12 MIDNIGHT GREENWICH MEAN TIME. ALL OTHER DATA AND FACING ASPECTARIAN PAGE IN **EASTERN TIME (BOLD)** AND PACIFIC TIME (REGULAR).

DECEMBER 2018

☽ Last Aspect day	ET / hr:mn / PT		asp	☽ Ingress sign	day	ET / hr:mn / PT	
1	**9:34 am**	6:34 am	⚹ ☿	♎	1	**9:49 am**	6:49 am
3	**1:16 pm**	10:16 am	☍ ♅	♏	3	**2:55 pm**	11:55 am
5	**4:53 pm**	1:53 pm	☌ ☿	♐	5	**9:49 pm**	6:49 pm
8	**5:00 am**	2:00 am	△ ♅	♑	8	**7:01 am**	4:01 am
10	**4:27 pm**	1:27 pm	□ ♅	♒	10	**6:39 pm**	3:39 pm
13	**5:20 am**	2:20 am	⚹ ♅	♓	13	**7:40 am**	4:40 am
15	**6:49 am**	3:49 am	□ ☉	♈	15	**7:44 pm**	4:44 pm
17		11:21 pm	☌ ♅	♉	18	**4:37 am**	1:37 am
18	**2:21 am**		☌ ♅	♉	18	**4:37 am**	1:37 am
19	**7:42 pm**	4:42 pm	⚹ ♂	♊	20	**9:34 am**	6:34 am

☽ Last Aspect day	ET / hr:mn / PT		asp	☽ Ingress sign	day	ET / hr:mn / PT	
22	**9:21 am**	6:21 am	⚹ ♅	♋	22	**11:28 am**	8:28 am
24	**9:50 am**	6:50 am	□ ♅	♌	24	**11:59 am**	8:59 am
26	**10:37 am**	7:37 am	△ ♅	♍	26	**12:50 pm**	9:50 am
28	**11:27 am**	8:27 am	☍ ♂	♎	28	**3:23 pm**	12:23 pm
30	**5:53 pm**	2:53 pm	☍ ♅	♏	30	**8:23 pm**	5:23 pm

☽ Phases & Eclipses phase	day	ET / hr:mn / PT	
New Moon	6		11:20 pm
New Moon	7	**2:20 am**	
2nd Quarter	15	**6:49 am**	3:49 am
Full Moon	22	**12:49 pm**	9:49 am
4th Quarter	29	**4:34 am**	1:34 am

Planet Ingress		day	ET / hr:mn / PT	
☿	♏	1	**6:12 am**	3:12 am
⚶	♒	1	**3:42 pm**	12:42 pm
♀	♏	2	**12:02 pm**	9:02 am
☿	♐	12	**6:43 pm**	3:43 pm
☉	♑	21	**5:23 pm**	2:23 pm
♂	♈	31	**9:20 pm**	6:20 pm

Planetary Motion		day	ET / hr:mn / PT	
☿	D	6	**4:22 pm**	1:22 pm
⚷	D	8		11:52 pm
⚷	D	9	**2:52 am**	
⚵	D	23	**9:56 pm**	6:56 pm

1 SATURDAY
☽ ⚻ ♅ **8:19 am** 5:19 am
☽ ⚺ ♀ **8:46 am** 5:46 am
☽ ⚹ ☿ **9:34 am** 6:34 am
☿ ⚺ ♀ **4:50 pm** 1:50 pm
☽ ⚹ ♃ **6:56 pm** 3:56 pm
☽ □ ♄ **11:44 pm** 8:44 pm

2 SUNDAY
☽ ⚹ ☉ **3:31 am** 12:31 am
☽ ⚻ ♂ **3:58 am** 12:58 am
☿ ⚻ ♅ **5:16 am** 2:16 am
☽ ⚻ ♆ **9:53 am** 6:53 am
☉ □ ♂ **7:34 pm** 4:34 pm
☽ □ ♇ **8:30 pm** 5:30 pm

3 MONDAY
☽ ⚺ ☿ **11:42 am** 8:42 am
☽ ☍ ♅ **1:16 pm** 10:16 am
☽ ☌ ♀ **4:05 pm** 1:05 pm
☽ ⚺ ♃ 10:14 pm

4 TUESDAY
☽ ⚺ ♃ **1:14 am**
☽ ⚹ ♄ **5:43 am** 2:43 am
☽ △ ♂ **12:24 pm** 9:24 am
☽ ⚺ ☉ **1:38 pm** 10:38 am
☽ △ ♆ **3:46 pm** 12:46 pm
☽ ⚹ ♇ 11:50 pm

5 WEDNESDAY
☽ ⚹ ♇ **2:50 am**
☽ ☌ ☿ **4:53 pm** 1:53 pm
☉ □ ♆ **5:22 pm** 2:22 pm
☽ ⚻ ♅ **7:59 pm** 4:59 pm
☽ ⚺ ♀ 10:43 pm

6 THURSDAY
☽ ⚺ ♀ **1:43 am**
☽ ☌ ♃ **9:31 am** 6:31 am
☽ ⚺ ♄ **1:41 pm** 10:41 am
☽ □ ♂ **11:11 pm** 8:11 pm
☽ □ ♆ **11:42 pm** 8:42 pm
☽ ☌ ☉ 11:20 pm

7 FRIDAY
☽ ☌ ☉ **2:20 am**
♂ ☌ ♆ **9:11 am** 6:11 am
☽ ⚺ ♇ **11:20 am** 8:20 am
☽ ⚺ ☿ 11:02 pm

8 SATURDAY
☽ ⚺ ☿ **2:02 am**
☽ △ ♅ **5:00 am** 2:00 am
☽ ⚹ ♀ **2:20 pm** 11:20 am
☽ ⚺ ♃ **8:19 pm** 5:19 pm
☽ ☌ ♄ 9:09 pm

9 SUNDAY
☽ ☌ ♄ **12:09 am**
☽ ⚹ ♆ **10:06 am** 7:06 am
☽ ⚹ ♂ **12:52 pm** 9:52 am

☽ ⚺ ☉ **6:12 pm** 3:12 pm
☽ ☌ ♇ **10:20 pm** 7:20 pm

10 MONDAY
☽ ⚹ ☿ **3:38 pm** 12:38 pm
☽ □ ♅ **4:27 pm** 1:27 pm

11 TUESDAY
☽ □ ♀ **6:01 am** 3:01 am
☿ ⚻ ♅ **6:38 am** 3:38 am
☽ ⚹ ♃ **9:34 am** 6:34 am
☽ ⚺ ♄ **12:56 pm** 9:56 am
☉ ⚺ ♇ **8:26 pm** 5:26 pm
☽ ⚺ ♆ **10:37 pm** 7:37 pm

12 WEDNESDAY
☽ ⚺ ♂ **4:59 am** 1:59 am
☽ ⚺ ♇ **11:15 am** 8:15 am
☽ ⚹ ☉ **12:36 pm** 9:36 am

13 THURSDAY
☽ ⚹ ♅ **5:20 am** 2:20 am
☽ □ ☿ **8:39 am** 5:39 am
☽ △ ♀ **11:10 pm** 8:10 pm
☽ □ ♃ **11:44 pm** 8:44 pm
☽ ⚹ ♄ 11:31 pm

14 FRIDAY
☽ ⚹ ♄ **2:31 am**
♀ ⚺ ♃ **10:59 am** 7:59 am
☽ ☌ ♆ **11:35 am** 8:35 am
☽ ☌ ♂ **9:19 pm** 6:19 pm
☽ ⚹ ♇ 9:05 pm

15 SATURDAY
☽ ⚹ ♇ **12:05 am**
☽ □ ☉ **6:49 am** 3:49 am
☽ ⚺ ♅ **5:23 pm** 2:23 pm
☽ △ ☿ 10:48 pm

16 SUNDAY
☽ △ ☿ **1:48 am**
♀ ⚹ ♄ **9:26 am** 6:26 am
☽ △ ♃ **12:12 pm** 9:12 am
☽ □ ♄ **2:21 pm** 11:21 am
☽ ⚻ ♀ **2:39 pm** 11:39 am
☽ ⚺ ♆ **10:27 pm** 7:27 pm
♂ ⚹ ♇ 10:57 pm

17 MONDAY
♂ ⚹ ♇ **1:57 am**
☽ □ ♇ **10:20 am** 7:20 am
☽ ⚺ ♂ **10:46 am** 7:46 am
☽ △ ☉ **9:27 pm** 6:27 pm
☽ ☌ ♅ 11:21 pm

18 TUESDAY
☽ ☌ ♅ **2:21 am**
☽ ⚻ ☿ **3:31 pm** 12:31 pm
☽ ⚻ ♃ **8:54 pm** 5:54 pm
☽ △ ♄ **10:27 pm** 7:27 pm
☽ ☍ ♀ 10:54 pm

19 WEDNESDAY
☽ ☍ ♀ **1:54 am**
☽ ⚹ ♆ **5:33 am** 2:33 am
☽ △ ♇ **4:41 pm** 1:41 pm
☽ ⚹ ♂ **7:42 pm** 4:42 pm

20 THURSDAY
☽ ⚻ ☉ **7:05 am** 4:05 am
☽ ⚺ ♅ **7:24 am** 4:24 am
☉ △ ♅ **11:22 am** 8:22 am
☽ ☍ ☿ 9:41 pm
☽ ☍ ♃ 10:35 pm
☽ ⚻ ♄ 11:40 pm

21 FRIDAY
☽ ☍ ☿ **12:41 am**
☽ ☍ ♃ **1:35 am**
☽ ⚻ ♄ **2:40 am**
☽ ⚻ ♀ **8:46 am** 5:46 am
☽ □ ♆ **8:58 am** 5:58 am
♀ △ ♆ **12:11 pm** 9:11 am
☿ ☌ ♃ **12:37 pm** 9:37 am
☽ ⚻ ♇ **7:31 pm** 4:31 pm
☽ □ ♂ 9:41 pm
☿ ⚺ ♄ 9:41 pm

22 SATURDAY
☽ □ ♂ **12:41 am**
☿ ⚺ ♄ **12:41 am**
☽ ⚹ ♅ **9:21 am** 6:21 am
☽ ☍ ☉ **12:49 pm** 9:49 am

23 SUNDAY
☽ ⚻ ♃ **3:35 am** 12:35 am
☽ ☍ ♄ **4:17 am** 1:17 am
☽ ⚻ ☿ **6:44 am** 3:44 am
☽ △ ♆ **10:03 am** 7:03 am
☽ △ ♀ **12:55 pm** 9:55 am
☽ ☍ ♇ **8:23 pm** 5:23 pm

24 MONDAY
☽ △ ♂ **3:37 am** 12:37 am
☽ □ ♅ **9:50 am** 6:50 am
☽ ⚻ ☉ **4:52 pm** 1:52 pm
☿ □ ♆ **7:32 pm** 4:32 pm

25 TUESDAY
☽ △ ♃ **4:44 am** 1:44 am
☽ ⚻ ♄ **5:07 am** 2:07 am
☽ ⚻ ♆ **10:34 am** 7:34 am
☽ △ ☿ **12:06 pm** 9:06 am
☽ □ ♀ **4:37 pm** 1:37 pm
☽ ⚻ ♇ **9:04 pm** 6:04 pm

26 WEDNESDAY
☽ ⚻ ♂ **6:38 am** 3:38 am
☽ △ ♅ **10:37 am** 7:37 am
☽ △ ☉ **9:33 pm** 6:33 pm

27 THURSDAY
☽ □ ♃ **6:48 am** 3:48 am
☽ △ ♄ **6:51 am** 3:51 am
☽ ☍ ♆ **12:09 pm** 9:09 am
♃ ⚺ ♄ **2:18 pm** 11:18 am
☽ □ ☿ **7:04 pm** 4:04 pm
☽ ⚹ ♀ **9:52 pm** 6:52 pm
☽ △ ♇ **11:04 pm** 8:04 pm

28 FRIDAY
☽ ☍ ♂ **11:27 am** 8:27 am
☽ ⚻ ♅ **1:02 pm** 10:02 am
♀ ⚹ ♇ **4:31 pm** 1:31 pm

29 SATURDAY
☽ □ ☉ **4:34 am** 1:34 am
☽ □ ♄ **10:41 am** 7:41 am
☽ ⚹ ♃ **11:00 am** 8:00 am
☿ ⚺ ♇ **11:44 am** 8:44 am
☽ ⚻ ♆ **3:52 pm** 12:52 pm
♂ ⚺ ♅ **8:14 pm** 5:14 pm

30 SUNDAY
☽ □ ♇ **3:23 am** 12:23 am
☽ ⚹ ☿ **5:13 am** 2:13 am
☽ ⚺ ♀ **5:59 am** 2:59 am
☽ ☍ ♅ **5:53 pm** 2:53 pm
☽ ⚻ ♂ **7:03 pm** 4:03 pm
☿ ⚺ ♀ 10:00 pm

31 MONDAY
☿ ⚺ ♀ **1:00 am**
☽ ⚹ ☉ **2:46 pm** 11:46 am
☽ ⚹ ♄ **5:09 pm** 2:09 pm
☽ ⚺ ♃ **5:52 pm** 2:52 pm
☽ △ ♆ **10:10 pm** 7:10 pm

Eastern time in bold type
Pacific time in medium type

DECEMBER 2018

DATE	SID.TIME	SUN	MOON	NODE	MERCURY	VENUS	MARS	JUPITER	SATURN	URANUS	NEPTUNE	PLUTO	CERES	PALLAS	JUNO	VESTA	CHIRON
1 Sa	4 39 12	8 ♐ 43 28	21 ♍ 29	28 ♋ 03 ℞	0 ♐ 29 ℞	29 ♎ 07	9 ♓ 28	5 ♐ 00	7 ♑ 49	29 ♈ 10 ℞	13 ♓ 42	19 ♑ 38	8 ♏ 18	10 ♎ 50	22 ♉ 41 ℞	29 ♑ 36	27 ♓ 56 ℞
2 Su	4 43 9	9 44 18	5 ♎ 15	28 00	29 ♏ 29	29 37	10 07	5 13	7 56	29 08	13 42	19 40	8 44	11 13	22 30	0 ♒ 04	27 55
3 M	4 47 5	10 45 08	18 51	27 55	28 40	0 ♏ 10	10 46	5 26	8 02	29 06	13 43	19 42	9 09	11 37	22 19	0 32	27 55
4 T	4 51 2	11 46 01	2 ♏ 16	27 48	28 02	0 43	11 24	5 40	8 09	29 05	13 43	19 43	9 35	12 00	22 09	1 00	27 55
5 W	4 54 58	12 46 54	15 29	27 40	27 36	1 18	12 03	5 53	8 16	29 03	13 43	19 45	10 00	12 22	21 59	1 28	27 54
6 Th	4 58 55	13 47 49	28 29	27 31	27 20 D	1 55	12 42	6 07	8 22	29 01	13 44	19 47	10 26	12 45	21 49	1 57	27 54
7 F	5 2 52	14 48 45	11 ♐ 16	27 24	27 16	2 33	13 21	6 20	8 29	29 00	13 44	19 48	10 51	13 08	21 40	2 25	27 54
8 Sa	5 6 48	15 49 42	23 48	27 17	27 23	3 12	14 00	6 33	8 36	28 58	13 45	19 50	11 16	13 30	21 31	2 53	27 54
9 Su	5 10 45	16 50 40	6 ♑ 07	27 13	27 38	3 52	14 40	6 47	8 42	28 57	13 45	19 52	11 42	13 52	21 22	3 22	27 54 D
10 M	5 14 41	17 51 39	18 14	27 11D	28 03	4 34	15 19	7 00	8 49	28 56	13 45	19 54	12 07	14 14	21 15	3 50	27 54
11 T	5 18 38	18 52 38	0 ♒ 10	27 10	28 35	5 17	15 58	7 13	8 56	28 54	13 46	19 55	12 32	14 36	21 07	4 19	27 54
12 W	5 22 34	19 53 38	12 00	27 11	29 15	6 00	16 37	7 27	9 03	28 53	13 47	19 57	12 57	14 58	21 00	4 47	27 54
13 Th	5 26 31	20 54 39	23 47	27 13	0 ♐ 01	6 45	17 17	7 40	9 09	28 52	13 47	19 59	13 22	15 19	20 54	5 16	27 54
14 F	5 30 27	21 55 41	5 ♓ 35	27 15	0 52	7 31	17 56	7 53	9 16	28 50	13 48	20 01	13 46	15 41	20 48	5 45	27 54
15 Sa	5 34 24	22 56 42	17 30	27 16 ℞	1 48	8 18	18 36	8 06	9 23	28 49	13 48	20 03	14 11	16 02	20 43	6 13	27 55
16 Su	5 38 21	23 57 45	29 38	27 16	2 49	9 05	19 16	8 19	9 30	28 48	13 49	20 05	14 36	16 23	20 38	6 42	27 55
17 M	5 42 17	24 58 48	12 ♈ 01	27 15	3 53	9 54	19 55	8 33	9 37	28 47	13 50	20 06	15 01	16 44	20 34	7 11	27 56
18 T	5 46 14	25 59 51	24 47	27 12	5 00	10 43	20 35	8 46	9 44	28 46	13 51	20 08	15 25	17 04	20 30	7 40	27 56
19 W	5 50 10	27 00 54	7 ♉ 56	27 08	6 10	11 33	21 15	8 59	9 51	28 45	13 51	20 10	15 50	17 25	20 27	8 09	27 56
20 Th	5 54 7	28 01 58	21 32	27 03	7 23	12 24	21 55	9 12	9 58	28 44	13 52	20 12	16 14	17 45	20 24	8 38	27 57
21 F	5 58 3	29 03 03	5 ♊ 33	26 58	8 38	13 16	22 35	9 25	10 05	28 43	13 53	20 14	16 38	18 05	20 22	9 07	27 58
22 Sa	6 2 0	0 ♑ 04 08	19 57	26 55	9 55	14 09	23 15	9 38	10 12	28 42	13 54	20 16	17 02	18 25	20 21	9 36	27 58
23 Su	6 5 56	1 05 13	4 ♋ 38	26 52	11 14	15 02	23 55	9 51	10 19	28 42	13 55	20 18	17 27	18 45	20 20	10 05	27 59
24 M	6 9 53	2 06 19	19 28	26 51D	12 34	15 56	24 35	10 04	10 26	28 41	13 56	20 20	17 51	19 04	20 19 D	10 34	28 00
25 T	6 13 50	3 07 25	4 ♌ 21	26 51	13 55	16 51	25 15	10 17	10 33	28 40	13 57	20 22	18 15	19 23	20 20	11 03	28 01
26 W	6 17 46	4 08 32	19 08	26 52	15 18	17 46	25 55	10 30	10 40	28 40	13 58	20 24	18 39	19 42	20 20	11 32	28 02
27 Th	6 21 43	5 09 39	3 ♍ 44	26 53	16 41	18 42	26 35	10 43	10 47	28 39	13 59	20 26	19 02	20 01	20 22	12 01	28 03
28 F	6 25 39	6 10 47	18 04	26 54	18 06	19 38	27 15	10 55	10 54	28 39	14 00	20 28	19 26	20 20	20 24	12 30	28 04
29 Sa	6 29 36	7 11 55	2 ♎ 06	26 55 ℞	19 31	20 35	27 55	11 08	11 01	28 38	14 01	20 30	19 50	20 38	20 26	13 00	28 05
30 Su	6 33 32	8 13 04	15 49	26 55	20 57	21 33	28 36	11 21	11 08	28 38	14 02	20 32	20 13	20 56	20 29	13 29	28 06
31 M	6 37 29	9 14 14	29 14	26 54	22 24	22 31	29 16	11 34	11 16	28 37	14 04	20 34	20 37	21 14	20 33	13 58	28 07

EPHEMERIS CALCULATED FOR 12 MIDNIGHT GREENWICH MEAN TIME. ALL OTHER DATA AND FACING ASPECTARIAN PAGE IN **EASTERN TIME (BOLD)** AND PACIFIC TIME (REGULAR).

JANUARY 2019

☽ Last Aspect day	ET / hr:mn / PT	asp	☽ Ingress sign	day	ET / hr:mn / PT
1	**5:26 pm** 2:26 pm	☌ ♀	♐	2	**3:58 am** 12:58 am
4	**12:41 pm** 9:41 am	☌ ☿	♑	4	**1:55 pm** 10:55 am
6	10:20 pm	⚹ ♀	♒	6	10:46 pm
7	**1:20 am**	⚹ ♀	♒	7	**1:46 am**
9	**11:53 am** 8:53 am	⚹ ♅	♓	9	**2:44 pm** 11:44 am
11	**9:25 am** 6:25 am	⚹ ☉	♈	12	**3:18 am** 12:18 am
14	**10:56 am** 7:56 am	☌ ♅	♉	14	**1:31 pm** 10:31 am
16	**1:34 pm** 10:34 am	△ ☉	♊	16	**8:00 pm** 5:00 pm
18	**8:32 pm** 5:32 pm	⚹ ♅	♋	18	**10:44 pm** 7:44 pm
20	**8:50 pm** 5:50 pm	□ ♅	♌	20	**10:54 pm** 7:54 pm
22	**8:19 pm** 5:19 pm	△ ♅	♍	22	**10:22 pm** 7:22 pm
24	**8:50 am** 5:50 am	△ ♇	♎	24	**11:02 pm** 8:02 pm
26	9:21 pm	☍ ♅	♏	26	11:31 pm
27	**12:21 am**	☍ ♅	♏	27	**2:31 am**
28	**5:39 pm** 2:39 pm	⚹ ♇	♐	29	**9:33 am** 6:33 am
31	**5:33 pm** 2:33 pm	△ ♅	♑	31	**7:47 pm** 4:47 pm

☽ Phases & Eclipses phase	day	ET / hr:mn / PT
New Moon	5	**8:28 pm** 5:28 pm
(solar eclipse)	5	15° ♑ 25'
2nd Quarter	13	10:46 pm
2nd Quarter	14	**1:46 am**
Full Moon	20	9:16 pm
Full Moon	21	**12:16 am**
(lunar eclipse)	20/21	0° ♌ 52'
4th Quarter	27	**4:10 pm** 1:10 pm

Planet Ingress		day	ET / hr:mn / PT
☿	♑	4	**10:40 pm** 7:40 pm
♀	♐	7	**6:18 am** 3:18 am
☉	♒	20	**4:00 am** 1:00 am
☿	♒	23	9:49 pm
☿	♒	24	**12:49 am**
⚳	♒	25	**1:08 pm** 10:08 am

Planetary Motion		day	ET / hr:mn / PT
♅	D	6	**3:27 pm** 12:27 pm

1 TUESDAY
☽ ⚹ ♇ **10:19 am** 7:19 am
☽ ☌ ♀ **5:26 pm** 2:26 pm
☽ ⊻ ☿ **7:09 pm** 4:09 pm
☉ ☌ ♄ 9:50 pm
☽ ⊼ ♅ 10:20 pm

2 WEDNESDAY
☉ ☌ ♄ **12:50 am**
☽ ⊼ ♅ **1:20 am**
☽ △ ♂ **5:41 am** 2:41 am
☉ ⊻ ♃ **3:49 pm** 12:49 pm
☽ ⊻ ♄ 11:13 pm

3 THURSDAY
☽ ⊻ ♄ **2:13 am**
☽ ☌ ♃ **3:23 am** 12:23 am
☽ ⊻ ☉ **4:13 am** 1:13 am
☽ □ ♆ **7:00 am** 4:00 am
☽ ⊻ ♇ **7:43 pm** 4:43 pm
☿ △ ♅ 9:13 pm

4 FRIDAY
☿ △ ♅ **12:13 am**
☽ ⊻ ♀ **8:04 am** 5:04 am
☽ △ ♅ **11:10 am** 8:10 am
☽ ☌ ☿ **12:41 pm** 9:41 am
☉ ⚹ ♆ **2:57 pm** 11:57 am
☽ □ ♂ **7:05 pm** 4:05 pm

5 SATURDAY
☽ ☌ ♄ **1:32 pm** 10:32 am
☽ ⊻ ♃ **3:12 pm** 12:12 pm
☽ ⚹ ♆ **6:01 pm** 3:01 pm
☽ ☌ ☉ **8:28 pm** 5:28 pm
♀ ⊼ ♅ **9:28 pm** 6:28 pm

6 SUNDAY
☽ ☌ ♇ **7:12 am** 4:12 am
☽ □ ♅ **10:56 pm** 7:56 pm
☽ ⚹ ♀ 10:20 pm

7 MONDAY
☽ ⚹ ♀ **1:20 am**
☽ ⊻ ☿ **9:12 am** 6:12 am
☽ ⚹ ♂ **10:42 am** 7:42 am
☽ ⊻ ♄ 11:34 pm

8 TUESDAY
☽ ⊻ ♄ **2:34 am**
☽ ⚹ ♃ **4:44 am** 1:44 am
☿ □ ♂ **5:05 am** 2:05 am
☽ ⊻ ♆ **6:39 am** 3:39 am
☽ ⊻ ☉ **2:46 pm** 11:46 am
☽ ⊻ ♇ **8:07 pm** 5:07 pm

9 WEDNESDAY
☽ ⚹ ♅ **11:53 am** 8:53 am
☽ □ ♀ **8:09 pm** 5:09 pm

10 THURSDAY
☽ ⊻ ♂ **3:25 am** 12:25 am
☽ ⚹ ☿ **7:16 am** 4:16 am
☽ ⚹ ♄ **4:13 pm** 1:13 pm
☽ □ ♃ **6:48 pm** 3:48 pm
☽ ☌ ♆ **7:47 pm** 4:47 pm

11 FRIDAY
☉ ☌ ♇ **6:38 am** 3:38 am
☽ ⚹ ♇ **9:11 am** 6:11 am
☽ ⚹ ☉ **9:25 am** 6:25 am
☽ ⊻ ♅ 9:32 pm

12 SATURDAY
☽ ⊻ ♅ **12:32 am**
☽ △ ♀ **2:20 pm** 11:20 am
☽ ☌ ♂ **7:12 pm** 4:12 pm

13 SUNDAY
☽ □ ☿ **4:05 am** 1:05 am
☽ □ ♄ **4:36 am** 1:36 am
☽ △ ♃ **7:31 am** 4:31 am
☽ ⊻ ♆ **7:36 am** 4:36 am
☿ ☌ ♄ **8:31 am** 5:31 am
♃ □ ♆ **1:58 pm** 10:58 am
☽ □ ♇ **8:28 pm** 5:28 pm
☽ □ ☉ 10:46 pm

14 MONDAY
☽ □ ☉ **1:46 am**
☿ ⚹ ♆ **8:13 am** 5:13 am
☿ ⊻ ♃ **10:30 am** 7:30 am
☽ ☌ ♅ **10:56 am** 7:56 am

15 TUESDAY
☽ ⊼ ♀ **5:05 am** 2:05 am
☽ ⊻ ♂ **7:39 am** 4:39 am
☽ △ ♄ **1:50 pm** 10:50 am
☽ ⚹ ♆ **4:15 pm** 1:15 pm
☽ ⊼ ♃ **4:54 pm** 1:54 pm
☽ △ ☿ **8:30 pm** 5:30 pm

16 WEDNESDAY
☽ △ ♇ **4:17 am** 1:17 am
☽ △ ☉ **1:34 pm** 10:34 am
☽ ⊻ ♅ **5:38 pm** 2:38 pm

17 THURSDAY
☽ ☍ ♀ **2:54 pm** 11:54 am
☽ ⚹ ♂ **3:32 pm** 12:32 pm
☽ ⊼ ♄ **7:02 pm** 4:02 pm
☽ □ ♆ **8:56 pm** 5:56 pm
☽ ☍ ♃ **10:10 pm** 7:10 pm

18 FRIDAY
☽ ⊼ ☿ **7:19 am** 4:19 am
☽ ⊼ ♇ **8:10 am** 5:10 am
♀ △ ♂ **11:49 am** 8:49 am
☿ ☌ ♇ **3:03 pm** 12:03 pm
☉ □ ♅ **8:31 pm** 5:31 pm
☽ ⚹ ♅ **8:32 pm** 5:32 pm
☽ ⊼ ☉ **8:32 pm** 5:32 pm

19 SATURDAY
☽ □ ♂ **7:28 pm** 4:28 pm
☽ ⊼ ♀ **8:24 pm** 5:24 pm
☽ ☍ ♄ **8:48 pm** 5:48 pm
☽ △ ♆ **10:19 pm** 7:19 pm
☽ ⊼ ♃ 9:02 pm
♀ ⊻ ♄ 11:29 pm

20 SUNDAY
☽ ⊼ ♃ **12:02 am**
♀ ⊻ ♄ **2:29 am**
☽ ☍ ♇ **9:01 am** 6:01 am
☽ ☍ ☿ **1:56 pm** 10:56 am
☽ □ ♅ **8:50 pm** 5:50 pm
♀ □ ♆ **11:15 pm** 8:15 pm
☽ ☍ ☉ 9:16 pm

21 MONDAY
☽ ☍ ☉ **12:16 am**
♂ □ ♄ **6:48 am** 3:48 am
☽ ⊼ ♄ **8:47 pm** 5:47 pm
☽ △ ♂ **9:19 pm** 6:19 pm
☽ ⊼ ♆ **10:00 pm** 7:00 pm
☽ △ ♀ **11:43 pm** 8:43 pm
☽ △ ♃ 9:12 pm

22 TUESDAY
☽ △ ♃ **12:12 am**
♀ ☌ ♃ **7:26 am** 4:26 am
☽ ⊼ ♇ **8:36 am** 5:36 am
♂ ⊻ ♆ **1:13 pm** 10:13 am
☽ ⊼ ☿ **7:07 pm** 4:07 pm
☽ △ ♅ **8:19 pm** 5:19 pm

23 WEDNESDAY
☽ ⊼ ☉ **3:11 am** 12:11 am
☿ □ ♅ **6:13 am** 3:13 am
☽ △ ♄ **8:56 pm** 5:56 pm
☽ ☍ ♆ **9:55 pm** 6:55 pm
☽ ⊼ ♂ **11:25 pm** 8:25 pm
☽ □ ♃ 9:41 pm

24 THURSDAY
☽ □ ♃ **12:41 am**
☽ □ ♀ **3:27 am** 12:27 am
☽ △ ♇ **8:50 am** 5:50 am
☽ ⊼ ♅ **8:57 pm** 5:57 pm
☽ △ ☿ 10:56 pm

25 FRIDAY
☽ △ ☿ **1:56 am**
☽ △ ☉ **7:48 am** 4:48 am
♂ △ ♃ **12:53 pm** 9:53 am
☽ □ ♄ **11:10 pm** 8:10 pm
☽ ⊼ ♆ **11:55 pm** 8:55 pm

26 SATURDAY
☽ ⚹ ♃ **3:23 am** 12:23 am
☽ ☍ ♂ **3:56 am** 12:56 am
☽ ⚹ ♀ **10:03 am** 7:03 am
☽ □ ♇ **11:30 am** 8:30 am
☽ ☍ ♅ 9:21 pm

27 SUNDAY
☽ ☍ ♅ **12:21 am**
♀ ⊻ ♇ **4:32 am** 1:32 am
☽ □ ☿ **12:59 pm** 9:59 am
☽ □ ☉ **4:10 pm** 1:10 pm

28 MONDAY
☽ ⚹ ♄ **4:46 am** 1:46 am
☽ △ ♆ **5:14 am** 2:14 am
☽ ⊻ ♃ **9:35 am** 6:35 am
☽ ⊼ ♂ **12:21 pm** 9:21 am
☽ ⚹ ♇ **5:39 pm** 2:39 pm
☽ ⊻ ♀ **9:05 pm** 6:05 pm

29 TUESDAY
☽ ⊼ ♅ **7:19 am** 4:19 am
☉ ☌ ☿ **9:52 pm** 6:52 pm

30 WEDNESDAY
☽ ⚹ ☉ **5:04 am** 2:04 am
☽ ⚹ ☿ **5:32 am** 2:32 am
☽ ⊻ ♄ **1:59 pm** 10:59 am
☽ □ ♆ **2:06 pm** 11:06 am
☽ ☌ ♃ **7:23 pm** 4:23 pm
☽ △ ♂ 9:50 pm

31 THURSDAY
☽ △ ♂ **12:50 am**
☽ ⊻ ♇ **3:14 am** 12:14 am
♄ ⚹ ♆ **9:15 am** 6:15 am
☽ ☌ ♀ **12:35 pm** 9:35 am
☽ △ ♅ **5:33 pm** 2:33 pm

Eastern time in bold type
Pacific time in medium type

JANUARY 2019

DATE	SID.TIME	SUN	MOON	NODE	MERCURY	VENUS	MARS	JUPITER	SATURN	URANUS	NEPTUNE	PLUTO	CERES	PALLAS	JUNO	VESTA	CHIRON
1 T	6 41 26	10 ♑ 15 24	12 ♏ 22	26 ♋ 52 ℞	23 ♐ 51	23 ♏ 30	29 ♓ 56	11 ♐ 46	11 ♑ 23	28 ♈ 37 ℞	14 ♓ 05	20 ♑ 36	21 ♏ 00	21 ♎ 32	20 ♉ 37	14 ♒ 28	28 ♓ 08
2 W	6 45 22	11 16 34	25 15	26 50	25 19	24 29	0 ♈ 36	11 59	11 30	28 37	14 06	20 38	21 23	21 49	20 41	14 57	28 09
3 Th	6 49 19	12 17 45	7 ♐ 53	26 48	26 48	25 28	1 17	12 11	11 37	28 36	14 07	20 40	21 46	22 06	20 46	15 26	28 11
4 F	6 53 15	13 18 55	20 20	26 45	28 17	26 28	1 57	12 24	11 44	28 36	14 09	20 42	22 09	22 23	20 52	15 56	28 12
5 Sa	6 57 12	14 20 06	2 ♑ 35	26 44	29 46	27 29	2 38	12 36	11 51	28 36	14 10	20 44	22 32	22 40	20 58	16 25	28 13
6 Su	7 1 8	15 21 17	14 41	26 43	1 ♑ 16	28 30	3 18	12 49	11 58	28 36 D	14 11	20 46	22 55	22 56	21 05	16 55	28 15
7 M	7 5 5	16 22 28	26 39	26 43 D	2 47	29 31	3 58	13 01	12 05	28 36	14 13	20 48	23 18	23 12	21 12	17 24	28 16
8 T	7 9 1	17 23 39	8 ♒ 31	26 43	4 18	0 ♐ 33	4 39	13 13	12 12	28 36	14 14	20 50	23 40	23 28	21 20	17 54	28 18
9 W	7 12 58	18 24 49	20 19	26 44	5 49	1 35	5 19	13 25	12 19	28 36	14 16	20 52	24 03	23 44	21 28	18 23	28 20
10 Th	7 16 55	19 25 59	2 ♓ 06	26 44	7 21	2 37	6 00	13 37	12 26	28 36	14 17	20 54	24 25	23 59	21 37	18 53	28 21
11 F	7 20 51	20 27 09	13 55	26 45	8 53	3 40	6 41	13 50	12 33	28 36	14 19	20 56	24 47	24 14	21 46	19 22	28 23
12 Sa	7 24 48	21 28 18	25 51	26 46	10 26	4 43	7 21	14 02	12 40	28 37	14 20	20 58	25 09	24 29	21 56	19 52	28 25
13 Su	7 28 44	22 29 26	7 ♈ 56	26 46	11 59	5 46	8 02	14 14	12 47	28 37	14 22	21 00	25 31	24 44	22 06	20 22	28 27
14 M	7 32 41	23 30 34	20 16	26 46 ℞	13 32	6 50	8 42	14 25	12 55	28 37	14 23	21 02	25 53	24 58	22 17	20 51	28 28
15 T	7 36 37	24 31 42	2 ♉ 55	26 46	15 06	7 54	9 23	14 37	13 02	28 38	14 25	21 04	26 15	25 12	22 28	21 21	28 30
16 W	7 40 34	25 32 48	15 57	26 46	16 41	8 58	10 03	14 49	13 09	28 38	14 26	21 06	26 36	25 25	22 40	21 51	28 32
17 Th	7 44 30	26 33 54	29 26	26 46 D	18 16	10 03	10 44	15 01	13 15	28 39	14 28	21 08	26 58	25 39	22 52	22 20	28 34
18 F	7 48 27	27 34 59	13 ♊ 21	26 46	19 51	11 08	11 25	15 12	13 22	28 39	14 30	21 10	27 19	25 52	23 05	22 50	28 36
19 Sa	7 52 24	28 36 04	27 44	26 46	21 28	12 13	12 05	15 24	13 29	28 40	14 32	21 12	27 40	26 04	23 18	23 20	28 38
20 Su	7 56 20	29 37 07	12 ♋ 29	26 47 ℞	23 04	13 18	12 46	15 35	13 36	28 41	14 33	21 14	28 02	26 17	23 31	23 49	28 41
21 M	8 0 17	0 ♒ 38 11	27 32	26 47	24 41	14 24	13 27	15 47	13 43	28 41	14 35	21 16	28 22	26 29	23 45	24 19	28 43
22 T	8 4 13	1 39 13	12 ♌ 43	26 46	26 19	15 29	14 07	15 58	13 50	28 42	14 37	21 18	28 43	26 40	23 59	24 49	28 45
23 W	8 8 10	2 40 15	27 53	26 46	27 57	16 36	14 48	16 09	13 57	28 43	14 39	21 20	29 04	26 52	24 13	25 18	28 47
24 Th	8 12 6	3 41 16	12 ♍ 52	26 45	29 36	17 42	15 29	16 20	14 04	28 44	14 40	21 22	29 24	27 03	24 28	25 48	28 49
25 F	8 16 3	4 42 16	27 34	26 44	1 ♒ 15	18 48	16 09	16 31	14 11	28 45	14 42	21 24	29 45	27 13	24 44	26 18	28 52
26 Sa	8 19 59	5 43 16	11 ♎ 52	26 44	2 55	19 55	16 50	16 42	14 17	28 46	14 44	21 26	0 ♐ 05	27 24	24 59	26 48	28 54
27 Su	8 23 56	6 44 15	25 45	26 43 D	4 36	21 02	17 30	16 53	14 24	28 47	14 46	21 28	0 25	27 34	25 16	27 17	28 57
28 M	8 27 53	7 45 14	9 ♏ 12	26 43	6 17	22 09	18 11	17 04	14 31	28 48	14 48	21 30	0 45	27 43	25 32	27 47	28 59
29 T	8 31 49	8 46 13	22 15	26 43	7 59	23 17	18 52	17 15	14 38	28 49	14 50	21 32	1 05	27 52	25 49	28 17	29 02
30 W	8 35 46	9 47 10	4 ♐ 58	26 44	9 42	24 24	19 32	17 25	14 44	28 50	14 52	21 34	1 24	28 01	26 06	28 47	29 04
31 Th	8 39 42	10 48 07	17 24	26 45	11 25	25 32	20 13	17 36	14 51	28 51	14 54	21 36	1 44	28 10	26 23	29 16	29 07

EPHEMERIS CALCULATED FOR 12 MIDNIGHT GREENWICH MEAN TIME. ALL OTHER DATA AND FACING ASPECTARIAN PAGE IN **EASTERN TIME (BOLD)** AND PACIFIC TIME (REGULAR).

FEBRUARY 2019

☽ Last Aspect				☽ Ingress			
day	ET / hr:mn / PT		asp	sign	day	ET / hr:mn / PT	
3	**5:53 am**	2:53 am	□♅	≈	3	**8:03 am**	5:03 am
5	**6:59 pm**	3:59 pm	✶♅	♓	5	**9:02 pm**	6:02 pm
7	**5:14 pm**	2:14 pm	✶♇	♈	8	**9:34 am**	6:34 am
10	**6:48 pm**	3:48 pm	☌♅	♉	10	**8:28 pm**	5:28 pm
12	**5:26 pm**	2:26 pm	□☉	♊	13	**4:32 am**	1:32 am
15	**7:48 am**	4:48 am	✶♅	♋	15	**9:03 am**	6:03 am
17	**9:17 am**	6:17 am	□♅	♌	17	**10:21 am**	7:21 am
19	**8:51 am**	5:51 am	△♅	♍	19	**9:47 am**	6:47 am
20	**8:52 pm**	5:52 pm	△♇	♎	21	**9:17 am**	6:17 am
23	**10:11 am**	7:11 am	☍♅	♏	23	**10:56 am**	7:56 am
25	**7:14 am**	4:14 am	✶♀	♐	25	**4:19 pm**	1:19 pm
27		10:17 pm	△♅	♑	27		10:48 pm
28	**1:17 am**		△♅	♑	28	**1:48 am**	

☽ Phases & Eclipses			
phase	day	ET / hr:mn / PT	
New Moon	4	**4:04 pm**	1:04 pm
2nd Quarter	12	**5:26 pm**	2:26 pm
Full Moon	19	**10:54 am**	7:54 am
4th Quarter	26	**6:28 am**	3:28 am

Planet Ingress			
	day	ET / hr:mn / PT	
⚶ ♓	1	**6:04 am**	3:04 am
♀ ♑	3	**5:29 pm**	2:29 pm
☿ ♓	10	**5:51 am**	2:51 am
⚵ ♊	10	**11:21 pm**	8:21 pm
♂ ♉	14	**5:51 am**	2:51 am
⚷ ♈	18	**4:10 am**	1:10 am
☉ ♓	18	**6:04 pm**	3:04 pm

Planetary Motion			
	day	ET / hr:mn / PT	
♀ ℞	18	**11:40 am**	8:40 am

1 FRIDAY
☿ ⚺ ♆ **7:49 pm** 4:49 pm
☿ ⚺ ♄ **9:25 pm** 6:25 pm
☽ ⚺ ☉ **9:37 pm** 6:37 pm
♂ □ ♇ **10:20 pm** 7:20 pm
☽ ✶ ♆ 10:41 pm
☽ ☌ ♄ 10:57 pm
☽ ⚺ ☿ 11:41 pm

2 SATURDAY
☽ ✶ ♆ **1:41 am**
☽ ☌ ♄ **1:57 am**
☽ ⚺ ☿ **2:41 am**
☽ ⚺ ♃ **7:51 am** 4:51 am
☽ ☌ ♇ **3:14 pm** 12:14 pm
☽ □ ♂ **4:12 pm** 1:12 pm
♀ △ ♅ **6:41 pm** 3:41 pm

3 SUNDAY
☽ □ ♅ **5:53 am** 2:53 am
☽ ⚺ ♀ **7:03 am** 4:03 am
☿ ✶ ♃ **4:54 pm** 1:54 pm
☉ ⚺ ♆ **11:00 pm** 8:00 pm

4 MONDAY
☉ ⚺ ♄ **6:09 am** 3:09 am
☽ ⚺ ♆ **2:38 pm** 11:38 am
☽ ⚺ ♄ **3:17 pm** 12:17 pm
☽ ☌ ☉ **4:04 pm** 1:04 pm
☽ ✶ ♃ **9:35 pm** 6:35 pm
☽ ☌ ☿ 11:11 pm

5 TUESDAY
☽ ☌ ☿ **2:11 am**
☽ ⚺ ♇ **4:18 am** 1:18 am
☽ ✶ ♂ **8:49 am** 5:49 am
☿ ⚺ ♇ **4:24 pm** 1:24 pm
☽ ✶ ♅ **6:59 pm** 3:59 pm
☽ ✶ ♀ 11:33 pm

6 WEDNESDAY
☽ ✶ ♀ **2:33 am**

7 THURSDAY
☽ ☌ ♆ **3:43 am** 12:43 am
☽ ✶ ♄ **4:44 am** 1:44 am
☽ ⚺ ☉ **10:37 am** 7:37 am
☽ □ ♃ **11:16 am** 8:16 am
☽ ✶ ♇ **5:14 pm** 2:14 pm
☉ ✶ ♃ **7:32 pm** 4:32 pm
☿ ✶ ♂ **8:24 pm** 5:24 pm
☽ ⚺ ♂ 10:11 pm
☽ ⚺ ☿ 10:43 pm

8 FRIDAY
☽ ⚺ ♂ **1:11 am**
☽ ⚺ ☿ **1:43 am**
☽ ⚺ ♅ **7:41 am** 4:41 am
☽ □ ♀ **9:21 pm** 6:21 pm

9 SATURDAY
☽ ⚺ ♆ **3:45 pm** 12:45 pm
☽ □ ♄ **5:06 pm** 2:06 pm
☿ ✶ ♅ **5:53 pm** 2:53 pm
☽ △ ♃ **11:42 pm** 8:42 pm

10 SUNDAY
☽ ✶ ☉ **3:39 am** 12:39 am
☽ □ ♇ **4:51 am** 1:51 am
☽ ☌ ♂ **3:48 pm** 12:48 pm
☉ ⚺ ♇ **6:36 pm** 3:36 pm
☽ ☌ ♅ **6:48 pm** 3:48 pm
☽ ✶ ☿ **10:57 pm** 7:57 pm

11 MONDAY
☽ △ ♀ **1:39 pm** 10:39 am
☽ ✶ ♆ 10:31 pm

12 TUESDAY
☽ ✶ ♆ **1:31 am**
☽ △ ♄ **3:05 am** 12:05 am
☽ ⚻ ♃ **9:36 am** 6:36 am
☽ △ ♇ **1:54 pm** 10:54 am
☽ □ ☉ **5:26 pm** 2:26 pm
♂ ☌ ♅ 10:21 pm

13 WEDNESDAY
♂ ☌ ♅ **1:21 am**
☽ ⚺ ♅ **3:05 am** 12:05 am
☽ ⚺ ♂ **3:10 am** 12:10 am
☽ □ ☿ **3:36 pm** 12:36 pm
☽ ⚻ ♀ 10:49 pm

14 THURSDAY
☽ ⚻ ♀ **1:49 am**
☽ □ ♆ **7:56 am** 4:56 am
☽ ⚻ ♄ **9:40 am** 6:40 am
☽ ☍ ♃ **3:56 pm** 12:56 pm
☽ ⚻ ♇ **7:30 pm** 4:30 pm
☽ △ ☉ 11:49 pm

15 FRIDAY
☽ △ ☉ **2:49 am**
☽ ✶ ♅ **7:48 am** 4:48 am
☽ ✶ ♂ **10:24 am** 7:24 am
☽ △ ☿ 11:39 pm

16 SATURDAY
☽ △ ☿ **2:39 am**
☽ ☍ ♀ **9:23 am** 6:23 am
☽ △ ♆ **10:48 am** 7:48 am
☽ ☍ ♄ **12:40 pm** 9:40 am
☽ ⚻ ♃ **6:42 pm** 3:42 pm
☽ ☍ ♇ **9:39 pm** 6:39 pm

17 SUNDAY
♀ ✶ ♆ **3:44 am** 12:44 am
☽ ⚻ ☉ **8:03 am** 5:03 am
☽ □ ♅ **9:17 am** 6:17 am
☽ □ ♂ **1:57 pm** 10:57 am
☉ ✶ ♅ 11:55 pm

18 MONDAY
☉ ✶ ♅ **2:55 am**
♀ ☌ ♄ **5:52 am** 2:52 am
☽ ⚻ ☿ **9:18 am** 6:18 am
☽ ⚻ ♆ **11:03 am** 8:03 am
☽ ⚻ ♄ **1:01 pm** 10:01 am
☽ ⚻ ♀ **1:34 pm** 10:34 am
☽ △ ♃ **7:00 pm** 4:00 pm
☽ ⚻ ♇ **9:30 pm** 6:30 pm
☿ ☌ ♆ 10:37 pm

19 TUESDAY
☿ ☌ ♆ **1:37 am**
☽ △ ♅ **8:51 am** 5:51 am
☽ ☍ ☉ **10:54 am** 7:54 am
☽ △ ♂ **3:31 pm** 12:31 pm
☿ ✶ ♄ **9:39 pm** 6:39 pm

20 WEDNESDAY
☽ ☍ ♆ **10:22 am** 7:22 am
☽ △ ♄ **12:32 pm** 9:32 am
☽ ☍ ☿ **2:11 pm** 11:11 am
☽ △ ♀ **4:45 pm** 1:45 pm
☽ □ ♃ **6:41 pm** 3:41 pm
☽ △ ♇ **8:52 pm** 5:52 pm

21 THURSDAY
☽ ⚻ ♅ **8:27 am** 5:27 am
☽ ⚻ ☉ **1:53 pm** 10:53 am
☽ ⚻ ♂ **5:27 pm** 2:27 pm
♀ ⚺ ♃ **8:44 pm** 5:44 pm

22 FRIDAY
☽ ⚻ ♆ **10:52 am** 7:52 am
☽ □ ♄ **1:20 pm** 10:20 am
☿ □ ♃ **3:40 pm** 12:40 pm
☽ ✶ ♃ **7:56 pm** 4:56 pm
☽ ⚻ ☿ **8:21 pm** 5:21 pm
☽ □ ♀ **9:46 pm** 6:46 pm
☽ □ ♇ **9:52 pm** 6:52 pm
♀ ☌ ♇ **10:53 pm** 7:53 pm

23 SATURDAY
☽ ☍ ♅ **10:11 am** 7:11 am
☿ ✶ ♇ **12:18 pm** 9:18 am
☽ △ ☉ **7:44 pm** 4:44 pm
☽ ☍ ♂ **10:12 pm** 7:12 pm

24 SUNDAY
☽ △ ♆ **2:29 pm** 11:29 am
☽ ✶ ♄ **5:21 pm** 2:21 pm
☽ ⚺ ♃ 9:37 pm
☽ ✶ ♇ 11:18 pm

25 MONDAY
☽ ⚺ ♃ **12:37 am**
☽ ✶ ♇ **2:18 am**
☽ △ ☿ **6:14 am** 3:14 am
☽ ✶ ♀ **7:14 am** 4:14 am
☽ ⚻ ♅ **3:40 pm** 12:40 pm

26 TUESDAY
☽ □ ☉ **6:28 am** 3:28 am
☽ ⚻ ♂ **7:32 am** 4:32 am
☽ □ ♆ **10:15 pm** 7:15 pm
☽ ⚺ ♄ 10:35 pm

27 WEDNESDAY
☽ ⚺ ♄ **1:35 am**
☽ ☌ ♃ **9:33 am** 6:33 am
☽ ⚺ ♇ **10:55 am** 7:55 am
☽ □ ☿ **8:11 pm** 5:11 pm
☉ ✶ ♂ **9:33 pm** 6:33 pm
☽ ⚺ ♀ **10:09 pm** 7:09 pm
☽ △ ♅ 10:17 pm

28 THURSDAY
☽ △ ♅ **1:17 am**
☽ △ ♂ **9:26 pm** 6:26 pm
☽ ✶ ☉ **10:09 pm** 7:09 pm

Eastern time in bold type
Pacific time in medium type

FEBRUARY 2019

DATE	SID.TIME	SUN	MOON	NODE	MERCURY	VENUS	MARS	JUPITER	SATURN	URANUS	NEPTUNE	PLUTO	CERES	PALLAS	JUNO	VESTA	CHIRON
1 F	8 43 39	11 ≈ 49 04	29 ♐ 36	26 ♋ 47	13 ≈ 09	26 ♐ 40	20 ♈ 54	17 ♐ 46	14 ♑ 57	28 ♈ 52	14 ♓ 56	21 ♑ 38	2 ♐ 03	28 ♎ 18	26 ♉ 41	29 ≈ 46	29 ♓ 09
2 Sa	8 47 35	12 49 59	11 ♑ 38	26 48	14 54	27 48	21 34	17 56	15 04	28 54	14 58	21 40	2 22	28 25	26 59	0 ♓ 16	29 12
3 Su	8 51 32	13 50 54	23 33	26 48 ℞	16 39	28 56	22 15	18 07	15 11	28 55	15 00	21 42	2 41	28 32	27 18	0 46	29 15
4 M	8 55 28	14 51 47	5 ≈ 24	26 48	18 25	0 ♑ 04	22 56	18 17	15 17	28 57	15 02	21 43	2 59	28 39	27 37	1 16	29 17
5 T	8 59 25	15 52 40	17 12	26 47	20 12	1 13	23 36	18 27	15 24	28 58	15 04	21 45	3 18	28 46	27 56	1 45	29 20
6 W	9 3 22	16 53 31	29 00	26 45	21 59	2 21	24 17	18 37	15 30	28 59	15 06	21 47	3 36	28 52	28 15	2 15	29 23
7 Th	9 7 18	17 54 21	10 ♓ 50	26 41	23 46	3 30	24 57	18 47	15 36	29 01	15 08	21 49	3 55	28 57	28 35	2 45	29 26
8 F	9 11 15	18 55 09	22 44	26 38	25 34	4 39	25 38	18 56	15 43	29 03	15 10	21 51	4 12	29 02	28 55	3 15	29 29
9 Sa	9 15 11	19 55 56	4 ♈ 44	26 34	27 22	5 48	26 19	19 06	15 49	29 04	15 12	21 53	4 30	29 07	29 15	3 45	29 32
10 Su	9 19 8	20 56 42	16 53	26 30	29 11	6 57	26 59	19 15	15 55	29 06	15 14	21 55	4 48	29 11	29 35	4 14	29 34
11 M	9 23 4	21 57 26	29 14	26 27	1 ♓ 00	8 07	27 40	19 25	16 01	29 08	15 16	21 56	5 05	29 15	29 56	4 44	29 37
12 T	9 27 1	22 58 09	11 ♉ 51	26 25 D	2 48	9 16	28 21	19 34	16 08	29 09	15 18	21 58	5 22	29 19	0 ♊ 17	5 14	29 40
13 W	9 30 57	23 58 50	24 46	26 25	4 36	10 25	29 01	19 43	16 14	29 11	15 20	22 00	5 39	29 22	0 39	5 44	29 43
14 Th	9 34 54	24 59 30	8 ♊ 04	26 25	6 24	11 35	29 42	19 52	16 20	29 13	15 23	22 02	5 56	29 24	1 00	6 13	29 46
15 F	9 38 51	26 00 07	21 46	26 27	8 12	12 45	0 ♉ 22	20 01	16 26	29 15	15 25	22 04	6 13	29 26	1 22	6 43	29 49
16 Sa	9 42 47	27 00 43	5 ♋ 55	26 28	9 58	13 55	1 03	20 10	16 32	29 17	15 27	22 05	6 29	29 28	1 44	7 13	29 53
17 Su	9 46 44	28 01 18	20 29	26 29 ℞	11 43	15 04	1 43	20 19	16 38	29 19	15 29	22 07	6 45	29 29	2 06	7 43	29 56
18 M	9 50 40	29 01 50	5 ♌ 25	26 29	13 26	16 14	2 24	20 27	16 44	29 21	15 31	22 09	7 01	29 29 ℞	2 29	8 12	29 59
19 T	9 54 37	0 ♓ 02 21	20 36	26 27	15 07	17 25	3 04	20 35	16 49	29 23	15 34	22 10	7 17	29 29	2 51	8 42	0 ♈ 02
20 W	9 58 33	1 02 51	5 ♍ 52	26 24	16 45	18 35	3 45	20 44	16 55	29 25	15 36	22 12	7 32	29 29	3 14	9 12	0 05
21 Th	10 2 30	2 03 18	21 04	26 19	18 20	19 45	4 25	20 52	17 01	29 27	15 38	22 14	7 48	29 28	3 37	9 41	0 08
22 F	10 6 26	3 03 44	6 ♎ 01	26 13	19 52	20 55	5 06	21 00	17 06	29 30	15 40	22 15	8 03	29 27	4 01	10 11	0 12
23 Sa	10 10 23	4 04 09	20 35	26 08	21 19	22 06	5 46	21 08	17 12	29 32	15 42	22 17	8 17	29 25	4 24	10 41	0 15
24 Su	10 14 20	5 04 33	4 ♏ 41	26 03	22 41	23 16	6 26	21 16	17 18	29 34	15 45	22 19	8 32	29 22	4 48	11 10	0 18
25 M	10 18 16	6 04 55	18 18	26 00	23 57	24 27	7 07	21 23	17 23	29 37	15 47	22 20	8 46	29 19	5 12	11 40	0 21
26 T	10 22 13	7 05 15	1 ♐ 27	25 58 D	25 07	25 38	7 47	21 31	17 29	29 39	15 49	22 22	9 00	29 16	5 36	12 10	0 25
27 W	10 26 9	8 05 35	14 10	25 58	26 10	26 49	8 28	21 38	17 34	29 41	15 51	22 23	9 14	29 12	6 00	12 39	0 28
28 Th	10 30 6	9 05 52	26 33	25 59	27 06	27 59	9 08	21 45	17 39	29 44	15 54	22 25	9 28	29 08	6 25	13 09	0 31

EPHEMERIS CALCULATED FOR 12 MIDNIGHT GREENWICH MEAN TIME. ALL OTHER DATA AND FACING ASPECTARIAN PAGE IN **EASTERN TIME (BOLD)** AND PACIFIC TIME (REGULAR).

MARCH 2019

☽ Last Aspect day	ET / hr:mn / PT		asp	☽ Ingress sign	day	ET / hr:mn / PT	
2	**1:47 pm**	10:47 am	□♅	♒	2	**2:06 pm**	11:06 am
5	**3:05 am**	12:05 am	✶♅	♓	5	**3:11 am**	12:11 am
7	**2:08 pm**	11:08 am	☌☿	♈	7	**3:27 pm**	12:27 pm
9	**12:14 pm**	9:14 am	△♃	♉	9		11:10 pm
9	**12:14 pm**	9:14 am	△♃	♉	10	**3:10 am**	
12	**5:31 am**	2:31 am	✶☿	♊	12	**11:48 am**	8:48 am
14	**8:30 am**	5:30 am	□☿	♋	14	**5:49 pm**	2:49 pm
16	**2:03 pm**	11:03 am	△☉	♌	16	**8:57 pm**	5:57 pm
18	**11:19 am**	8:19 am	△♃	♍	18	**9:41 pm**	6:41 pm
20	**11:22 am**	8:22 am	□♃	♎	20	**9:28 pm**	6:28 pm

☽ Last Aspect day	ET / hr:mn / PT		asp	☽ Ingress sign	day	ET / hr:mn / PT	
22	**2:10 pm**	11:10 am	△♀	♏	22	**10:16 pm**	7:16 pm
24	**10:24 pm**	7:24 pm	□♀	♐	24		11:06 pm
24	**10:24 pm**	7:24 pm	□♀	♐	25	**2:06 am**	
26	**10:37 pm**	7:37 pm	☌♃	♑	27	**10:07 am**	7:07 am
29	**8:05 pm**	5:05 pm	△♂	♒	29	**9:46 pm**	6:46 pm
31	**11:02 pm**	8:02 pm	✶♃	♓	4/1	**10:48 am**	7:48 am

☽ Phases & Eclipses phase	day	ET / hr:mn / PT	
New Moon	6	**11:04 am**	8:04 am
2nd Quarter	14	**6:27 am**	3:27 am
Full Moon	20	**9:43 pm**	6:43 pm
4th Quarter	27		9:10 pm
4th Quarter	28	**12:10 am**	

Planet Ingress		day	ET / hr:mn / PT	
♀	♒	1	**11:45 am**	8:45 am
♅	♉	6	**3:26 am**	12:26 am
☉	♈	20	**5:58 pm**	2:58 pm
♀	♓	26	**3:43 pm**	12:43 pm
♂	♊	30		11:12 pm
♂	♊	31	**2:12 am**	

Planetary Motion		day	ET / hr:mn / PT	
☿	℞	5	**1:19 pm**	10:19 am
☿	D	28	**9:59 am**	6:59 am

1 FRIDAY
♀□♅ **7:32 am** 4:32 am
☽✶♆ **9:39 am** 6:39 am
☽☌♄ **1:23 pm** 10:23 am
☽⚺♃ **9:52 pm** 6:52 pm
☽☌♇ **10:49 pm** 7:49 pm

2 SATURDAY
☽✶☿ **11:55 am** 8:55 am
☽□♅ **1:47 pm** 10:47 am
☽☌♀ **5:03 pm** 2:03 pm

3 SUNDAY
☽□♂ **1:54 pm** 10:54 am
☽⚺☉ **4:37 pm** 1:37 pm
☽⚺♆ **10:49 pm** 7:49 pm
☽⚺♄ 11:49 pm

4 MONDAY
☽⚺♄ **2:49 am**
☽✶♃ **11:30 am** 8:30 am
☽⚺♇ **12:00 pm** 9:00 am
☽⚺☿ 11:26 pm

5 TUESDAY
☽⚺☿ **2:26 am**
☽✶♅ **3:05 am** 12:05 am
☽⚺♀ **12:54 pm** 9:54 am

6 WEDNESDAY
☽✶♂ **6:26 am** 3:26 am
☽☌☉ **11:04 am** 8:04 am
☽☌♆ **11:47 am** 8:47 am
☽✶♄ **3:58 pm** 12:58 pm
☉☌♆ **8:00 pm** 5:00 pm
☽□♃ 9:37 pm
☽✶♇ 9:41 pm

7 THURSDAY
☽□♃ **12:37 am**
☽✶♇ **12:41 am**
♃⚺♇ **11:33 am** 8:33 am
☽☌☿ **2:08 pm** 11:08 am
☽⚺♅ **3:35 pm** 12:35 pm

8 FRIDAY
☽✶♀ **7:29 am** 4:29 am
☽⚺♂ **9:31 pm** 6:31 pm
☽⚺♆ **11:28 pm** 8:28 pm
☉✶♄ 11:10 pm

9 SATURDAY
☉✶♄ **2:10 am**
☽□♄ **3:44 am** 12:44 am
☽⚺☉ **3:52 am** 12:52 am
☽□♇ **11:56 am** 8:56 am
☽△♃ **12:14 pm** 9:14 am
☽⚺☿ **10:46 pm** 7:46 pm
☽☌♅ 11:31 pm

10 SUNDAY
☽☌♅ **3:31 am**
♂✶♆ **12:20 pm** 9:20 am
☽□♀ 9:45 pm

11 MONDAY
☽□♀ **12:45 am**
☽✶♆ **10:18 am** 7:18 am
☽☌♂ **11:27 am** 8:27 am
☽△♄ **2:34 pm** 11:34 am
☽✶☉ **7:13 pm** 4:13 pm
☽△♇ **10:13 pm** 7:13 pm
☽⚻♃ **10:49 pm** 7:49 pm

12 TUESDAY
☽✶☿ **5:31 am** 2:31 am
☽⚺♅ **12:20 pm** 9:20 am

13 WEDNESDAY
☉✶♇ **10:29 am** 7:29 am
☽△♀ **1:58 pm** 10:58 am
☽□♆ **5:44 pm** 2:44 pm
☉□♃ **9:29 pm** 6:29 pm
☽⚺♂ **9:34 pm** 6:34 pm
☽⚻♄ **9:57 pm** 6:57 pm

14 THURSDAY
☽⚻♇ **5:00 am** 2:00 am
☽☍♃ **5:50 am** 2:50 am
♂△♄ **6:02 am** 3:02 am
☽□☉ **6:27 am** 3:27 am
☽□☿ **8:30 am** 5:30 am
☽✶♅ **6:31 pm** 3:31 pm
☉☌☿ **9:48 pm** 6:48 pm

15 FRIDAY
♀⚺♆ **9:11 am** 6:11 am
☿□♃ **7:17 pm** 4:17 pm
☽△♆ **10:18 pm** 7:18 pm
☽⚻♀ **11:28 pm** 8:28 pm
☽☍♄ 11:24 pm

16 SATURDAY
☽☍♄ **2:24 am**
☽✶♂ **4:22 am** 1:22 am
☽☍♇ **8:53 am** 5:53 am
☽△☿ **8:54 am** 5:54 am
☿✶♇ **9:08 am** 6:08 am
☽⚻♃ **9:54 am** 6:54 am
☽△☉ **2:03 pm** 11:03 am
☽□♅ **9:47 pm** 6:47 pm

17 SUNDAY
♀⚺♄ **12:09 pm** 9:09 am
☿✶♂ **11:23 pm** 8:23 pm
☽⚻♆ 9:07 pm

18 MONDAY
☽⚻♆ **12:07 am**
☽⚻♄ **4:08 am** 1:08 am
☽☍♀ **5:27 am** 2:27 am
☽⚻☿ **7:14 am** 4:14 am
☽□♂ **8:06 am** 5:06 am
☽⚻♇ **10:10 am** 7:10 am
☽△♃ **11:19 am** 8:19 am
☽⚻☉ **6:33 pm** 3:33 pm
☿⚺♀ **6:56 pm** 3:56 pm
☽△♅ **10:40 pm** 7:40 pm

19 TUESDAY
☽☍♆ 9:13 pm

20 WEDNESDAY
☽☍♆ **12:13 am**
☽△♄ **4:15 am** 1:15 am
☽☍☿ **4:35 am** 1:35 am
♂△♇ **7:41 am** 4:41 am
☽⚻♀ **9:29 am** 6:29 am
☽△♇ **10:04 am** 7:04 am
☽△♂ **10:10 am** 7:10 am
☿✶♄ **10:27 am** 7:27 am
☽□♃ **11:22 am** 8:22 am
♀⚺♇ **4:54 pm** 1:54 pm
☽☍☉ **9:43 pm** 6:43 pm
☽⚻♅ **10:36 pm** 7:36 pm

21 THURSDAY
♀□♂ **4:07 am** 1:07 am
♀✶♃ **10:17 am** 7:17 am
☉⚺♅ **11:48 am** 8:48 am
♂⚻♃ **3:43 pm** 12:43 pm
☽⚻♆ 9:26 pm
☽⚻☿ 11:35 pm

22 FRIDAY
☽⚻♆ **12:26 am**
☽⚻☿ **2:35 am**
☽□♄ **4:39 am** 1:39 am
☽□♇ **10:29 am** 7:29 am
☽✶♃ **11:59 am** 8:59 am
☽⚻♂ **12:52 pm** 9:52 am
☽△♀ **2:10 pm** 11:10 am
☽☍♅ **11:38 pm** 8:38 pm
☽⚻☉ 11:09 pm

23 SATURDAY
☽⚻☉ **2:09 am**
☽△♆ 11:50 pm

24 SUNDAY
☽△♆ **2:50 am**
☽△☿ **3:10 am** 12:10 am
☽✶♄ **7:25 am** 4:25 am
☿☌♆ **1:28 pm** 10:28 am
☽✶♇ **1:30 pm** 10:30 am
☽⚺♃ **3:15 pm** 12:15 pm
☽☍♂ **6:38 pm** 3:38 pm
☽□♀ **10:24 pm** 7:24 pm

25 MONDAY
☽⚻♅ **3:46 am** 12:46 am
☽△☉ **10:30 am** 7:30 am

26 TUESDAY
☽□☿ **8:01 am** 5:01 am
☽□♆ **9:07 am** 6:07 am
☽⚺♄ **2:10 pm** 11:10 am
☽⚺♇ **8:35 pm** 5:35 pm
☽☌♃ **10:37 pm** 7:37 pm

27 WEDNESDAY
☽⚻♂ **5:10 am** 2:10 am
☽✶♀ **12:06 pm** 9:06 am
☽△♅ **12:10 pm** 9:10 am
♀✶♅ **12:45 pm** 9:45 am
☽□☉ 9:10 pm

28 THURSDAY
☽□☉ **12:10 am**
☽✶☿ **5:48 pm** 2:48 pm
☽✶♆ **7:33 pm** 4:33 pm
☽☌♄ 10:00 pm

29 FRIDAY
☽☌♄ **1:00 am**
☽☌♇ **7:35 am** 4:35 am
☽⚺♃ **9:53 am** 6:53 am
☽△♂ **8:05 pm** 5:05 pm
☽□♅ 9:10 pm

30 SATURDAY
☽□♅ **12:10 am**
☽⚺♀ **6:36 am** 3:36 am
☽✶☉ **5:53 pm** 2:53 pm

31 SUNDAY
☽⚺☿ **7:17 am** 4:17 am
☽⚺♆ **8:30 am** 5:30 am
☽⚺♄ **2:06 pm** 11:06 am
☽⚺♇ **8:36 pm** 5:36 pm
☽✶♃ **11:02 pm** 8:02 pm

Eastern time in bold type
Pacific time in medium type

MARCH 2019

DATE	SID.TIME	SUN	MOON	NODE	MERCURY	VENUS	MARS	JUPITER	SATURN	URANUS	NEPTUNE	PLUTO	CERES	PALLAS	JUNO	VESTA	CHIRON
1 F	10 34 2	10 ♓ 06 09	8 ♑ 39	26 ♋ 01	27 ♓ 54	29 ♑ 10	9 ♉ 48	21 ♐ 52	17 ♑ 44	29 ♈ 46	15 ♓ 56	22 ♑ 26	9 ♐ 41	29 ♎ 03 ℞	6 ♊ 49	13 ♓ 38	0 ♈ 35
2 Sa	10 37 59	11 06 24	20 35	26 02 ℞	28 33	0 ♒ 21	10 29	21 59	17 50	29 49	15 58	22 28	9 54	28 57	7 14	14 08	0 38
3 Su	10 41 55	12 06 37	2 ♒ 24	26 02	29 03	1 33	11 09	22 06	17 55	29 51	16 01	22 29	10 07	28 52	7 39	14 37	0 42
4 M	10 45 52	13 06 49	14 11	26 00	29 24	2 44	11 49	22 13	18 00	29 54	16 03	22 31	10 19	28 45	8 04	15 07	0 45
5 T	10 49 49	14 06 58	25 58	25 56	29 36 ℞	3 55	12 30	22 19	18 05	29 56	16 05	22 32	10 31	28 38	8 29	15 37	0 48
6 W	10 53 45	15 07 07	7 ♓ 49	25 49	29 39	5 06	13 10	22 25	18 10	29 59	16 07	22 34	10 43	28 31	8 55	16 06	0 52
7 Th	10 57 42	16 07 13	19 45	25 40	29 32	6 17	13 50	22 32	18 14	0 ♉ 02	16 10	22 35	10 55	28 23	9 20	16 35	0 55
8 F	11 1 38	17 07 17	1 ♈ 47	25 31	29 16	7 29	14 30	22 38	18 19	0 04	16 12	22 36	11 06	28 14	9 46	17 05	0 59
9 Sa	11 5 35	18 07 20	13 58	25 20	28 52	8 40	15 10	22 44	18 24	0 07	16 14	22 38	11 17	28 05	10 12	17 34	1 02
10 Su	11 9 31	19 07 20	26 17	25 10	28 20	9 52	15 51	22 49	18 28	0 10	16 16	22 39	11 28	27 56	10 38	18 04	1 06
11 M	11 13 28	20 07 18	8 ♉ 48	25 02	27 41	11 03	16 31	22 55	18 33	0 13	16 19	22 40	11 39	27 46	11 04	18 33	1 09
12 T	11 17 24	21 07 15	21 30	24 56	26 56	12 15	17 11	23 00	18 38	0 16	16 21	22 41	11 49	27 35	11 30	19 03	1 13
13 W	11 21 21	22 07 09	4 ♊ 27	24 52	26 06	13 26	17 51	23 05	18 42	0 18	16 23	22 43	11 59	27 24	11 56	19 32	1 16
14 Th	11 25 17	23 07 01	17 41	24 50 D	25 12	14 38	18 31	23 10	18 46	0 21	16 26	22 44	12 08	27 13	12 23	20 01	1 20
15 F	11 29 14	24 06 51	1 ♋ 15	24 50	24 16	15 50	19 11	23 15	18 50	0 24	16 28	22 45	12 17	27 01	12 49	20 30	1 23
16 Sa	11 33 11	25 06 38	15 09	24 51 ℞	23 18	17 01	19 51	23 20	18 55	0 27	16 30	22 46	12 26	26 49	13 16	21 00	1 27
17 Su	11 37 7	26 06 23	29 26	24 51	22 21	18 13	20 31	23 25	18 59	0 30	16 32	22 47	12 35	26 36	13 43	21 29	1 30
18 M	11 41 4	27 06 06	14 ♌ 03	24 50	21 25	19 25	21 11	23 29	19 03	0 33	16 35	22 48	12 43	26 23	14 10	21 58	1 34
19 T	11 45 0	28 05 47	28 57	24 46	20 31	20 37	21 51	23 33	19 07	0 36	16 37	22 49	12 51	26 09	14 37	22 27	1 37
20 W	11 48 57	29 05 26	14 ♍ 00	24 39	19 41	21 49	22 31	23 37	19 11	0 39	16 39	22 50	12 59	25 55	15 04	22 57	1 41
21 Th	11 52 53	0 ♈ 05 02	29 05	24 30	18 55	23 01	23 11	23 41	19 14	0 42	16 41	22 51	13 06	25 41	15 31	23 26	1 45
22 F	11 56 50	1 04 36	14 ♎ 01	24 20	18 14	24 13	23 51	23 45	19 18	0 45	16 44	22 52	13 13	25 26	15 58	23 55	1 48
23 Sa	12 0 46	2 04 09	28 38	24 10	17 38	25 25	24 31	23 48	19 22	0 48	16 46	22 53	13 20	25 11	16 26	24 24	1 52
24 Su	12 4 43	3 03 39	12 ♏ 51	24 01	17 08	26 37	25 11	23 52	19 25	0 52	16 48	22 54	13 26	24 56	16 53	24 53	1 55
25 M	12 8 40	4 03 08	26 35	23 53	16 44	27 49	25 51	23 55	19 29	0 55	16 50	22 55	13 32	24 40	17 21	25 22	1 59
26 T	12 12 36	5 02 35	9 ♐ 50	23 48	16 25	29 01	26 31	23 58	19 32	0 58	16 52	22 56	13 37	24 24	17 48	25 51	2 02
27 W	12 16 33	6 02 00	22 39	23 45	16 13	0 ♓ 13	27 11	24 01	19 35	1 01	16 55	22 57	13 43	24 07	18 16	26 20	2 06
28 Th	12 20 29	7 01 24	5 ♑ 04	23 45 D	16 07 D	1 25	27 50	24 03	19 38	1 04	16 57	22 58	13 48	23 50	18 44	26 49	2 09
29 F	12 24 26	8 00 45	17 12	23 45 ℞	16 06	2 37	28 30	24 06	19 41	1 07	16 59	22 59	13 52	23 33	19 12	27 18	2 13
30 Sa	12 28 22	9 00 05	29 08	23 45	16 11	3 49	29 10	24 08	19 44	1 11	17 01	22 59	13 56	23 16	19 40	27 46	2 16
31 Su	12 32 19	9 59 23	10 ♒ 56	23 43	16 22	5 02	29 50	24 10	19 47	1 14	17 03	23 00	14 00	22 58	20 08	28 15	2 20

EPHEMERIS CALCULATED FOR 12 MIDNIGHT GREENWICH MEAN TIME. ALL OTHER DATA AND FACING ASPECTARIAN PAGE IN **EASTERN TIME (BOLD)** AND PACIFIC TIME (REGULAR).

APRIL 2019

☽ Last Aspect day	ET / hr:mn / PT		asp	☽ Ingress sign	day	ET / hr:mn / PT	
3/31	**11:02 pm**	8:02 pm	⚹ ♃	♓	1	**10:48 am**	7:48 am
3	**11:36 am**	8:36 am	□ ♃	♈	3	**10:56 pm**	7:56 pm
5	**10:15 pm**	7:15 pm	△ ♃	♉	6	**9:06 am**	6:06 am
8	**4:29 am**	1:29 am	△ ♇	♊	8	**5:15 pm**	2:15 pm
10	**1:27 pm**	10:27 am	☍ ♃	♋	10	**11:31 pm**	8:31 pm
12	**7:33 pm**	4:33 pm	△ ☿	♌	13	**3:50 am**	12:50 am
14	**9:38 pm**	6:38 pm	△ ☉	♍	15	**6:14 am**	3:14 am
16		9:29 pm	☍ ♀	♎	17	**7:22 am**	4:22 am
17	**12:29 am**		☍ ♀	♎	17	**7:22 am**	4:22 am
19	**7:12 am**	4:12 am	☍ ☉	♏	19	**8:41 am**	5:41 am
20		9:00 pm	⚹ ♇	♐	21	**11:59 am**	8:59 am
21	**12:00 am**		⚹ ♇	♐	21	**11:59 am**	8:59 am
23	**7:44 am**	4:44 am	☌ ♃	♑	23	**6:50 pm**	3:50 pm
25	**3:48 pm**	12:48 pm	☌ ♇	♒	26	**5:27 am**	2:27 am
28	**5:44 am**	2:44 am	⚹ ♃	♓	28	**6:11 pm**	3:11 pm
30	**5:57 pm**	2:57 pm	□ ♃	♈	5/1	**6:24 am**	3:24 am

☽ Phases & Eclipses phase	day	ET / hr:mn / PT	
New Moon	5	**4:50 am**	1:50 am
2nd Quarter	12	**3:06 pm**	12:06 pm
Full Moon	19	**7:12 am**	4:12 am
4th Quarter	26	**6:18 pm**	3:18 pm

Planet Ingress		day	ET / hr:mn / PT	
⚶	♈	3	**11:28 am**	8:28 am
☿	♈	16		11:01 pm
☿	♈	17	**2:01 am**	
☉	♉	20	**4:55 am**	1:55 am
♀	♈	20	**12:11 pm**	9:11 am
⚵	♋	20	**12:38 pm**	9:38 am

Planetary Motion		day	ET / hr:mn / PT	
⚳	℞	8		9:35 pm
⚳	℞	9	**12:35 am**	
♃	℞	10	**1:01 pm**	10:01 am
♇	℞	24	**2:48 pm**	11:48 am
♄	℞	29	**8:54 pm**	5:54 pm

1 MONDAY
☽ □ ♂ **12:44 pm** 9:44 am
☽ ⚹ ♅ **1:30 pm** 10:30 am
☽ ☌ ♀ 11:31 pm

2 TUESDAY
☽ ☌ ♀ **2:31 am**
♂ ⚺ ♅ **3:29 am** 12:29 am
☿ ☌ ♆ **5:36 am** 2:36 am
☽ ⚺ ☉ **12:20 pm** 9:20 am
☽ ☌ ♆ **9:25 pm** 6:25 pm
☽ ☌ ☿ **9:58 pm** 6:58 pm
☽ ⚹ ♄ 11:58 pm

3 WEDNESDAY
☽ ⚹ ♄ **2:58 am**
☽ ⚹ ♇ **9:09 am** 6:09 am
☽ □ ♃ **11:36 am** 8:36 am
☽ ⚺ ♅ 10:50 pm

4 THURSDAY
☽ ⚺ ♅ **1:50 am**
☽ ⚹ ♂ **4:16 am** 1:16 am
☽ ⚺ ♀ **8:41 pm** 5:41 pm

5 FRIDAY
☽ ☌ ☉ **4:50 am** 1:50 am
☽ ⚺ ♆ **8:38 am** 5:38 am
☽ ⚺ ☿ **11:48 am** 8:48 am
☽ □ ♄ **2:02 pm** 11:02 am
☽ □ ♇ **7:51 pm** 4:51 pm
☽ △ ♃ **10:15 pm** 7:15 pm

6 SATURDAY
☽ ☌ ♅ **12:09 pm** 9:09 am
☽ ⚺ ♂ **5:26 pm** 2:26 pm

7 SUNDAY
☿ ⚹ ♄ **5:17 am** 2:17 am
☉ ⚺ ♆ **6:11 am** 3:11 am
☽ ⚹ ♀ **12:04 pm** 9:04 am
☽ ⚹ ♆ **5:46 pm** 2:46 pm
☽ ⚺ ☉ **6:42 pm** 3:42 pm
☽ △ ♄ **10:59 pm** 7:59 pm
☽ ⚹ ☿ 9:04 pm

8 MONDAY
☽ ⚹ ☿ **12:04 am**
☽ △ ♇ **4:29 am** 1:29 am
☽ ⚻ ♃ **6:49 am** 3:49 am
☽ ⚺ ♅ **8:26 pm** 5:26 pm

9 TUESDAY
☽ ☌ ♂ **4:16 am** 1:16 am
☽ □ ♀ 9:51 pm
☽ □ ♆ 9:58 pm
♀ ☌ ♆ 11:13 pm

10 WEDNESDAY
☽ □ ♀ **12:51 am**
☽ □ ♆ **12:58 am**
♀ ☌ ♆ **2:13 am**
☉ □ ♄ **4:47 am** 1:47 am
☽ ⚻ ♄ **6:01 am** 3:01 am
☽ ⚹ ☉ **6:06 am** 3:06 am
☽ □ ☿ **10:43 am** 7:43 am

☽ ⚻ ♇ **11:13 am** 8:13 am
☽ ☍ ♃ **1:27 pm** 10:27 am
☿ ⚹ ♇ **5:45 pm** 2:45 pm
☽ ⚹ ♅ 11:49 pm

11 THURSDAY
☽ ⚹ ♅ **2:49 am**
☽ ⚺ ♂ **12:53 pm** 9:53 am
☿ □ ♃ 9:18 pm

12 FRIDAY
☿ □ ♃ **12:18 am**
☽ △ ♆ **6:15 am** 3:15 am
☽ △ ♀ **11:05 am** 8:05 am
☽ ☍ ♄ **11:05 am** 8:05 am
♀ ⚹ ♄ **11:08 am** 8:08 am
☽ □ ☉ **3:06 pm** 12:06 pm
☽ ☍ ♇ **4:01 pm** 1:01 pm
☽ ⚻ ♃ **6:07 pm** 3:07 pm
☽ △ ☿ **7:33 pm** 4:33 pm

13 SATURDAY
☉ □ ♇ **4:07 am** 1:07 am
☽ □ ♅ **7:14 am** 4:14 am
☽ ⚹ ♂ **7:13 pm** 4:13 pm

14 SUNDAY
☽ ⚻ ♆ **9:31 am** 6:31 am
☉ △ ♃ **9:41 am** 6:41 am
☽ ⚻ ♄ **2:10 pm** 11:10 am
☽ ⚻ ♀ **6:45 pm** 3:45 pm
☽ ⚻ ♇ **6:50 pm** 3:50 pm
♀ ⚹ ♇ **7:52 pm** 4:52 pm

☽ △ ♃ **8:49 pm** 5:49 pm
☽ △ ☉ **9:38 pm** 6:38 pm
☽ ⚻ ☿ 11:22 pm

15 MONDAY
☽ ⚻ ☿ **2:22 am**
☽ △ ♅ **9:42 am** 6:42 am
♀ □ ♃ **7:15 pm** 4:15 pm
☽ □ ♂ **11:28 pm** 8:28 pm

16 TUESDAY
☽ ☍ ♆ **11:09 am** 8:09 am
☽ △ ♄ **3:40 pm** 12:40 pm
☽ △ ♇ **8:10 pm** 5:10 pm
☽ □ ♃ **10:03 pm** 7:03 pm
☽ ☍ ♀ 9:29 pm
☽ ⚻ ☉ 11:25 pm

17 WEDNESDAY
☽ ☍ ♀ **12:29 am**
☽ ⚻ ☉ **2:25 am**
☽ ☍ ☿ **7:51 am** 4:51 am
☽ ⚻ ♅ **11:00 am** 8:00 am
☽ △ ♂ 11:46 pm

18 THURSDAY
☽ △ ♂ **2:46 am**
☽ ⚻ ♆ **12:17 pm** 9:17 am
☽ □ ♄ **4:48 pm** 1:48 pm
☽ □ ♇ **9:18 pm** 6:18 pm
☿ ⚺ ♅ **10:17 pm** 7:17 pm
☽ ⚹ ♃ **11:07 pm** 8:07 pm

19 FRIDAY
☽ ⚻ ♀ **6:09 am** 3:09 am
☽ ☍ ☉ **7:12 am** 4:12 am
☽ ☍ ♅ **12:35 pm** 9:35 am
☽ ⚻ ☿ **1:56 pm** 10:56 am

20 SATURDAY
☽ ⚻ ♂ **7:05 am** 4:05 am
☽ △ ♆ **2:39 pm** 11:39 am
☽ ⚹ ♄ **7:20 pm** 4:20 pm
☽ ⚹ ♇ 9:00 pm
☽ ⚺ ♃ 10:47 pm

21 SUNDAY
☽ ⚹ ♇ **12:00 am**
☽ ⚺ ♃ **1:47 am**
☽ △ ♀ **2:19 pm** 11:19 am
☽ ⚻ ☉ **2:23 pm** 11:23 am
☽ ⚻ ♅ **4:21 pm** 1:21 pm
☉ ⚺ ♀ **6:19 pm** 3:19 pm
☽ △ ☿ **11:18 pm** 8:18 pm

22 MONDAY
♀ ⚺ ♅ **2:03 pm** 11:03 am
☽ ☍ ♂ **2:35 pm** 11:35 am
☉ ☌ ♅ **7:07 pm** 4:07 pm
☽ □ ♆ **8:03 pm** 5:03 pm
☽ ⚺ ♄ 10:00 pm

23 TUESDAY
☽ ⚺ ♄ **1:00 am**
☽ ⚺ ♇ **5:58 am** 2:58 am
☽ ☌ ♃ **7:44 am** 4:44 am
☽ △ ♅ **11:46 pm** 8:46 pm
☽ △ ☉ 11:02 pm

24 WEDNESDAY
☽ △ ☉ **2:02 am**
☽ □ ♀ **3:12 am** 12:12 am
☽ □ ☿ **2:14 pm** 11:14 am
☽ ⚻ ♂ 11:35 pm

25 THURSDAY
☽ ⚻ ♂ **2:35 am**
☽ ⚹ ♆ **5:22 am** 2:22 am
☽ ☌ ♄ **10:33 am** 7:33 am
☽ ☌ ♇ **3:48 pm** 12:48 pm
☽ ⚺ ♃ **5:28 pm** 2:28 pm

26 FRIDAY
☽ □ ♅ **10:57 am** 7:57 am
☽ □ ☉ **6:18 pm** 3:18 pm
☽ ⚹ ♀ **8:58 pm** 5:58 pm

27 SATURDAY
♂ □ ♆ **9:03 am** 6:03 am
☽ ⚹ ☿ **10:35 am** 7:35 am
☽ ⚺ ♆ **5:42 pm** 2:42 pm
☽ △ ♂ **6:11 pm** 3:11 pm
☽ ⚺ ♄ **10:55 pm** 7:55 pm

28 SUNDAY
☽ ⚺ ♇ **4:16 am** 1:16 am
☽ ⚹ ♃ **5:44 am** 2:44 am
☽ ⚹ ♅ 9:02 pm

29 MONDAY
☽ ⚹ ♅ **12:02 am**
☽ ⚹ ☉ **12:34 pm** 9:34 am
☿ ⚺ ♆ **4:08 pm** 1:08 pm
☽ ⚺ ♀ **4:44 pm** 1:44 pm

30 TUESDAY
☽ ☌ ♆ **6:33 am** 3:33 am
☽ ⚺ ☿ **8:47 am** 5:47 am
☽ □ ♂ **10:22 am** 7:22 am
☽ ⚹ ♄ **11:34 am** 8:34 am
☽ ⚹ ♇ **4:48 pm** 1:48 pm
☽ □ ♃ **5:57 pm** 2:57 pm
☿ ⚹ ♂ 11:37 pm

Eastern time in bold type
Pacific time in medium type

APRIL 2019

DATE	SID.TIME	SUN	MOON	NODE	MERCURY	VENUS	MARS	JUPITER	SATURN	URANUS	NEPTUNE	PLUTO	CERES	PALLAS	JUNO	VESTA	CHIRON
1 M	12 36 15	10 ♈ 58 40	22 ♒ 43	23 ♋ 40 ℞	16 ♓ 38	6 ♓ 14	0 ♊ 29	24 ♐ 12	19 ♑ 50	1 ♉ 17	17 ♓ 05	23 ♑ 01	14 ♐ 03	22 ♎ 41 ℞	20 ♊ 36	28 ♓ 44	2 ♈ 23
2 T	12 40 12	11 57 54	4 ♓ 32	23 34	16 59	7 26	1 09	24 14	19 53	1 20	17 07	23 01	14 06	22 23	21 04	29 13	2 27
3 W	12 44 9	12 57 06	16 27	23 25	17 24	8 39	1 49	24 15	19 56	1 24	17 10	23 02	14 09	22 05	21 32	29 42	2 31
4 Th	12 48 5	13 56 17	28 31	23 14	17 54	9 51	2 28	24 17	19 58	1 27	17 12	23 03	14 11	21 46	22 00	0 ♈ 10	2 34
5 F	12 52 2	14 55 26	10 ♈ 44	23 00	18 28	11 03	3 08	24 18	20 01	1 30	17 14	23 03	14 13	21 28	22 29	0 39	2 37
6 Sa	12 55 58	15 54 32	23 09	22 46	19 07	12 16	3 48	24 19	20 03	1 34	17 16	23 04	14 14	21 09	22 57	1 07	2 41
7 Su	12 59 55	16 53 37	5 ♉ 44	22 33	19 49	13 28	4 27	24 20	20 05	1 37	17 18	23 04	14 15	20 51	23 26	1 36	2 44
8 M	13 3 51	17 52 39	18 31	22 21	20 35	14 41	5 07	24 20	20 07	1 40	17 20	23 05	14 16	20 32	23 54	2 05	2 48
9 T	13 7 48	18 51 39	1 ♊ 30	22 12	21 24	15 53	5 46	24 21	20 09	1 44	17 22	23 05	14 16 ℞	20 13	24 23	2 33	2 51
10 W	13 11 44	19 50 37	14 39	22 06	22 16	17 06	6 26	24 21 ℞	20 11	1 47	17 24	23 06	14 16	19 55	24 51	3 01	2 55
11 Th	13 15 41	20 49 33	28 01	22 03	23 12	18 18	7 06	24 21	20 13	1 51	17 26	23 06	14 16	19 36	25 20	3 30	2 58
12 F	13 19 37	21 48 27	11 ♋ 36	22 02	24 10	19 31	7 45	24 21	20 15	1 54	17 28	23 07	14 15	19 17	25 49	3 58	3 02
13 Sa	13 23 34	22 47 18	25 26	22 02	25 11	20 43	8 25	24 21	20 17	1 57	17 30	23 07	14 13	18 59	26 17	4 27	3 05
14 Su	13 27 31	23 46 07	9 ♌ 30	22 01	26 15	21 56	9 04	24 20	20 19	2 01	17 32	23 07	14 12	18 40	26 46	4 55	3 08
15 M	13 31 27	24 44 54	23 50	21 59	27 22	23 08	9 43	24 19	20 20	2 04	17 34	23 08	14 10	18 22	27 15	5 23	3 12
16 T	13 35 24	25 43 38	8 ♍ 22	21 55	28 31	24 21	10 23	24 18	20 21	2 08	17 35	23 08	14 07	18 04	27 44	5 51	3 15
17 W	13 39 20	26 42 20	23 02	21 48	29 42	25 33	11 02	24 17	20 23	2 11	17 37	23 08	14 04	17 45	28 13	6 19	3 18
18 Th	13 43 17	27 41 00	7 ♎ 44	21 38	0 ♈ 55	26 46	11 41	24 16	20 24	2 15	17 39	23 08	14 01	17 27	28 42	6 48	3 22
19 F	13 47 13	28 39 38	22 22	21 27	2 11	27 58	12 21	24 15	20 25	2 18	17 41	23 09	13 57	17 10	29 11	7 16	3 25
20 Sa	13 51 10	29 38 14	6 ♏ 46	21 15	3 29	29 11	13 00	24 13	20 26	2 21	17 43	23 09	13 53	16 52	29 40	7 44	3 28
21 Su	13 55 6	0 ♉ 36 48	20 50	21 05	4 49	0 ♈ 24	13 39	24 11	20 27	2 25	17 45	23 09	13 49	16 35	0 ♋ 09	8 12	3 32
22 M	13 59 3	1 35 20	4 ♐ 31	20 56	6 11	1 36	14 19	24 09	20 28	2 28	17 46	23 09	13 44	16 17	0 38	8 40	3 35
23 T	14 3 0	2 33 50	17 46	20 49	7 35	2 49	14 58	24 07	20 29	2 32	17 48	23 09	13 39	16 01	1 07	9 07	3 38
24 W	14 6 56	3 32 19	0 ♑ 37	20 46	9 01	4 02	15 37	24 05	20 29	2 35	17 50	23 09 ℞	13 33	15 44	1 36	9 35	3 41
25 Th	14 10 53	4 30 47	13 05	20 44 D	10 28	5 14	16 16	24 02	20 30	2 39	17 52	23 09	13 27	15 28	2 05	10 03	3 44
26 F	14 14 49	5 29 12	25 16	20 44 ℞	11 58	6 27	16 55	23 59	20 30	2 42	17 53	23 09	13 21	15 12	2 35	10 31	3 47
27 Sa	14 18 46	6 27 36	7 ♒ 14	20 44	13 30	7 40	17 35	23 56	20 31	2 46	17 55	23 09	13 14	14 56	3 04	10 58	3 51
28 Su	14 22 42	7 25 59	19 05	20 44	15 03	8 53	18 14	23 53	20 31	2 49	17 57	23 09	13 07	14 41	3 33	11 26	3 54
29 M	14 26 39	8 24 19	0 ♓ 54	20 41	16 38	10 05	18 53	23 50	20 31	2 52	17 58	23 09	13 00	14 26	4 02	11 54	3 57
30 T	14 30 35	9 22 39	12 46	20 37	18 15	11 18	19 32	23 47	20 31 ℞	2 56	18 00	23 09	12 52	14 11	4 31	12 21	4 00

EPHEMERIS CALCULATED FOR 12 MIDNIGHT GREENWICH MEAN TIME. ALL OTHER DATA AND FACING ASPECTARIAN PAGE IN **EASTERN TIME (BOLD)** AND PACIFIC TIME (REGULAR).

MAY 2019

☽ Last Aspect day	ET / hr:mn / PT		asp	☽ Ingress sign	day	ET / hr:mn / PT	
4/30	**5:57 pm**	2:57 pm	□♃	♈	1	**6:24 am**	3:24 am
3	**4:47 am**	1:47 am	☌☿	♉	3	**4:18 pm**	1:18 pm
5	**11:10 am**	8:10 am	△♇	♊	5	**11:40 pm**	8:40 pm
7	**7:50 pm**	4:50 pm	☌♂	♋	8	**5:06 am**	2:06 am
9	**10:06 pm**	7:06 pm	□♀	♌	10	**9:14 am**	6:14 am
12	**8:24 am**	5:24 am	⚹♂	♍	12	**12:22 pm**	9:22 am
14	**1:19 pm**	10:19 am	□♂	♎	14	**2:51 pm**	11:51 am
16	**5:37 am**	2:37 am	□♇	♏	16	**5:26 pm**	2:26 pm
18	**5:11 pm**	2:11 pm	☍☉	♐	18	**9:21 pm**	6:21 pm
20	**1:05 pm**	10:05 am	☌♃	♑	21	**3:56 am**	12:56 am
22	**11:58 pm**	8:58 pm	☌♇	♒	23	**1:49 pm**	10:49 am
25	**8:51 am**	5:51 am	⚹♃	♓	25		11:08 pm
25	**8:51 am**	5:51 am	⚹♃	♓	26	**2:08 am**	
27		9:21 pm	⚹♇	♈	28	**2:32 pm**	11:32 am
28	**12:21 am**		⚹♇	♈	28	**2:32 pm**	11:32 am
30	**11:08 am**	8:08 am	□♇	♉	30		9:43 pm
30	**11:08 am**	8:08 am	□♇	♉	31	**12:43 am**	

☽ Phases & Eclipses phase	day	ET / hr:mn / PT	
New Moon	4	**6:45 pm**	3:45 pm
2nd Quarter	11	**9:12 pm**	6:12 pm
Full Moon	18	**5:11 pm**	2:11 pm
4th Quarter	26	**12:34 pm**	9:34 am

Planet Ingress		day	ET / hr:mn / PT	
☿	♉	6	**2:25 pm**	11:25 am
♀	♉	15	**5:46 am**	2:46 am
♂	♋	15	**11:09 pm**	8:09 pm
☉	♊	21	**3:59 am**	12:59 am
☿	♊	21	**6:52 am**	3:52 am

Planetary Motion		day	ET / hr:mn / PT	
♀	D	30	**10:52 pm**	7:52 pm

1 WEDNESDAY
☿ ⚹ ♂ **2:37 am**
☿ □ ♄ **4:50 am** 1:50 am
♂ ⚻ ♄ **8:17 am** 5:17 am
☽ ⚺ ♅ **12:22 pm** 9:22 am

2 THURSDAY
☽ ⚺ ☉ **5:17 am** 2:17 am
☽ ☌ ♀ **10:39 am** 7:39 am
☽ ⚺ ♆ **5:36 pm** 2:36 pm
☿ □ ♇ **5:51 pm** 2:51 pm
☽ □ ♄ **10:17 pm** 7:17 pm
☿ △ ♃ **11:59 pm** 8:59 pm
☽ ⚹ ♂ 9:22 pm

3 FRIDAY
☽ ⚹ ♂ **12:22 am**
☽ □ ♇ **3:17 am** 12:17 am
☽ △ ♃ **4:06 am** 1:06 am
☽ ☌ ☿ **4:47 am** 1:47 am
☽ ☌ ♅ **10:15 pm** 7:15 pm

4 SATURDAY
☽ ☌ ☉ **6:45 pm** 3:45 pm
☽ ⚺ ♀ 10:06 pm
☽ ⚹ ♆ 11:02 pm

5 SUNDAY
☽ ⚺ ♀ **1:06 am**
☽ ⚹ ♆ **2:02 am**
☽ △ ♄ **6:22 am** 3:22 am
♂ ⚻ ♇ **8:29 am** 5:29 am
☽ △ ♇ **11:10 am** 8:10 am
♀ ⚺ ♆ **11:18 am** 8:18 am
☽ ⚺ ♂ **11:19 am** 8:19 am
☽ ⚻ ♃ **11:41 am** 8:41 am
♂ ☍ ♃ **5:57 pm** 2:57 pm
☽ ⚺ ☿ **9:18 pm** 6:18 pm

6 MONDAY
☽ ⚺ ♅ **5:37 am** 2:37 am

7 TUESDAY
☽ ⚺ ☉ **5:20 am** 2:20 am
☽ □ ♆ **8:15 am** 5:15 am
♀ □ ♄ **9:26 am** 6:26 am
☽ ⚻ ♄ **12:18 pm** 9:18 am
☽ ⚹ ♀ **12:35 pm** 9:35 am
☽ ⚻ ♇ **4:58 pm** 1:58 pm
☽ ☍ ♃ **5:11 pm** 2:11 pm
☽ ☌ ♂ **7:50 pm** 4:50 pm

8 WEDNESDAY
☿ ☌ ♅ **10:23 am** 7:23 am
☽ ⚹ ♅ **11:07 am** 8:07 am
☽ ⚹ ☿ **11:13 am** 8:13 am
☉ ⚹ ♆ **10:52 pm** 7:52 pm

9 THURSDAY
♃ ⚺ ♇ **6:30 am** 3:30 am
☽ △ ♆ **12:55 pm** 9:55 am
♀ △ ♃ **12:56 pm** 9:56 am
♀ □ ♇ **1:20 pm** 10:20 am
☽ ⚹ ☉ **1:57 pm** 10:57 am
☽ ☍ ♄ **4:44 pm** 1:44 pm
☽ ⚻ ♃ **9:15 pm** 6:15 pm
☽ ☍ ♇ **9:20 pm** 6:20 pm
☽ □ ♀ **10:06 pm** 7:06 pm
☽ ⚺ ♂ 11:43 pm

10 FRIDAY
☽ ⚺ ♂ **2:43 am**
☽ □ ♅ **3:19 pm** 12:19 pm
☽ □ ☿ **11:33 pm** 8:33 pm

11 SATURDAY
☉ △ ♄ **5:19 am** 2:19 am
☽ ⚻ ♆ **4:29 pm** 1:29 pm
☽ ⚻ ♄ **8:06 pm** 5:06 pm
☽ □ ☉ **9:12 pm** 6:12 pm
☽ △ ♃ 9:16 pm
☽ ⚻ ♇ 9:38 pm

12 SUNDAY
☽ △ ♃ **12:16 am**
☽ ⚻ ♇ **12:38 am**
☽ △ ♀ **6:14 am** 3:14 am
☽ ⚹ ♂ **8:24 am** 5:24 am
☽ △ ♅ **6:33 pm** 3:33 pm

13 MONDAY
☽ △ ☿ **10:48 am** 7:48 am
☉ ⚻ ♃ **2:27 pm** 11:27 am
☽ ☍ ♆ **7:14 pm** 4:14 pm
☽ △ ♄ **10:39 pm** 7:39 pm
☉ △ ♇ **11:07 pm** 8:07 pm
☽ □ ♃ 11:32 pm

14 TUESDAY
☽ □ ♃ **2:32 am**
☽ △ ♇ **3:12 am** 12:12 am
☽ △ ☉ **3:30 am** 12:30 am
♀ ⚹ ♂ **9:58 am** 6:58 am
☽ □ ♂ **1:19 pm** 10:19 am
☽ ⚻ ♀ **1:28 pm** 10:28 am
☽ ⚻ ♅ **9:11 pm** 6:11 pm

15 WEDNESDAY
☿ ⚹ ♆ **9:20 pm** 6:20 pm
☽ ⚻ ♆ **9:44 pm** 6:44 pm
☽ ⚻ ☿ **9:48 pm** 6:48 pm
☽ □ ♄ 10:00 pm

16 THURSDAY
☽ □ ♄ **1:00 am**
☽ ⚹ ♃ **4:39 am** 1:39 am
☽ □ ♇ **5:37 am** 2:37 am
☽ ⚻ ☉ **9:39 am** 6:39 am
☽ △ ♂ **6:18 pm** 3:18 pm
☿ △ ♄ **7:09 pm** 4:09 pm
☽ ☍ ♀ **8:47 pm** 5:47 pm
☽ ☍ ♅ 9:04 pm

17 FRIDAY
☽ ☍ ♅ **12:04 am**
☿ ⚻ ♃ **5:49 pm** 2:49 pm
☽ △ ♆ 10:02 pm
☿ △ ♇ 10:48 pm

18 SATURDAY
☽ △ ♆ **1:02 am**
☿ △ ♇ **1:48 am**
☽ ⚹ ♄ **4:15 am** 1:15 am
☽ ⚺ ♃ **7:43 am** 4:43 am
☽ ⚹ ♇ **9:04 am** 6:04 am
☽ ☍ ☿ **10:26 am** 7:26 am
♀ ☌ ♅ **12:17 pm** 9:17 am
☽ ☍ ☉ **5:11 pm** 2:11 pm
☽ ⚻ ♂ 9:52 pm

19 SUNDAY
☽ ⚻ ♂ **12:52 am**
☽ ⚻ ♅ **4:28 am** 1:28 am
☽ ⚻ ♀ **6:00 am** 3:00 am

20 MONDAY
☽ □ ♆ **6:32 am** 3:32 am
☽ ⚺ ♄ **9:43 am** 6:43 am
☽ ☌ ♃ **1:05 pm** 10:05 am
☽ ⚺ ♇ **2:54 pm** 11:54 am

21 TUESDAY
☽ ⚻ ☿ **3:20 am** 12:20 am
☽ ⚻ ☉ **3:56 am** 12:56 am
☉ ☌ ☿ **9:07 am** 6:07 am
☽ ☍ ♂ **10:35 am** 7:35 am
☽ △ ♅ **11:43 am** 8:43 am
☽ △ ♀ **6:58 pm** 3:58 pm

22 WEDNESDAY
♂ ⚹ ♅ **10:46 am** 7:46 am
☽ ⚹ ♆ **3:14 pm** 12:14 pm
☽ ☌ ♄ **6:23 pm** 3:23 pm
☽ ⚺ ♃ **9:36 pm** 6:36 pm
☽ ☌ ♇ **11:58 pm** 8:58 pm

23 THURSDAY
☿ ⚺ ♅ **5:05 am** 2:05 am
☿ ⚺ ♂ **12:04 pm** 9:04 am
☽ △ ☉ **6:49 pm** 3:49 pm
☽ □ ♅ **10:17 pm** 7:17 pm
☽ ⚻ ♂ 9:07 pm
☽ △ ☿ 11:01 pm

24 FRIDAY
☽ ⚻ ♂ **12:07 am**
☽ △ ☿ **2:01 am**
☽ □ ♀ **12:17 pm** 9:17 am
☽ ⚺ ♆ 11:54 pm

25 SATURDAY
☽ ⚺ ♆ **2:54 am**
☽ ⚺ ♄ **5:54 am** 2:54 am
☽ ⚹ ♃ **8:51 am** 5:51 am
☽ ⚺ ♇ **11:48 am** 8:48 am
☉ ⚺ ♅ **4:40 pm** 1:40 pm

26 SUNDAY
☽ ⚹ ♅ **11:02 am** 8:02 am
☽ □ ☉ **12:34 pm** 9:34 am
☽ △ ♂ **4:07 pm** 1:07 pm

27 MONDAY
☽ □ ☿ **4:07 am** 1:07 am
☽ ⚹ ♀ **7:52 am** 4:52 am
☽ ☌ ♆ **3:39 pm** 12:39 pm
☽ ⚹ ♄ **6:22 pm** 3:22 pm
☽ □ ♃ **8:54 pm** 5:54 pm
☽ ⚹ ♇ 9:21 pm

28 TUESDAY
☽ ⚹ ♇ **12:21 am**
☽ ⚺ ♅ **11:29 pm** 8:29 pm
☿ ⚺ ♀ 9:01 pm

29 WEDNESDAY
☿ ⚺ ♀ **12:01 am**
☽ ⚹ ☉ **5:51 am** 2:51 am
☽ □ ♂ **7:30 am** 4:30 am
☿ □ ♆ **9:22 am** 6:22 am
☽ ⚺ ♀ 10:53 pm
☽ ⚺ ♆ 11:56 pm

30 THURSDAY
☽ ⚺ ♀ **1:53 am**
☽ ⚺ ♆ **2:56 am**
☽ ⚹ ☿ **4:03 am** 1:03 am
☽ □ ♄ **5:16 am** 2:16 am
☽ △ ♃ **7:21 am** 4:21 am
☽ □ ♇ **11:08 am** 8:08 am
☿ ⚻ ♄ **11:19 am** 8:19 am
♀ ⚹ ♆ **12:50 pm** 9:50 am
☿ ☍ ♃ **11:12 pm** 8:12 pm

31 FRIDAY
☽ ☌ ♅ **9:26 am** 6:26 am
♀ △ ♄ **11:26 am** 8:26 am
☉ ⚺ ♂ **6:02 pm** 3:02 pm
☽ ⚹ ♂ **7:49 pm** 4:49 pm
☽ ⚺ ☉ **7:52 pm** 4:52 pm
☿ ⚻ ♇ **11:14 pm** 8:14 pm

Eastern time in bold type
Pacific time in medium type

MAY 2019

DATE	SID.TIME	SUN	MOON	NODE	MERCURY	VENUS	MARS	JUPITER	SATURN	URANUS	NEPTUNE	PLUTO	CERES	PALLAS	JUNO	VESTA	CHIRON
1 W	14 34 32	10♉20 56	24♓45	20♋30℞	19♈54	12♈31	20♊11	23♐43℞	20♑31℞	2♉59	18♓01	23♑09℞	12♐44℞	13♎57℞	5♋01	12♈49	4♈03
2 Th	14 38 29	11 19 12	6♈56	20 20	21 35	13 44	20 50	23 39	20 31	3 03	18 03	23 08	12 36	13 43	5 30	13 16	4 06
3 F	14 42 25	12 17 27	19 19	20 09	23 17	14 56	21 29	23 35	20 31	3 06	18 04	23 08	12 27	13 30	5 59	13 43	4 09
4 Sa	14 46 22	13 15 40	1♉58	19 57	25 02	16 09	22 08	23 31	20 30	3 10	18 06	23 08	12 18	13 17	6 29	14 11	4 12
5 Su	14 50 18	14 13 51	14 51	19 46	26 48	17 22	22 47	23 27	20 30	3 13	18 07	23 08	12 08	13 04	6 58	14 38	4 15
6 M	14 54 15	15 12 00	27 59	19 36	28 36	18 35	23 26	23 22	20 29	3 16	18 09	23 07	11 59	12 52	7 27	15 05	4 17
7 T	14 58 11	16 10 08	11♊19	19 28	0♉26	19 48	24 05	23 18	20 29	3 20	18 10	23 07	11 49	12 40	7 57	15 32	4 20
8 W	15 2 8	17 08 14	24 50	19 23	2 17	21 00	24 44	23 13	20 28	3 23	18 12	23 07	11 38	12 29	8 26	15 59	4 23
9 Th	15 6 4	18 06 18	8♋30	19 21 D	4 11	22 13	25 23	23 08	20 27	3 27	18 13	23 06	11 28	12 18	8 56	16 26	4 26
10 F	15 10 1	19 04 21	22 20	19 20	6 06	23 26	26 02	23 03	20 26	3 30	18 14	23 06	11 17	12 08	9 25	16 53	4 29
11 Sa	15 13 58	20 02 21	6♌17	19 21	8 03	24 39	26 41	22 58	20 25	3 33	18 16	23 05	11 06	11 58	9 54	17 20	4 31
12 Su	15 17 54	21 00 20	20 21	19 21℞	10 02	25 52	27 20	22 53	20 24	3 37	18 17	23 05	10 55	11 49	10 24	17 47	4 34
13 M	15 21 51	21 58 16	4♍31	19 21	12 03	27 05	27 58	22 47	20 23	3 40	18 18	23 04	10 43	11 40	10 53	18 14	4 37
14 T	15 25 47	22 56 11	18 47	19 18	14 05	28 17	28 37	22 41	20 22	3 43	18 20	23 04	10 31	11 32	11 23	18 41	4 39
15 W	15 29 44	23 54 04	3♎04	19 13	16 09	29 30	29 16	22 36	20 20	3 46	18 21	23 03	10 19	11 24	11 52	19 07	4 42
16 Th	15 33 40	24 51 55	17 20	19 06	18 15	0♉43	29 55	22 30	20 19	3 50	18 22	23 03	10 07	11 16	12 22	19 34	4 44
17 F	15 37 37	25 49 44	1♏31	18 58	20 22	1 56	0♋34	22 24	20 17	3 53	18 23	23 02	9 55	11 09	12 51	20 00	4 47
18 Sa	15 41 33	26 47 32	15 30	18 50	22 30	3 09	1 12	22 18	20 16	3 56	18 24	23 01	9 42	11 03	13 20	20 27	4 49
19 Su	15 45 30	27 45 19	29 14	18 42	24 39	4 22	1 51	22 12	20 14	3 59	18 25	23 01	9 30	10 57	13 50	20 53	4 52
20 M	15 49 27	28 43 04	12♐40	18 35	26 50	5 35	2 30	22 05	20 12	4 03	18 26	23 00	9 17	10 51	14 19	21 19	4 54
21 T	15 53 23	29 40 48	25 45	18 31	29 01	6 48	3 09	21 59	20 10	4 06	18 27	22 59	9 04	10 46	14 49	21 46	4 56
22 W	15 57 20	0♊38 30	8♑30	18 28 D	1♊12	8 01	3 47	21 52	20 08	4 09	18 28	22 59	8 51	10 42	15 18	22 12	4 59
23 Th	16 1 16	1 36 12	20 56	18 28	3 24	9 14	4 26	21 46	20 06	4 12	18 29	22 58	8 38	10 38	15 48	22 38	5 01
24 F	16 5 13	2 33 52	3♒07	18 29	5 35	10 27	5 05	21 39	20 04	4 15	18 30	22 57	8 25	10 34	16 17	23 04	5 03
25 Sa	16 9 9	3 31 32	15 06	18 30	7 46	11 39	5 43	21 32	20 02	4 18	18 31	22 56	8 11	10 31	16 46	23 30	5 05
26 Su	16 13 6	4 29 10	26 59	18 31℞	9 57	12 52	6 22	21 25	19 59	4 22	18 32	22 55	7 58	10 29	17 16	23 56	5 08
27 M	16 17 2	5 26 47	8♓49	18 32	12 07	14 05	7 00	21 18	19 57	4 25	18 33	22 55	7 45	10 26	17 45	24 22	5 10
28 T	16 20 59	6 24 23	20 43	18 30	14 15	15 18	7 39	21 11	19 54	4 28	18 34	22 54	7 31	10 25	18 15	24 47	5 12
29 W	16 24 56	7 21 59	2♈46	18 27	16 23	16 31	8 17	21 04	19 52	4 31	18 34	22 53	7 18	10 24	18 44	25 13	5 14
30 Th	16 28 52	8 19 33	15 00	18 23	18 28	17 44	8 56	20 56	19 49	4 34	18 35	22 52	7 04	10 23	19 13	25 39	5 16
31 F	16 32 49	9 17 06	27 30	18 17	20 32	18 57	9 35	20 49	19 46	4 37	18 36	22 51	6 51	10 23 D	19 43	26 04	5 18

EPHEMERIS CALCULATED FOR 12 MIDNIGHT GREENWICH MEAN TIME. ALL OTHER DATA AND FACING ASPECTARIAN PAGE IN **EASTERN TIME (BOLD)** AND PACIFIC TIME (REGULAR).

JUNE 2019

☽ Last Aspect day	ET / hr:mn / PT	asp	☽ Ingress sign day	ET / hr:mn / PT
1	**6:53 pm** 3:53 pm	△♇	♊ 2	**7:48 am** 4:48 am
4	**11:42 am** 8:42 am	☌☿	♋ 4	**12:17 pm** 9:17 am
6	**10:10 am** 7:10 am	⚹♀	♌ 6	**3:16 pm** 12:16 pm
8	**5:23 pm** 2:23 pm	□♀	♍ 8	**5:45 pm** 2:45 pm
10	**8:01 am** 5:01 am	△♇	♎ 10	**8:29 pm** 5:29 pm
12	**11:15 am** 8:15 am	□♇	♏ 12	9:02 pm
12	**11:15 am** 8:15 am	□♇	♏ 13	**12:02 am**
14	**3:46 pm** 12:46 pm	⚹♇	♐ 15	**5:03 am** 2:03 am
17	**4:31 am** 1:31 am	☍☉	♑ 17	**12:13 pm** 9:13 am
19	**7:19 am** 4:19 am	☍☿	♒ 19	**10:01 pm** 7:01 pm
21	**10:02 am** 7:02 am	⚹♃	♓ 22	**10:01 am** 7:01 am
24	**7:10 pm** 4:10 pm	△☿	♈ 24	**10:38 pm** 7:38 pm
27	**3:51 am** 12:51 am	□♂	♉ 27	**9:32 am** 6:32 am
29	**2:38 pm** 11:38 am	⚹♂	♊ 29	**5:09 pm** 2:09 pm

☽ Phases & Eclipses phase	day	ET / hr:mn / PT
New Moon	3	**6:02 am** 3:02 am
2nd Quarter	9	10:59 pm
2nd Quarter	10	**1:59 am**
Full Moon	17	**4:31 am** 1:31 am
4th Quarter	25	**5:46 am** 2:46 am

Planet Ingress	day	ET / hr:mn / PT
☿ ♋	4	**4:05 pm** 1:05 pm
♀ ♊	8	**9:37 pm** 6:37 pm
⚶ ♉	9	**5:55 am** 2:55 am
⚵ ♌	20	**10:37 pm** 7:37 pm
☉ ♋	21	**11:54 am** 8:54 am
☿ ♌	26	**8:19 pm** 5:19 pm

Planetary Motion	day	ET / hr:mn / PT
♆ ℞	21	**10:36 am** 7:36 am

1 SATURDAY
♀⊼♃ **5:20 am** 2:20 am
☽⚹♆ **11:15 am** 8:15 am
☽△♄ **1:12 pm** 10:12 am
☽⊼♃ **2:52 pm** 11:52 am
☽☌♀ **3:55 pm** 12:55 pm
☽△♇ **6:53 pm** 3:53 pm
☽⊻☿ **10:22 pm** 7:22 pm

2 SUNDAY
☽⊻♅ **4:15 pm** 1:15 pm
♀△♇ **11:42 pm** 8:42 pm

3 MONDAY
☽⊻♂ **4:34 am** 1:34 am
☽☌☉ **6:02 am** 3:02 am
☽□♆ **4:39 pm** 1:39 pm
☽⊼♄ **6:17 pm** 3:17 pm
☽☍♃ **7:35 pm** 4:35 pm
☽⊼♇ **11:50 pm** 8:50 pm
☽⊻♀ 11:11 pm

4 TUESDAY
☽⊻♀ **2:11 am**
☽☌☿ **11:42 am** 8:42 am
☽⚹♅ **8:36 pm** 5:36 pm

5 WEDNESDAY
☽☌♂ **10:48 am** 7:48 am
☽⊻☉ **1:31 pm** 10:31 am
☽△♆ **8:06 pm** 5:06 pm
☽☍♄ **9:28 pm** 6:28 pm
☽⊼♃ **10:28 pm** 7:28 pm

6 THURSDAY
☽☍♇ **3:00 am** 12:00 am
☽⚹♀ **10:10 am** 7:10 am
☽⊻☿ **10:09 pm** 7:09 pm
☽□♅ **11:37 pm** 8:37 pm

7 FRIDAY
☿⚹♅ **10:16 am** 7:16 am
☽⊻♂ **3:50 pm** 12:50 pm
☽⚹☉ **7:47 pm** 4:47 pm
☽⊼♆ **10:42 pm** 7:42 pm
☽⊼♄ **11:50 pm** 8:50 pm
☽△♃ 9:35 pm

8 SATURDAY
☽△♃ **12:35 am**
☽⊼♇ **5:28 am** 2:28 am
☽□♀ **5:23 pm** 2:23 pm
☽△♅ 11:16 pm

9 SUNDAY
☽△♅ **2:16 am**
☽⚹☿ **7:33 am** 4:33 am
☉□♆ **3:34 pm** 12:34 pm
☽⚹♂ **8:45 pm** 5:45 pm
☽☍♆ 10:17 pm
☽□☉ 10:59 pm
☽△♄ 11:12 pm
☽□♃ 11:42 pm

10 MONDAY
☽☍♆ **1:17 am**
☽□☉ **1:59 am**
☽△♄ **2:12 am**
☽□♃ **2:42 am**
☉⊼♄ **5:04 am** 2:04 am
☽△♇ **8:01 am** 5:01 am
☉☍♃ **11:28 am** 8:28 am
☽△♀ 9:55 pm

11 TUESDAY
☽△♀ **12:55 am**
☽⊼♅ **5:15 am** 2:15 am
☽□☿ **5:03 pm** 2:03 pm
☽□♂ 11:19 pm

12 WEDNESDAY
☽□♂ **2:19 am**
☽⊼♆ **4:29 am** 1:29 am
☽□♄ **5:11 am** 2:11 am
☽⚹♃ **5:27 am** 2:27 am
☽△☉ **8:57 am** 5:57 am
☽□♇ **11:15 am** 8:15 am

13 THURSDAY
♀⊻♅ **4:41 am** 1:41 am
☽☍♅ **9:11 am** 6:11 am
☽⊼♀ **9:36 am** 6:36 am
☉⊼♇ **5:45 pm** 2:45 pm
♂△♆ 11:11 pm

14 FRIDAY
♂△♆ **2:11 am**
☽△☿ **3:33 am** 12:33 am
☽△♆ **8:53 am** 5:53 am
☽△♂ **9:13 am** 6:13 am
☽⚹♄ **9:21 am** 6:21 am
☽⊻♃ **9:22 am** 6:22 am
♂☍♄ **11:50 am** 8:50 am
♂⊼♃ **11:53 am** 8:53 am
♃⊻♄ **12:28 pm** 9:28 am
☽⚹♇ **3:46 pm** 12:46 pm
☽⊼☉ **5:29 pm** 2:29 pm

15 SATURDAY
☽⊼♅ **2:41 pm** 11:41 am
☽☍♀ **8:23 pm** 5:23 pm

16 SUNDAY
☿△♆ **7:43 am** 4:43 am
☿⊼♃ **8:02 am** 5:02 am
☿☍♄ **10:00 am** 7:00 am
♃□♆ **11:22 am** 8:22 am
☽☌♃ **3:09 pm** 12:09 pm
☽□♆ **3:11 pm** 12:11 pm
☽⊻♄ **3:23 pm** 12:23 pm
☽⊼☿ **4:02 pm** 1:02 pm
☽⊼♂ **6:19 pm** 3:19 pm
☽⊻♇ **10:15 pm** 7:15 pm

17 MONDAY
☽☍☉ **4:31 am** 1:31 am
☽△♅ **10:29 pm** 7:29 pm

18 TUESDAY
♄⚹♆ **7:47 am** 4:47 am
☽⊼♀ **10:17 am** 7:17 am
☿☌♂ **12:04 pm** 9:04 am
☽⊻♃ **11:22 pm** 8:22 pm
☽☌♄ **11:53 pm** 8:53 pm
☽⚹♆ **11:59 pm** 8:59 pm

19 WEDNESDAY
☽☍♂ **6:22 am** 3:22 am
☿☍♇ **6:56 am** 3:56 am
☽☌♇ **7:17 am** 4:17 am
☽☍☿ **7:19 am** 4:19 am
☽⊼☉ **6:48 pm** 3:48 pm
♂☍♇ **11:26 pm** 8:26 pm

20 THURSDAY
☽□♅ **8:56 am** 5:56 am

21 FRIDAY
☽△♀ **3:42 am** 12:42 am
☽⚹♃ **10:02 am** 7:02 am
☽⊻♄ **10:52 am** 7:52 am
☽⊻♆ **11:17 am** 8:17 am
☽⊻♇ **6:44 pm** 3:44 pm
☽⊼♂ **9:16 pm** 6:16 pm
☽⊼☿ 10:06 pm

22 SATURDAY
☽⊼☿ **1:06 am**
☽△☉ **11:57 am** 8:57 am
☽⚹♅ **9:25 pm** 6:25 pm

23 SUNDAY
♀☍♃ **12:45 pm** 9:45 am
☽□♃ **10:03 pm** 7:03 pm
♀⊼♄ **10:32 pm** 7:32 pm
☽⚹♄ **11:09 pm** 8:09 pm
☽□♀ **11:14 pm** 8:14 pm
☽☌♆ **11:55 pm** 8:55 pm

24 MONDAY
♀□♆ **5:58 am** 2:58 am
☽⚹♇ **7:17 am** 4:17 am
☽△♂ **1:22 pm** 10:22 am
☽△☿ **7:10 pm** 4:10 pm

25 TUESDAY
☽□☉ **5:46 am** 2:46 am
☽⊻♅ **10:03 am** 7:03 am

26 WEDNESDAY
☽△♃ **9:20 am** 6:20 am
☽□♄ **10:38 am** 7:38 am
☽⊻♆ **11:42 am** 8:42 am
☽⚹♀ **5:38 pm** 2:38 pm
☽□♇ **6:43 pm** 3:43 pm

27 THURSDAY
☽□♂ **3:51 am** 12:51 am
♀⊼♇ **4:20 am** 1:20 am
☽□☿ **10:23 am** 7:23 am
☉⚹♅ **1:45 pm** 10:45 am
☽☌♅ **8:34 pm** 5:34 pm
☽⚹☉ **9:06 pm** 6:06 pm

28 FRIDAY
☽⊼♃ **5:55 pm** 2:55 pm
☽△♄ **7:20 pm** 4:20 pm
☽⚹♆ **8:38 pm** 5:38 pm

29 SATURDAY
☽△♇ **3:08 am** 12:08 am
☽⊻♀ **8:01 am** 5:01 am
☽⚹♂ **2:38 pm** 11:38 am
☽⚹☿ **8:51 pm** 5:51 pm

30 SUNDAY
☽⊻♅ **3:38 am** 12:38 am
☽⊻☉ **8:09 am** 5:09 am
☽☍♃ **11:06 pm** 8:06 pm
☽⊼♄ 9:34 pm
☽□♆ 11:03 pm

Eastern time in bold type
Pacific time in medium type

JUNE 2019

DATE	SID.TIME	SUN	MOON	NODE	MERCURY	VENUS	MARS	JUPITER	SATURN	URANUS	NEPTUNE	PLUTO	CERES	PALLAS	JUNO	VESTA	CHIRON
1 Sa	16 36 45	10 ♊ 14 39	10 ♉ 19	18 ♋ 11 ℞	22 ♊ 34	20 ♉ 10	10 ♋ 13	20 ♐ 42 ℞	19 ♑ 43 ℞	4 ♉ 40	18 ♓ 37	22 ♑ 50 ℞	6 ♐ 38 ℞	10 ♎ 23	20 ♋ 12	26 ♈ 29	5 ♈ 20
2 Su	16 40 42	11 12 11	23 26	18 05	24 33	21 24	10 52	20 34	19 41	4 43	18 37	22 49	6 24	10 23	20 42	26 55	5 22
3 M	16 44 38	12 09 42	6 ♊ 52	17 59	26 31	22 37	11 30	20 27	19 38	4 46	18 38	22 48	6 11	10 24	21 11	27 20	5 23
4 T	16 48 35	13 07 12	20 34	17 55	28 26	23 50	12 09	20 19	19 34	4 48	18 38	22 47	5 58	10 26	21 40	27 45	5 25
5 W	16 52 31	14 04 40	4 ♋ 30	17 53 D	0 ♋ 18	25 03	12 47	20 12	19 31	4 51	18 39	22 46	5 45	10 28	22 10	28 10	5 27
6 Th	16 56 28	15 02 08	18 36	17 52	2 08	26 16	13 26	20 04	19 28	4 54	18 39	22 45	5 32	10 30	22 39	28 35	5 29
7 F	17 0 25	15 59 35	2 ♌ 49	17 53	3 56	27 29	14 04	19 57	19 25	4 57	18 40	22 44	5 19	10 33	23 08	29 00	5 30
8 Sa	17 4 21	16 57 01	17 04	17 54	5 41	28 42	14 42	19 49	19 22	5 00	18 40	22 43	5 07	10 36	23 38	29 25	5 32
9 Su	17 8 18	17 54 25	1 ♍ 20	17 56	7 23	29 55	15 21	19 41	19 18	5 02	18 41	22 42	4 54	10 40	24 07	29 50	5 33
10 M	17 12 14	18 51 48	15 34	17 56 ℞	9 03	1 ♊ 08	15 59	19 34	19 15	5 05	18 41	22 40	4 42	10 44	24 36	0 ♉ 14	5 35
11 T	17 16 11	19 49 10	29 43	17 56	10 40	2 21	16 38	19 26	19 11	5 08	18 42	22 39	4 30	10 49	25 05	0 39	5 36
12 W	17 20 7	20 46 31	13 ♎ 46	17 55	12 14	3 34	17 16	19 18	19 08	5 10	18 42	22 38	4 18	10 53	25 35	1 03	5 38
13 Th	17 24 4	21 43 51	27 40	17 52	13 45	4 48	17 54	19 11	19 04	5 13	18 42	22 37	4 06	10 59	26 04	1 28	5 39
14 F	17 28 0	22 41 10	11 ♏ 25	17 49	15 14	6 01	18 33	19 03	19 00	5 16	18 43	22 36	3 55	11 04	26 33	1 52	5 40
15 Sa	17 31 57	23 38 28	24 57	17 45	16 40	7 14	19 11	18 55	18 57	5 18	18 43	22 34	3 44	11 10	27 02	2 16	5 41
16 Su	17 35 54	24 35 46	8 ♐ 16	17 42	18 03	8 27	19 49	18 48	18 53	5 21	18 43	22 33	3 33	11 17	27 31	2 40	5 43
17 M	17 39 50	25 33 02	21 19	17 39	19 24	9 40	20 28	18 40	18 49	5 23	18 43	22 32	3 22	11 24	28 00	3 04	5 44
18 T	17 43 47	26 30 19	4 ♑ 07	17 37	20 41	10 53	21 06	18 33	18 45	5 26	18 43	22 31	3 12	11 31	28 30	3 28	5 45
19 W	17 47 43	27 27 34	16 40	17 37 D	21 56	12 07	21 44	18 25	18 41	5 28	18 43	22 29	3 01	11 38	28 59	3 52	5 46
20 Th	17 51 40	28 24 49	28 59	17 37	23 07	13 20	22 22	18 18	18 37	5 31	18 43	22 28	2 51	11 46	29 28	4 16	5 47
21 F	17 55 36	29 22 04	11 ♒ 06	17 38	24 16	14 33	23 01	18 10	18 33	5 33	18 43 ℞	22 27	2 42	11 54	29 57	4 39	5 48
22 Sa	17 59 33	0 ♋ 19 19	23 03	17 40	25 21	15 46	23 39	18 03	18 29	5 35	18 43	22 26	2 33	12 03	0 ♌ 26	5 03	5 49
23 Su	18 3 30	1 16 33	4 ♓ 56	17 41	26 24	17 00	24 17	17 56	18 25	5 37	18 43	22 24	2 23	12 12	0 55	5 26	5 50
24 M	18 7 26	2 13 47	16 47	17 42	27 23	18 13	24 55	17 49	18 21	5 40	18 43	22 23	2 15	12 21	1 24	5 49	5 51
25 T	18 11 23	3 11 00	28 41	17 43 ℞	28 18	19 26	25 34	17 41	18 17	5 42	18 43	22 22	2 06	12 30	1 53	6 12	5 51
26 W	18 15 19	4 08 14	10 ♈ 44	17 43	29 11	20 39	26 12	17 34	18 13	5 44	18 43	22 20	1 58	12 40	2 22	6 35	5 52
27 Th	18 19 16	5 05 28	22 59	17 42	29 59	21 53	26 50	17 27	18 08	5 46	18 43	22 19	1 51	12 50	2 51	6 58	5 53
28 F	18 23 12	6 02 42	5 ♉ 30	17 41	0 ♌ 44	23 06	27 28	17 20	18 04	5 48	18 43	22 17	1 43	13 01	3 20	7 21	5 53
29 Sa	18 27 9	6 59 55	18 22	17 40	1 26	24 20	28 07	17 13	18 00	5 50	18 43	22 16	1 36	13 11	3 49	7 44	5 54
30 Su	18 31 5	7 57 09	1 ♊ 36	17 38	2 03	25 33	28 45	17 07	17 56	5 52	18 42	22 15	1 29	13 22	4 18	8 06	5 54

EPHEMERIS CALCULATED FOR 12 MIDNIGHT GREENWICH MEAN TIME. ALL OTHER DATA AND FACING ASPECTARIAN PAGE IN **EASTERN TIME (BOLD)** AND PACIFIC TIME (REGULAR).

JULY 2019

☽ Last Aspect day	ET / hr:mn / PT		asp	☽ Ingress sign	day	ET / hr:mn / PT	
1	**5:48 pm**	2:48 pm	☌ ♀	♋	1	**9:24 pm**	6:24 pm
3	**10:25 am**	7:25 am	☍ ♇	♌	3	**11:19 pm**	8:19 pm
4		11:24 pm	△ ♃	♍	5		9:25 pm
5	**2:24 am**		△ ♃	♍	6	**12:25 am**	
7	**12:50 pm**	9:50 am	△ ♇	♎	7		11:07 pm
7	**12:50 pm**	9:50 am	△ ♇	♎	8	**2:07 am**	
9	**3:36 pm**	12:36 pm	□ ♇	♏	10	**5:29 am**	2:29 am
11	**8:28 pm**	5:28 pm	✶ ♇	♐	12	**11:05 am**	8:05 am
13	**9:30 pm**	6:30 pm	□ ♆	♑	14	**7:05 pm**	4:05 pm
16	**5:38 pm**	2:38 pm	☍ ☉	♒	17	**5:19 am**	2:19 am

☽ Last Aspect day	ET / hr:mn / PT		asp	☽ Ingress sign	day	ET / hr:mn / PT	
18	**11:53 am**	8:53 am	✶ ♃	♓	19	**5:19 pm**	2:19 pm
22	**4:34 am**	1:34 am	△ ☉	♈	22	**6:02 am**	3:02 am
24	**10:48 am**	7:48 am	□ ☿	♉	24	**5:42 pm**	2:42 pm
26		9:28 pm	✶ ♀	♊	26		11:29 pm
27	**12:28 am**		✶ ♀	♊	27	**2:29 am**	
28	**11:24 am**	8:24 am	□ ♆	♋	29	**7:31 am**	4:31 am
30	**11:32 pm**	8:32 pm	☌ ☿	♌	31	**9:18 am**	6:18 am

☽ Phases & Eclipses phase	day	ET / hr:mn / PT	
New Moon	2	**3:16 pm**	12:16 pm
●	2	10° ♋	38'
2nd Quarter	9	**6:55 am**	3:55 am
Full Moon	16	**5:38 pm**	2:38 pm
●	16	24° ♑	04'
4th Quarter	24	**9:18 pm**	6:18 pm
New Moon	31	**11:12 pm**	8:12 pm

Planet Ingress		day	ET / hr:mn / PT	
♂	♌	1	**7:19 pm**	4:19 pm
♀	♋	3	**11:18 am**	8:18 am
☿	♋	19	**3:06 am**	12:06 am
☉	♌	22	**10:50 pm**	7:50 pm
♀	♌	27	**9:54 pm**	6:54 pm

Planetary Motion		day	ET / hr:mn / PT	
☿	℞	7	**7:14 pm**	4:14 pm
⚷	℞	8	**7:40 pm**	4:40 pm
⚳	D	17	**3:06 pm**	12:06 pm
☿	D	31	**11:58 pm**	8:58 pm

1 MONDAY
☽ ⚻ ♄ **12:34 am**
☽ □ ♆ **2:03 am**
☽ ⚻ ♇ **8:06 am** 5:06 am
☽ ☌ ♀ **5:48 pm** 2:48 pm
☽ ⚺ ♂ **9:30 pm** 6:30 pm
☽ ⚺ ☿ 11:50 pm

2 TUESDAY
☽ ⚺ ☿ **2:50 am**
☽ ✶ ♅ **7:27 am** 4:27 am
☽ ☌ ☉ **3:16 pm** 12:16 pm
☽ ⚻ ♃ 10:29 pm

3 WEDNESDAY
☽ ⚻ ♃ **1:29 am**
☽ ☍ ♄ **3:01 am** 12:01 am
☽ △ ♆ **4:40 am** 1:40 am
☽ ☍ ♇ **10:25 am** 7:25 am
☽ ⚺ ♀ 9:25 pm
☽ ☌ ♂ 10:41 pm

4 THURSDAY
☽ ⚺ ♀ **12:25 am**
☽ ☌ ♂ **1:41 am**
☽ ☌ ☿ **5:50 am** 2:50 am
☽ □ ♅ **9:11 am** 6:11 am
☽ ⚺ ☉ **8:10 pm** 5:10 pm
☽ △ ♃ 11:24 pm

5 FRIDAY
☽ △ ♃ **2:24 am**
☽ ⚻ ♄ **4:02 am** 1:02 am
☽ ⚻ ♆ **5:53 am** 2:53 am
♀ ⚺ ♂ **6:32 am** 3:32 am
☽ ⚻ ♇ **11:30 am** 8:30 am

6 SATURDAY
☽ ⚺ ♂ **5:01 am** 2:01 am
☽ ✶ ♀ **6:00 am** 3:00 am
☽ ⚺ ☿ **7:36 am** 4:36 am
☽ △ ♅ **10:24 am** 7:24 am
☽ ✶ ☉ 9:49 pm
☿ ⚺ ♀ 11:26 pm

7 SUNDAY
☽ ✶ ☉ **12:49 am**
☿ ⚺ ♀ **2:26 am**
☽ □ ♃ **3:20 am** 12:20 am
☽ △ ♄ **5:04 am** 2:04 am
☽ ☍ ♆ **7:11 am** 4:11 am
☽ △ ♇ **12:50 pm** 9:50 am

8 MONDAY
☽ ✶ ♂ **9:09 am** 6:09 am
☽ ✶ ☿ **9:37 am** 6:37 am
♀ ✶ ♅ **11:32 am** 8:32 am
☉ ⚻ ♃ **11:48 am** 8:48 am
☽ ⚻ ♅ **12:28 pm** 9:28 am
☽ □ ♀ **12:33 pm** 9:33 am
☿ ☌ ♂ **6:27 pm** 3:27 pm

9 TUESDAY
☽ ✶ ♃ **5:30 am** 2:30 am
☽ □ ☉ **6:55 am** 3:55 am
☽ □ ♄ **7:22 am** 4:22 am
☽ ⚻ ♆ **9:47 am** 6:47 am
☉ ☍ ♄ **1:07 pm** 10:07 am
☽ □ ♇ **3:36 pm** 12:36 pm

10 WEDNESDAY
☽ □ ☿ **12:48 pm** 9:48 am
☽ □ ♂ **3:20 pm** 12:20 pm
☽ ☍ ♅ **4:21 pm** 1:21 pm
☽ △ ♀ **9:29 pm** 6:29 pm
☉ △ ♆ 9:31 pm

11 THURSDAY
☉ △ ♆ **12:31 am**
☽ ⚺ ♃ **9:40 am** 6:40 am
☽ ✶ ♄ **11:42 am** 8:42 am
♂ □ ♅ **2:01 pm** 11:01 am
☽ △ ♆ **2:28 pm** 11:28 am
☽ △ ☉ **3:33 pm** 12:33 pm
☽ ✶ ♇ **8:28 pm** 5:28 pm

12 FRIDAY
☽ △ ☿ **5:33 pm** 2:33 pm
☽ ⚻ ♅ **10:33 pm** 7:33 pm
☽ △ ♂ 9:10 pm

13 SATURDAY
☽ △ ♂ **12:10 am**
☽ ⚻ ♀ **9:30 am** 6:30 am
☽ ☌ ♃ **4:11 pm** 1:11 pm
☽ ⚺ ♄ **6:21 pm** 3:21 pm
☽ □ ♆ **9:30 pm** 6:30 pm

14 SUNDAY
☽ ⚻ ☉ **3:08 am** 12:08 am
☽ ⚺ ♇ **3:44 am** 12:44 am
☉ ☍ ♇ **10:51 am** 7:51 am
☽ ⚻ ☿ **11:53 pm** 8:53 pm

15 MONDAY
☽ △ ♅ **7:08 am** 4:08 am
☽ ⚻ ♂ **11:44 am** 8:44 am
☽ ☍ ♀ 9:42 pm
☽ ⚺ ♃ 10:01 pm

16 TUESDAY
☽ ☍ ♀ **12:42 am**
☽ ⚺ ♃ **1:01 am**
☽ ☌ ♄ **3:18 am** 12:18 am
♀ ⚻ ♃ **3:44 am** 12:44 am
☽ ✶ ♆ **6:52 am** 3:52 am
☽ ☌ ♇ **1:16 pm** 10:16 am
☽ ☍ ☉ **5:38 pm** 2:38 pm
♀ ☍ ♄ 10:34 pm

17 WEDNESDAY
♀ ☍ ♄ **1:34 am**
☽ ☍ ☿ **7:39 am** 4:39 am
☽ □ ♅ **5:54 pm** 2:54 pm
☽ ☍ ♂ 10:50 pm

18 THURSDAY
☽ ☍ ♂ **1:50 am**
☽ ✶ ♃ **11:53 am** 8:53 am
♀ △ ♆ **2:03 pm** 11:03 am
☽ ⚺ ♄ **2:15 pm** 11:15 am
☽ ⚺ ♆ **6:13 pm** 3:13 pm
☽ ⚻ ♀ **6:42 pm** 3:42 pm
☽ ⚺ ♇ 9:45 pm

19 FRIDAY
☽ ⚺ ♇ **12:45 am**
☽ ⚻ ☉ **10:33 am** 7:33 am
☽ ⚻ ☿ **4:33 pm** 1:33 pm

20 SATURDAY
☽ ✶ ♅ **6:16 am** 3:16 am
☽ ⚻ ♂ **5:39 pm** 2:39 pm
☽ □ ♃ 9:06 pm
☽ ✶ ♄ 11:28 pm

21 SUNDAY
☽ □ ♃ **12:06 am**
☽ ✶ ♄ **2:28 am**
♀ ☍ ♇ **4:32 am** 1:32 am
☽ ☌ ♆ **6:46 am** 3:46 am
☉ ☌ ☿ **8:34 am** 5:34 am
☽ ✶ ♇ **1:18 pm** 10:18 am
☽ △ ♀ **2:20 pm** 11:20 am
☽ △ ☿ 10:58 pm

22 MONDAY
☽ △ ☿ **1:58 am**
☽ △ ☉ **4:34 am** 1:34 am
☽ ⚺ ♅ **7:01 pm** 4:01 pm

23 TUESDAY
☽ △ ♂ **9:34 am** 6:34 am
☽ △ ♃ **12:14 pm** 9:14 am
☽ □ ♄ **2:31 pm** 11:31 am
☽ ⚺ ♆ **6:59 pm** 3:59 pm
☽ □ ♇ 10:20 pm

24 WEDNESDAY
☽ □ ♇ **1:20 am**
☽ □ ♀ **9:12 am** 6:12 am
☽ □ ☿ **10:48 am** 7:48 am
☿ ☌ ♀ **8:26 pm** 5:26 pm
☽ □ ☉ **9:18 pm** 6:18 pm

25 THURSDAY
☽ ☌ ♅ **6:17 am** 3:17 am
♂ △ ♃ **8:23 am** 5:23 am
☽ ⚻ ♃ **10:24 pm** 7:24 pm
☽ □ ♂ **11:12 pm** 8:12 pm
☽ △ ♄ 9:29 pm

26 FRIDAY
☽ △ ♄ **12:29 am**
☽ ✶ ♆ **4:59 am** 1:59 am
☽ △ ♇ **10:57 am** 7:57 am
☽ ✶ ☿ **5:44 pm** 2:44 pm
♂ ⚻ ♄ **10:41 pm** 7:41 pm
☽ ✶ ♀ 9:28 pm

27 SATURDAY
☽ ✶ ♀ **12:28 am**
☽ ✶ ☉ **10:16 am** 7:16 am
☽ ⚺ ♅ **2:20 pm** 11:20 am

28 SUNDAY
☽ ☍ ♃ **5:08 am** 2:08 am
☽ ⚻ ♄ **7:00 am** 4:00 am
☽ ✶ ♂ **8:45 am** 5:45 am
☽ □ ♆ **11:24 am** 8:24 am
☽ ⚻ ♇ **4:57 pm** 1:57 pm
☽ ⚺ ☿ **9:55 pm** 6:55 pm

29 MONDAY
☽ ⚺ ♀ **10:44 am** 7:44 am
☽ ⚺ ☉ **6:34 pm** 3:34 pm
☽ ✶ ♅ **6:37 pm** 3:37 pm
☉ □ ♅ **7:14 pm** 4:14 pm

30 TUESDAY
☽ ⚻ ♃ **8:17 am** 5:17 am
☽ ☍ ♄ **9:57 am** 6:57 am
☽ ⚺ ♂ **2:09 pm** 11:09 am
☽ △ ♆ **2:15 pm** 11:15 am
♂ ⚻ ♆ **4:09 pm** 1:09 pm
☽ ☍ ♇ **7:27 pm** 4:27 pm
☽ ☌ ☿ **11:32 pm** 8:32 pm

31 WEDNESDAY
☽ ☌ ♀ **4:51 pm** 1:51 pm
☽ □ ♅ **7:54 pm** 4:54 pm
☽ ☌ ☉ **11:12 pm** 8:12 pm

Eastern time in bold type
Pacific time in medium type

JULY 2019

DATE	SID.TIME	SUN	MOON	NODE	MERCURY	VENUS	MARS	JUPITER	SATURN	URANUS	NEPTUNE	PLUTO	CERES	PALLAS	JUNO	VESTA	CHIRON
1 M	18 35 2	8 ♋ 54 23	15 ♊ 12	17 ♋ 37 ℞	2 ♌ 36	26 ♊ 46	29 ♋ 23	17 ♐ 00 ℞	17 ♑ 51 ℞	5 ♉ 54	18 ♓ 42 ℞	22 ♑ 13 ℞	1 ♐ 23 ℞	13 ♎ 34	4 ♌ 46	8 ♉ 28	5 ♈ 55
2 T	18 38 59	9 51 37	29 11	17 37	3 06	28 00	0 ♌ 01	16 53	17 47	5 56	18 42	22 12	1 17	13 45	5 15	8 51	5 55
3 W	18 42 55	10 48 50	13 ♋ 28	17 36D	3 31	29 13	0 39	16 47	17 43	5 58	18 41	22 10	1 11	13 57	5 44	9 13	5 55
4 Th	18 46 52	11 46 04	27 59	17 36	3 51	0 ♋ 27	1 17	16 41	17 38	6 00	18 41	22 09	1 06	14 10	6 13	9 35	5 56
5 F	18 50 48	12 43 18	12 ♌ 38	17 37	4 07	1 40	1 56	16 34	17 34	6 02	18 41	22 08	1 01	14 22	6 42	9 57	5 56
6 Sa	18 54 45	13 40 31	27 18	17 37	4 19	2 54	2 34	16 28	17 29	6 04	18 40	22 06	0 57	14 35	7 10	10 19	5 56
7 Su	18 58 41	14 37 44	11 ♍ 54	17 37	4 26 ℞	4 07	3 12	16 22	17 25	6 05	18 40	22 05	0 52	14 48	7 39	10 40	5 56
8 M	19 2 38	15 34 57	26 21	17 38	4 28	5 21	3 50	16 16	17 21	6 07	18 39	22 03	0 49	15 01	8 08	11 02	5 56 ℞
9 T	19 6 34	16 32 09	10 ♎ 35	17 38 ℞	4 25	6 34	4 28	16 11	17 16	6 09	18 39	22 02	0 45	15 15	8 36	11 23	5 56
10 W	19 10 31	17 29 21	24 33	17 38D	4 18	7 48	5 06	16 05	17 12	6 10	18 38	22 00	0 42	15 29	9 05	11 44	5 56
11 Th	19 14 28	18 26 33	8 ♏ 16	17 38	4 06	9 01	5 44	16 00	17 07	6 12	18 37	21 59	0 39	15 43	9 34	12 05	5 56
12 F	19 18 24	19 23 45	21 42	17 38	3 50	10 15	6 23	15 54	17 03	6 13	18 37	21 57	0 37	15 57	10 02	12 26	5 56
13 Sa	19 22 21	20 20 58	4 ♐ 52	17 38	3 29	11 28	7 01	15 49	16 58	6 15	18 36	21 56	0 35	16 11	10 31	12 47	5 56
14 Su	19 26 17	21 18 10	17 47	17 38	3 04	12 42	7 39	15 44	16 54	6 16	18 35	21 54	0 33	16 26	10 59	13 08	5 56
15 M	19 30 14	22 15 22	0 ♑ 29	17 39	2 36	13 56	8 17	15 39	16 50	6 18	18 35	21 53	0 32	16 41	11 28	13 28	5 55
16 T	19 34 10	23 12 34	12 58	17 39 ℞	2 04	15 09	8 55	15 34	16 45	6 19	18 34	21 52	0 31	16 56	11 56	13 48	5 55
17 W	19 38 7	24 09 47	25 16	17 39	1 29	16 23	9 33	15 30	16 41	6 20	18 33	21 50	0 31 D	17 12	12 25	14 08	5 55
18 Th	19 42 3	25 07 00	7 ♒ 25	17 39	0 51	17 36	10 11	15 25	16 37	6 21	18 32	21 49	0 31	17 27	12 53	14 28	5 54
19 F	19 46 0	26 04 14	19 25	17 38	0 12	18 50	10 49	15 21	16 32	6 23	18 32	21 47	0 31	17 43	13 21	14 48	5 54
20 Sa	19 49 57	27 01 28	1 ♓ 20	17 37	29 ♋ 31	20 04	11 27	15 17	16 28	6 24	18 31	21 46	0 32	17 59	13 50	15 08	5 53
21 Su	19 53 53	27 58 42	13 11	17 35	28 50	21 18	12 05	15 13	16 24	6 25	18 30	21 44	0 33	18 16	14 18	15 27	5 53
22 M	19 57 50	28 55 58	25 02	17 34	28 09	22 31	12 43	15 09	16 19	6 26	18 29	21 43	0 34	18 32	14 46	15 47	5 52
23 T	20 1 46	29 53 13	6 ♈ 56	17 32	27 29	23 45	13 21	15 06	16 15	6 27	18 28	21 41	0 36	18 49	15 15	16 06	5 51
24 W	20 5 43	0 ♌ 50 30	18 58	17 31	26 51	24 59	13 59	15 02	16 11	6 28	18 27	21 40	0 38	19 06	15 43	16 25	5 51
25 Th	20 9 39	1 47 48	1 ♉ 11	17 31 D	26 15	26 13	14 38	14 59	16 07	6 29	18 26	21 39	0 40	19 23	16 11	16 44	5 50
26 F	20 13 36	2 45 06	13 40	17 31	25 41	27 26	15 16	14 56	16 03	6 30	18 25	21 37	0 43	19 40	16 39	17 02	5 49
27 Sa	20 17 32	3 42 26	26 28	17 32	25 12	28 40	15 54	14 53	15 58	6 31	18 24	21 36	0 46	19 57	17 07	17 21	5 48
28 Su	20 21 29	4 39 46	9 ♊ 41	17 33	24 47	29 54	16 32	14 50	15 54	6 31	18 23	21 34	0 49	20 15	17 35	17 39	5 47
29 M	20 25 26	5 37 08	23 18	17 35	24 26	1 ♌ 08	17 10	14 47	15 50	6 32	18 22	21 33	0 53	20 33	18 03	17 57	5 46
30 T	20 29 22	6 34 30	7 ♋ 22	17 36 ℞	24 11	2 22	17 48	14 45	15 46	6 33	18 21	21 31	0 57	20 51	18 31	18 15	5 45
31 W	20 33 19	7 31 53	21 50	17 36	24 01	3 36	18 26	14 43	15 42	6 33	18 20	21 30	1 02	21 09	18 59	18 32	5 44

EPHEMERIS CALCULATED FOR 12 MIDNIGHT GREENWICH MEAN TIME. ALL OTHER DATA AND FACING ASPECTARIAN PAGE IN **EASTERN TIME (BOLD)** AND PACIFIC TIME (REGULAR).

AUGUST 2019

☽ Last Aspect day	ET / hr:mn / PT		asp	☽ Ingress sign	day	ET / hr:mn / PT	
1	**4:48 pm**	1:48 pm	☌♂	♍	2	**9:20 am**	6:20 am
3		9:27 pm	⚹☿	♎	4	**9:30 am**	6:30 am
4	**12:27 am**		⚹☿	♎	4	**9:30 am**	6:30 am
6	**3:36 am**	12:36 am	□☿	♏	6	**11:31 am**	8:31 am
8	**10:58 am**	7:58 am	△☿	♐	8	**4:35 pm**	1:35 pm
10	**3:50 pm**	12:50 pm	△♂	♑	10		9:50 pm
10	**3:50 pm**	12:50 pm	△♂	♑	11	**12:50 am**	
12	**6:11 pm**	3:11 pm	☌♇	♒	13	**11:35 am**	8:35 am
15	**9:02 pm**	6:02 pm	☍♂	♓	15	**11:49 pm**	8:49 pm
17	**6:35 pm**	3:35 pm	⚹♇	♈	18	**12:33 pm**	9:33 am
20		9:06 pm	△♀	♉	20		9:37 pm
21	**12:06 am**		△♀	♉	21	**12:37 am**	
22	**5:33 pm**	2:33 pm	△♇	♊	23	**10:34 am**	7:34 am
24		11:58 pm	⚹☿	♋	25	**5:05 pm**	2:05 pm
25	**2:58 am**		⚹☿	♋	25	**5:05 pm**	2:05 pm
27	**4:55 am**	1:55 am	☍♇	♌	27	**7:53 pm**	4:53 pm
28	**8:07 pm**	5:07 pm	△♃	♍	29	**7:57 pm**	4:57 pm
31	**4:46 am**	1:46 am	△♇	♎	31	**7:08 pm**	4:08 pm

☽ Phases & Eclipses phase	day	ET / hr:mn / PT	
2nd Quarter	7	**1:31 pm**	10:31 am
Full Moon	15	**8:29 am**	5:29 am
4th Quarter	23	**10:56 am**	7:56 am
New Moon	30	**6:37 am**	3:37 am

Planet Ingress		day	ET / hr:mn / PT	
☿	♌	11	**3:46 pm**	12:46 pm
♂	♍	17		10:18 pm
♂	♍	18	**1:18 am**	
♀	♍	21	**5:06 am**	2:06 am
☉	♍	23	**6:02 am**	3:02 am
✳	♍	23	**8:00 pm**	5:00 pm
♀	♏	26	**4:56 am**	1:56 am
☿	♍	29	**3:48 am**	12:48 am

Planetary Motion		day	ET / hr:mn / PT	
♃	D	11	**9:37 am**	6:37 am
♅	℞	11	**10:27 pm**	7:27 pm

1 THURSDAY
☽△♃ **8:53 am** 5:53 am
☽⚻♄ **10:23 am** 7:23 am
☽⚻♆ **2:41 pm** 11:41 am
☽☌♂ **4:48 pm** 1:48 pm
☽⚻♇ **7:44 pm** 4:44 pm
☽⚺☿ **11:47 pm** 8:47 pm

2 FRIDAY
♀□♅ **6:00 am** 3:00 am
☽△♅ **7:50 pm** 4:50 pm
☽⚺♀ **9:03 pm** 6:03 pm
☽⚺☉ 11:20 pm

3 SATURDAY
☽⚺☉ **2:20 am**
☽□♃ **8:39 am** 5:39 am
☽△♄ **10:03 am** 7:03 am
☽☍♆ **2:30 pm** 11:30 am
☽⚺♂ **6:50 pm** 3:50 pm
☽△♇ **7:35 pm** 4:35 pm
☽⚹☿ 9:27 pm

4 SUNDAY
☽⚹☿ **12:27 am**
♂⚻♇ **11:59 am** 8:59 am
☽⚻♅ **8:17 pm** 5:17 pm
☽⚹♀ 11:00 pm

5 MONDAY
☽⚹♀ **2:00 am**
☽⚹☉ **6:25 am** 3:25 am
☽⚹♃ **9:27 am** 6:27 am
☽□♄ **10:46 am** 7:46 am
☽⚻♆ **3:33 pm** 12:33 pm
☽□♇ **8:51 pm** 5:51 pm
☽⚹♂ **10:26 pm** 7:26 pm

6 TUESDAY
☽□☿ **3:36 am** 12:36 am
☽☍♅ **10:55 pm** 7:55 pm

7 WEDNESDAY
☉△♃ **3:31 am** 12:31 am
☽□♀ **10:01 am** 7:01 am
☽⚺♃ **12:48 pm** 9:48 am
☽□☉ **1:31 pm** 10:31 am
☽⚹♄ **2:02 pm** 11:02 am
☽△♆ **7:15 pm** 4:15 pm
☉⚻♄ **8:24 pm** 5:24 pm
☽⚹♇ 9:53 pm

8 THURSDAY
☽⚹♇ **12:53 am**
☽□♂ **5:16 am** 2:16 am
☽△☿ **10:58 am** 7:58 am
♀△♃ **4:28 pm** 1:28 pm

9 FRIDAY
♀⚻♄ **4:24 am** 1:24 am
☽⚻♅ **4:43 am** 1:43 am
☽☌♃ **7:25 pm** 4:25 pm
☽⚺♄ **8:30 pm** 5:30 pm
☽△♀ **10:19 pm** 7:19 pm
☽△☉ 9:39 pm
☽□♆ 11:12 pm

10 SATURDAY
☽△☉ **12:39 am**
☽□♆ **2:12 am**
☽⚺♇ **8:09 am** 5:09 am
☽△♂ **3:50 pm** 12:50 pm
☉⚻♆ **8:44 pm** 5:44 pm
☽⚻☿ **11:24 pm** 8:24 pm

11 SUNDAY
☽△♅ **1:37 pm** 10:37 am
♀⚻♆ **1:43 pm** 10:43 am

12 MONDAY
☽⚺♃ **5:00 am** 2:00 am
☽☌♄ **5:53 am** 2:53 am
☽⚹♆ **11:58 am** 8:58 am
☽⚻♀ **2:31 pm** 11:31 am
☽⚻☉ **3:24 pm** 12:24 pm
☽☌♇ **6:11 pm** 3:11 pm

13 TUESDAY
☽⚻♂ **5:30 am** 2:30 am
☽☍☿ **4:33 pm** 1:33 pm
☽□♅ 9:47 pm
☉☌♀ 11:07 pm
♀⚻♇ 11:08 pm
☉⚻♇ 11:08 pm

14 WEDNESDAY
☽□♅ **12:47 am**
☉☌♀ **2:07 am**
♀⚻♇ **2:08 am**
☉⚻♇ **2:08 am**
☽⚹♃ **4:37 pm** 1:37 pm
☽⚺♄ **5:15 pm** 2:15 pm
☽⚺♆ **11:37 pm** 8:37 pm

15 THURSDAY
☽⚺♇ **6:00 am** 3:00 am
☽☍☉ **8:29 am** 5:29 am
☽☍♀ **9:16 am** 6:16 am
☽☍♂ **9:02 pm** 6:02 pm

16 FRIDAY
☿□♅ **1:07 pm** 10:07 am
☽⚹♅ **1:11 pm** 10:11 am
☽⚻☿ **1:12 pm** 10:12 am

17 SATURDAY
☽□♃ **5:17 am** 2:17 am
☽⚹♄ **5:36 am** 2:36 am
☽☌♆ **12:08 pm** 9:08 am
☽⚹♇ **6:35 pm** 3:35 pm
☽⚻☉ 11:32 pm

18 SUNDAY
☽⚻☉ **2:32 am**
☽⚻♀ **5:02 am** 2:02 am
☽⚻♂ **1:11 pm** 10:11 am
☽⚺♅ 10:51 pm

19 MONDAY
☽⚺♅ **1:51 am**
♃⚺♄ **10:47 am** 7:47 am
☽△☿ **11:41 am** 8:41 am
☽□♄ **5:56 pm** 2:56 pm
☽△♃ **5:58 pm** 2:58 pm
☽⚺♆ 9:30 pm

20 TUESDAY
☽⚺♆ **12:30 am**
☽□♇ **6:53 am** 3:53 am
☽△☉ **8:01 pm** 5:01 pm
☽△♀ 9:06 pm

21 WEDNESDAY
☽△♀ **12:06 am**
☿⚻♄ **4:26 am** 1:26 am
☽△♂ **4:33 am** 1:33 am
☿△♃ **6:05 am** 3:05 am
☽☌♅ **1:33 pm** 10:33 am

22 THURSDAY
☽△♄ **4:57 am** 1:57 am
☽⚻♃ **5:21 am** 2:21 am
☽□☿ **9:22 am** 6:22 am
☽⚹♆ **11:23 am** 8:23 am
☽△♇ **5:33 pm** 2:33 pm
☿⚻♆ **10:26 pm** 7:26 pm

23 FRIDAY
☽□☉ **10:56 am** 7:56 am
☽□♀ **4:17 pm** 1:17 pm
☽□♂ **5:19 pm** 2:19 pm
☽⚺♅ **10:48 pm** 7:48 pm

24 SATURDAY
♀☌♂ **1:05 pm** 10:05 am
☽⚻♄ **1:12 pm** 10:12 am
☽☍♃ **1:53 pm** 10:53 am
☿⚻♇ **2:14 pm** 11:14 am
☽□♆ **7:18 pm** 4:18 pm
☽⚻♇ 10:06 pm
☽⚹☿ 11:58 pm

25 SUNDAY
☽⚻♇ **1:06 am**
☽⚹☿ **2:58 am**
☽⚹☉ **9:33 pm** 6:33 pm
☽⚹♂ 10:59 pm

26 MONDAY
☽⚹♂ **1:59 am**
☽⚹♀ **3:44 am** 12:44 am
☽⚹♅ **4:27 am** 1:27 am
♀△♅ **11:38 am** 8:38 am
☽☍♄ **5:45 pm** 2:45 pm
☽⚻♃ **6:42 pm** 3:42 pm
☽△♆ **11:28 pm** 8:28 pm

27 TUESDAY
☽☍♇ **4:55 am** 1:55 am
☽⚺☿ **2:52 pm** 11:52 am

28 WEDNESDAY
☽⚺☉ **3:36 am** 12:36 am
☽⚺♂ **6:28 am** 3:28 am
☽□♅ **6:29 am** 3:29 am
♂△♅ **6:53 am** 3:53 am
☽⚺♀ **10:26 am** 7:26 am
☽⚻♄ **6:57 pm** 3:57 pm
☽△♃ **8:07 pm** 5:07 pm
☽⚻♆ 9:23 pm

29 THURSDAY
☽⚻♆ **12:23 am**
☽⚻♇ **5:35 am** 2:35 am
☽☌☿ **10:22 pm** 7:22 pm
☉△♅ **11:14 pm** 8:14 pm

30 FRIDAY
☽△♅ **6:09 am** 3:09 am
☽☌☉ **6:37 am** 3:37 am
☽☌♂ **8:15 am** 5:15 am
☽☌♀ **2:13 pm** 11:13 am
☽△♄ **6:14 pm** 3:14 pm
☽□♃ **7:39 pm** 4:39 pm
☽☍♆ **11:35 pm** 8:35 pm

31 SATURDAY
☽△♇ **4:46 am** 1:46 am

Eastern time in bold type
Pacific time in medium type

AUGUST 2019

DATE	SID.TIME	SUN	MOON	NODE	MERCURY	VENUS	MARS	JUPITER	SATURN	URANUS	NEPTUNE	PLUTO	CERES	PALLAS	JUNO	VESTA	CHIRON
1 Th	20 37 15	8 ♌ 29 18	6 ♌ 38	17 ♋ 35 ℞	23 ♋ 57 D	4 ♌ 50	19 ♌ 04	14 ♐ 41 ℞	15 ♑ 38 ℞	6 ♉ 34	18 ♓ 19 ℞	21 ♑ 29 ℞	1 ♐ 06	21 ♎ 27	19 ♌ 27	18 ♉ 50	5 ♈ 43 ℞
2 F	20 41 12	9 26 43	21 38	17 33	23 59	6 04	19 42	14 39	15 35	6 34	18 17	21 27	1 12	21 46	19 55	19 07	5 42
3 Sa	20 45 8	10 24 08	6 ♍ 41	17 31	24 07	7 18	20 20	14 37	15 31	6 35	18 16	21 26	1 17	22 04	20 23	19 24	5 40
4 Su	20 49 5	11 21 35	21 40	17 28	24 22	8 32	20 58	14 36	15 27	6 35	18 15	21 25	1 23	22 23	20 51	19 41	5 39
5 M	20 53 1	12 19 02	6 ♎ 25	17 25	24 43	9 46	21 36	14 34	15 23	6 36	18 14	21 23	1 29	22 42	21 19	19 58	5 38
6 T	20 56 58	13 16 30	20 52	17 22	25 11	11 00	22 14	14 33	15 20	6 36	18 12	21 22	1 35	23 01	21 47	20 14	5 37
7 W	21 0 55	14 13 58	4 ♏ 55	17 21 D	25 45	12 14	22 53	14 32	15 16	6 36	18 11	21 21	1 42	23 20	22 14	20 30	5 35
8 Th	21 4 51	15 11 27	18 35	17 20	26 26	13 28	23 31	14 31	15 12	6 37	18 10	21 19	1 49	23 40	22 42	20 46	5 34
9 F	21 8 48	16 08 57	1 ♐ 52	17 21	27 13	14 42	24 09	14 31	15 09	6 37	18 09	21 18	1 56	23 59	23 10	21 02	5 32
10 Sa	21 12 44	17 06 28	14 49	17 23	28 07	15 56	24 47	14 31	15 06	6 37	18 07	21 17	2 04	24 19	23 37	21 17	5 31
11 Su	21 16 41	18 04 00	27 29	17 24	29 06	17 10	25 25	14 30 D	15 02	6 37	18 06	21 15	2 12	24 39	24 05	21 32	5 29
12 M	21 20 37	19 01 33	9 ♑ 54	17 25 ℞	0 ♌ 12	18 24	26 03	14 30	14 59	6 37 ℞	18 04	21 14	2 20	24 59	24 32	21 47	5 27
13 T	21 24 34	19 59 06	22 08	17 26	1 24	19 38	26 41	14 30	14 56	6 37	18 03	21 13	2 28	25 19	25 00	22 02	5 26
14 W	21 28 30	20 56 41	4 ♒ 13	17 24	2 41	20 52	27 19	14 31	14 53	6 37	18 02	21 12	2 37	25 39	25 27	22 17	5 24
15 Th	21 32 27	21 54 16	16 12	17 21	4 03	22 07	27 57	14 31	14 50	6 37	18 00	21 10	2 46	26 00	25 55	22 31	5 22
16 F	21 36 24	22 51 53	28 06	17 17	5 31	23 21	28 35	14 32	14 47	6 37	17 59	21 09	2 55	26 20	26 22	22 45	5 20
17 Sa	21 40 20	23 49 31	9 ♓ 58	17 11	7 03	24 35	29 13	14 33	14 44	6 36	17 57	21 08	3 05	26 41	26 50	22 59	5 19
18 Su	21 44 17	24 47 11	21 49	17 04	8 40	25 49	29 52	14 34	14 41	6 36	17 56	21 07	3 15	27 02	27 17	23 12	5 17
19 M	21 48 13	25 44 51	3 ♈ 42	16 57	10 21	27 03	0 ♍ 30	14 35	14 38	6 36	17 54	21 06	3 25	27 23	27 44	23 25	5 15
20 T	21 52 10	26 42 34	15 37	16 51	12 05	28 18	1 08	14 37	14 35	6 35	17 53	21 05	3 35	27 44	28 11	23 38	5 13
21 W	21 56 6	27 40 17	27 40	16 45	13 53	29 32	1 46	14 38	14 33	6 35	17 51	21 04	3 46	28 05	28 39	23 51	5 11
22 Th	22 0 3	28 38 03	9 ♉ 52	16 42	15 44	0 ♍ 46	2 24	14 40	14 30	6 34	17 50	21 02	3 57	28 26	29 06	24 03	5 09
23 F	22 3 59	29 35 50	22 19	16 40 D	17 37	2 00	3 02	14 42	14 28	6 34	17 48	21 01	4 08	28 47	29 33	24 15	5 07
24 Sa	22 7 56	0 ♍ 33 39	5 ♊ 03	16 40	19 31	3 15	3 40	14 45	14 25	6 33	17 47	21 00	4 19	29 09	0 ♍ 00	24 27	5 05
25 Su	22 11 53	1 31 30	18 09	16 41	21 28	4 29	4 19	14 47	14 23	6 33	17 45	20 59	4 31	29 30	0 27	24 38	5 03
26 M	22 15 49	2 29 22	1 ♋ 40	16 42	23 25	5 43	4 57	14 49	14 21	6 32	17 44	20 58	4 43	29 52	0 54	24 50	5 00
27 T	22 19 46	3 27 16	15 38	16 43 ℞	25 24	6 58	5 35	14 52	14 19	6 31	17 42	20 57	4 55	0 ♏ 14	1 21	25 00	4 58
28 W	22 23 42	4 25 12	0 ♌ 04	16 42	27 22	8 12	6 13	14 55	14 16	6 31	17 40	20 56	5 07	0 36	1 48	25 11	4 56
29 Th	22 27 39	5 23 10	14 54	16 39	29 21	9 26	6 51	14 58	14 14	6 30	17 39	20 55	5 19	0 58	2 15	25 21	4 54
30 F	22 31 35	6 21 09	0 ♍ 02	16 34	1 ♍ 20	10 41	7 29	15 01	14 13	6 29	17 37	20 54	5 32	1 20	2 42	25 31	4 51
31 Sa	22 35 32	7 19 10	15 18	16 28	3 19	11 55	8 08	15 05	14 11	6 28	17 36	20 54	5 45	1 42	3 08	25 41	4 49

EPHEMERIS CALCULATED FOR 12 MIDNIGHT GREENWICH MEAN TIME. ALL OTHER DATA AND FACING ASPECTARIAN PAGE IN **EASTERN TIME (BOLD)** AND PACIFIC TIME (REGULAR).

SEPTEMBER 2019

☽ Last Aspect day	ET / hr:mn / PT	asp	☽ Ingress sign	day	ET / hr:mn / PT
2	**4:34 am** 1:34 am	□♇	♏	2	**7:35 pm** 4:35 pm
4	**6:58 am** 3:58 am	✶♇	♐	4	**11:08 pm** 8:08 pm
6	**12:03 pm** 9:03 am	□♀	♑	7	**6:37 am** 3:37 am
9	**4:30 am** 1:30 am	△♀	♒	9	**5:24 pm** 2:24 pm
10	10:22 pm	✶♃	♓	12	**5:52 am** 2:52 am
11	**1:22 am**	✶♃	♓	12	**5:52 am** 2:52 am
13	9:33 pm	☍☉	♈	14	**6:32 pm** 3:32 pm
14	**12:33 am**	☍☉	♈	14	**6:32 pm** 3:32 pm
16	**12:03 pm** 9:03 am	□♇	♉	17	**6:31 am** 3:31 am
19	**9:57 am** 6:57 am	△☉	♊	19	**4:58 pm** 1:58 pm
21	**10:41 pm** 7:41 pm	□☉	♋	21	9:50 pm
21	**10:41 pm** 7:41 pm	□☉	♋	22	**12:50 am**
23	**6:05 pm** 3:05 pm	✶♂	♌	24	**5:19 am** 2:19 am
25	**12:14 pm** 9:14 am	✶☿	♍	26	**6:37 am** 3:37 am
27	**11:58 pm** 8:58 pm	☌♂	♎	28	**6:03 am** 3:03 am
29	**10:06 pm** 7:06 pm	☌☿	♏	30	**5:42 am** 2:42 am

☽ Phases & Eclipses phase	day	ET / hr:mn / PT
2nd Quarter	5	**11:10 pm** 8:10 pm
Full Moon	13	9:33 pm
Full Moon	14	**12:33 am**
4th Quarter	21	**10:41 pm** 7:41 pm
New Moon	28	**2:26 pm** 11:26 am

Planet Ingress	day	ET / hr:mn / PT
☿ ♎	14	**3:14 am** 12:14 am
♀ ♎	14	**9:43 am** 6:43 am
☉ ♎	23	**3:50 am** 12:50 am

Planetary Motion		day	ET / hr:mn / PT
♄	D	18	**4:47 am** 1:47 am
⚴	R	23	**11:43 pm** 8:43 pm

1 SUNDAY
☽ ⚺ ☿ **4:39 am** 1:39 am
☽ ⚻ ♅ **5:22 am** 2:22 am
☽ ⚺ ☉ **9:09 am** 6:09 am
☽ ⚺ ♂ **9:39 am** 6:39 am
☿ △ ♅ **10:11 am** 7:11 am
♀ △ ♄ **2:49 pm** 11:49 am
☽ □ ♄ **5:40 pm** 2:40 pm
☽ ⚺ ♀ **5:56 pm** 2:56 pm
☽ ✶ ♃ **7:24 pm** 4:24 pm
☽ ⚻ ♆ **11:10 pm** 8:10 pm

2 MONDAY
☽ □ ♇ **4:34 am** 1:34 am
☉ ☌ ♂ **6:42 am** 3:42 am
♀ □ ♃ **12:26 pm** 9:26 am

3 TUESDAY
☽ ☍ ♅ **6:18 am** 3:18 am
☿ ☌ ♂ **11:40 am** 8:40 am
☽ ✶ ♂ **1:12 pm** 10:12 am
☽ ✶ ☿ **1:21 pm** 10:21 am
☽ ✶ ☉ **1:58 pm** 10:58 am
☽ ✶ ♄ **7:18 pm** 4:18 pm
☽ ⚺ ♃ **9:28 pm** 6:28 pm
☉ ☌ ☿ **9:40 pm** 6:40 pm
☽ ✶ ♀ 9:32 pm
☽ △ ♆ 10:09 pm

4 WEDNESDAY
☽ ✶ ♀ **12:32 am**
☽ △ ♆ **1:09 am**
☽ ✶ ♇ **6:58 am** 3:58 am
♀ ☍ ♆ **7:26 am** 4:26 am

5 THURSDAY
☿ △ ♄ **8:37 am** 5:37 am
☽ ⚻ ♅ **10:36 am** 7:36 am
☽ □ ♂ **8:49 pm** 5:49 pm
☽ □ ☉ **11:10 pm** 8:10 pm
☽ ⚺ ♄ 9:36 pm

6 FRIDAY
☽ ⚺ ♄ **12:36 am**
☿ □ ♃ **3:11 am** 12:11 am
☽ ☌ ♃ **3:20 am** 12:20 am
☽ □ ☿ **3:21 am** 12:21 am
☽ □ ♆ **6:53 am** 3:53 am
☽ □ ♀ **12:03 pm** 9:03 am
☽ ⚺ ♇ **1:12 pm** 10:12 am
☉ △ ♄ **5:56 pm** 2:56 pm
♀ △ ♇ **11:46 pm** 8:46 pm

7 SATURDAY
☿ ☍ ♆ **3:18 am** 12:18 am
☽ △ ♅ **6:47 pm** 3:47 pm

8 SUNDAY
☽ △ ♂ **8:53 am** 5:53 am
☽ ☌ ♄ **9:42 am** 6:42 am
☉ □ ♃ **11:27 am** 8:27 am
☽ ⚺ ♃ **1:04 pm** 10:04 am
☽ △ ☉ **1:11 pm** 10:11 am
☽ ✶ ♆ **4:18 pm** 1:18 pm
☽ △ ☿ **11:02 pm** 8:02 pm
☽ ☌ ♇ **11:03 pm** 8:03 pm
☿ △ ♇ **11:09 pm** 8:09 pm
♂ △ ♄ 9:14 pm

9 MONDAY
♂ △ ♄ **12:14 am**
☽ △ ♀ **4:30 am** 1:30 am

10 TUESDAY
☉ ☍ ♆ **3:24 am** 12:24 am
☽ □ ♅ **5:57 am** 2:57 am
☽ ⚺ ♄ **9:25 am** 6:25 am
☽ ⚻ ♂ 9:02 pm
☽ ✶ ♃ 10:22 pm

11 WEDNESDAY
☽ ⚻ ♂ **12:02 am**
☽ ✶ ♃ **1:22 am**
☽ ⚺ ♆ **4:08 am** 1:08 am
☽ ⚻ ☉ **6:24 am** 3:24 am
☽ ⚺ ♇ **11:08 am** 8:08 am
☽ ⚻ ☿ **9:58 pm** 6:58 pm
☽ ⚻ ♀ **11:47 pm** 8:47 pm

12 THURSDAY
♂ □ ♃ **5:06 am** 2:06 am
☽ ✶ ♅ **6:27 pm** 3:27 pm

13 FRIDAY
☽ ✶ ♄ **10:04 am** 7:04 am
☿ ☌ ♀ **11:11 am** 8:11 am
☽ □ ♃ **2:35 pm** 11:35 am
☉ △ ♇ **3:42 pm** 12:42 pm
☽ ☍ ♂ **4:12 pm** 1:12 pm
☽ ☌ ♆ **4:43 pm** 1:43 pm
☽ ✶ ♇ **11:49 pm** 8:49 pm
☽ ☍ ☉ 9:33 pm
♂ ☍ ♆ 10:25 pm

14 SATURDAY
☽ ☍ ☉ **12:33 am**
♂ ☍ ♆ **1:25 am**
☽ ☍ ♀ **7:34 pm** 4:34 pm
☽ ☍ ☿ **9:08 pm** 6:08 pm

15 SUNDAY
☽ ⚺ ♅ **6:55 am** 3:55 am
☽ □ ♄ **10:29 pm** 7:29 pm

16 MONDAY
☽ △ ♃ **3:29 am** 12:29 am
☽ ⚺ ♆ **4:57 am** 1:57 am
☽ ⚻ ♂ **7:58 am** 4:58 am
☽ □ ♇ **12:03 pm** 9:03 am
☽ ⚻ ☉ **6:06 pm** 3:06 pm

17 TUESDAY
☽ ⚻ ♀ **2:21 pm** 11:21 am
☿ ⚻ ♅ **4:57 pm** 1:57 pm
☽ ☌ ♅ **6:31 pm** 3:31 pm
☽ ⚻ ☿ **6:46 pm** 3:46 pm

18 WEDNESDAY
☽ △ ♄ **9:52 am** 6:52 am
☽ ⚻ ♃ **3:15 pm** 12:15 pm
☽ ✶ ♆ **4:02 pm** 1:02 pm
☽ △ ♂ **10:20 pm** 7:20 pm
☽ △ ♇ **11:02 pm** 8:02 pm

19 THURSDAY
♀ ⚻ ♅ **6:27 am** 3:27 am
☽ △ ☉ **9:57 am** 6:57 am
♂ △ ♇ **11:53 am** 8:53 am

20 FRIDAY
☽ ⚺ ♅ **4:24 am** 1:24 am
☽ △ ♀ **6:50 am** 3:50 am
☽ △ ☿ **1:24 pm** 10:24 am
☽ ⚻ ♄ **7:16 pm** 4:16 pm
☽ ☍ ♃ 9:54 pm
☽ □ ♆ 10:02 pm

21 SATURDAY
☽ ☍ ♃ **12:54 am**
☽ □ ♆ **1:02 am**
☽ ⚻ ♇ **7:47 am** 4:47 am
☽ □ ♂ **10:05 am** 7:05 am
♃ □ ♆ **12:44 pm** 9:44 am
☽ □ ☉ **10:41 pm** 7:41 pm

22 SUNDAY
☽ ✶ ♅ **11:31 am** 8:31 am
☿ □ ♄ **12:19 pm** 9:19 am
☽ □ ♀ **7:30 pm** 4:30 pm
☽ ☍ ♄ 10:39 pm

23 MONDAY
☽ ☍ ♄ **1:39 am**
☽ □ ☿ **3:23 am** 12:23 am
☽ △ ♆ **6:55 am** 3:55 am
☽ ⚻ ♃ **7:22 am** 4:22 am
☽ ☍ ♇ **1:21 pm** 10:21 am
☽ ✶ ♂ **6:05 pm** 3:05 pm

24 TUESDAY
☽ ✶ ☉ **7:12 am** 4:12 am
☿ ⚻ ♆ **9:57 am** 6:57 am
☽ □ ♅ **3:12 pm** 12:12 pm
☿ ✶ ♃ **5:01 pm** 2:01 pm

25 WEDNESDAY
☽ ✶ ♀ **3:35 am** 12:35 am
☽ ⚻ ♄ **4:35 am** 1:35 am
☽ ⚻ ♆ **9:25 am** 6:25 am
☽ △ ♃ **10:21 am** 7:21 am
☽ ✶ ☿ **12:14 pm** 9:14 am
♀ □ ♄ **3:20 pm** 12:20 pm
☽ ⚻ ♇ **3:32 pm** 12:32 pm
☽ ⚺ ♂ **10:15 pm** 7:15 pm

26 THURSDAY
☽ ⚺ ☉ **11:50 am** 8:50 am
☽ △ ♅ **3:53 pm** 12:53 pm
☿ □ ♇ **7:52 pm** 4:52 pm

27 FRIDAY
☽ △ ♄ **4:50 am** 1:50 am
☽ ⚺ ♀ **8:08 am** 5:08 am
☽ ☍ ♆ **9:21 am** 6:21 am
☽ □ ♃ **10:45 am** 7:45 am
☽ △ ♇ **3:20 pm** 12:20 pm
☽ ⚺ ☿ **5:29 pm** 2:29 pm
♀ ⚻ ♆ **10:50 pm** 7:50 pm
☽ ☌ ♂ **11:58 pm** 8:58 pm

28 SATURDAY
☽ ☌ ☉ **2:26 pm** 11:26 am
☽ ⚻ ♅ **3:05 pm** 12:05 pm
♀ ✶ ♃ **7:41 pm** 4:41 pm
☉ ⚻ ♅ 9:14 pm

29 SUNDAY
☉ ⚻ ♅ **12:14 am**
☽ □ ♄ **4:08 am** 1:08 am
☽ ⚻ ♆ **8:33 am** 5:33 am
☽ ✶ ♃ **10:27 am** 7:27 am
☽ ☌ ♀ **11:38 am** 8:38 am
☽ □ ♇ **2:40 pm** 11:40 am
☽ ☌ ☿ **10:06 pm** 7:06 pm
☽ ⚺ ♂ 10:36 pm

30 MONDAY
☽ ⚺ ♂ **1:36 am**
☽ ☍ ♅ **2:56 pm** 11:56 am
☽ ⚺ ☉ **5:48 pm** 2:48 pm
♀ □ ♇ 9:18 pm

Eastern time in bold type
Pacific time in medium type

SEPTEMBER 2019

DATE	SID.TIME	SUN	MOON	NODE	MERCURY	VENUS	MARS	JUPITER	SATURN	URANUS	NEPTUNE	PLUTO	CERES	PALLAS	JUNO	VESTA	CHIRON
1 Su	22 39 28	8 ♍ 17 13	0 ♎ 33	16 ♋ 20 ℞	5 ♍ 17	13 ♍ 10	8 ♍ 46	15 ♐ 08	14 ♑ 09 ℞	6 ♉ 27 ℞	17 ♓ 34 ℞	20 ♑ 53 ℞	5 ♐ 58	2 ♏ 04	3 ♍ 35	25 ♉ 50	4 ♈ 47 ℞
2 M	22 43 25	9 15 16	15 35	16 12	7 15	14 24	9 24	15 12	14 08	6 26	17 32	20 52	6 12	2 27	4 02	25 59	4 44
3 T	22 47 22	10 13 22	0 ♏ 15	16 06	9 12	15 38	10 02	15 16	14 06	6 25	17 31	20 51	6 25	2 49	4 28	26 07	4 42
4 W	22 51 18	11 11 29	14 29	16 01	11 07	16 53	10 41	15 20	14 05	6 24	17 29	20 50	6 39	3 12	4 55	26 15	4 40
5 Th	22 55 15	12 09 37	28 14	15 58	13 02	18 07	11 19	15 25	14 03	6 23	17 27	20 49	6 53	3 34	5 21	26 23	4 37
6 F	22 59 11	13 07 46	11 ♐ 32	15 57 D	14 56	19 22	11 57	15 29	14 02	6 22	17 26	20 49	7 08	3 57	5 48	26 31	4 35
7 Sa	23 3 8	14 05 58	24 25	15 57	16 49	20 36	12 35	15 34	14 01	6 21	17 24	20 48	7 22	4 20	6 14	26 38	4 32
8 Su	23 7 4	15 04 10	6 ♑ 57	15 58 ℞	18 41	21 51	13 14	15 38	14 00	6 19	17 22	20 47	7 37	4 43	6 41	26 45	4 30
9 M	23 11 1	16 02 24	19 14	15 58	20 32	23 05	13 52	15 43	13 59	6 18	17 21	20 46	7 51	5 06	7 07	26 51	4 27
10 T	23 14 57	17 00 40	1 ♒ 18	15 57	22 22	24 19	14 30	15 49	13 58	6 17	17 19	20 46	8 06	5 29	7 33	26 57	4 25
11 W	23 18 54	17 58 57	13 15	15 53	24 10	25 34	15 09	15 54	13 57	6 16	17 17	20 45	8 22	5 52	7 59	27 03	4 22
12 Th	23 22 51	18 57 16	25 08	15 47	25 57	26 48	15 47	15 59	13 57	6 14	17 16	20 45	8 37	6 15	8 26	27 08	4 20
13 F	23 26 47	19 55 37	6 ♓ 59	15 39	27 43	28 03	16 25	16 05	13 56	6 13	17 14	20 44	8 53	6 39	8 52	27 13	4 17
14 Sa	23 30 44	20 53 59	18 50	15 28	29 29	29 17	17 03	16 11	13 56	6 11	17 13	20 43	9 08	7 02	9 18	27 17	4 14
15 Su	23 34 40	21 52 23	0 ♈ 43	15 15	1 ♎ 12	0 ♎ 32	17 42	16 17	13 55	6 10	17 11	20 43	9 24	7 25	9 44	27 21	4 12
16 M	23 38 37	22 50 49	12 40	15 03	2 55	1 46	18 20	16 23	13 55	6 08	17 09	20 42	9 40	7 49	10 10	27 25	4 09
17 T	23 42 33	23 49 17	24 42	14 51	4 37	3 01	18 59	16 29	13 55	6 06	17 08	20 42	9 57	8 13	10 36	27 28	4 06
18 W	23 46 30	24 47 47	6 ♉ 50	14 41	6 18	4 15	19 37	16 35	13 55 D	6 05	17 06	20 41	10 13	8 36	11 01	27 31	4 04
19 Th	23 50 26	25 46 19	19 07	14 33	7 57	5 30	20 15	16 42	13 55	6 03	17 04	20 41	10 29	9 00	11 27	27 33	4 01
20 F	23 54 23	26 44 53	1 ♊ 36	14 28	9 36	6 44	20 54	16 48	13 55	6 01	17 03	20 41	10 46	9 24	11 53	27 35	3 58
21 Sa	23 58 19	27 43 30	14 19	14 25	11 14	7 59	21 32	16 55	13 55	6 00	17 01	20 40	11 03	9 48	12 19	27 37	3 56
22 Su	0 2 16	28 42 09	27 20	14 24 D	12 50	9 14	22 11	17 02	13 55	5 58	16 59	20 40	11 20	10 12	12 44	27 38	3 53
23 M	0 6 13	29 40 50	10 ♋ 43	14 25 ℞	14 26	10 28	22 49	17 09	13 56	5 56	16 58	20 40	11 37	10 36	13 10	27 39	3 50
24 T	0 10 9	0 ♎ 39 33	24 31	14 24	16 01	11 43	23 28	17 16	13 56	5 54	16 56	20 39	11 55	11 00	13 35	27 39 ℞	3 48
25 W	0 14 6	1 38 19	8 ♌ 45	14 23	17 34	12 57	24 06	17 24	13 57	5 52	16 55	20 39	12 12	11 24	14 01	27 39	3 45
26 Th	0 18 2	2 37 07	23 24	14 18	19 07	14 12	24 44	17 31	13 57	5 50	16 53	20 39	12 30	11 48	14 26	27 38	3 42
27 F	0 21 59	3 35 57	8 ♍ 24	14 11	20 39	15 26	25 23	17 39	13 58	5 48	16 52	20 39	12 48	12 12	14 51	27 37	3 39
28 Sa	0 25 55	4 34 49	23 37	14 02	22 10	16 41	26 02	17 47	13 59	5 46	16 50	20 38	13 06	12 37	15 17	27 36	3 37
29 Su	0 29 52	5 33 43	8 ♎ 52	13 51	23 40	17 56	26 40	17 55	14 00	5 44	16 48	20 38	13 24	13 01	15 42	27 34	3 34
30 M	0 33 48	6 32 39	23 58	13 40	25 09	19 10	27 19	18 03	14 01	5 42	16 47	20 38	13 42	13 25	16 07	27 32	3 31

EPHEMERIS CALCULATED FOR 12 MIDNIGHT GREENWICH MEAN TIME. ALL OTHER DATA AND FACING ASPECTARIAN PAGE IN **EASTERN TIME (BOLD)** AND PACIFIC TIME (REGULAR).

OCTOBER 2019

☽ Last Aspect day	ET / hr:mn / PT		asp	☽ Ingress sign	day	ET / hr:mn / PT	
2	**5:46 am**	2:46 am	✶♂	♐	2	**7:44 am**	4:44 am
4	**3:34 am**	12:34 am	✶♀	♑	4	**1:43 pm**	10:43 am
6	**7:25 pm**	4:25 pm	□♀	♒	6	**11:42 pm**	8:42 pm
8	**2:27 pm**	11:27 am	✶♃	♓	9	**12:05 pm**	9:05 am
11	**5:55 am**	2:55 am	✶♇	♈	11		9:46 pm
11	**5:55 am**	2:55 am	✶♇	♈	12	**12:46 am**	
13	**5:59 pm**	2:59 pm	□♇	♉	14	**12:24 pm**	9:24 am
16	**4:37 am**	1:37 am	△♇	♊	16	**10:30 pm**	7:30 pm
18	**10:14 pm**	7:14 pm	△☉	♋	19	**6:43 am**	3:43 am
21	**8:39 am**	5:39 am	□☉	♌	21	**12:29 pm**	9:29 am
23	**5:14 am**	2:14 am	□☿	♍	23	**3:29 pm**	12:29 pm
25	**9:00 am**	6:00 am	✶☿	♎	25	**4:20 pm**	1:20 pm
27	**4:22 am**	1:22 am	✶♃	♏	27	**4:29 pm**	1:29 pm
29	**1:34 pm**	10:34 am	☌☿	♐	29	**5:58 pm**	2:58 pm
31	**10:30 am**	7:30 am	☌♃	♑	31	**10:38 pm**	7:38 pm

☽ Phases & Eclipses phase	day	ET / hr:mn / PT	
2nd Quarter	5	**12:47 pm**	9:47 am
Full Moon	13	**5:08 pm**	2:08 pm
4th Quarter	21	**8:39 am**	5:39 am
New Moon	27	**11:39 pm**	8:39 pm

Planet Ingress	day	ET / hr:mn / PT	
☿ ♏	3	**4:14 am**	1:14 am
♂ ♎	3		9:22 pm
♂ ♎	4	**12:22 am**	
♀ ♏	8	**1:06 pm**	10:06 am
☉ ♏	23	**1:20 pm**	10:20 am

Planetary Motion	day	ET / hr:mn / PT	
♇ D	2		11:39 pm
♇ D	3	**2:39 am**	
☿ ℞	31	**11:41 am**	8:41 am

1 TUESDAY

♀□♇	**12:18 am**	
☽✶♄	**4:43 am**	1:43 am
☽△♆	**9:12 am**	6:12 am
☽⚺♃	**11:46 am**	8:46 am
☽✶♇	**3:45 pm**	12:45 pm
☽⚺♀	**5:14 pm**	2:14 pm

2 WEDNESDAY

☽⚺☿	**5:23 am**	2:23 am
☽✶♂	**5:46 am**	2:46 am
☿⚺♂	**11:45 am**	8:45 am
☽⚻♅	**5:30 pm**	2:30 pm
☽✶☉		9:42 pm

3 THURSDAY

☽✶☉	**12:42 am**	
☽⚺♄	**8:34 am**	5:34 am
☽□♆	**1:14 pm**	10:14 am
☽☌♃	**4:40 pm**	1:40 pm
☽⚺♇	**8:24 pm**	5:24 pm

4 FRIDAY

☽✶♀	**3:34 am**	12:34 am
☽□♂	**2:26 pm**	11:26 am
☽✶☿	**5:52 pm**	2:52 pm
☽△♅		9:08 pm

5 SATURDAY

☽△♅	**12:08 am**	
☽□☉	**12:47 pm**	9:47 am
☽☌♄	**4:40 pm**	1:40 pm
☽✶♆	**9:26 pm**	6:26 pm
☽⚺♃		10:55 pm

6 SUNDAY

☽⚺♃	**1:55 am**	
☽☌♇	**5:15 am**	2:15 am
☽□♀	**7:25 pm**	4:25 pm
☿☍♅		11:17 pm

7 MONDAY

☿☍♅	**2:17 am**	
☽△♂	**3:43 am**	12:43 am
☽□♅	**10:32 am**	7:32 am
☽□☿	**11:36 am**	8:36 am
☉□♄	**3:07 pm**	12:07 pm

8 TUESDAY

☽⚺♄	**4:12 am**	1:12 am
☽△☉	**5:20 am**	2:20 am
☽⚺♆	**8:54 am**	5:54 am
☽✶♃	**2:27 pm**	11:27 am
☽⚺♇	**5:08 pm**	2:08 pm

9 WEDNESDAY

☽△♀	**2:47 pm**	11:47 am
☽⚻♂	**7:40 pm**	4:40 pm
☽✶♅	**10:55 pm**	7:55 pm
☉⚻♆	**11:24 pm**	8:24 pm

10 THURSDAY

☽△☿	**7:49 am**	4:49 am
☽✶♄	**5:08 pm**	2:08 pm
☽☌♆	**9:34 pm**	6:34 pm
☽⚻☉	**11:37 pm**	8:37 pm

11 FRIDAY

☽□♃	**4:02 am**	1:02 am
☽✶♇	**5:55 am**	2:55 am

12 SATURDAY

♂⚻♅	**4:00 am**	1:00 am
☽⚻♀	**10:28 am**	7:28 am
☽⚺♅	**11:17 am**	8:17 am
☽☍♂	**11:43 am**	8:43 am
♀☍♅	**6:07 pm**	3:07 pm

13 SUNDAY

☽⚻☿	**3:18 am**	12:18 am
☽□♄	**5:36 am**	2:36 am
☽⚺♆	**9:39 am**	6:39 am
♀⚺♂	**10:17 am**	7:17 am
☉✶♃	**2:02 pm**	11:02 am
☽△♃	**4:55 pm**	1:55 pm
☽☍☉	**5:08 pm**	2:08 pm
☽□♇	**5:59 pm**	2:59 pm
☿✶♄		11:56 pm

14 MONDAY

☿✶♄	**2:56 am**	
☉□♇	**3:38 am**	12:38 am
☽☌♅	**10:29 pm**	7:29 pm
☽⚻♂		11:24 pm

15 TUESDAY

☽⚻♂	**2:24 am**	
☽☍♀	**4:33 am**	1:33 am
☽△♄	**4:44 pm**	1:44 pm
☿△♆	**6:45 pm**	3:45 pm
☽✶♆	**8:23 pm**	5:23 pm
☽☍☿	**8:33 pm**	5:33 pm

16 WEDNESDAY

☽⚻♃	**4:21 am**	1:21 am
☽△♇	**4:37 am**	1:37 am
☽⚻☉	**8:49 am**	5:49 am
♃⚺♇		10:45 pm

17 THURSDAY

♃⚺♇	**1:45 am**	
☽⚺♅	**8:07 am**	5:07 am
☽△♂	**3:11 pm**	12:11 pm
☽⚻♀	**8:25 pm**	5:25 pm
☽⚻♄		11:12 pm

18 FRIDAY

☽⚻♄	**2:12 am**	
☽□♆	**5:25 am**	2:25 am
☽⚻☿	**11:02 am**	8:02 am
☽⚻♇	**1:30 pm**	10:30 am
☽☍♃	**1:58 pm**	10:58 am
☽△☉	**10:14 pm**	7:14 pm

19 SATURDAY

☽✶♅	**3:47 pm**	12:47 pm
☿✶♇	**6:21 pm**	3:21 pm
☽□♂		10:35 pm

20 SUNDAY

☽□♂	**1:35 am**	
☿⚺♃	**7:23 am**	4:23 am
☽△♀	**9:26 am**	6:26 am
☽☍♄	**9:29 am**	6:29 am
♀✶♄	**9:58 am**	6:58 am
☽△♆	**12:17 pm**	9:17 am
☽☍♇	**8:07 pm**	5:07 pm
☽⚻♃	**9:14 pm**	6:14 pm
☽△☿	**10:06 pm**	7:06 pm

21 MONDAY

☽□☉	**8:39 am**	5:39 am
♀△♆	**3:40 pm**	12:40 pm
☽□♅	**8:56 pm**	5:56 pm

22 TUESDAY

☽✶♂	**8:58 am**	5:58 am
☽⚻♄	**2:05 pm**	11:05 am
☽⚻♆	**4:28 pm**	1:28 pm
☽□♀	**6:54 pm**	3:54 pm
☽⚻♇		9:01 pm
☽△♃		10:41 pm

23 WEDNESDAY

☽⚻♇	**12:01 am**	
☽△♃	**1:41 am**	
☽□☿	**5:14 am**	2:14 am
☽✶☉	**3:39 pm**	12:39 pm
☽△♅	**11:24 pm**	8:24 pm

24 THURSDAY

☽⚺♂	**1:18 pm**	10:18 am
☽△♄	**4:05 pm**	1:05 pm
☽☍♆	**6:07 pm**	3:07 pm
☽✶♀		10:02 pm
☽△♇		10:26 pm

25 FRIDAY

☽✶♀	**1:02 am**	
☽△♇	**1:26 am**	
☽□♃	**3:37 am**	12:37 am
♀✶♇	**5:52 am**	2:52 am
☽✶☿	**9:00 am**	6:00 am
☽⚺☉	**7:58 pm**	4:58 pm
☽⚻♅	**11:52 pm**	8:52 pm

26 SATURDAY

♀⚺♃	**12:47 pm**	9:47 am
☽☌♂	**3:48 pm**	12:48 pm
☽□♄	**4:32 pm**	1:32 pm
☽⚻♆	**6:18 pm**	3:18 pm
☽□♇		10:38 pm

27 SUNDAY

☽□♇	**1:38 am**	
☽✶♃	**4:22 am**	1:22 am
☽⚺♀	**5:34 am**	2:34 am
♂□♄	**10:31 am**	7:31 am
☽⚺☿	**11:03 am**	8:03 am
☽☌☉	**11:39 pm**	8:39 pm
☽☍♅	**11:58 pm**	8:58 pm

28 MONDAY

☉☍♅	**4:15 am**	1:15 am
☽✶♄	**5:19 pm**	2:19 pm
☽⚺♂	**6:37 pm**	3:37 pm
☽△♆	**6:52 pm**	3:52 pm
♂⚻♆	**11:57 pm**	8:57 pm
☽✶♇		11:32 pm

29 TUESDAY

☽✶♇	**2:32 am**	
☽⚺♃	**5:58 am**	2:58 am
☽☌♀	**11:14 am**	8:14 am
☽☌☿	**1:34 pm**	10:34 am
☽⚻♅		10:41 pm

30 WEDNESDAY

☽⚻♅	**1:41 am**	
☽⚺☉	**5:19 am**	2:19 am
☿☌♀	**6:05 pm**	3:05 pm
☽⚺♄	**8:28 pm**	5:28 pm
☽□♆	**9:49 pm**	6:49 pm
☽✶♂		9:10 pm

31 THURSDAY

☽✶♂	**12:10 am**	
☽⚺♇	**6:07 am**	3:07 am
☽☌♃	**10:30 am**	7:30 am
☽⚺☿	**6:20 pm**	3:20 pm
☽⚺♀	**8:47 pm**	5:47 pm

Eastern time in bold type
Pacific time in medium type

OCTOBER 2019

DATE	SID.TIME	SUN	MOON	NODE	MERCURY	VENUS	MARS	JUPITER	SATURN	URANUS	NEPTUNE	PLUTO	CERES	PALLAS	JUNO	VESTA	CHIRON
1 T	0 37 45	7 ♎ 31 37	8 ♏ 47	13 ♋ 30 R	26 ♎ 37	20 ♎ 25	27 ♍ 57	18 ♐ 11	14 ♑ 02	5 ♉ 40 R	16 ♓ 45 R	20 ♑ 38 R	14 ♐ 00	13 ♏ 50	16 ♍ 32	27 ♉ 29 R	3 ♈ 29 R
2 W	0 41 42	8 30 37	23 09	13 22	28 04	21 39	28 36	18 19	14 04	5 38	16 44	20 38	14 19	14 14	16 57	27 25	3 26
3 Th	0 45 38	9 29 38	7 ♐ 02	13 16	29 31	22 54	29 14	18 28	14 05	5 36	16 42	20 38D	14 37	14 39	17 22	27 22	3 23
4 F	0 49 35	10 28 42	20 25	13 13	0 ♏ 56	24 09	29 53	18 36	14 07	5 34	16 41	20 38	14 56	15 04	17 47	27 18	3 20
5 Sa	0 53 31	11 27 47	3 ♑ 21	13 12	2 20	25 23	0 ♎ 32	18 45	14 08	5 32	16 39	20 38	15 15	15 28	18 11	27 13	3 18
6 Su	0 57 28	12 26 55	15 53	13 12	3 43	26 38	1 10	18 54	14 10	5 30	16 38	20 38	15 34	15 53	18 36	27 08	3 15
7 M	1 1 24	13 26 04	28 08	13 12	5 06	27 52	1 49	19 03	14 12	5 27	16 36	20 38	15 53	16 18	19 01	27 02	3 12
8 T	1 5 21	14 25 14	10 ♒ 10	13 10	6 27	29 07	2 28	19 12	14 14	5 25	16 35	20 38	16 12	16 43	19 25	26 56	3 10
9 W	1 9 17	15 24 27	22 04	13 06	7 46	0 ♏ 21	3 06	19 21	14 16	5 23	16 34	20 39	16 32	17 08	19 50	26 50	3 07
10 Th	1 13 14	16 23 41	3 ♓ 54	12 59	9 05	1 36	3 45	19 30	14 18	5 21	16 32	20 39	16 51	17 33	20 14	26 43	3 05
11 F	1 17 11	17 22 57	15 45	12 49	10 23	2 51	4 24	19 40	14 20	5 18	16 31	20 39	17 11	17 57	20 39	26 36	3 02
12 Sa	1 21 7	18 22 15	27 38	12 37	11 39	4 05	5 02	19 49	14 22	5 16	16 30	20 39	17 30	18 22	21 03	26 28	2 59
13 Su	1 25 4	19 21 35	9 ♈ 36	12 23	12 54	5 20	5 41	19 59	14 24	5 14	16 28	20 39	17 50	18 47	21 27	26 20	2 57
14 M	1 29 0	20 20 57	21 41	12 09	14 07	6 34	6 20	20 09	14 27	5 11	16 27	20 40	18 10	19 13	21 51	26 11	2 54
15 T	1 32 57	21 20 21	3 ♉ 53	11 55	15 18	7 49	6 59	20 18	14 29	5 09	16 26	20 40	18 30	19 38	22 15	26 02	2 52
16 W	1 36 53	22 19 47	16 13	11 44	16 28	9 03	7 37	20 28	14 32	5 07	16 24	20 40	18 50	20 03	22 39	25 53	2 49
17 Th	1 40 50	23 19 15	28 41	11 35	17 36	10 18	8 16	20 38	14 35	5 04	16 23	20 41	19 10	20 28	23 03	25 43	2 47
18 F	1 44 46	24 18 45	11 ♊ 20	11 28	18 42	11 33	8 55	20 49	14 37	5 02	16 22	20 41	19 30	20 53	23 27	25 33	2 44
19 Sa	1 48 43	25 18 18	24 11	11 25	19 45	12 47	9 34	20 59	14 40	4 59	16 21	20 42	19 51	21 18	23 51	25 23	2 42
20 Su	1 52 39	26 17 53	7 ♋ 17	11 24 D	20 46	14 02	10 13	21 09	14 43	4 57	16 19	20 42	20 11	21 44	24 14	25 12	2 39
21 M	1 56 36	27 17 31	20 39	11 24 R	21 45	15 16	10 52	21 20	14 46	4 55	16 18	20 43	20 32	22 09	24 38	25 00	2 37
22 T	2 0 33	28 17 10	4 ♌ 20	11 24	22 40	16 31	11 31	21 30	14 50	4 52	16 17	20 43	20 53	22 34	25 01	24 49	2 34
23 W	2 4 29	29 16 52	18 21	11 23	23 32	17 45	12 09	21 41	14 53	4 50	16 16	20 44	21 13	23 00	25 25	24 37	2 32
24 Th	2 8 26	0 ♏ 16 37	2 ♍ 43	11 19	24 20	19 00	12 48	21 52	14 56	4 47	16 15	20 44	21 34	23 25	25 48	24 24	2 30
25 F	2 12 22	1 16 23	17 24	11 13	25 04	20 15	13 27	22 03	15 00	4 45	16 14	20 45	21 55	23 51	26 11	24 12	2 27
26 Sa	2 16 19	2 16 12	2 ♎ 17	11 05	25 44	21 29	14 06	22 14	15 03	4 42	16 13	20 46	22 16	24 16	26 34	23 59	2 25
27 Su	2 20 15	3 16 02	17 16	10 54	26 19	22 44	14 45	22 25	15 07	4 40	16 12	20 46	22 37	24 41	26 57	23 45	2 23
28 M	2 24 12	4 15 55	2 ♏ 10	10 44	26 48	23 58	15 24	22 36	15 10	4 37	16 11	20 47	22 59	25 07	27 20	23 32	2 21
29 T	2 28 8	5 15 50	16 51	10 34	27 11	25 13	16 03	22 47	15 14	4 35	16 10	20 48	23 20	25 33	27 43	23 18	2 19
30 W	2 32 5	6 15 47	1 ♐ 12	10 26	27 27	26 27	16 42	22 58	15 18	4 32	16 09	20 49	23 41	25 58	28 06	23 04	2 16
31 Th	2 36 2	7 15 45	15 06	10 21	27 37 R	27 42	17 22	23 10	15 22	4 30	16 08	20 49	24 03	26 24	28 28	22 49	2 14

EPHEMERIS CALCULATED FOR 12 MIDNIGHT GREENWICH MEAN TIME. ALL OTHER DATA AND FACING ASPECTARIAN PAGE IN **EASTERN TIME (BOLD)** AND PACIFIC TIME (REGULAR).

NOVEMBER 2019

☽ Last Aspect day	ET / hr:mn / PT		asp	☽ Ingress sign	day	ET / hr:mn / PT	
2		10:46 pm	⚹ ☿	♒	3	**6:19 am**	3:19 am
3	**1:46 am**		⚹ ☿	♒	3	**6:19 am**	3:19 am
5	**9:37 am**	6:37 am	□ ☿	♓	5	**6:08 pm**	3:08 pm
7	**8:13 pm**	5:13 pm	□ ♃	♈	8	**6:49 am**	3:49 am
10	**9:00 am**	6:00 am	△ ♃	♉	10	**6:18 pm**	3:18 pm
12	**10:48 am**	7:48 am	△ ♇	♊	13	**3:46 am**	12:46 am
15	**6:40 am**	3:40 am	△ ♂	♋	15	**11:15 am**	8:15 am
17	**3:14 pm**	12:14 pm	□ ♂	♌	17	**4:57 pm**	1:57 pm
19	**4:11 pm**	1:11 pm	□ ☉	♍	19	**8:54 pm**	5:54 pm
21	**10:31 pm**	7:31 pm	⚹ ☉	♎	21	**11:20 pm**	8:20 pm

☽ Last Aspect day	ET / hr:mn / PT		asp	☽ Ingress sign	day	ET / hr:mn / PT	
23	**9:49 pm**	6:49 pm	⚹ ♃	♏	23		9:58 pm
23	**9:49 pm**	6:49 pm	⚹ ♃	♏	24	**12:58 am**	
25	**12:30 pm**	9:30 am	⚹ ♇	♐	26	**3:11 am**	12:11 am
28	**5:50 am**	2:50 am	☌ ♃	♑	28	**7:33 am**	4:33 am
29	**10:57 pm**	7:57 pm	☌ ♇	♒	30	**3:13 pm**	12:13 pm

☽ Phases & Eclipses phase	day	ET / hr:mn / PT	
2nd Quarter	4	**5:23 am**	2:23 am
Full Moon	12	**8:34 am**	5:34 am
4th Quarter	19	**4:11 pm**	1:11 pm
New Moon	26	**10:06 am**	7:06 am

Planet Ingress		day	ET / hr:mn / PT	
♀	♐	1	**4:25 pm**	1:25 pm
⚵	♎	3	**9:28 pm**	6:28 pm
⚴	♐	8	**5:18 am**	2:18 am
⚳	♑	15	**11:36 pm**	8:36 pm
♂	♏	18		11:40 pm
♂	♏	19	**2:40 am**	
☉	♐	22	**9:59 am**	6:59 am
♀	♑	25	**7:28 pm**	4:28 pm

Planetary Motion		day	ET / hr:mn / PT	
☿	D	20	**2:12 pm**	11:12 am
♆	D	27	**7:32 am**	4:32 am

1 FRIDAY
☽ △ ♅ **6:47 am** 3:47 am
☽ ⚹ ☉ **3:21 pm** 12:21 pm

2 SATURDAY
☽ ☌ ♄ **3:29 am** 12:29 am
☽ ⚹ ♆ **4:35 am** 1:35 am
☽ □ ♂ **10:11 am** 7:11 am
☽ ☌ ♇ **1:39 pm** 10:39 am
☽ ⚺ ♃ **7:10 pm** 4:10 pm
☽ ⚹ ☿ 10:46 pm

3 SUNDAY
☽ ⚹ ☿ **1:46 am**
☽ ⚹ ♀ **10:42 am** 7:42 am
☽ □ ♅ **2:50 pm** 11:50 am

4 MONDAY
☽ □ ☉ **5:23 am** 2:23 am
☽ ⚺ ♄ **1:21 pm** 10:21 am
☽ ⚺ ♆ **2:06 pm** 11:06 am
☽ △ ♂ **11:28 pm** 8:28 pm
☽ ⚺ ♇ **11:47 pm** 8:47 pm
♀ ⚻ ♅ 11:09 pm

5 TUESDAY
♀ ⚻ ♅ **2:09 am**
♂ □ ♇ **5:28 am** 2:28 am
☽ ⚹ ♃ **6:29 am** 3:29 am
☽ □ ☿ **9:37 am** 6:37 am
☽ ⚹ ♅ 11:43 pm

6 WEDNESDAY
☽ ⚹ ♅ **2:43 am**
☽ □ ♀ **5:41 am** 2:41 am
☿ ⚺ ♃ **7:48 pm** 4:48 pm
☽ △ ☉ **11:25 pm** 8:25 pm
☽ ⚹ ♄ 11:18 pm
☽ ☌ ♆ 11:37 pm

7 THURSDAY
☽ ⚹ ♄ **2:18 am**
☽ ☌ ♆ **2:37 am**
☽ ⚹ ♇ **12:33 pm** 9:33 am
☽ ⚻ ♂ **3:40 pm** 12:40 pm
☽ △ ☿ **5:52 pm** 2:52 pm
☽ □ ♃ **8:13 pm** 5:13 pm

8 FRIDAY
☿ ⚺ ♂ **7:38 am** 4:38 am
☉ ⚹ ♄ **12:06 pm** 9:06 am
☉ △ ♆ **12:56 pm** 9:56 am
☽ ⚺ ♅ **3:07 pm** 12:07 pm
♄ ⚹ ♆ **9:45 pm** 6:45 pm
☽ △ ♀ 10:15 pm

9 SATURDAY
☽ △ ♀ **1:15 am**
☽ ⚺ ♆ **2:48 pm** 11:48 am
☽ □ ♄ **2:55 pm** 11:55 am
☽ ⚻ ☉ **5:09 pm** 2:09 pm
☿ ⚹ ♇ **9:09 pm** 6:09 pm
☽ ⚻ ☿ 9:17 pm
☽ □ ♇ 9:37 pm

10 SUNDAY
☽ ⚻ ☿ **12:17 am**
☽ □ ♇ **12:37 am**
☽ ☍ ♂ **6:58 am** 3:58 am
☽ △ ♃ **9:00 am** 6:00 am
☽ ☌ ♅ 11:10 pm

11 MONDAY
☽ ☌ ♅ **2:10 am**
☉ ☌ ☿ **10:22 am** 7:22 am
☽ ⚻ ♀ **6:40 pm** 3:40 pm
☽ ⚹ ♆ 10:11 pm
☽ △ ♄ 10:44 pm

12 TUESDAY
☽ ⚹ ♆ **1:11 am**
☽ △ ♄ **1:44 am**
☽ ☍ ☿ **4:51 am** 1:51 am
☽ ☍ ☉ **8:34 am** 5:34 am
☽ △ ♇ **10:48 am** 7:48 am
♂ ⚹ ♃ **1:21 pm** 10:21 am
☽ ⚻ ♃ **7:45 pm** 4:45 pm
☽ ⚻ ♂ **7:59 pm** 4:59 pm

13 WEDNESDAY
☿ ⚹ ♄ **9:35 am** 6:35 am
☽ ⚺ ♅ **11:11 am** 8:11 am
☉ ⚹ ♇ **1:00 pm** 10:00 am
☿ △ ♆ **5:34 pm** 2:34 pm

14 THURSDAY
☿ ⚺ ♀ **3:09 am** 12:09 am
☽ ⚻ ☿ **8:14 am** 5:14 am
☽ ☍ ♀ **9:16 am** 6:16 am
☽ □ ♆ **9:32 am** 6:32 am
☽ ⚻ ♄ **10:27 am** 7:27 am
♀ □ ♆ **12:06 pm** 9:06 am
☽ ⚻ ♇ **6:56 pm** 3:56 pm
☽ ⚻ ☉ **9:23 pm** 6:23 pm
♀ ⚺ ♄ **10:32 pm** 7:32 pm

15 FRIDAY
☽ ☍ ♃ **4:24 am** 1:24 am
☽ △ ♂ **6:40 am** 3:40 am
☽ ⚹ ♅ **6:16 pm** 3:16 pm

16 SATURDAY
☽ △ ☿ **11:08 am** 8:08 am
☽ △ ♆ **4:02 pm** 1:02 pm
☽ ☍ ♄ **5:18 pm** 2:18 pm
☽ ⚻ ♀ **9:21 pm** 6:21 pm
☽ ☍ ♇ 10:15 pm

17 SUNDAY
☽ ☍ ♇ **1:15 am**
☽ △ ☉ **7:53 am** 4:53 am
☽ ⚻ ♃ **11:10 am** 8:10 am
☽ □ ♂ **3:14 pm** 12:14 pm
☽ □ ♅ **11:35 pm** 8:35 pm

18 MONDAY
☽ □ ☿ **1:53 pm** 10:53 am
♀ ⚺ ♇ **4:25 pm** 1:25 pm
☽ ⚻ ♆ **8:47 pm** 5:47 pm
☽ ⚻ ♄ **10:21 pm** 7:21 pm

19 TUESDAY
☽ ⚻ ♇ **5:48 am** 2:48 am
☽ △ ♀ **7:04 am** 4:04 am
☉ ⚺ ♃ **2:54 pm** 11:54 am
☽ △ ♃ **4:06 pm** 1:06 pm
☽ □ ☉ **4:11 pm** 1:11 pm
☽ ⚹ ♂ **9:48 pm** 6:48 pm

20 WEDNESDAY
☽ △ ♅ **3:12 am** 12:12 am
☽ ⚹ ☿ **4:32 pm** 1:32 pm
☽ ☍ ♆ **11:51 pm** 8:51 pm
☽ △ ♄ 10:43 pm

21 THURSDAY
☽ △ ♄ **1:43 am**
☽ △ ♇ **8:42 am** 5:42 am
☽ □ ♀ **2:39 pm** 11:39 am
☽ □ ♃ **7:25 pm** 4:25 pm
☽ ⚹ ☉ **10:31 pm** 7:31 pm
☽ ⚺ ♂ 11:36 pm

22 FRIDAY
☽ ⚺ ♂ **2:36 am**
☽ ⚻ ♅ **5:21 am** 2:21 am
☽ ⚺ ☿ **7:14 pm** 4:14 pm
☽ ⚻ ♆ 10:43 pm

23 SATURDAY
☽ ⚻ ♆ **1:43 am**
☽ □ ♄ **3:53 am** 12:53 am
☽ □ ♇ **10:32 am** 7:32 am
☽ ⚹ ♀ **9:00 pm** 6:00 pm
☽ ⚹ ♃ **9:49 pm** 6:49 pm

24 SUNDAY
☽ ⚺ ☉ **3:54 am** 12:54 am
☽ ☌ ♂ **6:36 am** 3:36 am
☽ ☍ ♅ **6:51 am** 3:51 am
♀ ☌ ♃ **8:33 am** 5:33 am
♂ ☍ ♅ **11:51 am** 8:51 am
☽ ☌ ☿ **10:50 pm** 7:50 pm

25 MONDAY
☽ △ ♆ **3:27 am** 12:27 am
☽ ⚹ ♄ **5:59 am** 2:59 am
☽ ⚹ ♇ **12:30 pm** 9:30 am
☉ ⚻ ♅ **9:00 pm** 6:00 pm
☽ ⚺ ♃ 9:44 pm

26 TUESDAY
☽ ⚺ ♃ **12:44 am**
☽ ⚺ ♀ **3:56 am** 12:56 am
☽ ⚻ ♅ **9:07 am** 6:07 am
☽ ☌ ☉ **10:06 am** 7:06 am
☽ ⚺ ♂ **11:28 am** 8:28 am

27 WEDNESDAY
☽ ⚺ ☿ **4:57 am** 1:57 am
☽ □ ♆ **6:37 am** 3:37 am
☽ ⚺ ♄ **9:38 am** 6:38 am
☽ ⚺ ♇ **4:11 pm** 1:11 pm

28 THURSDAY
☿ △ ♆ **4:51 am** 1:51 am
☽ ☌ ♃ **5:50 am** 2:50 am
♀ △ ♅ **1:27 pm** 10:27 am
☽ △ ♅ **1:41 pm** 10:41 am
☽ ☌ ♀ **1:43 pm** 10:43 am
☉ ⚺ ♂ **2:21 pm** 11:21 am
☽ ⚹ ♂ **7:06 pm** 4:06 pm
☽ ⚺ ☉ **7:14 pm** 4:14 pm

29 FRIDAY
☽ ⚹ ♆ **12:39 pm** 9:39 am
☽ ⚹ ☿ **3:30 pm** 12:30 pm
☽ ☌ ♄ **4:17 pm** 1:17 pm
☽ ☌ ♇ **10:57 pm** 7:57 pm
☿ ⚹ ♄ 10:13 pm

30 SATURDAY
☿ ⚹ ♄ **1:13 am**
☽ ⚺ ♃ **2:23 pm** 11:23 am
☽ □ ♅ **9:38 pm** 6:38 pm

Eastern time in bold type
Pacific time in medium type

NOVEMBER 2019

DATE	SID.TIME	SUN	MOON	NODE	MERCURY	VENUS	MARS	JUPITER	SATURN	URANUS	NEPTUNE	PLUTO	CERES	PALLAS	JUNO	VESTA	CHIRON
1 F	2 39 58	8 ♏ 15 46	28 ♐ 33	10 ♋ 19 D	27 ♏ 38 ℞	28 ♏ 57	18 ♎ 01	23 ♐ 21	15 ♑ 26	4 ♉ 28 ℞	16 ♓ 07 ℞	20 ♑ 50	24 ♐ 24	26 ♏ 49	28 ♍ 51	22 ♉ 35 ℞	2 ♈ 12 ℞
2 Sa	2 43 55	9 15 48	11 ♑ 33	10 18	27 31	0 ♐ 11	18 40	23 33	15 30	4 25	16 06	20 51	24 46	27 15	29 13	22 20	2 10
3 Su	2 47 51	10 15 51	24 10	10 18	27 14	1 26	19 19	23 44	15 34	4 23	16 06	20 52	25 08	27 41	29 36	22 05	2 08
4 M	2 51 48	11 15 56	6 ♒ 27	10 19 ℞	26 49	2 40	19 58	23 56	15 38	4 20	16 05	20 53	25 29	28 06	29 58	21 50	2 06
5 T	2 55 44	12 16 03	18 31	10 19	26 13	3 55	20 37	24 08	15 43	4 18	16 04	20 54	25 51	28 32	0 ♎ 20	21 35	2 04
6 W	2 59 41	13 16 11	0 ♓ 26	10 17	25 28	5 09	21 16	24 20	15 47	4 15	16 03	20 55	26 13	28 58	0 42	21 20	2 02
7 Th	3 3 37	14 16 21	12 17	10 13	24 34	6 24	21 56	24 32	15 52	4 13	16 03	20 56	26 35	29 23	1 04	21 04	2 01
8 F	3 7 34	15 16 32	24 08	10 07	23 31	7 38	22 35	24 44	15 56	4 10	16 02	20 57	26 57	29 49	1 26	20 48	1 59
9 Sa	3 11 31	16 16 45	6 ♈ 05	9 58	22 21	8 53	23 14	24 56	16 01	4 08	16 01	20 58	27 19	0 ♐ 15	1 47	20 33	1 57
10 Su	3 15 27	17 17 00	18 08	9 49	21 06	10 07	23 53	25 08	16 05	4 06	16 01	20 59	27 41	0 40	2 09	20 17	1 55
11 M	3 19 24	18 17 16	0 ♉ 22	9 39	19 47	11 22	24 32	25 20	16 10	4 03	16 00	21 00	28 04	1 06	2 30	20 01	1 54
12 T	3 23 20	19 17 34	12 46	9 29	18 27	12 36	25 12	25 32	16 15	4 01	16 00	21 01	28 26	1 32	2 51	19 46	1 52
13 W	3 27 17	20 17 53	25 21	9 20	17 09	13 51	25 51	25 45	16 20	3 59	15 59	21 02	28 48	1 58	3 13	19 30	1 50
14 Th	3 31 13	21 18 14	8 ♊ 08	9 14	15 54	15 05	26 30	25 57	16 25	3 56	15 59	21 03	29 11	2 23	3 34	19 14	1 49
15 F	3 35 10	22 18 37	21 07	9 10	14 47	16 20	27 10	26 10	16 30	3 54	15 58	21 05	29 33	2 49	3 55	18 59	1 47
16 Sa	3 39 6	23 19 02	4 ♋ 16	9 09 D	13 47	17 34	27 49	26 22	16 35	3 52	15 58	21 06	29 56	3 15	4 16	18 43	1 46
17 Su	3 43 3	24 19 29	17 37	9 09	12 58	18 49	28 29	26 35	16 40	3 49	15 57	21 07	0 ♑ 18	3 41	4 36	18 28	1 45
18 M	3 47 0	25 19 58	1 ♌ 10	9 10	12 20	20 03	29 08	26 47	16 45	3 47	15 57	21 08	0 41	4 07	4 57	18 12	1 43
19 T	3 50 56	26 20 28	14 55	9 11 ℞	11 54	21 18	29 47	27 00	16 51	3 45	15 57	21 10	1 04	4 32	5 17	17 57	1 42
20 W	3 54 53	27 21 00	28 53	9 12	11 39 D	22 32	0 ♏ 27	27 13	16 56	3 43	15 57	21 11	1 26	4 58	5 38	17 42	1 41
21 Th	3 58 49	28 21 34	13 ♍ 03	9 11	11 35	23 46	1 06	27 26	17 02	3 41	15 56	21 12	1 49	5 24	5 58	17 27	1 39
22 F	4 2 46	29 22 10	27 24	9 08	11 43	25 01	1 46	27 39	17 07	3 38	15 56	21 14	2 12	5 50	6 18	17 12	1 38
23 Sa	4 6 42	0 ♐ 22 47	11 ♎ 52	9 04	12 01	26 15	2 25	27 51	17 13	3 36	15 56	21 15	2 35	6 16	6 38	16 58	1 37
24 Su	4 10 39	1 23 26	26 23	8 58	12 28	27 30	3 05	28 04	17 18	3 34	15 56	21 17	2 58	6 41	6 58	16 43	1 36
25 M	4 14 35	2 24 07	10 ♏ 52	8 52	13 03	28 44	3 44	28 17	17 24	3 32	15 56	21 18	3 21	7 07	7 17	16 29	1 35
26 T	4 18 32	3 24 49	25 10	8 46	13 46	29 59	4 24	28 30	17 30	3 30	15 56	21 19	3 44	7 33	7 37	16 15	1 34
27 W	4 22 29	4 25 33	9 ♐ 14	8 42	14 36	1 ♑ 13	5 04	28 44	17 35	3 28	15 56 D	21 21	4 07	7 59	7 56	16 02	1 33
28 Th	4 26 25	5 26 18	22 58	8 39	15 31	2 27	5 43	28 57	17 41	3 26	15 56	21 22	4 30	8 25	8 15	15 48	1 32
29 F	4 30 22	6 27 05	6 ♑ 20	8 38 D	16 32	3 42	6 23	29 10	17 47	3 24	15 56	21 24	4 53	8 51	8 35	15 35	1 32
30 Sa	4 34 18	7 27 52	19 20	8 39	17 37	4 56	7 03	29 23	17 53	3 22	15 56	21 26	5 16	9 16	8 53	15 22	1 31

EPHEMERIS CALCULATED FOR 12 MIDNIGHT GREENWICH MEAN TIME. ALL OTHER DATA AND FACING ASPECTARIAN PAGE IN **EASTERN TIME (BOLD)** AND PACIFIC TIME (REGULAR).

DECEMBER 2019

☽ Last Aspect day	ET / hr:mn / PT		asp	☽ Ingress sign	day	ET / hr:mn / PT	
2	**7:27 am**	4:27 am	□☿	♓	2		11:11 pm
2	**7:27 am**	4:27 am	□☿	♓	3	**2:11 am**	
5	**3:15 am**	12:15 am	△☿	♈	5	**2:44 pm**	11:44 am
7	**10:01 am**	7:01 am	□♇	♉	7		11:29 pm
7	**10:01 am**	7:01 am	□♇	♉	8	**2:29 am**	
9	**8:13 pm**	5:13 pm	△♇	♊	10	**11:47 am**	8:47 am
11		9:12 pm	☍☉	♋	12	**6:23 pm**	3:23 pm
12	**12:12 am**		☍☉	♋	12	**6:23 pm**	3:23 pm
14	**10:57 am**	7:57 am	☍♀	♌	14	**10:56 pm**	7:56 pm
16	**5:10 pm**	2:10 pm	△☉	♍	16		11:16 pm
16	**5:10 pm**	2:10 pm	△☉	♍	17	**2:16 am**	
19	**3:07 am**	12:07 am	△♀	♎	19	**5:04 am**	2:04 am
21	**6:45 am**	3:45 am	✶☉	♏	21	**7:57 am**	4:57 am
22	**10:27 pm**	7:27 pm	☌♂	♐	23	**11:34 am**	8:34 am
25	**6:18 am**	3:18 am	☌☿	♑	25	**4:45 pm**	1:45 pm
27	**4:03 pm**	1:03 pm	✶♂	♒	27		9:21 pm
27	**4:03 pm**	1:03 pm	✶♂	♒	28	**12:21 am**	
30	**5:24 am**	2:24 am	□♂	♓	30	**10:41 am**	7:41 am

☽ Phases & Eclipses phase	day	ET / hr:mn / PT	
2nd Quarter	3		10:58 pm
2nd Quarter	4	**1:58 am**	
Full Moon	11		9:12 pm
Full Moon	12	**12:12 am**	
4th Quarter	18	**11:57 pm**	8:57 pm
New Moon	25		9:13 pm
New Moon	26	**12:13 am**	
●	25/26	4° ♑ 07'	

Planet Ingress	day	ET / hr:mn / PT	
♃ ♑	2	**1:20 pm**	10:20 am
☿ ♐	9	**4:42 am**	1:42 am
♀ ♒	19		10:42 pm
♀ ♒	20	**1:42 am**	
☉ ♑	21	**11:19 pm**	8:19 pm
☿ ♑	28	**11:55 pm**	8:55 pm

Planetary Motion	day	ET / hr:mn / PT	
⚷ D	12	**10:48 pm**	7:48 pm
⚶ D	29	**5:40 pm**	2:40 pm

1 SUNDAY
☽⚺♀ **4:01 am** 1:01 am
☽□♂ **6:43 am** 3:43 am
☽✶☉ **8:43 am** 5:43 am
☽⚺♆ **10:12 pm** 7:12 pm
☽⚺♄ 11:30 pm

2 MONDAY
☽⚺♄ **2:30 am**
☽□☿ **7:27 am** 4:27 am
☽⚺♇ **9:12 am** 6:12 am
☿✶♇ 9:23 pm
☽✶♃ 11:25 pm

3 TUESDAY
☿✶♇ **12:23 am**
☽✶♃ **2:25 am**
☽✶♅ **8:43 am** 5:43 am
♀✶♂ **10:47 am** 7:47 am
☽△♂ **9:51 pm** 6:51 pm
☽✶♀ **10:26 pm** 7:26 pm
☽□☉ 10:58 pm

4 WEDNESDAY
☽□☉ **1:58 am**
☽☌♆ **10:19 am** 7:19 am
☽✶♄ **3:14 pm** 12:14 pm
☽✶♇ **9:41 pm** 6:41 pm

5 THURSDAY
☽△☿ **3:15 am** 12:15 am
☽□♃ **4:09 pm** 1:09 pm
☽⚺♅ **9:10 pm** 6:10 pm

6 FRIDAY
☽⚻♂ **1:57 pm** 10:57 am
☽□♀ **5:57 pm** 2:57 pm
☽△☉ **8:04 pm** 5:04 pm
☽⚺♆ **10:45 pm** 7:45 pm

7 SATURDAY
☽□♄ **4:05 am** 1:05 am
☽□♇ **10:01 am** 7:01 am
☽⚻☿ **11:02 pm** 8:02 pm

8 SUNDAY
☉□♆ **4:00 am** 1:00 am
☽△♃ **4:58 am** 1:58 am
☽☌♅ **8:34 am** 5:34 am
♀✶♆ **4:48 pm** 1:48 pm

9 MONDAY
☽☍♂ **4:10 am** 1:10 am
☽✶♆ **9:20 am** 6:20 am
☽△♀ **11:07 am** 8:07 am
☽⚻☉ **11:53 am** 8:53 am
☽△♄ **2:54 pm** 11:54 am
☽△♇ **8:13 pm** 5:13 pm

10 TUESDAY
☿⚺♃ **9:58 am** 6:58 am
☽⚻♃ **3:10 pm** 12:10 pm
☽☍☿ **3:43 pm** 12:43 pm
☽⚺♅ **5:28 pm** 2:28 pm

11 WEDNESDAY
☉⚺♀ **3:26 am** 12:26 am
♀☌♄ **5:05 am** 2:05 am
☉⚺♄ **5:29 am** 2:29 am
☿⚻♅ **6:55 am** 3:55 am
☽⚻♂ **3:12 pm** 12:12 pm
☽□♆ **5:11 pm** 2:11 pm
☽⚻♄ **10:55 pm** 7:55 pm
☽☍☉ 9:12 pm
☽⚻♀ 9:35 pm

12 THURSDAY
☽☍☉ **12:12 am**
☽⚻♀ **12:35 am**
☽⚻♇ **3:38 am** 12:38 am
☽☍♃ **10:33 pm** 7:33 pm
☽✶♅ **11:43 pm** 8:43 pm

13 FRIDAY
☽⚻☿ **4:48 am** 1:48 am
♂△♆ **6:55 am** 3:55 am
♀☌♇ **10:16 am** 7:16 am
☉⚺♇ **10:27 pm** 7:27 pm
☽△♆ **10:37 pm** 7:37 pm
☽△♂ **11:25 pm** 8:25 pm

14 SATURDAY
☽☍♄ **4:32 am** 1:32 am
☽☍♇ **8:47 am** 5:47 am
☽⚻☉ **9:35 am** 6:35 am
☽☍♀ **10:57 am** 7:57 am

15 SUNDAY
☽⚻♃ **3:51 am** 12:51 am
☽□♅ **4:02 am** 1:02 am
♃△♅ **2:01 pm** 11:01 am
☽△☿ **3:18 pm** 12:18 pm
☽⚻♆ 11:28 pm

16 MONDAY
☽⚻♆ **2:28 am**
☽□♂ **5:47 am** 2:47 am
☽⚻♄ **8:37 am** 5:37 am
☽⚻♇ **12:29 pm** 9:29 am
☽△☉ **5:10 pm** 2:10 pm
☽⚻♀ **7:26 pm** 4:26 pm

17 TUESDAY
☽△♅ **7:12 am** 4:12 am
☽△♃ **7:56 am** 4:56 am
☽□☿ 9:29 pm

18 WEDNESDAY
☽□☿ **12:29 am**
☽☍♆ **5:29 am** 2:29 am
☽✶♂ **11:14 am** 8:14 am
☽△♄ **11:56 am** 8:56 am
☽△♇ **3:29 pm** 12:29 pm
☽□☉ **11:57 pm** 8:57 pm

19 THURSDAY
☽△♀ **3:07 am** 12:07 am
♂✶♄ **5:00 am** 2:00 am
☽⚻♅ **9:55 am** 6:55 am
☽□♃ **11:34 am** 8:34 am
☿□♆ **11:19 pm** 8:19 pm

20 FRIDAY
☽⚻♆ **8:18 am** 5:18 am
☽✶☿ **9:22 am** 6:22 am
☽□♄ **3:08 pm** 12:08 pm
☽⚺♂ **4:33 pm** 1:33 pm
☽□♇ **6:24 pm** 3:24 pm

21 SATURDAY
☽✶☉ **6:45 am** 3:45 am
☽□♀ **10:51 am** 7:51 am
☽☍♅ **12:47 pm** 9:47 am
☽✶♃ **3:21 pm** 12:21 pm

22 SUNDAY
♀□♅ **8:30 am** 5:30 am
♂✶♇ **9:32 am** 6:32 am
☽△♆ **11:32 am** 8:32 am
☿⚺♄ **6:24 pm** 3:24 pm
☽✶♄ **6:51 pm** 3:51 pm
☽⚺☿ **6:54 pm** 3:54 pm
☽✶♇ **9:52 pm** 6:52 pm
☽☌♂ **10:27 pm** 7:27 pm

23 MONDAY
☽⚺☉ **2:28 pm** 11:28 am
☽⚻♅ **4:26 pm** 1:26 pm
☽✶♀ **7:38 pm** 4:38 pm
☽⚺♃ **8:01 pm** 5:01 pm
☿⚺♇ **10:08 pm** 7:08 pm
♀⚺♃ 9:51 pm

24 TUESDAY
♀⚺♃ **12:51 am**
☽□♆ **3:56 pm** 12:56 pm
☉△♅ **4:44 pm** 1:44 pm
☽⚺♄ **11:53 pm** 8:53 pm
☿⚺♂ 9:53 pm
☽⚺♇ 11:40 pm

25 WEDNESDAY
☿⚺♂ **12:53 am**
☽⚺♇ **2:40 am**
☽⚺♂ **5:56 am** 2:56 am
☽☌☿ **6:18 am** 3:18 am
☽△♅ **9:45 pm** 6:45 pm
☽☌☉ 9:13 pm
☽☌♃ 11:29 pm

26 THURSDAY
☽☌☉ **12:13 am**
☽☌♃ **2:29 am**
☽⚺♀ **6:39 am** 3:39 am
☽✶♆ **10:23 pm** 7:23 pm

27 FRIDAY
☽☌♄ **7:08 am** 4:08 am
☽☌♇ **9:42 am** 6:42 am
☉☌♃ **1:25 pm** 10:25 am
☽✶♂ **4:03 pm** 1:03 pm
☽⚺☿ **9:02 pm** 6:02 pm

28 SATURDAY
☽□♅ **5:33 am** 2:33 am
☽⚺♃ **11:37 am** 8:37 am
☽⚺☉ **1:09 pm** 10:09 am
☽☌♀ **9:07 pm** 6:07 pm

29 SUNDAY
☽⚺♆ **7:34 am** 4:34 am
☽⚺♄ **5:13 pm** 2:13 pm
☽⚺♇ **7:31 pm** 4:31 pm

30 MONDAY
☽□♂ **5:24 am** 2:24 am
☽✶☿ **3:52 pm** 12:52 pm
☽✶♅ **4:04 pm** 1:04 pm
☿△♅ **5:22 pm** 2:22 pm
☽✶♃ **11:37 pm** 8:37 pm

31 TUESDAY
☽✶☉ **5:32 am** 2:32 am
☽⚺♀ **3:07 pm** 12:07 pm
☽☌♆ **7:15 pm** 4:15 pm

Eastern time in bold type
Pacific time in medium type

DECEMBER 2019

DATE	SID.TIME	SUN	MOON	NODE	MERCURY	VENUS	MARS	JUPITER	SATURN	URANUS	NEPTUNE	PLUTO	CERES	PALLAS	JUNO	VESTA	CHIRON
1 Su	4 38 15	8 ♐ 28 41	1 ♒ 58	8 ♋ 40	18 ♏ 46	6 ♑ 10	7 ♏ 42	29 ♐ 36	17 ♑ 59	3 ♉ 20 R	15 ♓ 56	21 ♑ 27	5 ♑ 40	9 ♐ 42	9 ♎ 12	15 ♉ 10 R	1 ♈ 30 R
2 M	4 42 11	9 29 30	14 19	8 42	19 58	7 25	8 22	29 50	18 05	3 18	15 56	21 29	6 03	10 08	9 31	14 58	1 29
3 T	4 46 8	10 30 21	26 25	8 43	21 13	8 39	9 02	0 ♑ 03	18 11	3 17	15 56	21 30	6 26	10 34	9 49	14 46	1 29
4 W	4 50 5	11 31 12	8 ♓ 22	8 44 R	22 31	9 53	9 42	0 17	18 17	3 15	15 56	21 32	6 50	10 59	10 07	14 35	1 28
5 Th	4 54 1	12 32 04	20 14	8 44	23 51	11 08	10 21	0 30	18 23	3 13	15 57	21 34	7 13	11 25	10 26	14 24	1 28
6 F	4 57 58	13 32 57	2 ♈ 07	8 42	25 12	12 22	11 01	0 43	18 30	3 11	15 57	21 35	7 37	11 51	10 44	14 13	1 27
7 Sa	5 1 54	14 33 51	14 04	8 40	26 35	13 36	11 41	0 57	18 36	3 10	15 57	21 37	8 00	12 17	11 01	14 03	1 27
8 Su	5 5 51	15 34 45	26 11	8 37	28 00	14 50	12 21	1 10	18 42	3 08	15 57	21 39	8 23	12 42	11 19	13 53	1 27
9 M	5 9 47	16 35 40	8 ♉ 30	8 33	29 25	16 05	13 01	1 24	18 49	3 06	15 58	21 40	8 47	13 08	11 36	13 43	1 27
10 T	5 13 44	17 36 37	21 04	8 29	0 ♐ 52	17 19	13 40	1 38	18 55	3 05	15 58	21 42	9 11	13 34	11 53	13 34	1 26
11 W	5 17 40	18 37 34	3 ♊ 53	8 26	2 19	18 33	14 20	1 51	19 01	3 03	15 59	21 44	9 34	13 59	12 11	13 26	1 26
12 Th	5 21 37	19 38 31	16 59	8 24	3 47	19 47	15 00	2 05	19 08	3 02	15 59	21 45	9 58	14 25	12 27	13 18	1 26
13 F	5 25 34	20 39 30	0 ♋ 21	8 23 D	5 16	21 01	15 40	2 18	19 14	3 00	16 00	21 47	10 21	14 50	12 44	13 10	1 26 D
14 Sa	5 29 30	21 40 30	13 56	8 23	6 45	22 15	16 20	2 32	19 21	2 59	16 00	21 49	10 45	15 16	13 01	13 03	1 26
15 Su	5 33 27	22 41 30	27 43	8 24	8 14	23 29	17 00	2 46	19 27	2 58	16 01	21 51	11 09	15 41	13 17	12 56	1 26
16 M	5 37 23	23 42 32	11 ♌ 40	8 25	9 44	24 43	17 40	2 59	19 34	2 56	16 01	21 53	11 32	16 07	13 33	12 49	1 26
17 T	5 41 20	24 43 34	25 44	8 26	11 15	25 57	18 20	3 13	19 41	2 55	16 02	21 54	11 56	16 33	13 49	12 43	1 26
18 W	5 45 16	25 44 37	9 ♍ 52	8 27	12 46	27 11	19 00	3 27	19 47	2 54	16 03	21 56	12 20	16 58	14 05	12 38	1 27
19 Th	5 49 13	26 45 42	24 03	8 27 R	14 17	28 25	19 40	3 41	19 54	2 53	16 04	21 58	12 44	17 23	14 20	12 32	1 27
20 F	5 53 9	27 46 47	8 ♎ 14	8 27	15 48	29 39	20 20	3 54	20 01	2 51	16 04	22 00	13 08	17 49	14 35	12 28	1 27
21 Sa	5 57 6	28 47 53	22 23	8 26	17 20	0 ♒ 53	21 00	4 08	20 08	2 50	16 05	22 02	13 31	18 14	14 51	12 23	1 28
22 Su	6 1 3	29 48 59	6 ♏ 28	8 25	18 51	2 07	21 41	4 22	20 14	2 49	16 06	22 04	13 55	18 40	15 05	12 20	1 28
23 M	6 4 59	0 ♑ 50 07	20 27	8 24	20 23	3 21	22 21	4 36	20 21	2 48	16 07	22 06	14 19	19 05	15 20	12 16	1 29
24 T	6 8 56	1 51 15	4 ♐ 15	8 24	21 56	4 35	23 01	4 50	20 28	2 47	16 08	22 08	14 43	19 30	15 35	12 13	1 29
25 W	6 12 52	2 52 24	17 52	8 23	23 28	5 49	23 41	5 03	20 35	2 47	16 09	22 09	15 07	19 56	15 49	12 11	1 30
26 Th	6 16 49	3 53 34	1 ♑ 14	8 23 D	25 01	7 03	24 21	5 17	20 42	2 46	16 09	22 11	15 31	20 21	16 03	12 09	1 31
27 F	6 20 45	4 54 44	14 21	8 23	26 34	8 16	25 02	5 31	20 49	2 45	16 10	22 13	15 55	20 46	16 17	12 07	1 31
28 Sa	6 24 42	5 55 54	27 11	8 23	28 07	9 30	25 42	5 45	20 56	2 44	16 11	22 15	16 19	21 11	16 30	12 06	1 32
29 Su	6 28 38	6 57 04	9 ♒ 45	8 23	29 41	10 44	26 22	5 59	21 03	2 43	16 13	22 17	16 42	21 36	16 43	12 06 D	1 33
30 M	6 32 35	7 58 14	22 04	8 23 R	1 ♑ 15	11 57	27 02	6 13	21 10	2 43	16 14	22 19	17 06	22 01	16 56	12 05	1 34
31 T	6 36 32	8 59 24	4 ♓ 10	8 23	2 49	13 11	27 43	6 26	21 17	2 42	16 15	22 21	17 30	22 27	17 09	12 06	1 35

EPHEMERIS CALCULATED FOR 12 MIDNIGHT GREENWICH MEAN TIME. ALL OTHER DATA AND FACING ASPECTARIAN PAGE IN **EASTERN TIME (BOLD)** AND PACIFIC TIME (REGULAR).

JANUARY 2020

☽ Last Aspect day	ET / hr:mn / PT	asp	☽ Ingress sign	day	ET / hr:mn / PT
1	**9:14 pm** 6:14 pm	△♂	♈	1	**11:00 pm** 8:00 pm
3	**8:18 pm** 5:18 pm	□♇	♉	4	**11:15 am** 8:15 am
6	**7:08 am** 4:08 am	△♇	♊	6	**9:11 pm** 6:11 pm
8	**5:16 pm** 2:16 pm	△♀	♋	9	**3:43 am** 12:43 am
10	**6:58 pm** 3:58 pm	☍♇	♌	11	**7:16 am** 4:16 am
13	**8:42 am** 5:42 am	☍♀	♍	13	**9:06 am** 6:06 am
15	**7:12 am** 4:12 am	△☿	♎	15	**10:43 am** 7:43 am
17	**7:58 am** 4:58 am	□☉	♏	17	**1:20 pm** 10:20 am
19	**4:22 pm** 1:22 pm	✶☉	♐	19	**5:41 pm** 2:41 pm
20	**11:46 pm** 8:46 pm	□♆	♑	21	9:00 pm

☽ Last Aspect day	ET / hr:mn / PT	asp	☽ Ingress sign	day	ET / hr:mn / PT
20	**11:46 pm** 8:46 pm	□♆	♑	22	**12:00 am**
23	**9:08 pm** 6:08 pm	☌♄	♒	24	**8:20 am** 5:20 am
25	**2:06 pm** 11:06 am	☌☿	♓	26	**6:44 pm** 3:44 pm
28	**8:08 pm** 5:08 pm	✶♄	♈	29	**6:51 am** 3:51 am
31	**10:10 am** 7:10 am	✶☿	♉	31	**7:28 pm** 4:28 pm

☽ Phases & Eclipses phase	day	ET / hr:mn / PT
2nd Quarter	2	**11:45 pm** 8:45 pm
Full Moon	10	**2:21 pm** 11:21 am
●	10	20° ♋ 00'
4th Quarter	17	**7:58 am** 4:58 am
New Moon	24	**4:42 pm** 1:42 pm

Planet Ingress	day	ET / hr:mn / PT
♂ ♐	3	**4:37 am** 1:37 am
♀ ♓	13	**1:39 pm** 10:39 am
☿ ♒	16	**1:31 pm** 10:31 am
⚵ ♑	18	**5:33 am** 2:33 am
☉ ♒	20	**9:55 am** 6:55 am
⚳ ♒	31	**3:01 am** 12:01 am

Planetary Motion	day	ET / hr:mn / PT
♅ D	10	**8:49 pm** 5:49 pm

1 WEDNESDAY
☽ ✶ ♄ **5:43 am** 2:43 am
☽ ✶ ♇ **7:39 am** 4:39 am
☽ △ ♂ **9:14 pm** 6:14 pm

2 THURSDAY
☽ ⚺ ♅ **4:26 am** 1:26 am
♀ ⚺ ♆ **7:56 am** 4:56 am
☿ ☌ ♃ **11:42 am** 8:42 am
☽ □ ♃ **1:19 pm** 10:19 am
☽ □ ☿ **1:32 pm** 10:32 am
☽ □ ☉ **11:45 pm** 8:45 pm

3 FRIDAY
☽ ⚺ ♆ **7:56 am** 4:56 am
☽ ✶ ♀ **10:38 am** 7:38 am
☽ □ ♄ **6:50 pm** 3:50 pm
☽ □ ♇ **8:18 pm** 5:18 pm

4 SATURDAY
☽ ⚻ ♂ **1:03 pm** 10:03 am
☽ ☌ ♅ **4:31 pm** 1:31 pm
☽ △ ♃ 11:20 pm

5 SUNDAY
☽ △ ♃ **2:20 am**
☽ △ ☿ **10:18 am** 7:18 am
☽ △ ☉ **4:37 pm** 1:37 pm
☽ ✶ ♆ **7:15 pm** 4:15 pm

6 MONDAY
☽ □ ♀ **4:08 am** 1:08 am
☽ △ ♄ **6:07 am** 3:07 am
☽ △ ♇ **7:08 am** 4:08 am
☉ ✶ ♆ 10:21 pm
☽ ☍ ♂ 11:05 pm
☽ ⚺ ♅ 11:09 pm
♀ ⚺ ♄ 11:39 pm

7 TUESDAY
☉ ✶ ♆ **1:21 am**
☽ ☍ ♂ **2:05 am**
☽ ⚺ ♅ **2:09 am**
♀ ⚺ ♄ **2:39 am**
♂ ⚻ ♅ **3:13 am** 12:13 am
♀ ⚺ ♇ **11:53 am** 8:53 am
☽ ⚻ ♃ **12:28 pm** 9:28 am
☽ ⚻ ☿ 11:49 pm

8 WEDNESDAY
☽ ⚻ ☿ **2:49 am**
☽ □ ♆ **3:27 am** 12:27 am
☽ ⚻ ☉ **5:35 am** 2:35 am
☿ ✶ ♆ **8:03 am** 5:03 am
☽ ⚻ ♄ **2:04 pm** 11:04 am
☽ ⚻ ♇ **2:40 pm** 11:40 am
☽ △ ♀ **5:16 pm** 2:16 pm

9 THURSDAY
☽ ✶ ♅ **8:23 am** 5:23 am
☽ ⚻ ♂ **11:09 am** 8:09 am
☽ ☍ ♃ **7:00 pm** 4:00 pm

10 FRIDAY
☽ △ ♆ **8:19 am** 5:19 am
☉ ☌ ☿ **10:19 am** 7:19 am
☽ ☍ ☉ **2:21 pm** 11:21 am
☽ ☍ ☿ **2:33 pm** 11:33 am
☽ ☍ ♄ **6:43 pm** 3:43 pm
☽ ☍ ♇ **6:58 pm** 3:58 pm
☽ ⚻ ♀ 11:12 pm

11 SATURDAY
☽ ⚻ ♀ **2:12 am**
☽ □ ♅ **11:43 am** 8:43 am
☽ △ ♂ **4:54 pm** 1:54 pm
☽ ⚻ ♃ **10:43 pm** 7:43 pm

12 SUNDAY
☿ ☌ ♄ **4:51 am** 1:51 am
☿ ☌ ♇ **5:14 am** 2:14 am
☽ ⚻ ♆ **10:50 am** 7:50 am
♄ ☌ ♇ **11:59 am** 8:59 am
☽ ⚻ ☉ **8:23 pm** 5:23 pm
☽ ⚻ ♇ **9:12 pm** 6:12 pm
☽ ⚻ ♄ **9:15 pm** 6:15 pm
☽ ⚻ ☿ **11:13 pm** 8:13 pm

13 MONDAY
☉ ☌ ♇ **8:21 am** 5:21 am
☽ ☍ ♀ **8:42 am** 5:42 am
☉ ☌ ♄ **10:15 am** 7:15 am
☽ △ ♅ **1:29 pm** 10:29 am
☽ □ ♂ **9:00 pm** 6:00 pm
☽ △ ♃ 10:07 pm

14 TUESDAY
☽ △ ♃ **1:07 am**
☽ ☍ ♆ **12:27 pm** 9:27 am
☽ △ ♇ **10:51 pm** 7:51 pm
☽ △ ♄ **11:12 pm** 8:12 pm
☽ △ ☉ 10:41 pm

15 WEDNESDAY
☽ △ ☉ **1:41 am**
☽ △ ☿ **7:12 am** 4:12 am
☽ ⚻ ♀ **2:52 pm** 11:52 am
☽ ⚻ ♅ **3:09 pm** 12:09 pm
♀ ✶ ♅ **6:18 pm** 3:18 pm
☽ ✶ ♂ 10:14 pm

16 THURSDAY
☽ ✶ ♂ **1:14 am**
☽ □ ♃ **3:45 am** 12:45 am
☽ ⚻ ♆ **2:36 pm** 11:36 am
☽ □ ♇ 10:16 pm
☽ □ ♄ 10:56 pm

17 FRIDAY
☽ □ ♇ **1:16 am**
☽ □ ♄ **1:56 am**
☽ □ ☉ **7:58 am** 4:58 am
☽ □ ☿ **4:36 pm** 1:36 pm
☽ ☍ ♅ **5:55 pm** 2:55 pm
☽ △ ♀ **10:26 pm** 7:26 pm

18 SATURDAY
☿ □ ♅ **3:32 am** 12:32 am
☽ ⚺ ♂ **6:56 am** 3:56 am
☽ ✶ ♃ **7:45 am** 4:45 am
☽ △ ♆ **6:13 pm** 3:13 pm

19 SUNDAY
☽ ✶ ♇ **5:18 am** 2:18 am
☽ ✶ ♄ **6:19 am** 3:19 am
♂ ⚺ ♃ **7:46 am** 4:46 am
☽ ✶ ☉ **4:22 pm** 1:22 pm
☽ ⚻ ♅ **10:28 pm** 7:28 pm

20 MONDAY
☽ ✶ ☿ **4:40 am** 1:40 am
☽ □ ♀ **8:20 am** 5:20 am
☽ ⚺ ♃ **1:42 pm** 10:42 am
☽ ☌ ♂ **2:47 pm** 11:47 am
☽ □ ♆ **11:46 pm** 8:46 pm

21 TUESDAY
☽ ⚺ ♇ **11:17 am** 8:17 am
☽ ⚺ ♄ **12:41 pm** 9:41 am

22 WEDNESDAY
☽ ⚺ ☉ **3:14 am** 12:14 am
☽ △ ♅ **5:00 am** 2:00 am
☽ ⚺ ☿ **7:47 pm** 4:47 pm
☽ ✶ ♀ **8:52 pm** 5:52 pm
☽ ☌ ♃ **9:45 pm** 6:45 pm
☽ ⚺ ♂ 9:58 pm
☉ □ ♅ 10:54 pm

23 THURSDAY
☽ ⚺ ♂ **12:58 am**
☉ □ ♅ **1:54 am**
☽ ✶ ♆ **7:20 am** 4:20 am
♀ ✶ ♃ **8:07 am** 5:07 am
☿ ⚺ ♃ **12:17 pm** 9:17 am
☽ ☌ ♇ **7:18 pm** 4:18 pm
☿ ⚺ ♀ **8:07 pm** 5:07 pm
☽ ☌ ♄ **9:08 pm** 6:08 pm

24 FRIDAY
☽ □ ♅ **1:34 pm** 10:34 am
☽ ☌ ☉ **4:42 pm** 1:42 pm

25 SATURDAY
☽ ⚺ ♃ **7:56 am** 4:56 am
☿ ✶ ♂ **8:09 am** 5:09 am
☽ ⚺ ♀ **12:08 pm** 9:08 am
☽ ✶ ♂ **1:34 pm** 10:34 am
☽ ☌ ☿ **2:06 pm** 11:06 am
☽ ⚺ ♆ **4:58 pm** 1:58 pm

26 SUNDAY
☽ ⚺ ♇ **5:23 am** 2:23 am
☽ ⚺ ♄ **7:42 am** 4:42 am
☿ ⚺ ♆ **10:50 am** 7:50 am
♀ □ ♂ **8:37 pm** 5:37 pm
☽ ✶ ♅ 9:12 pm

27 MONDAY
☽ ✶ ♅ **12:12 am**
☽ ⚺ ☉ **8:47 am** 5:47 am
♀ ☌ ♆ **3:00 pm** 12:00 pm
☽ ✶ ♃ **8:13 pm** 5:13 pm

28 TUESDAY
☽ □ ♂ **4:30 am** 1:30 am
☽ ☌ ♆ **4:34 am** 1:34 am
♂ □ ♆ **5:34 am** 2:34 am
☽ ☌ ♀ **6:02 am** 3:02 am
☽ ⚺ ☿ **11:27 am** 8:27 am
☽ ✶ ♇ **5:21 pm** 2:21 pm
☽ ✶ ♄ **8:08 pm** 5:08 pm

29 WEDNESDAY
☽ ⚺ ♅ **12:31 pm** 9:31 am
☽ ✶ ☉ 11:50 pm

30 THURSDAY
☽ ✶ ☉ **2:50 am**
☿ ⚺ ♇ **5:26 am** 2:26 am
☽ □ ♃ **9:54 am** 6:54 am
☽ ⚺ ♆ **5:21 pm** 2:21 pm
☽ △ ♂ **8:49 pm** 5:49 pm
☽ ⚺ ♀ 10:26 pm

31 FRIDAY
☽ ⚺ ♀ **1:26 am**
☿ ⚺ ♄ **4:26 am** 1:26 am
☽ □ ♇ **6:11 am** 3:11 am
☽ □ ♄ **9:24 am** 6:24 am
☽ ✶ ☿ **10:10 am** 7:10 am
☽ ☌ ♅ 10:10 pm

Eastern time in bold type
Pacific time in medium type

JANUARY 2020

DATE	SID.TIME	SUN	MOON	NODE	MERCURY	VENUS	MARS	JUPITER	SATURN	URANUS	NEPTUNE	PLUTO	CERES	PALLAS	JUNO	VESTA	CHIRON
1 W	6 40 28	10♑00 34	16♓08	8♋23℞	4♑23	14♒25	28♏23	6♑40	21♑24	2♉42℞	16♓16	22♑23	17♑54	22♐52	17♎22	12♉06	1♈36
2 Th	6 44 25	11 01 44	28 01	8 23	5 58	15 38	29 03	6 54	21 31	2 41	16 17	22 25	18 18	23 17	17 34	12 08	1 37
3 F	6 48 21	12 02 54	9♈53	8 23D	7 33	16 52	29 44	7 08	21 38	2 41	16 18	22 27	18 42	23 41	17 46	12 09	1 38
4 Sa	6 52 18	13 04 04	21 50	8 23	9 08	18 05	0♐24	7 22	21 45	2 40	16 19	22 29	19 06	24 06	17 58	12 11	1 39
5 Su	6 56 14	14 05 13	3♉55	8 23	10 44	19 18	1 05	7 35	21 52	2 40	16 21	22 31	19 30	24 31	18 09	12 13	1 40
6 M	7 0 11	15 06 22	16 14	8 24	12 20	20 32	1 45	7 49	21 59	2 40	16 22	22 33	19 54	24 56	18 21	12 16	1 42
7 T	7 4 7	16 07 31	28 50	8 24	13 56	21 45	2 25	8 03	22 06	2 39	16 23	22 35	20 18	25 21	18 32	12 20	1 43
8 W	7 8 4	17 08 39	11♊47	8 25	15 33	22 58	3 06	8 17	22 13	2 39	16 25	22 37	20 42	25 45	18 42	12 23	1 44
9 Th	7 12 1	18 09 48	25 05	8 26	17 10	24 11	3 46	8 31	22 20	2 39	16 26	22 39	21 06	26 10	18 53	12 27	1 46
10 F	7 15 57	19 10 56	8♋44	8 26℞	18 47	25 24	4 27	8 44	22 27	2 39	16 27	22 41	21 30	26 35	19 03	12 32	1 47
11 Sa	7 19 54	20 12 03	22 44	8 26	20 25	26 37	5 08	8 58	22 34	2 39D	16 29	22 43	21 54	26 59	19 13	12 37	1 49
12 Su	7 23 50	21 13 11	7♌00	8 25	22 04	27 50	5 48	9 12	22 42	2 39	16 30	22 45	22 18	27 24	19 22	12 42	1 50
13 M	7 27 47	22 14 18	21 27	8 23	23 43	29 03	6 29	9 25	22 49	2 39	16 32	22 47	22 42	27 48	19 32	12 47	1 52
14 T	7 31 43	23 15 25	6♍00	8 21	25 22	0♓16	7 09	9 39	22 56	2 39	16 33	22 49	23 06	28 12	19 41	12 53	1 54
15 W	7 35 40	24 16 31	20 32	8 19	27 02	1 29	7 50	9 53	23 03	2 39	16 35	22 51	23 30	28 37	19 50	13 00	1 55
16 Th	7 39 36	25 17 38	4♎58	8 18	28 42	2 42	8 31	10 06	23 10	2 40	16 36	22 53	23 54	29 01	19 58	13 06	1 57
17 F	7 43 33	26 18 44	19 14	8 17D	0♒23	3 54	9 11	10 20	23 17	2 40	16 38	22 55	24 18	29 25	20 06	13 14	1 59
18 Sa	7 47 30	27 19 51	3♏18	8 17	2 04	5 07	9 52	10 34	23 24	2 40	16 40	22 57	24 42	29 49	20 14	13 21	2 01
19 Su	7 51 26	28 20 57	17 08	8 18	3 46	6 20	10 33	10 47	23 31	2 41	16 41	22 59	25 06	0♑13	20 21	13 29	2 03
20 M	7 55 23	29 22 03	0♐44	8 19	5 28	7 32	11 13	11 01	23 38	2 41	16 43	23 01	25 30	0 38	20 28	13 37	2 05
21 T	7 59 19	0♒23 08	14 07	8 21	7 10	8 44	11 54	11 14	23 45	2 42	16 45	23 03	25 54	1 01	20 35	13 45	2 07
22 W	8 3 16	1 24 13	27 17	8 22℞	8 53	9 57	12 35	11 28	23 53	2 42	16 46	23 05	26 18	1 25	20 42	13 54	2 09
23 Th	8 7 12	2 25 18	10♑14	8 22	10 36	11 09	13 16	11 41	24 00	2 43	16 48	23 07	26 41	1 49	20 48	14 04	2 11
24 F	8 11 9	3 26 22	23 00	8 21	12 20	12 21	13 57	11 54	24 07	2 43	16 50	23 09	27 05	2 13	20 54	14 13	2 13
25 Sa	8 15 6	4 27 26	5♒33	8 19	14 03	13 33	14 37	12 08	24 14	2 44	16 52	23 11	27 29	2 37	20 59	14 23	2 15
26 Su	8 19 2	5 28 28	17 56	8 16	15 46	14 45	15 18	12 21	24 21	2 45	16 53	23 13	27 53	3 00	21 04	14 33	2 17
27 M	8 22 59	6 29 30	0♓08	8 11	17 30	15 57	15 59	12 34	24 28	2 46	16 55	23 15	28 17	3 24	21 09	14 44	2 19
28 T	8 26 55	7 30 30	12 12	8 05	19 13	17 09	16 40	12 48	24 35	2 46	16 57	23 17	28 41	3 47	21 14	14 54	2 22
29 W	8 30 52	8 31 30	24 08	8 00	20 56	18 20	17 21	13 01	24 42	2 47	16 59	23 19	29 05	4 11	21 18	15 06	2 24
30 Th	8 34 48	9 32 28	6♈00	7 55	22 38	19 32	18 02	13 14	24 49	2 48	17 01	23 21	29 28	4 34	21 22	15 17	2 26
31 F	8 38 45	10 33 26	17 52	7 51	24 19	20 44	18 43	13 27	24 56	2 49	17 03	23 23	29 52	4 57	21 25	15 29	2 29

EPHEMERIS CALCULATED FOR 12 MIDNIGHT GREENWICH MEAN TIME. ALL OTHER DATA AND FACING ASPECTARIAN PAGE IN **EASTERN TIME (BOLD)** AND PACIFIC TIME (REGULAR).

FEBRUARY 2020

☽ Last Aspect day	ET / hr:mn / PT	asp	☽ Ingress sign	day	ET / hr:mn / PT
3	**6:28 am** 3:28 am	□☿	♊	3	**6:29 am** 3:29 am
5	**9:20 am** 6:20 am	□♀	♋	5	**2:03 pm** 11:03 am
7	**10:43 am** 7:43 am	☍♄	♌	7	**5:45 pm** 2:45 pm
9	**11:08 am** 8:08 am	△♂	♍	9	**6:39 pm** 3:39 pm
11	**1:26 pm** 10:26 am	□♂	♎	11	**6:37 pm** 3:37 pm
13	**4:40 pm** 1:40 pm	⚹♂	♏	13	**7:37 pm** 4:37 pm
15	**5:20 pm** 2:20 pm	⚹♄	♐	15	**11:07 pm** 8:07 pm
18	**4:03 am** 1:03 am	⚹☉	♑	18	**5:37 am** 2:37 am
20	**9:18 am** 6:18 am	☌♄	♒	20	**2:42 pm** 11:42 am
21	**11:08 pm** 8:08 pm	⚹♀	♓	22	10:37 pm
21	**11:08 pm** 8:08 pm	⚹♀	♓	23	**1:37 am**
25	**9:12 am** 6:12 am	⚹♄	♈	25	**1:47 pm** 10:47 am
27	**10:25 pm** 7:25 pm	□♄	♉	27	11:30 pm
27	**10:25 pm** 7:25 pm	□♄	♉	28	**2:30 am**

☽ Phases & Eclipses phase	day	ET / hr:mn / PT
2nd Quarter	1	**8:42 pm** 5:42 pm
Full Moon	8	11:33 pm
Full Moon	9	**2:33 am**
4th Quarter	15	**5:17 pm** 2:17 pm
New Moon	23	**10:32 am** 7:32 am

Planet Ingress	day	ET / hr:mn / PT
☿ ♓	3	**6:37 am** 3:37 am
♀ ♈	7	**3:02 pm** 12:02 pm
♂ ♑	16	**6:33 am** 3:33 am
☉ ♓	18	**11:57 pm** 8:57 pm

Planetary Motion	day	ET / hr:mn / PT
✷ ℞	8	**12:59 pm** 9:59 am
☿ ℞	16	**7:54 pm** 4:54 pm

1 SATURDAY
☽ ☌ ♅ **1:10 am**
☽ □ ☉ **8:42 pm** 5:42 pm
☽ △ ♃ **11:12 pm** 8:12 pm
♀ ⚹ ♇ 11:07 pm

2 SUNDAY
♀ ⚹ ♇ **2:07 am**
☽ ⚹ ♆ **5:30 am** 2:30 am
☽ ⚻ ♂ **12:14 pm** 9:14 am
☽ △ ♇ **5:54 pm** 2:54 pm
☽ ⚹ ♀ **7:32 pm** 4:32 pm
☽ △ ♄ **9:24 pm** 6:24 pm

3 MONDAY
☽ □ ☿ **6:28 am** 3:28 am
☉ ⚺ ♃ **10:00 am** 7:00 am
☽ ⚺ ♅ **12:01 pm** 9:01 am
♀ ⚹ ♄ **5:01 pm** 2:01 pm

4 TUESDAY
☽ ⚻ ♃ **9:45 am** 6:45 am
☽ △ ☉ **11:20 am** 8:20 am
☽ □ ♆ **2:50 pm** 11:50 am
☽ ☍ ♂ 9:07 pm
☽ ⚻ ♇ 11:27 pm

5 WEDNESDAY
☽ ☍ ♂ **12:07 am**
☽ ⚻ ♇ **2:27 am**
☿ ⚹ ♅ **4:43 am** 1:43 am
☽ ⚻ ♄ **6:04 am** 3:04 am
☽ □ ♀ **9:20 am** 6:20 am
☽ ⚹ ♅ **7:17 pm** 4:17 pm
☽ △ ☿ **9:00 pm** 6:00 pm

6 THURSDAY
☉ ⚺ ♆ **9:39 am** 6:39 am
☽ ☍ ♃ **4:14 pm** 1:14 pm
☽ △ ♆ **8:15 pm** 5:15 pm
☽ ⚻ ☉ **9:03 pm** 6:03 pm
♂ ⚺ ♇ **11:03 pm** 8:03 pm

7 FRIDAY
☽ ☍ ♇ **7:02 am** 4:02 am
☽ ⚻ ♂ **7:26 am** 4:26 am
☽ ☍ ♄ **10:43 am** 7:43 am
☽ △ ♀ **5:59 pm** 2:59 pm
☽ □ ♅ **10:43 pm** 7:43 pm

8 SATURDAY
☽ ⚻ ☿ **5:26 am** 2:26 am
☽ ⚻ ♃ **7:04 pm** 4:04 pm
☽ ⚻ ♆ **10:15 pm** 7:15 pm
☽ ☍ ☉ 11:33 pm

9 SUNDAY
☽ ☍ ☉ **2:33 am**
☽ ⚻ ♇ **8:30 am** 5:30 am
☽ △ ♂ **11:08 am** 8:08 am
☽ ⚻ ♄ **12:17 pm** 9:17 am
☽ ⚻ ♀ **11:02 pm** 8:02 pm
☽ △ ♅ **11:31 pm** 8:31 pm

10 MONDAY
♀ ⚺ ♅ **5:23 am** 2:23 am
☽ ☍ ☿ **9:51 am** 6:51 am
♂ ⚺ ♄ **4:30 pm** 1:30 pm
☽ △ ♃ **7:55 pm** 4:55 pm
☽ ☍ ♆ **10:29 pm** 7:29 pm

11 TUESDAY
☽ ⚻ ☉ **6:05 am** 3:05 am
☽ △ ♇ **8:36 am** 5:36 am
☽ △ ♄ **12:37 pm** 9:37 am
☽ □ ♂ **1:26 pm** 10:26 am
☽ ⚻ ♅ **11:36 pm** 8:36 pm

12 WEDNESDAY
☽ ☍ ♀ **3:06 am** 12:06 am
☽ ⚻ ☿ **12:55 pm** 9:55 am
☉ ⚺ ♇ **8:25 pm** 5:25 pm
☽ □ ♃ **8:54 pm** 5:54 pm
☽ ⚻ ♆ **10:57 pm** 7:57 pm

13 THURSDAY
☽ □ ♇ **9:20 am** 6:20 am
☽ △ ☉ **10:17 am** 7:17 am
☽ □ ♄ **1:46 pm** 10:46 am
☽ ⚹ ♂ **4:40 pm** 1:40 pm
☽ ☍ ♅ 9:54 pm

14 FRIDAY
☽ ☍ ♅ **12:54 am**
☽ ⚻ ♀ **8:52 am** 5:52 am
☽ △ ☿ **4:43 pm** 1:43 pm
☽ ⚹ ♃ **11:52 pm** 8:52 pm
☽ △ ♆ 10:25 pm

15 SATURDAY
☽ △ ♆ **1:25 am**
☽ ⚹ ♇ **12:21 pm** 9:21 am
☽ □ ☉ **5:17 pm** 2:17 pm
☽ ⚹ ♄ **5:20 pm** 2:20 pm
☉ ⚺ ♄ **5:57 pm** 2:57 pm
☽ ⚺ ♂ **10:43 pm** 7:43 pm

16 SUNDAY
☽ ⚻ ♅ **4:49 am** 1:49 am
☽ △ ♀ **6:06 pm** 3:06 pm
☽ □ ☿ **10:10 pm** 7:10 pm

17 MONDAY
☽ ⚺ ♃ **5:52 am** 2:52 am
☽ □ ♆ **6:49 am** 3:49 am
☽ ⚺ ♇ **6:22 pm** 3:22 pm
☽ ⚺ ♄ **11:58 pm** 8:58 pm

18 TUESDAY
☽ ⚹ ☉ **4:03 am** 1:03 am
☽ ☌ ♂ **8:16 am** 5:16 am
☽ △ ♅ **11:45 am** 8:45 am
☿ ⚺ ♀ **12:02 pm** 9:02 am

19 WEDNESDAY
☽ ⚹ ☿ **4:56 am** 1:56 am
☽ □ ♀ **7:08 am** 4:08 am
☽ ☌ ♃ **2:50 pm** 11:50 am
☽ ⚹ ♆ **3:05 pm** 12:05 pm

20 THURSDAY
☽ ☌ ♇ **3:07 am** 12:07 am
☽ ☌ ♄ **9:18 am** 6:18 am
♃ ⚹ ♆ **10:56 am** 7:56 am
☽ ⚺ ☉ **6:08 pm** 3:08 pm
☽ ⚺ ♂ **8:50 pm** 5:50 pm
☽ □ ♅ **9:13 pm** 6:13 pm

21 FRIDAY
♂ △ ♅ **4:10 am** 1:10 am
☽ ⚺ ☿ **12:15 pm** 9:15 am
☽ ⚹ ♀ **11:08 pm** 8:08 pm
☽ ⚺ ♆ 10:31 pm
☽ ⚺ ♃ 11:02 pm

22 SATURDAY
☽ ⚺ ♆ **1:31 am**
☽ ⚺ ♃ **2:02 am**
☉ ⚹ ♅ **9:13 am** 6:13 am
☽ ⚺ ♇ **1:51 pm** 10:51 am
☽ ⚺ ♄ **8:36 pm** 5:36 pm
♀ ⚺ ♆ 10:27 pm

23 SUNDAY
♀ ⚺ ♆ **1:27 am**
☽ ⚹ ♅ **8:29 am** 5:29 am
☽ ☌ ☉ **10:32 am** 7:32 am
☽ ⚹ ♂ **11:30 am** 8:30 am
♀ □ ♃ **11:59 am** 8:59 am
☽ ☌ ☿ **7:39 pm** 4:39 pm

24 MONDAY
☽ ☌ ♆ **1:26 pm** 10:26 am
☽ ⚹ ♃ **2:45 pm** 11:45 am
☽ ⚺ ♀ **5:05 pm** 2:05 pm
☉ ⚹ ♂ **9:06 pm** 6:06 pm
☽ ⚹ ♇ 10:57 pm

25 TUESDAY
☽ ⚹ ♇ **1:57 am**
☽ ⚹ ♄ **9:12 am** 6:12 am
☉ ☌ ☿ **8:45 pm** 5:45 pm
☽ ⚺ ♅ **8:56 pm** 5:56 pm
☿ ⚹ ♂ 9:59 pm

26 WEDNESDAY
☿ ⚹ ♂ **12:59 am**
☽ ⚺ ☿ **3:11 am** 12:11 am
☽ □ ♂ **3:32 am** 12:32 am
☽ ⚺ ☉ **4:26 am** 1:26 am
☽ ⚺ ♆ 11:14 pm

27 THURSDAY
☽ ⚺ ♆ **2:14 am**
☽ □ ♃ **4:22 am** 1:22 am
☽ ☌ ♀ **12:05 pm** 9:05 am
☽ □ ♇ **2:47 pm** 11:47 am
☽ □ ♄ **10:25 pm** 7:25 pm

28 FRIDAY
☽ ☌ ♅ **9:50 am** 6:50 am
☽ ⚹ ☿ **10:51 am** 7:51 am
♀ □ ♇ **5:08 pm** 2:08 pm
☽ △ ♂ **7:56 pm** 4:56 pm
☿ ⚹ ♅ **10:13 pm** 7:13 pm
☽ ⚹ ☉ **10:40 pm** 7:40 pm

29 SATURDAY
☽ ⚹ ♆ **2:50 pm** 11:50 am
☽ △ ♃ **5:41 pm** 2:41 pm

Eastern time in bold type
Pacific time in medium type

FEBRUARY 2020

DATE	SID.TIME	SUN	MOON	NODE	MERCURY	VENUS	MARS	JUPITER	SATURN	URANUS	NEPTUNE	PLUTO	CERES	PALLAS	JUNO	VESTA	CHIRON
1 Sa	8 42 41	11♒34 22	29♈46	7♋49℞	25♒59	21♓55	19♐24	13♑40	25♑03	2♉50	17♓05	23♑25	0♒16	5♑20	21♎28	15♉41	2♈31
2 Su	8 46 38	12 35 17	11♉48	7 48D	27 37	23 06	20 05	13 53	25 10	2 51	17 07	23 27	0 40	5 43	21 31	15 53	2 34
3 M	8 50 34	13 36 10	24 03	7 48	29 14	24 17	20 46	14 06	25 16	2 53	17 09	23 29	1 03	6 06	21 33	16 05	2 36
4 T	8 54 31	14 37 02	6♊35	7 50	0♓48	25 29	21 27	14 19	25 23	2 54	17 11	23 31	1 27	6 29	21 35	16 18	2 39
5 W	8 58 28	15 37 53	19 28	7 51	2 20	26 40	22 08	14 32	25 30	2 55	17 13	23 33	1 50	6 52	21 37	16 31	2 42
6 Th	9 2 24	16 38 43	2♋47	7 53℞	3 48	27 50	22 49	14 45	25 37	2 56	17 15	23 34	2 14	7 15	21 38	16 45	2 44
7 F	9 6 21	17 39 31	16 33	7 52	5 11	29 01	23 30	14 58	25 44	2 58	17 17	23 36	2 38	7 37	21 39	16 58	2 47
8 Sa	9 10 17	18 40 18	0♌45	7 50	6 31	0♈12	24 11	15 10	25 50	2 59	17 19	23 38	3 01	8 00	21 39℞	17 12	2 50
9 Su	9 14 14	19 41 03	15 21	7 46	7 44	1 22	24 52	15 23	25 57	3 01	17 21	23 40	3 25	8 22	21 39	17 26	2 52
10 M	9 18 10	20 41 47	0♍13	7 40	8 52	2 32	25 33	15 35	26 04	3 02	17 23	23 42	3 48	8 44	21 39	17 41	2 55
11 T	9 22 7	21 42 30	15 14	7 34	9 53	3 43	26 14	15 48	26 11	3 04	17 25	23 44	4 12	9 07	21 38	17 56	2 58
12 W	9 26 4	22 43 11	0♎14	7 27	10 46	4 53	26 55	16 00	26 17	3 05	17 27	23 46	4 35	9 29	21 37	18 10	3 01
13 Th	9 30 0	23 43 52	15 04	7 20	11 30	6 03	27 36	16 13	26 24	3 07	17 29	23 47	4 59	9 51	21 36	18 25	3 04
14 F	9 33 57	24 44 31	29 38	7 16	12 06	7 12	28 18	16 25	26 30	3 09	17 31	23 49	5 22	10 13	21 34	18 41	3 07
15 Sa	9 37 53	25 45 09	13♏50	7 13D	12 32	8 22	28 59	16 37	26 37	3 10	17 33	23 51	5 45	10 35	21 32	18 56	3 10
16 Su	9 41 50	26 45 46	27 40	7 12	12 48	9 31	29 40	16 50	26 43	3 12	17 36	23 53	6 08	10 56	21 29	19 12	3 12
17 M	9 45 46	27 46 22	11♐08	7 13	12 53℞	10 41	0♑21	17 02	26 50	3 14	17 38	23 54	6 32	11 18	21 26	19 28	3 15
18 T	9 49 43	28 46 57	24 17	7 14	12 49	11 50	1 03	17 14	26 56	3 16	17 40	23 56	6 55	11 39	21 23	19 44	3 18
19 W	9 53 39	29 47 31	7♑09	7 15℞	12 33	12 59	1 44	17 26	27 03	3 18	17 42	23 58	7 18	12 01	21 19	20 01	3 22
20 Th	9 57 36	0♓48 03	19 47	7 14	12 08	14 08	2 25	17 38	27 09	3 20	17 44	24 00	7 41	12 22	21 15	20 17	3 25
21 F	10 1 33	1 48 34	2♒13	7 11	11 34	15 16	3 07	17 50	27 15	3 22	17 46	24 01	8 04	12 43	21 11	20 34	3 28
22 Sa	10 5 29	2 49 03	14 30	7 05	10 51	16 25	3 48	18 01	27 22	3 24	17 49	24 03	8 27	13 04	21 06	20 51	3 31
23 Su	10 9 26	3 49 31	26 40	6 57	10 01	17 33	4 29	18 13	27 28	3 26	17 51	24 05	8 50	13 25	21 00	21 08	3 34
24 M	10 13 22	4 49 57	8♓43	6 46	9 04	18 41	5 11	18 25	27 34	3 28	17 53	24 06	9 13	13 46	20 55	21 26	3 37
25 T	10 17 19	5 50 22	20 41	6 34	8 04	19 49	5 52	18 36	27 40	3 30	17 55	24 08	9 36	14 07	20 49	21 43	3 40
26 W	10 21 15	6 50 44	2♈35	6 22	7 00	20 57	6 33	18 48	27 46	3 32	17 58	24 09	9 59	14 27	20 42	22 01	3 44
27 Th	10 25 12	7 51 05	14 26	6 11	5 55	22 05	7 15	18 59	27 52	3 34	18 00	24 11	10 22	14 48	20 35	22 19	3 47
28 F	10 29 8	8 51 24	26 17	6 01	4 50	23 12	7 56	19 10	27 58	3 37	18 02	24 12	10 45	15 08	20 28	22 37	3 50
29 Sa	10 33 5	9 51 42	8♉11	5 54	3 48	24 19	8 38	19 22	28 04	3 39	18 04	24 14	11 08	15 28	20 21	22 56	3 53

EPHEMERIS CALCULATED FOR 12 MIDNIGHT GREENWICH MEAN TIME. ALL OTHER DATA AND FACING ASPECTARIAN PAGE IN **EASTERN TIME (BOLD)** AND PACIFIC TIME (REGULAR).

MARCH 2020

☽ Last Aspect day	ET / hr:mn / PT	asp	☽ Ingress sign	day	ET / hr:mn / PT
1	**10:52 am** 7:52 am	△♄	♊	1	**2:21 pm** 11:21 am
3	**9:20 pm** 6:20 pm	⚹♀	♋	3	**11:25 pm** 8:25 pm
5	11:11 pm	☍♄	♌	6	**4:27 am** 1:27 am
6	**2:11 am**	☍♄	♌	6	**4:27 am** 1:27 am
8	**4:12 am** 12:12 am	☍☿	♍	8	**6:47 am** 3:47 am
10	**4:32 am** 1:32 am	△♄	♎	10	**6:03 am** 3:03 am
12	**4:12 am** 1:12 am	□♄	♏	12	**5:28 am** 2:28 am
14	**6:06 am** 3:06 am	⚹♄	♐	14	**7:09 am** 4:09 am
16	**5:34 am** 2:34 am	□☉	♑	16	**12:25 pm** 9:25 am
18	**8:48 pm** 5:48 pm	☌♄	♒	18	**9:16 pm** 6:16 pm

☽ Last Aspect day	ET / hr:mn / PT	asp	☽ Ingress sign	day	ET / hr:mn / PT
20	**5:00 am** 2:00 am	□♀	♓	21	**8:33 am** 5:33 am
23	**10:51 am** 7:51 am	⚹♂	♈	23	**8:58 pm** 5:58 pm
26	**3:16 am** 12:16 am	□♂	♉	26	**9:37 am** 6:37 am
28	**7:05 pm** 4:05 pm	△♂	♊	28	**9:38 pm** 6:38 pm
30	**11:10 am** 8:10 am	□♆	♋	31	**7:43 am** 4:43 am

☽ Phases & Eclipses phase	day	ET / hr:mn / PT
2nd Quarter	2	**2:57 pm** 11:57 am
Full Moon	9	**1:48 pm** 10:48 am
4th Quarter	16	**5:34 am** 2:34 am
New Moon	24	**5:28 am** 2:28 am

Planet Ingress	day	ET / hr:mn / PT
☿ ♒	4	**6:08 am** 3:08 am
♀ ♉	4	**10:07 pm** 7:07 pm
☿ ♓	16	**3:42 am** 12:42 am
☉ ♈	19	**11:50 pm** 8:50 pm
⚶ ♊	20	10:10 pm
⚶ ♊	21	**1:10 am**
♄ ♒	21	**11:58 pm** 8:58 pm
♂ ♒	30	**3:43 pm** 12:43 pm

Planetary Motion	day	ET / hr:mn / PT
☿ D	9	**11:49 pm** 8:49 pm

1 SUNDAY
☽△♇ **3:04 am** 12:04 am
☽⚺♀ **6:25 am** 3:25 am
☽△♄ **10:52 am** 7:52 am
☽□☿ **6:05 pm** 3:05 pm
☽⚺♅ **9:38 pm** 6:38 pm

2 MONDAY
☽⚻♂ **10:39 am** 7:39 am
☽□☉ **2:57 pm** 11:57 am
☽□♆ 10:24 pm

3 TUESDAY
☽□♆ **1:24 am**
☽⚻♃ **4:47 am** 1:47 am
♀□♄ **11:44 am** 8:44 am
☽⚻♇ **12:55 pm** 9:55 am
☽⚻♄ **8:35 pm** 5:35 pm
☽⚹♀ **9:20 pm** 6:20 pm
☽△☿ **11:44 pm** 8:44 pm

4 WEDNESDAY
☽⚹♅ **6:26 am** 3:26 am
☿⚹♀ **4:24 pm** 1:24 pm
☽☍♂ **9:25 pm** 6:25 pm
☽△☉ 11:49 pm

5 THURSDAY
☽△☉ **2:49 am**
☽△♆ **8:14 am** 5:14 am
☽☍♃ **11:56 am** 8:56 am
☽☍♇ **6:50 pm** 3:50 pm
☽☍♄ 11:11 pm

☽⚻☿ 11:47 pm

6 FRIDAY
☽☍♄ **2:11 am**
☽⚻☿ **2:47 am**
☽□♀ **7:00 am** 4:00 am
☽□♅ **11:06 am** 8:06 am
☿⚺♄ **8:08 pm** 5:08 pm

7 SATURDAY
☽⚻♂ **3:23 am** 12:23 am
☽⚻☉ **9:35 am** 6:35 am
☽⚻♆ **11:00 am** 8:00 am
☽⚻♃ **2:55 pm** 11:55 am
☽⚻♇ **8:50 pm** 5:50 pm

8 SUNDAY
☽☍☿ **4:12 am** 12:12 am
☽⚻♄ **4:57 am** 12:57 am
☉☌♆ **8:23 am** 5:23 am
☽△♀ **1:00 pm** 10:00 am
☽△♅ **1:11 pm** 10:11 am
♀☌♅ **3:38 pm** 12:38 pm

9 MONDAY
☽△♂ **6:48 am** 3:48 am
☽☍♆ **11:57 am** 8:57 am
☽☍☉ **1:48 pm** 10:48 am
☽△♃ **4:08 pm** 1:08 pm
☽△♇ **9:24 pm** 6:24 pm

10 TUESDAY
☽⚻☿ **3:15 am** 12:15 am

☽△♄ **4:32 am** 1:32 am
☽⚻♅ **12:28 pm** 9:28 am
☽⚻♀ **3:43 pm** 12:43 pm

11 WEDNESDAY
☽□♂ **8:06 am** 5:06 am
☉⚹♃ **8:27 am** 5:27 am
☽⚻♆ **11:09 am** 8:09 am
☽□♃ **3:48 pm** 12:48 pm
☽⚻☉ **4:14 pm** 1:14 pm
☽□♇ **8:41 pm** 5:41 pm
☽△☿ 11:58 pm

12 THURSDAY
☽△☿ **2:58 am**
☽□♄ **4:12 am** 1:12 am
☽☍♅ **12:14 pm** 9:14 am
☽☍♀ **7:10 pm** 4:10 pm

13 FRIDAY
☽⚹♂ **11:00 am** 8:00 am
☽△♆ **11:53 am** 8:53 am
☽⚹♃ **5:14 pm** 2:14 pm
☽△☉ **8:47 pm** 5:47 pm
☽⚹♇ **9:53 pm** 6:53 pm

14 SATURDAY
☽□☿ **5:36 am** 2:36 am
☽⚹♄ **6:06 am** 3:06 am
♂⚹♆ **6:32 am** 3:32 am
☉⚹♇ **12:47 pm** 9:47 am
☽⚻♅ **2:32 pm** 11:32 am
☿⚺♄ 10:50 pm
☽⚻♀ 11:00 pm

15 SUNDAY
☿⚺♄ **1:50 am**
☽⚻♀ **2:00 am**
☽□♆ **3:51 pm** 12:51 pm
☽⚺♂ **5:35 pm** 2:35 pm
☽⚺♃ **10:05 pm** 7:05 pm
☽⚺♇ 11:33 pm

16 MONDAY
☽⚺♇ **2:33 am**
☽□☉ **5:34 am** 2:34 am
☽⚺♄ **11:38 am** 8:38 am
☽⚹☿ **12:49 pm** 9:49 am
☽△♅ **8:33 pm** 5:33 pm

17 TUESDAY
☽△♀ **1:31 pm** 10:31 am
☽⚹♆ **11:36 pm** 8:36 pm

18 WEDNESDAY
☽☌♂ **4:32 am** 1:32 am
☽☌♃ **6:47 am** 3:47 am
☽☌♇ **10:53 am** 7:53 am
☽⚹☉ **6:57 pm** 3:57 pm
☽☌♄ **8:48 pm** 5:48 pm
☽⚺☿ 9:54 pm

19 THURSDAY
☽⚺☿ **12:54 am**
☽□♅ **6:04 am** 3:04 am
☉⚹♄ **7:50 pm** 4:50 pm

20 FRIDAY
☽□♀ **5:00 am** 2:00 am
♂☌♃ **7:35 am** 4:35 am

☽⚺♆ **10:20 am** 7:20 am
☽⚺♃ **6:21 pm** 3:21 pm
☽⚺♂ **6:52 pm** 3:52 pm
☽⚺♇ **9:56 pm** 6:56 pm

21 SATURDAY
☽⚺♄ **8:27 am** 5:27 am
☽⚺☉ **11:31 am** 8:31 am
☽☌☿ **4:39 pm** 1:39 pm
☽⚹♅ **5:51 pm** 2:51 pm

22 SUNDAY
☿⚹♅ **9:19 am** 6:19 am
☽⚹♀ **10:36 pm** 7:36 pm
☽☌♆ **10:38 pm** 7:38 pm
♀⚹♆ **11:08 pm** 8:08 pm
♂☌♇ 10:21 pm

23 MONDAY
♂☌♇ **1:21 am**
☽⚹♃ **7:20 am** 4:20 am
☽⚹♇ **10:18 am** 7:18 am
☽⚹♂ **10:51 am** 7:51 am
☽⚹♄ **9:15 pm** 6:15 pm

24 TUESDAY
☽☌☉ **5:28 am** 2:28 am
☽⚺♅ **6:36 am** 3:36 am
☽⚺☿ **10:27 am** 7:27 am
☉⚺♅ **7:44 pm** 4:44 pm

25 WEDNESDAY
☽⚺♆ **11:28 am** 8:28 am
☽⚺♀ **4:46 pm** 1:46 pm

☽□♃ **8:43 pm** 5:43 pm
☽□♇ **11:03 pm** 8:03 pm

26 THURSDAY
☽□♂ **3:16 am** 12:16 am
☽□♄ **10:15 am** 7:15 am
☽☌♅ **7:29 pm** 4:29 pm
☽⚺☉ **11:35 pm** 8:35 pm

27 FRIDAY
☽⚹☿ **5:03 am** 2:03 am
☽⚹♆ 9:02 pm
♀△♃ 9:24 pm

28 SATURDAY
☽⚹♆ **12:02 am**
♀△♃ **12:24 am**
☽△♃ **9:39 am** 6:39 am
☽☌♀ **10:20 am** 7:20 am
☽△♇ **11:20 am** 8:20 am
☽△♂ **7:05 pm** 4:05 pm
☽△♄ **10:36 pm** 7:36 pm
♀△♇ **10:57 pm** 7:57 pm

29 SUNDAY
☽⚺♅ **7:33 am** 4:33 am
☽⚹☉ **4:32 pm** 1:32 pm
☽□☿ **10:58 pm** 7:58 pm

30 MONDAY
☽□♆ **11:10 am** 8:10 am
☽⚻♃ **8:52 pm** 5:52 pm
☽⚻♇ **9:55 pm** 6:55 pm
☽⚺♀ 10:40 pm

31 TUESDAY
☽⚺♀ **1:40 am**
☽⚻♂ **8:39 am** 5:39 am
☽⚻♄ **8:56 am** 5:56 am
♂☌♄ **2:31 pm** 11:31 am
☽⚹♅ **5:24 pm** 2:24 pm

Eastern time in bold type
Pacific time in medium type

MARCH 2020

DATE	SID.TIME	SUN	MOON	NODE	MERCURY	VENUS	MARS	JUPITER	SATURN	URANUS	NEPTUNE	PLUTO	CERES	PALLAS	JUNO	VESTA	CHIRON
1 Su	10 37 1	10♓51 57	20♉12	5♋49℞	2♓48℞	25♈26	9♑19	19♑33	28♑10	3♉41	18♓07	24♑16	11♒30	15♑48	20♎13℞	23♉14	3♈57
2 M	10 40 58	11 52 10	2♊23	5 47D	1 53	26 33	10 01	19 44	28 16	3 44	18 09	24 17	11 53	16 08	20 05	23 33	4 00
3 T	10 44 55	12 52 21	14 49	5 47	1 03	27 39	10 42	19 55	28 21	3 46	18 11	24 18	12 15	16 28	19 56	23 52	4 03
4 W	10 48 51	13 52 30	27 36	5 47℞	0 18	28 45	11 23	20 05	28 27	3 49	18 13	24 20	12 38	16 47	19 47	24 11	4 07
5 Th	10 52 48	14 52 37	10♋48	5 47	29♒41	29 51	12 05	20 16	28 33	3 51	18 16	24 21	13 00	17 07	19 38	24 30	4 10
6 F	10 56 44	15 52 42	24 28	5 46	29 09	0♉57	12 46	20 27	28 38	3 54	18 18	24 23	13 23	17 26	19 29	24 49	4 13
7 Sa	11 0 41	16 52 45	8♌39	5 42	28 45	2 03	13 28	20 37	28 44	3 56	18 20	24 24	13 45	17 45	19 19	25 09	4 17
8 Su	11 4 37	17 52 45	23 17	5 36	28 28	3 08	14 09	20 48	28 49	3 59	18 23	24 25	14 07	18 04	19 09	25 28	4 20
9 M	11 8 34	18 52 44	8♍19	5 27	28 17	4 13	14 51	20 58	28 55	4 02	18 25	24 27	14 30	18 23	18 58	25 48	4 24
10 T	11 12 30	19 52 40	23 35	5 16	28 13D	5 17	15 33	21 08	29 00	4 04	18 27	24 28	14 52	18 42	18 47	26 08	4 27
11 W	11 16 27	20 52 35	8♎54	5 05	28 15	6 22	16 14	21 18	29 05	4 07	18 29	24 29	15 14	19 00	18 36	26 28	4 31
12 Th	11 20 24	21 52 28	24 05	4 55	28 23	7 26	16 56	21 28	29 11	4 10	18 32	24 31	15 36	19 19	18 25	26 48	4 34
13 F	11 24 20	22 52 19	8♏58	4 47	28 37	8 30	17 37	21 38	29 16	4 12	18 34	24 32	15 58	19 37	18 14	27 08	4 37
14 Sa	11 28 17	23 52 08	23 26	4 42	28 56	9 33	18 19	21 48	29 21	4 15	18 36	24 33	16 20	19 55	18 02	27 29	4 41
15 Su	11 32 13	24 51 56	7♐26	4 39	29 21	10 36	19 01	21 58	29 26	4 18	18 38	24 34	16 42	20 13	17 50	27 49	4 44
16 M	11 36 10	25 51 42	20 59	4 38D	29 50	11 39	19 42	22 07	29 31	4 21	18 41	24 35	17 03	20 31	17 37	28 10	4 48
17 T	11 40 6	26 51 27	4♑06	4 38℞	0♓23	12 42	20 24	22 17	29 36	4 24	18 43	24 37	17 25	20 48	17 25	28 31	4 51
18 W	11 44 3	27 51 09	16 52	4 38	1 01	13 44	21 05	22 26	29 41	4 27	18 45	24 38	17 47	21 06	17 12	28 52	4 55
19 Th	11 47 59	28 50 50	29 21	4 36	1 43	14 46	21 47	22 35	29 45	4 30	18 47	24 39	18 08	21 23	16 59	29 13	4 58
20 F	11 51 56	29 50 29	11♒37	4 31	2 29	15 47	22 29	22 45	29 50	4 32	18 50	24 40	18 30	21 40	16 46	29 34	5 02
21 Sa	11 55 53	0♈50 07	23 43	4 24	3 18	16 48	23 10	22 54	29 55	4 35	18 52	24 41	18 51	21 57	16 33	29 55	5 06
22 Su	11 59 49	1 49 42	5♓43	4 14	4 10	17 49	23 52	23 02	29 59	4 38	18 54	24 42	19 12	22 13	16 19	0♊17	5 09
23 M	12 3 46	2 49 16	17 38	4 01	5 05	18 49	24 34	23 11	0♒04	4 42	18 56	24 43	19 34	22 30	16 06	0 38	5 13
24 T	12 7 42	3 48 47	29 31	3 46	6 03	19 49	25 16	23 20	0 08	4 45	18 59	24 44	19 55	22 46	15 52	1 00	5 16
25 W	12 11 39	4 48 17	11♈23	3 32	7 04	20 48	25 57	23 28	0 12	4 48	19 01	24 45	20 16	23 02	15 38	1 22	5 20
26 Th	12 15 35	5 47 44	23 15	3 17	8 08	21 47	26 39	23 37	0 17	4 51	19 03	24 46	20 37	23 18	15 24	1 44	5 23
27 F	12 19 32	6 47 09	5♉09	3 05	9 14	22 46	27 21	23 45	0 21	4 54	19 05	24 47	20 58	23 34	15 10	2 06	5 27
28 Sa	12 23 28	7 46 33	17 07	2 56	10 22	23 44	28 02	23 53	0 25	4 57	19 07	24 47	21 19	23 49	14 56	2 28	5 30
29 Su	12 27 25	8 45 54	29 10	2 49	11 33	24 41	28 44	24 01	0 29	5 00	19 10	24 48	21 39	24 04	14 41	2 50	5 34
30 M	12 31 21	9 45 12	11♊23	2 45	12 46	25 38	29 26	24 09	0 33	5 03	19 12	24 49	22 00	24 19	14 27	3 12	5 37
31 T	12 35 18	10 44 29	23 49	2 44D	14 00	26 35	0♒07	24 16	0 37	5 07	19 14	24 50	22 21	24 34	14 13	3 34	5 41

EPHEMERIS CALCULATED FOR 12 MIDNIGHT GREENWICH MEAN TIME. ALL OTHER DATA AND FACING ASPECTARIAN PAGE IN **EASTERN TIME (BOLD)** AND PACIFIC TIME (REGULAR).

APRIL 2020

☽ Last Aspect day	ET / hr:mn / PT	asp	☽ Ingress sign day	ET / hr:mn / PT
2	**12:49 pm** 9:49 am	✶ ♀	♌ 2	**2:26 pm** 11:26 am
3	**3:29 pm** 12:29 pm	△ ☉	♍ 4	**5:18 pm** 2:18 pm
6	**9:29 am** 6:29 am	△ ♃	♎ 6	**5:16 pm** 2:16 pm
8	**8:50 am** 5:50 am	□ ♃	♏ 8	**4:17 pm** 1:17 pm
10	**3:35 pm** 12:35 pm	△ ☿	♐ 10	**4:35 pm** 1:35 pm
12	**7:46 am** 4:46 am	△ ☉	♑ 12	**8:05 pm** 5:05 pm
14	**7:47 pm** 4:47 pm	☌ ♃	♒ 15	**3:37 am** 12:37 am
17	**10:34 am** 7:34 am	✶ ☉	♓ 17	**2:29 pm** 11:29 am
19	**7:31 pm** 4:31 pm	✶ ♃	♈ 20	**3:00 am** 12:00 am
22	**8:32 am** 5:32 am	□ ♃	♉ 22	**3:36 pm** 12:36 pm
24	**8:43 pm** 5:43 pm	△ ♃	♊ 25	**3:20 am** 12:20 am
27	**1:00 pm** 10:00 am	✶ ☿	♋ 27	**1:28 pm** 10:28 am
29	**3:29 pm** 12:29 pm	☍ ♃	♌ 29	**9:06 pm** 6:06 pm

☽ Phases & Eclipses phase	day	ET / hr:mn / PT
2nd Quarter	1	**6:21 am** 3:21 am
Full Moon	7	**10:35 pm** 7:35 pm
4th Quarter	14	**6:56 pm** 3:56 pm
New Moon	22	**10:26 pm** 7:26 pm
2nd Quarter	30	**4:38 pm** 1:38 pm

Planet Ingress	day	ET / hr:mn / PT
♀ ♊	3	**1:11 pm** 10:11 am
☿ ♈	10	9:48 pm
☿ ♈	11	**12:48 am**
☉ ♉	19	**10:45 am** 7:45 am
⚳ ♓	23	**4:20 pm** 1:20 pm
☿ ♉	27	**3:53 pm** 12:53 pm
⚴ ♒	29	**8:29 pm** 5:29 pm

Planetary Motion	day	ET / hr:mn / PT
♇ ℞	25	**2:54 pm** 11:54 am

1 WEDNESDAY
☽ □ ☉ **6:21 am** 3:21 am
☽ △ ☿ **1:51 pm** 10:51 am
☽ △ ♆ **7:23 pm** 4:23 pm

2 THURSDAY
☽ ☍ ♃ **4:49 am** 1:49 am
☽ ☍ ♇ **5:20 am** 2:20 am
☽ ✶ ♀ **12:49 pm** 9:49 am
☽ ☍ ♄ **3:49 pm** 12:49 pm
☽ ☍ ♂ **6:13 pm** 3:13 pm
☽ □ ♅ **11:40 pm** 8:40 pm

3 FRIDAY
☽ △ ☉ **3:29 pm** 12:29 pm
☿ ☌ ♆ **9:15 pm** 6:15 pm
☽ ⚻ ♆ **11:42 pm** 8:42 pm
☽ ⚻ ☿ **11:58 pm** 8:58 pm

4 SATURDAY
☽ ⚻ ♃ **8:46 am** 5:46 am
☽ ⚻ ♇ **8:52 am** 5:52 am
♀ △ ♄ **1:09 pm** 10:09 am
☽ ⚻ ♄ **6:48 pm** 3:48 pm
☽ □ ♀ **7:08 pm** 4:08 pm
♃ ☌ ♇ **10:45 pm** 7:45 pm
☽ ⚻ ♂ **11:20 pm** 8:20 pm
☽ △ ♅ 11:06 pm

5 SUNDAY
☽ △ ♅ **2:06 am**
☽ ⚻ ☉ **8:12 pm** 5:12 pm
☽ ☍ ♆ 9:38 pm

6 MONDAY
☽ ☍ ♆ **12:38 am**
☽ ☍ ☿ **5:49 am** 2:49 am
☽ △ ♇ **9:15 am** 6:15 am
☽ △ ♃ **9:29 am** 6:29 am
☽ △ ♄ **6:52 pm** 3:52 pm
☽ △ ♀ **9:56 pm** 6:56 pm
☽ △ ♂ 10:20 pm
☽ ⚻ ♅ 10:54 pm

7 TUESDAY
☽ △ ♂ **1:20 am**
☽ ⚻ ♅ **1:54 am**
♂ □ ♅ **2:50 pm** 11:50 am
☿ ✶ ♇ **5:28 pm** 2:28 pm
☿ ✶ ♃ **10:20 pm** 7:20 pm
☽ ☍ ☉ **10:35 pm** 7:35 pm
☽ ⚻ ♆ **11:49 pm** 8:49 pm

8 WEDNESDAY
☽ □ ♇ **8:17 am** 5:17 am
☽ □ ♃ **8:50 am** 5:50 am
☽ ⚻ ☿ **9:54 am** 6:54 am
☽ □ ♄ **6:03 pm** 3:03 pm
☉ ⚺ ♆ **6:34 pm** 3:34 pm
☽ ⚻ ♀ **11:46 pm** 8:46 pm
☽ ☍ ♅ 10:09 pm
☽ □ ♂ 11:41 pm

9 THURSDAY
☽ ☍ ♅ **1:09 am**
☽ □ ♂ **2:41 am**

☽ △ ♆ **11:32 pm** 8:32 pm
☽ ⚻ ☉ 10:32 pm
♀ ⚺ ♅ 11:40 pm

10 FRIDAY
☽ ⚻ ☉ **1:32 am**
♀ ⚺ ♅ **2:40 am**
☽ ✶ ♇ **8:15 am** 5:15 am
☽ ✶ ♃ **9:08 am** 6:08 am
☽ △ ☿ **3:35 pm** 12:35 pm
☽ ✶ ♄ **6:37 pm** 3:37 pm
☽ ⚻ ♅ 11:08 pm

11 SATURDAY
☽ ⚻ ♅ **2:08 am**
☽ ☍ ♀ **3:28 am** 12:28 am
☽ ✶ ♂ **6:03 am** 3:03 am
☿ ✶ ♄ **7:58 pm** 4:58 pm
☽ □ ♆ 10:53 pm

12 SUNDAY
☽ □ ♆ **1:53 am**
☽ △ ☉ **7:46 am** 4:46 am
☽ ⚺ ♇ **11:09 am** 8:09 am
☽ ⚺ ♃ **12:26 pm** 9:26 am
☽ ⚺ ♄ **10:27 pm** 7:27 pm
☽ □ ☿ 11:00 pm

13 MONDAY
☽ □ ☿ **2:00 am**
☽ △ ♅ **6:36 am** 3:36 am
☽ ⚻ ♀ **11:10 am** 8:10 am
☽ ⚺ ♂ **1:33 pm** 10:33 am

14 TUESDAY
☉ □ ♇ **7:07 am** 4:07 am
☽ ✶ ♆ **8:10 am** 5:10 am
☿ ⚺ ♅ **4:06 pm** 1:06 pm
☽ ☌ ♇ **6:02 pm** 3:02 pm
☽ □ ☉ **6:56 pm** 3:56 pm
☽ ☌ ♃ **7:47 pm** 4:47 pm

15 WEDNESDAY
☽ ☌ ♄ **6:21 am** 3:21 am
☉ □ ♃ **6:59 am** 3:59 am
☽ □ ♅ **3:09 pm** 12:09 pm
☽ ✶ ☿ **6:41 pm** 3:41 pm
☽ △ ♀ **11:29 pm** 8:29 pm
☽ ☌ ♂ 10:42 pm

16 THURSDAY
☽ ☌ ♂ **1:42 am**
☽ ⚺ ♆ **6:13 pm** 3:13 pm

17 FRIDAY
☽ ⚺ ♇ **4:28 am** 1:28 am
☽ ⚺ ♃ **6:43 am** 3:43 am
☽ ✶ ☉ **10:34 am** 7:34 am
☽ ⚺ ♄ **5:32 pm** 2:32 pm
☿ ✶ ♀ 10:36 pm
☽ ✶ ♅ 11:47 pm

18 SATURDAY
☿ ✶ ♀ **1:36 am**
☽ ✶ ♅ **2:47 am**
☽ □ ♀ **2:57 pm** 11:57 am
☽ ⚺ ☿ **4:22 pm** 1:22 pm
☽ ⚺ ♂ **5:07 pm** 2:07 pm
☿ ✶ ♂ **11:55 pm** 8:55 pm

19 SUNDAY
☽ ☌ ♆ **6:32 am** 3:32 am
☽ ✶ ♇ **4:51 pm** 1:51 pm
☽ ✶ ♃ **7:31 pm** 4:31 pm

20 MONDAY
☽ ⚺ ☉ **4:28 am** 1:28 am
☽ ✶ ♄ **6:16 am** 3:16 am
☽ ⚺ ♅ **3:43 pm** 12:43 pm

21 TUESDAY
☉ □ ♄ **3:00 am** 12:00 am
☽ ✶ ♀ **7:17 am** 4:17 am
☽ ✶ ♂ **9:35 am** 6:35 am
☽ ☌ ☿ **4:06 pm** 1:06 pm
☽ ⚺ ♆ **7:23 pm** 4:23 pm

22 WEDNESDAY
☽ □ ♇ **5:31 am** 2:31 am
☽ □ ♃ **8:32 am** 5:32 am
☿ ⚺ ♆ **1:11 pm** 10:11 am
☽ □ ♄ **6:59 pm** 3:59 pm
☽ ☌ ☉ **10:26 pm** 7:26 pm

23 THURSDAY
☽ ☌ ♅ **4:29 am** 1:29 am
☽ ⚺ ♀ **10:50 pm** 7:50 pm
☽ □ ♂ 10:30 pm

24 FRIDAY
☽ □ ♂ **1:30 am**
☽ ✶ ♆ **7:38 am** 4:38 am
☽ ⚺ ☿ **3:30 pm** 12:30 pm
☽ △ ♇ **5:27 pm** 2:27 pm
☽ △ ♃ **8:43 pm** 5:43 pm

25 SATURDAY
☿ □ ♇ **3:36 am** 12:36 am
☽ △ ♄ **6:47 am** 3:47 am
☽ ⚺ ☉ **3:10 pm** 12:10 pm
☽ ⚺ ♅ **4:13 pm** 1:13 pm
☿ □ ♃ 9:31 pm

26 SUNDAY
☿ □ ♃ **12:31 am**
☉ ☌ ♅ **5:01 am** 2:01 am
☽ ☌ ♀ **12:39 pm** 9:39 am
☽ △ ♂ **3:55 pm** 12:55 pm
☽ □ ♆ **6:31 pm** 3:31 pm

27 MONDAY
☽ ⚻ ♇ **3:54 am** 12:54 am
☽ ⚻ ♃ **7:20 am** 4:20 am
☽ ✶ ☿ **1:00 pm** 10:00 am
☽ ⚻ ♄ **4:54 pm** 1:54 pm
☽ ✶ ♅ 11:08 pm

28 TUESDAY
☽ ✶ ♅ **2:08 am**
☽ ✶ ☉ **5:38 am** 2:38 am
☿ □ ♄ **1:28 pm** 10:28 am
♂ ⚺ ♆ **4:48 pm** 1:48 pm
☽ ⚺ ♀ **11:45 pm** 8:45 pm

29 WEDNESDAY
☽ △ ♆ **3:12 am** 12:12 am
☽ ⚻ ♂ **3:46 am** 12:46 am
☽ ☍ ♇ **12:01 pm** 9:01 am
☽ ☍ ♃ **3:29 pm** 12:29 pm
☽ ☍ ♄ 9:27 pm

30 THURSDAY
☽ ☍ ♄ **12:27 am**
☽ □ ☿ **6:46 am** 3:46 am
☽ □ ♅ **9:21 am** 6:21 am
☽ □ ☉ **4:38 pm** 1:38 pm
☿ ☌ ♅ **11:41 pm** 8:41 pm

Eastern time in bold type
Pacific time in medium type

APRIL 2020

DATE	SID.TIME	SUN	MOON	NODE	MERCURY	VENUS	MARS	JUPITER	SATURN	URANUS	NEPTUNE	PLUTO	CERES	PALLAS	JUNO	VESTA	CHIRON
1 W	12 39 15	11♈43 43	6♋33	2♋44℞	15♓17	27♉31	0♒49	24♑24	0♒40	5♉10	19♓16	24♑51	22♒41	24♑49	13♎59℞	3♊57	5♈44
2 Th	12 43 11	12 42 55	19 39	2 44	16 36	28 26	1 31	24 31	0 44	5 13	19 18	24 51	23 01	25 03	13 44	4 19	5 48
3 F	12 47 8	13 42 05	3♌11	2 42	17 56	29 21	2 13	24 38	0 48	5 16	19 20	24 52	23 22	25 17	13 30	4 42	5 51
4 Sa	12 51 4	14 41 12	17 10	2 39	19 18	0♊15	2 54	24 46	0 51	5 20	19 23	24 53	23 42	25 31	13 16	5 05	5 55
5 Su	12 55 1	15 40 17	1♍39	2 33	20 42	1 09	3 36	24 52	0 55	5 23	19 25	24 53	24 02	25 45	13 01	5 28	5 58
6 M	12 58 57	16 39 19	16 32	2 25	22 08	2 02	4 18	24 59	0 58	5 26	19 27	24 54	24 22	25 58	12 47	5 50	6 02
7 T	13 2 54	17 38 19	1♎44	2 15	23 35	2 54	4 59	25 06	1 01	5 29	19 29	24 54	24 42	26 12	12 33	6 13	6 05
8 W	13 6 50	18 37 18	17 05	2 04	25 04	3 46	5 41	25 12	1 04	5 33	19 31	24 55	25 02	26 24	12 19	6 36	6 09
9 Th	13 10 47	19 36 14	2♏21	1 54	26 35	4 37	6 23	25 19	1 08	5 36	19 33	24 55	25 21	26 37	12 05	7 00	6 12
10 F	13 14 44	20 35 08	17 24	1 46	28 07	5 27	7 04	25 25	1 11	5 40	19 35	24 56	25 41	26 50	11 51	7 23	6 16
11 Sa	13 18 40	21 34 00	2♐03	1 41	29 41	6 16	7 46	25 31	1 13	5 43	19 37	24 56	26 00	27 02	11 37	7 46	6 19
12 Su	13 22 37	22 32 51	16 15	1 38	1♈16	7 05	8 28	25 37	1 16	5 46	19 39	24 57	26 20	27 14	11 24	8 09	6 23
13 M	13 26 33	23 31 40	29 57	1 37D	2 53	7 52	9 10	25 43	1 19	5 50	19 41	24 57	26 39	27 25	11 10	8 33	6 26
14 T	13 30 30	24 30 27	13♑11	1 37℞	4 32	8 39	9 51	25 48	1 22	5 53	19 43	24 58	26 58	27 37	10 57	8 56	6 29
15 W	13 34 26	25 29 13	26 00	1 38	6 12	9 25	10 33	25 54	1 24	5 56	19 45	24 58	27 17	27 48	10 44	9 20	6 33
16 Th	13 38 23	26 27 56	8♒29	1 37	7 54	10 10	11 15	25 59	1 27	6 00	19 47	24 58	27 36	27 59	10 31	9 44	6 36
17 F	13 42 19	27 26 39	20 43	1 34	9 37	10 54	11 56	26 04	1 29	6 03	19 49	24 58	27 55	28 10	10 18	10 07	6 39
18 Sa	13 46 16	28 25 19	2♓45	1 29	11 22	11 37	12 38	26 09	1 31	6 07	19 50	24 59	28 13	28 20	10 06	10 31	6 43
19 Su	13 50 13	29 23 57	14 41	1 21	13 09	12 19	13 20	26 14	1 34	6 10	19 52	24 59	28 32	28 30	9 53	10 55	6 46
20 M	13 54 9	0♉22 34	26 32	1 12	14 57	13 00	14 01	26 18	1 36	6 14	19 54	24 59	28 50	28 40	9 41	11 19	6 49
21 T	13 58 6	1 21 09	8♈24	1 01	16 47	13 40	14 43	26 23	1 38	6 17	19 56	24 59	29 09	28 49	9 29	11 43	6 53
22 W	14 2 2	2 19 42	20 16	0 49	18 38	14 19	15 25	26 27	1 40	6 20	19 58	24 59	29 27	28 58	9 18	12 07	6 56
23 Th	14 5 59	3 18 13	2♉11	0 38	20 31	14 56	16 06	26 31	1 41	6 24	20 00	24 59	29 45	29 07	9 06	12 31	6 59
24 F	14 9 55	4 16 43	14 11	0 29	22 26	15 33	16 48	26 35	1 43	6 27	20 01	24 59	0♓03	29 15	8 55	12 55	7 02
25 Sa	14 13 52	5 15 11	26 17	0 21	24 22	16 08	17 29	26 39	1 45	6 31	20 03	25 00℞	0 20	29 24	8 44	13 20	7 06
26 Su	14 17 48	6 13 36	8♊30	0 16	26 20	16 41	18 11	26 42	1 46	6 34	20 05	25 00	0 38	29 32	8 34	13 44	7 09
27 M	14 21 45	7 12 00	20 52	0 14D	28 20	17 13	18 52	26 45	1 48	6 38	20 07	25 00	0 56	29 39	8 24	14 08	7 12
28 T	14 25 42	8 10 22	3♋27	0 14	0♉21	17 44	19 34	26 49	1 49	6 41	20 08	24 59	1 13	29 46	8 14	14 33	7 15
29 W	14 29 38	9 08 41	16 16	0 14	2 23	18 13	20 15	26 52	1 50	6 45	20 10	24 59	1 30	29 53	8 04	14 57	7 18
30 Th	14 33 35	10 06 59	29 23	0 16℞	4 27	18 41	20 57	26 54	1 51	6 48	20 12	24 59	1 47	0♒00	7 55	15 22	7 21

EPHEMERIS CALCULATED FOR 12 MIDNIGHT GREENWICH MEAN TIME. ALL OTHER DATA AND FACING ASPECTARIAN PAGE IN **EASTERN TIME (BOLD)** AND PACIFIC TIME (REGULAR).

MAY 2020

☽ Last Aspect day	ET / hr:mn / PT		asp	☽ Ingress sign	day	ET / hr:mn / PT	
1	**12:04 pm**	9:04 am	☍♂	♍	1		10:35 pm
1	**12:04 pm**	9:04 am	☍♂	♍	2	**1:35 am**	
3	**10:25 pm**	7:25 pm	△♃	♎	4	**3:09 am**	12:09 am
5	**10:31 pm**	7:31 pm	□♃	♏	6	**3:05 am**	12:05 am
7	**10:39 pm**	7:39 pm	⚹♃	♐	8	**3:15 am**	12:15 am
9		11:11 pm	⚹♂	♑	10	**5:39 am**	2:39 am
10	**2:11 am**		⚹♂	♑	10	**5:39 am**	2:39 am
12	**6:30 am**	3:30 am	☌♃	♒	12	**11:39 am**	8:39 am
14	**10:03 am**	7:03 am	□☉	♓	14	**9:24 pm**	6:24 pm
17	**3:59 am**	12:59 am	⚹♃	♈	17	**9:36 am**	6:36 am
19	**4:33 pm**	1:33 pm	□♃	♉	19	**10:10 pm**	7:10 pm
22	**4:01 am**	1:01 am	△♃	♊	22	**9:36 am**	6:36 am
24	**7:09 am**	4:09 am	☌☿	♋	24	**7:09 pm**	4:09 pm
26	**9:06 pm**	6:06 pm	☍♃	♌	26		11:33 pm
26	**9:06 pm**	6:06 pm	☍♃	♌	27	**2:33 am**	
28	**9:30 am**	6:30 am	⚹♀	♍	29	**7:40 am**	4:40 am
31	**5:17 am**	2:17 am	△♃	♎	31	**10:38 am**	7:38 am

☽ Phases & Eclipses phase	day	ET / hr:mn / PT	
Full Moon	7	**6:45 am**	3:45 am
4th Quarter	14	**10:03 am**	7:03 am
New Moon	22	**1:39 pm**	10:39 am
2nd Quarter	29	**11:30 pm**	8:30 pm

Planet Ingress		day	ET / hr:mn / PT	
☿	♊	11	**5:58 pm**	2:58 pm
♂	♓	12		9:17 pm
♂	♓	13	**12:17 am**	
☉	♊	20	**9:49 am**	6:49 am
☿	♋	28	**2:09 pm**	11:09 am

Planetary Motion		day	ET / hr:mn / PT	
♄	℞	10		9:09 pm
♄	℞	11	**12:09 am**	
♀	℞	12		11:45 pm
♀	℞	13	**2:45 am**	
♃	℞	14	**10:32 am**	7:32 am
♀	℞	17	**4:29 am**	1:29 am
⚵	D	26	**10:51 pm**	7:51 pm

1 FRIDAY
☽⚹♀ **7:16 am** 4:16 am
☽⚻♆ **8:51 am** 5:51 am
☽☍♂ **12:04 pm** 9:04 am
☽⚻♇ **5:02 pm** 2:02 pm
☽⚻♃ **8:28 pm** 5:28 pm

2 SATURDAY
☽⚻♄ **4:48 am** 1:48 am
☽△♅ **1:19 pm** 10:19 am
☽△☿ **7:38 pm** 4:38 pm
☽△☉ **11:40 pm** 8:40 pm

3 SUNDAY
☽□♀ **11:06 am** 8:06 am
☽☍♆ **11:22 am** 8:22 am
☽⚻♂ **4:47 pm** 1:47 pm
☽△♇ **7:01 pm** 4:01 pm
☽△♃ **10:25 pm** 7:25 pm
♀□♆ **11:52 pm** 8:52 pm

4 MONDAY
☽△♄ **6:15 am** 3:15 am
☽⚻♅ **2:32 pm** 11:32 am
☉☌☿ **5:41 pm** 2:41 pm

5 TUESDAY
☽⚻☉ **3:39 am** 12:39 am
☽⚻☿ **4:34 am** 1:34 am
☽⚻♆ **11:43 am** 8:43 am
☽△♀ **12:23 pm** 9:23 am
♂⚺♇ **4:11 pm** 1:11 pm
☽□♇ **7:05 pm** 4:05 pm
☽△♂ **7:13 pm** 4:13 pm
☽□♃ **10:31 pm** 7:31 pm

6 WEDNESDAY
☽□♄ **6:10 am** 3:10 am
☽☍♅ **2:31 pm** 11:31 am

7 THURSDAY
☿⚹♆ **6:42 am** 3:42 am
☽☍☉ **6:45 am** 3:45 am
☽△♆ **11:40 am** 8:40 am
☽☍☿ **12:30 pm** 9:30 am
☽⚻♀ **1:04 pm** 10:04 am
☿⚺♀ **4:39 pm** 1:39 pm
☽⚹♇ **7:03 pm** 4:03 pm
☽□♂ **9:33 pm** 6:33 pm
☽⚹♃ **10:39 pm** 7:39 pm

8 FRIDAY
☽⚹♄ **6:27 am** 3:27 am
☽⚻♅ **3:15 pm** 12:15 pm
♂⚺♃ **9:53 pm** 6:53 pm

9 SATURDAY
☿△♇ **9:17 am** 6:17 am
☽⚻☉ **11:35 am** 8:35 am
☽□♆ **1:14 pm** 10:14 am
☽☍♀ **3:13 pm** 12:13 pm
☽⚺♇ **8:55 pm** 5:55 pm
☽⚻☿ **11:03 pm** 8:03 pm
☽⚺♃ 9:49 pm
☽⚹♂ 11:11 pm

10 SUNDAY
☽⚺♃ **12:49 am**
☽⚹♂ **2:11 am**
☽⚺♄ **9:03 am** 6:03 am
☿△♃ **10:36 am** 7:36 am
☉⚹♆ **12:16 pm** 9:16 am
☽△♅ **6:38 pm** 3:38 pm

11 MONDAY
☿□♂ **3:33 am** 12:33 am
☽⚹♆ **6:05 pm** 3:05 pm
☽△☉ **8:24 pm** 5:24 pm
☽⚻♀ **8:30 pm** 5:30 pm
☉⚺♀ **9:57 pm** 6:57 pm
☽☌♇ 11:14 pm

12 TUESDAY
☽☌♇ **2:14 am**
☽☌♃ **6:30 am** 3:30 am
☽⚺♂ **10:56 am** 7:56 am
☽△☿ **3:07 pm** 12:07 pm
☽☌♄ **3:18 pm** 12:18 pm
☿△♄ **4:14 pm** 1:14 pm
☽□♅ 10:52 pm

13 WEDNESDAY
☽□♅ **1:52 am**
☽⚺♆ 11:50 pm

14 THURSDAY
☽⚺♆ **2:50 am**
☽△♀ **5:20 am** 2:20 am
☽□☉ **10:03 am** 7:03 am
☽⚺♇ **11:23 am** 8:23 am
☽⚺♃ **3:58 pm** 12:58 pm
☽☌♂ 9:06 pm
☽⚺♄ 10:15 pm
☉△♇ 11:49 pm

15 FRIDAY
☽☌♂ **12:06 am**
☽⚺♄ **1:15 am**
☉△♇ **2:49 am**
☿⚺♅ **11:17 am** 8:17 am
☽⚹♅ **12:41 pm** 9:41 am
☽□☿ **12:57 pm** 9:57 am
♂⚺♄ **8:25 pm** 5:25 pm

16 SATURDAY
☽☌♆ **2:34 pm** 11:34 am
☽□♀ **4:35 pm** 1:35 pm
☽⚹♇ **11:15 pm** 8:15 pm

17 SUNDAY
☽⚹☉ **3:13 am** 12:13 am
☽⚹♃ **3:59 am** 12:59 am
☉△♃ **12:40 pm** 9:40 am
☽⚹♄ **1:29 pm** 10:29 am
☽⚺♂ **4:01 pm** 1:01 pm
☽⚺♅ 10:27 pm

18 MONDAY
☽⚺♅ **1:27 am**
☽⚹☿ **1:17 pm** 10:17 am

19 TUESDAY
☽⚺♆ **3:20 am** 12:20 am
☽⚹♀ **4:17 am** 1:17 am
☽□♇ **11:51 am** 8:51 am
☽□♃ **4:33 pm** 1:33 pm
☽⚺☉ **9:09 pm** 6:09 pm
☽□♄ 10:58 pm

20 WEDNESDAY
☽□♄ **1:58 am**
☽⚹♂ **8:10 am** 5:10 am
☽☌♅ **2:07 pm** 11:07 am
♀□♆ **7:03 pm** 4:03 pm

21 THURSDAY
☽⚺☿ **12:01 pm** 9:01 am
☽⚺♀ **2:46 pm** 11:46 am
☽⚹♆ **3:19 pm** 12:19 pm
☽△♇ **11:29 pm** 8:29 pm

22 FRIDAY
☽△♃ **4:01 am** 1:01 am
☿☌♀ **4:41 am** 1:41 am
☉△♄ **8:02 am** 5:02 am
☿□♆ **11:43 am** 8:43 am
☽△♄ **1:12 pm** 10:12 am
☽☌☉ **1:39 pm** 10:39 am
☽□♂ **10:43 pm** 7:43 pm
☽⚺♅ 10:20 pm

23 SATURDAY
☽⚺♅ **1:20 am**
☽☌♀ **11:15 pm** 8:15 pm
☽□♆ 10:34 pm

24 SUNDAY
☽□♆ **1:34 am**
☽☌☿ **7:09 am** 4:09 am
☽⚻♇ **9:19 am** 6:19 am
☽⚻♃ **1:38 pm** 10:38 am
☽⚻♄ **10:32 pm** 7:32 pm
☿⚻♇ 9:26 pm
♂⚹♅ 11:48 pm

25 MONDAY
☿⚻♇ **12:26 am**
♂⚹♅ **2:48 am**
☽⚺☉ **3:43 am** 12:43 am
☽⚹♅ **10:34 am** 7:34 am
☽△♂ **10:58 am** 7:58 am

26 TUESDAY
☽⚺♀ **5:31 am** 2:31 am
☽△♆ **9:43 am** 6:43 am
☿⚻♃ **11:35 am** 8:35 am
☽☍♇ **5:03 pm** 2:03 pm
☽☍♃ **9:06 pm** 6:06 pm
☽⚺☿ **10:19 pm** 7:19 pm

27 WEDNESDAY
☽☍♄ **5:42 am** 2:42 am
☽⚹☉ **3:02 pm** 12:02 pm
☽□♅ **5:34 pm** 2:34 pm
☽⚻♂ **8:36 pm** 5:36 pm

28 THURSDAY
☽⚹♀ **9:30 am** 6:30 am
☽⚻♆ **3:36 pm** 12:36 pm
☽⚻♇ **10:31 pm** 7:31 pm
☽⚻♃ 11:17 pm

29 FRIDAY
☽⚻♃ **2:17 am**
☉⚺♅ **4:13 am** 1:13 am
☽⚹☿ **9:32 am** 6:32 am
☽⚻♄ **10:35 am** 7:35 am
☿⚻♄ **8:25 pm** 5:25 pm
☽△♅ **10:15 pm** 7:15 pm
☽□☉ **11:30 pm** 8:30 pm

30 SATURDAY
☽☍♂ **3:34 am** 12:34 am
☽□♀ **11:18 am** 8:18 am
☽☍♆ **7:14 pm** 4:14 pm
☽△♇ 10:46 pm

31 SUNDAY
☽△♇ **1:46 am**
☽△♃ **5:17 am** 2:17 am
☽△♄ **1:20 pm** 10:20 am
☽□☿ **5:16 pm** 2:16 pm
☽⚻♅ 9:52 pm

Eastern time in bold type
Pacific time in medium type

MAY 2020

DATE	SID.TIME	SUN	MOON	NODE	MERCURY	VENUS	MARS	JUPITER	SATURN	URANUS	NEPTUNE	PLUTO	CERES	PALLAS	JUNO	VESTA	CHIRON
1 F	14 37 31	11♉05 14	12♌52	0♋16℞	6♉33	19♊07	21♒38	26♑57	1♒52	6♉52	20♓13	24♑59℞	2♓04	0♒06	7♎45℞	15♊46	7♈24
2 Sa	14 41 28	12 03 28	26 43	0 15	8 39	19 31	22 19	26 59	1 53	6 55	20 15	24 59	2 21	0 12	7 37	16 11	7 28
3 Su	14 45 24	13 01 39	10♍58	0 12	10 47	19 54	23 01	27 02	1 54	6 58	20 16	24 59	2 37	0 18	7 28	16 35	7 31
4 M	14 49 21	13 59 48	25 35	0 07	12 55	20 15	23 42	27 04	1 55	7 02	20 18	24 59	2 54	0 23	7 20	17 00	7 34
5 T	14 53 17	14 57 56	10♎29	0 01	15 05	20 34	24 23	27 06	1 56	7 05	20 19	24 58	3 10	0 28	7 12	17 25	7 36
6 W	14 57 14	15 56 01	25 33	29♊55	17 15	20 51	25 05	27 07	1 56	7 09	20 21	24 58	3 26	0 32	7 05	17 50	7 39
7 Th	15 1 11	16 54 05	10♏37	29 48	19 25	21 06	25 46	27 09	1 57	7 12	20 22	24 58	3 42	0 36	6 58	18 14	7 42
8 F	15 5 7	17 52 07	25 33	29 43	21 35	21 19	26 27	27 10	1 57	7 16	20 24	24 57	3 58	0 40	6 51	18 39	7 45
9 Sa	15 9 4	18 50 07	10♐10	29 40	23 45	21 29	27 08	27 11	1 57	7 19	20 25	24 57	4 14	0 43	6 45	19 04	7 48
10 Su	15 13 0	19 48 06	24 24	29 39D	25 55	21 38	27 49	27 12	1 57	7 22	20 26	24 57	4 29	0 47	6 39	19 29	7 51
11 M	15 16 57	20 46 04	8♑12	29 39	28 03	21 44	28 31	27 13	1 57℞	7 26	20 28	24 56	4 44	0 49	6 33	19 54	7 54
12 T	15 20 53	21 44 00	21 32	29 40	0♊11	21 48	29 12	27 14	1 57	7 29	20 29	24 56	4 59	0 51	6 28	20 19	7 56
13 W	15 24 50	22 41 55	4♒27	29 41	2 17	21 50℞	29 53	27 14	1 57	7 32	20 30	24 55	5 14	0 53	6 23	20 44	7 59
14 Th	15 28 46	23 39 49	17 01	29 43℞	4 22	21 50	0♓34	27 14℞	1 57	7 36	20 32	24 55	5 29	0 55	6 18	21 10	8 02
15 F	15 32 43	24 37 41	29 17	29 43	6 24	21 47	1 15	27 14	1 57	7 39	20 33	24 54	5 44	0 56	6 14	21 35	8 05
16 Sa	15 36 40	25 35 32	11♓21	29 41	8 25	21 42	1 56	27 14	1 56	7 42	20 34	24 54	5 58	0 57	6 10	22 00	8 07
17 Su	15 40 36	26 33 22	23 17	29 39	10 23	21 34	2 36	27 14	1 56	7 46	20 35	24 53	6 12	0 57℞	6 06	22 25	8 10
18 M	15 44 33	27 31 11	5♈08	29 35	12 19	21 24	3 17	27 13	1 55	7 49	20 37	24 53	6 26	0 57	6 03	22 51	8 12
19 T	15 48 29	28 28 58	17 00	29 30	14 12	21 11	3 58	27 13	1 54	7 52	20 38	24 52	6 40	0 57	6 00	23 16	8 15
20 W	15 52 26	29 26 44	28 55	29 24	16 02	20 56	4 39	27 12	1 54	7 56	20 39	24 51	6 54	0 56	5 57	23 41	8 17
21 Th	15 56 22	0♊24 29	10♉55	29 19	17 50	20 39	5 19	27 11	1 53	7 59	20 40	24 51	7 07	0 54	5 55	24 07	8 20
22 F	16 0 19	1 22 13	23 04	29 15	19 35	20 19	6 00	27 09	1 52	8 02	20 41	24 50	7 20	0 53	5 53	24 32	8 22
23 Sa	16 4 15	2 19 56	5♊21	29 12	21 16	19 58	6 40	27 08	1 51	8 05	20 42	24 49	7 33	0 51	5 51	24 58	8 25
24 Su	16 8 12	3 17 37	17 48	29 10D	22 55	19 34	7 21	27 06	1 49	8 09	20 43	24 48	7 46	0 48	5 50	25 23	8 27
25 M	16 12 9	4 15 17	0♋27	29 09	24 30	19 07	8 01	27 04	1 48	8 12	20 44	24 48	7 59	0 45	5 49	25 49	8 29
26 T	16 16 5	5 12 56	13 18	29 10	26 02	18 39	8 42	27 02	1 47	8 15	20 45	24 47	8 11	0 42	5 49	26 14	8 31
27 W	16 20 2	6 10 33	26 23	29 11	27 31	18 09	9 22	27 00	1 45	8 18	20 46	24 46	8 23	0 38	5 48D	26 40	8 34
28 Th	16 23 58	7 08 09	9♌43	29 13	28 57	17 38	10 02	26 57	1 44	8 21	20 46	24 45	8 35	0 34	5 48	27 05	8 36
29 F	16 27 55	8 05 44	23 18	29 14	0♋20	17 05	10 42	26 55	1 42	8 24	20 47	24 44	8 47	0 29	5 49	27 31	8 38
30 Sa	16 31 51	9 03 17	7♍09	29 14℞	1 39	16 30	11 22	26 52	1 40	8 27	20 48	24 43	8 58	0 24	5 50	27 57	8 40
31 Su	16 35 48	10 00 48	21 16	29 14	2 55	15 55	12 02	26 49	1 39	8 31	20 49	24 42	9 09	0 19	5 51	28 22	8 42

EPHEMERIS CALCULATED FOR 12 MIDNIGHT GREENWICH MEAN TIME. ALL OTHER DATA AND FACING ASPECTARIAN PAGE IN **EASTERN TIME (BOLD)** AND PACIFIC TIME (REGULAR).

JUNE 2020

☽ Last Aspect				☽ Ingress			
day	ET / hr:mn / PT		asp	sign	day	ET / hr:mn / PT	
2	**6:40 am**	3:40 am	□♃	♏	2	**12:06 pm**	9:06 am
4	**7:36 am**	4:36 am	✶♃	♐	4	**1:17 pm**	10:17 am
5		9:10 pm	□♆	♑	6	**3:44 pm**	12:44 pm
6	**12:10 am**		□♆	♑	6	**3:44 pm**	12:44 pm
8	**2:06 pm**	11:06 am	☌♃	♒	8	**8:54 pm**	5:54 pm
10	**10:35 am**	7:35 am	△☉	♓	11	**5:32 am**	2:32 am
13	**8:45 am**	5:45 am	✶♃	♈	13	**5:03 pm**	2:03 pm
15	**8:49 pm**	5:49 pm	□♃	♉	16	**5:35 am**	2:35 am
18	**8:02 am**	5:02 am	△♃	♊	18	**5:00 pm**	2:00 pm
20	**5:48 pm**	2:48 pm	□♂	♋	20		11:02 pm
20	**5:48 pm**	2:48 pm	□♂	♋	21	**2:02 am**	
23	**3:20 am**	12:20 am	△♂	♌	23	**8:33 am**	5:33 am
23		10:34 pm	□♅	♍	25	**1:05 pm**	10:05 am
24	**1:34 am**		□♅	♍	25	**1:05 pm**	10:05 am
27	**4:02 pm**	1:02 pm	☍♂	♎	27	**4:16 pm**	1:16 pm
29	**9:02 am**	6:02 am	□♃	♏	29	**6:48 pm**	3:48 pm

☽ Phases & Eclipses			
phase	day	ET / hr:mn / PT	
Full Moon	5	**3:12 pm**	12:12 pm
●	5	15° ♐ 34'	
4th Quarter	12		11:24 pm
4th Quarter	13	**2:24 am**	
New Moon	20		11:41 pm
New Moon	21	**2:41 am**	
●	20/21	0° ♋ 21'	
2nd Quarter	28	**4:16 am**	1:16 am

Planet Ingress			
	day	ET / hr:mn / PT	
♀ ♑	2	**8:55 pm**	5:55 pm
⚶ ♋	3	**2:55 pm**	11:55 am
☉ ♋	20	**5:44 pm**	2:44 pm
♂ ♈	27	**9:45 pm**	6:45 pm

Planetary Motion			
	day	ET / hr:mn / PT	
☿ ℞	17		9:59 pm
☿ ℞	18	**12:59 am**	
♆ ℞	22		9:32 pm
♆ ℞	23	**12:32 am**	
♀ D	24		11:48 pm
♀ D	25	**2:48 am**	

1 MONDAY
☽ ⚻ ♅ **12:52 am**
☽ △ ☉ **5:28 am** 2:28 am
☽ ⚻ ♂ **8:15 am** 5:15 am
☽ △ ♀ **11:20 am** 8:20 am
☽ ⚻ ♆ **9:05 pm** 6:05 pm

2 TUESDAY
☽ □ ♇ **3:22 am** 12:22 am
☽ □ ♃ **6:40 am** 3:40 am
☽ □ ♄ **2:38 pm** 11:38 am
♀ □ ♂ **8:41 pm** 5:41 pm
☽ △ ☿ **10:41 pm** 7:41 pm
☽ ☍ ♅ 11:17 pm

3 WEDNESDAY
☽ ☍ ♅ **2:17 am**
☽ ⚻ ☉ **10:05 am** 7:05 am
☽ ⚻ ♀ **10:28 am** 7:28 am
☽ △ ♂ **11:44 am** 8:44 am
☉ ☌ ♀ **1:44 pm** 10:44 am
☽ △ ♆ **10:14 pm** 7:14 pm

4 THURSDAY
☽ ✶ ♇ **4:27 am** 1:27 am
☽ ✶ ♃ **7:36 am** 4:36 am
☽ ✶ ♄ **3:43 pm** 12:43 pm

5 FRIDAY
☽ ⚻ ☿ **3:38 am** 12:38 am
☽ ⚻ ♅ **3:50 am** 12:50 am
☿ ✶ ♅ **7:05 am** 4:05 am
☽ ☍ ♀ **9:57 am** 6:57 am
☽ ☍ ☉ **3:12 pm** 12:12 pm
☽ □ ♂ **3:44 pm** 12:44 pm
☽ □ ♆ 9:10 pm

6 SATURDAY
☽ □ ♆ **12:10 am**
☽ ⚺ ♇ **6:30 am** 3:30 am
☽ ⚺ ♃ **9:36 am** 6:36 am
☉ □ ♂ **3:11 pm** 12:11 pm
☽ ⚺ ♄ **6:08 pm** 3:08 pm

7 SUNDAY
☽ △ ♅ **7:08 am** 4:08 am
☽ ☍ ☿ **10:06 am** 7:06 am
☽ ⚻ ♀ **11:11 am** 8:11 am
☿ ⚺ ♀ **9:29 pm** 6:29 pm
☽ ✶ ♂ **10:07 pm** 7:07 pm
☽ ⚻ ☉ **10:51 pm** 7:51 pm

8 MONDAY
☽ ✶ ♆ **4:25 am** 1:25 am
☽ ☌ ♇ **11:01 am** 8:01 am
☽ ☌ ♃ **2:06 pm** 11:06 am
☽ ☌ ♄ **11:17 pm** 8:17 pm

9 TUESDAY
☽ □ ♅ **1:30 pm** 10:30 am
☽ △ ♀ **3:15 pm** 12:15 pm
☽ ⚻ ☿ **7:33 pm** 4:33 pm

10 WEDNESDAY
☽ ⚺ ♂ **8:15 am** 5:15 am
☽ △ ☉ **10:35 am** 7:35 am
☽ ⚺ ♆ **12:01 pm** 9:01 am
☽ ⚺ ♇ **6:56 pm** 3:56 pm
☽ ⚺ ♃ **9:56 pm** 6:56 pm

11 THURSDAY
☉ □ ♆ **5:37 am** 2:37 am
♀ ⚺ ♅ **5:50 am** 2:50 am
☽ ⚺ ♄ **7:51 am** 4:51 am
☽ □ ♀ **10:35 pm** 7:35 pm
☽ ✶ ♅ **11:20 pm** 8:20 pm

12 FRIDAY
☽ △ ☿ **8:07 am** 5:07 am
☽ ☌ ♂ **10:13 pm** 7:13 pm
☽ ☌ ♆ **10:51 pm** 7:51 pm
☽ □ ☉ 11:24 pm

13 SATURDAY
☽ □ ☉ **2:24 am**
☽ ✶ ♇ **5:56 am** 2:56 am
☽ ✶ ♃ **8:45 am** 5:45 am
♂ ☌ ♆ **10:13 am** 7:13 am
☽ ✶ ♄ **7:12 pm** 4:12 pm

14 SUNDAY
☽ ✶ ♀ **8:24 am** 5:24 am
☽ ⚺ ♅ **11:38 am** 8:38 am
☉ ⚻ ♇ **9:58 pm** 6:58 pm
☽ □ ☿ **10:07 pm** 7:07 pm

15 MONDAY
☽ ⚺ ♆ **11:21 am** 8:21 am
☽ ⚺ ♂ **2:08 pm** 11:08 am
☽ □ ♇ **6:22 pm** 3:22 pm
☽ ✶ ☉ **8:11 pm** 5:11 pm
☽ □ ♃ **8:49 pm** 5:49 pm

16 TUESDAY
☉ ⚻ ♃ **3:33 am** 12:33 am
☽ □ ♄ **7:29 am** 4:29 am
☽ ⚺ ♀ **7:01 pm** 4:01 pm
☽ ☌ ♅ 9:15 pm

17 WEDNESDAY
☽ ☌ ♅ **12:15 am**
☽ ✶ ☿ **11:03 am** 8:03 am
☽ ✶ ♆ **11:18 pm** 8:18 pm

18 THURSDAY
☽ ✶ ♂ **5:16 am** 2:16 am
☽ △ ♇ **6:01 am** 3:01 am
☽ △ ♃ **8:02 am** 5:02 am
☽ ⚺ ☉ **12:54 pm** 9:54 am
☽ △ ♄ **6:34 pm** 3:34 pm
♂ ✶ ♇ **7:08 pm** 4:08 pm

19 FRIDAY
☽ ☌ ♀ **4:40 am** 1:40 am
☽ ⚺ ♅ **11:12 am** 8:12 am
☽ ⚺ ☿ **9:09 pm** 6:09 pm

20 SATURDAY
♂ ✶ ♃ **3:56 am** 12:56 am
☽ □ ♆ **9:07 am** 6:07 am
☽ ⚻ ♇ **3:26 pm** 12:26 pm
☽ ⚻ ♃ **5:01 pm** 2:01 pm
☽ □ ♂ **5:48 pm** 2:48 pm
☽ ☌ ☉ 11:41 pm

21 SUNDAY
☽ ☌ ☉ **2:41 am**
☽ ⚻ ♄ **3:17 am** 12:17 am
☉ ⚻ ♄ **10:14 am** 7:14 am
☽ ⚺ ♀ **12:22 pm** 9:22 am
☽ ✶ ♅ **7:35 pm** 4:35 pm

22 MONDAY
☽ ☌ ☿ **4:01 am** 1:01 am
☽ △ ♆ **4:22 pm** 1:22 pm
☽ ☍ ♇ **10:19 pm** 7:19 pm
☽ ☍ ♃ **11:29 pm** 8:29 pm

23 TUESDAY
☽ △ ♂ **3:20 am** 12:20 am
☽ ☍ ♄ **9:31 am** 6:31 am
☽ ⚺ ☉ **1:20 pm** 10:20 am
☽ ✶ ♀ **6:05 pm** 3:05 pm
☽ □ ♅ 10:34 pm

24 WEDNESDAY
☽ □ ♅ **1:34 am**
☽ ⚺ ☿ **8:09 am** 5:09 am
☽ ⚻ ♆ **9:25 pm** 6:25 pm

25 THURSDAY
☽ ⚻ ♇ **3:05 am** 12:05 am
☽ ⚻ ♃ **3:53 am** 12:53 am
☽ ⚻ ♂ **10:29 am** 7:29 am
☽ ⚻ ♄ **1:47 pm** 10:47 am
☽ ✶ ☉ **9:33 pm** 6:33 pm
☽ □ ♀ **10:17 pm** 7:17 pm

26 FRIDAY
☽ △ ♅ **5:44 am** 2:44 am
☉ ⚺ ♀ **8:41 am** 5:41 am
☽ ✶ ☿ **10:18 am** 7:18 am
☽ ☍ ♆ 9:56 pm

27 SATURDAY
☽ ☍ ♆ **12:56 am**
☽ △ ♇ **6:24 am** 3:24 am
☽ △ ♃ **6:51 am** 3:51 am
☽ ☍ ♂ **4:02 pm** 1:02 pm
☽ △ ♄ **4:44 pm** 1:44 pm
☽ △ ♀ 10:34 pm

28 SUNDAY
☽ △ ♀ **1:34 am**
☽ □ ☉ **4:16 am** 1:16 am
♂ ✶ ♄ **6:59 am** 3:59 am
☽ ⚻ ♅ **8:47 am** 5:47 am
☽ □ ☿ **11:14 am** 8:14 am

29 MONDAY
☽ ⚻ ♆ **3:35 am** 12:35 am
☽ □ ♇ **8:55 am** 5:55 am
☽ □ ♃ **9:02 am** 6:02 am
☽ □ ♄ **7:01 pm** 4:01 pm
☽ ⚻ ♂ **8:47 pm** 5:47 pm
♃ ☌ ♇ 10:46 pm

30 TUESDAY
♃ ☌ ♇ **1:46 am**
☽ ⚻ ♀ **4:34 am** 1:34 am
☽ △ ☉ **10:20 am** 7:20 am
☽ ☍ ♅ **11:21 am** 8:21 am
☽ △ ☿ **11:39 am** 8:39 am
☿ ✶ ♅ **6:12 pm** 3:12 pm
☉ ☌ ☿ **10:53 pm** 7:53 pm
☉ ✶ ♅ 11:07 pm

Eastern time in bold type
Pacific time in medium type

JUNE 2020

DATE	SID.TIME	SUN	MOON	NODE	MERCURY	VENUS	MARS	JUPITER	SATURN	URANUS	NEPTUNE	PLUTO	CERES	PALLAS	JUNO	VESTA	CHIRON
1 M	16 39 44	10♊58 18	5♎38	29♊13℞	4♋07	15♊18℞	12♓42	26♑46℞	1♒37℞	8♉34	20♓50	24♑42℞	9♓20	0♒13℞	5♎52	28♊48	8♈44
2 T	16 43 41	11 55 47	20 11	29 11	5 16	14 41	13 22	26 43	1 35	8 37	20 50	24 41	9 31	0 07	5 54	29 14	8 46
3 W	16 47 38	12 53 14	4♏50	29 09	6 21	14 04	14 01	26 39	1 33	8 40	20 51	24 40	9 42	0 00	5 56	29 40	8 48
4 Th	16 51 34	13 50 41	19 30	29 07	7 23	13 26	14 41	26 35	1 30	8 43	20 52	24 39	9 52	29♑53	5 59	0♋05	8 50
5 F	16 55 31	14 48 06	4♐04	29 06	8 21	12 48	15 20	26 32	1 28	8 46	20 52	24 38	10 02	29 46	6 01	0 31	8 52
6 Sa	16 59 27	15 45 31	18 25	29 05D	9 16	12 11	16 00	26 28	1 26	8 48	20 53	24 37	10 12	29 38	6 04	0 57	8 54
7 Su	17 3 24	16 42 54	2♑28	29 05	10 06	11 34	16 39	26 23	1 23	8 51	20 53	24 36	10 21	29 30	6 08	1 23	8 55
8 M	17 7 20	17 40 17	16 11	29 05	10 53	10 58	17 19	26 19	1 21	8 54	20 54	24 34	10 30	29 21	6 11	1 49	8 57
9 T	17 11 17	18 37 39	29 30	29 06	11 35	10 23	17 58	26 15	1 18	8 57	20 54	24 33	10 39	29 12	6 15	2 15	8 59
10 W	17 15 13	19 35 00	12♒28	29 07	12 14	9 49	18 37	26 10	1 16	9 00	20 55	24 32	10 48	29 02	6 19	2 41	9 00
11 Th	17 19 10	20 32 21	25 05	29 08	12 48	9 17	19 16	26 05	1 13	9 03	20 55	24 31	10 56	28 53	6 24	3 07	9 02
12 F	17 23 7	21 29 41	7♓24	29 08	13 19	8 46	19 55	26 00	1 10	9 05	20 56	24 30	11 05	28 42	6 28	3 33	9 03
13 Sa	17 27 3	22 27 01	19 30	29 09℞	13 44	8 17	20 33	25 55	1 07	9 08	20 56	24 29	11 13	28 32	6 33	3 59	9 05
14 Su	17 31 0	23 24 20	1♈28	29 09	14 06	7 50	21 12	25 50	1 04	9 11	20 56	24 28	11 20	28 21	6 39	4 25	9 06
15 M	17 34 56	24 21 39	13 21	29 08	14 22	7 25	21 50	25 44	1 01	9 14	20 57	24 26	11 27	28 10	6 44	4 51	9 08
16 T	17 38 53	25 18 58	25 14	29 08	14 35	7 02	22 29	25 39	0 58	9 16	20 57	24 25	11 34	27 58	6 50	5 17	9 09
17 W	17 42 49	26 16 16	7♉11	29 07	14 43	6 41	23 07	25 33	0 55	9 19	20 57	24 24	11 41	27 46	6 56	5 43	9 10
18 Th	17 46 46	27 13 34	19 17	29 07	14 46℞	6 23	23 45	25 27	0 52	9 21	20 57	24 23	11 48	27 34	7 03	6 09	9 12
19 F	17 50 42	28 10 51	1♊33	29 07D	14 44	6 07	24 23	25 21	0 48	9 24	20 57	24 21	11 54	27 21	7 10	6 35	9 13
20 Sa	17 54 39	29 08 09	14 02	29 07	14 39	5 53	25 01	25 15	0 45	9 26	20 57	24 20	12 00	27 08	7 16	7 01	9 14
21 Su	17 58 36	0♋05 25	26 46	29 07℞	14 29	5 42	25 38	25 09	0 41	9 29	20 58	24 19	12 05	26 55	7 24	7 27	9 15
22 M	18 2 32	1 02 42	9♋45	29 07	14 14	5 33	26 16	25 03	0 38	9 31	20 58	24 18	12 10	26 41	7 31	7 53	9 16
23 T	18 6 29	1 59 58	22 59	29 07	13 56	5 26	26 53	24 56	0 34	9 34	20 58℞	24 16	12 15	26 27	7 39	8 20	9 17
24 W	18 10 25	2 57 13	6♌27	29 06	13 34	5 22	27 30	24 50	0 31	9 36	20 58	24 15	12 20	26 13	7 47	8 46	9 18
25 Th	18 14 22	3 54 28	20 08	29 06	13 08	5 20D	28 07	24 43	0 27	9 39	20 58	24 14	12 24	25 59	7 55	9 12	9 19
26 F	18 18 18	4 51 42	4♍01	29 05	12 40	5 21	28 44	24 36	0 23	9 41	20 57	24 12	12 28	25 44	8 03	9 38	9 20
27 Sa	18 22 15	5 48 56	18 03	29 05	12 09	5 24	29 21	24 29	0 20	9 43	20 57	24 11	12 32	25 29	8 12	10 04	9 20
28 Su	18 26 12	6 46 09	2♎12	29 05D	11 36	5 29	29 57	24 22	0 16	9 45	20 57	24 10	12 35	25 14	8 21	10 31	9 21
29 M	18 30 8	7 43 22	16 26	29 05	11 01	5 36	0♈34	24 15	0 12	9 48	20 57	24 08	12 38	24 59	8 30	10 57	9 22
30 T	18 34 5	8 40 34	0♏43	29 05	10 25	5 45	1 10	24 08	0 08	9 50	20 57	24 07	12 41	24 43	8 39	11 23	9 23

EPHEMERIS CALCULATED FOR 12 MIDNIGHT GREENWICH MEAN TIME. ALL OTHER DATA AND FACING ASPECTARIAN PAGE IN **EASTERN TIME (BOLD)** AND PACIFIC TIME (REGULAR).

JULY 2020

☽ Last Aspect day	ET / hr:mn / PT	asp	☽ Ingress sign	day	ET / hr:mn / PT
1	**9:20 pm** 6:20 pm	⚹ ♄	♐	1	**9:21 pm** 6:21 pm
3	**9:06 am** 6:06 am	□ ♆	♑	3	9:48 pm
3	**9:06 am** 6:06 am	□ ♆	♑	4	**12:48 am**
6	**5:35 am** 2:35 am	☌ ♄	♒	6	**6:08 am** 3:08 am
6	9:37 pm	□ ♅	♓	8	**2:13 pm** 11:13 am
7	**12:37 am**	□ ♅	♓	8	**2:13 pm** 11:13 am
10	**11:49 pm** 8:49 pm	⚹ ♄	♈	10	10:06 pm
10	**11:49 pm** 8:49 pm	⚹ ♄	♈	11	**1:06 am**
13	**11:54 am** 8:54 am	□ ♄	♉	13	**1:34 pm** 10:34 am
15	**11:21 pm** 8:21 pm	△ ♄	♊	15	10:19 pm
15	**11:21 pm** 8:21 pm	△ ♄	♊	16	**1:19 am**
17	**5:14 pm** 2:14 pm	□ ♆	♋	18	**10:24 am** 7:24 am
20	**1:55 pm** 10:55 am	☍ ♄	♌	20	**4:16 pm** 1:16 pm
21	**8:27 pm** 5:27 pm	⚹ ♀	♍	22	**7:40 pm** 4:40 pm
24	**7:08 pm** 4:08 pm	△ ♄	♎	24	**9:54 pm** 6:54 pm
26	**9:09 pm** 6:09 pm	□ ♄	♏	26	9:12 pm
26	**9:09 pm** 6:09 pm	□ ♄	♏	27	**12:12 am**
28	9:01 pm	⚹ ♄	♐	29	**3:25 am** 12:25 am
29	**12:01 am**	⚹ ♄	♐	29	**3:25 am** 12:25 am
30	**8:08 pm** 5:08 pm	☍ ♀	♑	31	**7:58 am** 4:58 am

☽ Phases & Eclipses phase	day	ET / hr:mn / PT
Full Moon	4	9:44 pm
Full Moon	5	**12:44 am**
☍	4/5	13° ♑ 38'
4th Quarter	12	**7:29 pm** 4:29 pm
New Moon	20	**1:33 pm** 10:33 am
2nd Quarter	27	**8:33 am** 5:33 am

Planet Ingress	day	ET / hr:mn / PT
♄ ♑	1	**7:39 pm** 4:39 pm
☉ ♌	22	**4:37 am** 1:37 am

Planetary Motion	day	ET / hr:mn / PT
⚳ ℞	6	9:01 pm
⚳ ℞	7	**12:01 am**
⚷ ℞	11	**5:09 pm** 2:09 pm

1 WEDNESDAY
☉ ⚹ ♅ **2:07 am**
☽ △ ♆ **6:02 am** 3:02 am
☽ ⚹ ♃ **11:06 am** 8:06 am
☽ ⚹ ♇ **11:20 am** 8:20 am
☽ ⚹ ♄ **9:20 pm** 6:20 pm
☽ △ ♂ 10:35 pm

2 THURSDAY
☽ △ ♂ **1:35 am**
☽ ☍ ♀ **8:02 am** 5:02 am
☽ ⚻ ☿ **12:20 pm** 9:20 am
☽ ⚻ ♅ **2:13 pm** 11:13 am
☽ ⚻ ☉ **4:45 pm** 1:45 pm

3 FRIDAY
☽ □ ♆ **9:06 am** 6:06 am
☽ ⚺ ♃ **1:51 pm** 10:51 am
☽ ⚺ ♇ **2:26 pm** 11:26 am
☽ ⚺ ♄ 9:32 pm

4 SATURDAY
☽ ⚺ ♄ **12:32 am**
☽ □ ♂ **7:28 am** 4:28 am
☽ ⚻ ♀ **12:55 pm** 9:55 am
☽ ☍ ☿ **2:13 pm** 11:13 am
☽ △ ♅ **6:19 pm** 3:19 pm
☽ ☍ ☉ 9:44 pm

5 SUNDAY
☽ ☍ ☉ **12:44 am**
☿ ⚺ ♀ **10:45 am** 7:45 am
☽ ⚹ ♆ **1:44 pm** 10:44 am

☽ ☌ ♃ **6:13 pm** 3:13 pm
☽ ☌ ♇ **7:14 pm** 4:14 pm

6 MONDAY
☽ ☌ ♄ **5:35 am** 2:35 am
☽ ⚹ ♂ **3:37 pm** 12:37 pm
☽ ⚻ ☿ **6:20 pm** 3:20 pm
☽ △ ♀ **8:22 pm** 5:22 pm
☽ □ ♅ 9:37 pm

7 TUESDAY
☽ □ ♅ **12:37 am**
☽ ⚻ ☉ **11:37 am** 8:37 am
☽ ⚺ ♆ **8:53 pm** 5:53 pm
☽ ⚺ ♃ 10:05 pm
☽ ⚺ ♇ 11:36 pm

8 WEDNESDAY
☽ ⚺ ♃ **1:05 am**
☽ ⚺ ♇ **2:36 am**
☿ □ ♂ **6:42 am** 3:42 am
☽ ⚺ ♄ **1:19 pm** 10:19 am
☽ △ ☿ 10:35 pm
☽ ⚺ ♂ 11:56 pm

9 THURSDAY
☽ △ ☿ **1:35 am**
☽ ⚺ ♂ **2:56 am**
☽ □ ♀ **7:15 am** 4:15 am
☽ ⚹ ♅ **9:50 am** 6:50 am
☽ △ ☉ 11:09 pm

10 FRIDAY
☽ △ ☉ **2:09 am**
☽ ☌ ♆ **6:57 am** 3:57 am
☽ ⚹ ♃ **10:47 am** 7:47 am
☽ ⚹ ♇ **12:52 pm** 9:52 am
☽ ⚹ ♄ **11:49 pm** 8:49 pm

11 SATURDAY
☽ □ ☿ **12:09 pm** 9:09 am
☽ ☌ ♂ **5:16 pm** 2:16 pm
☽ ⚹ ♀ **9:21 pm** 6:21 pm
☽ ⚺ ♅ **9:36 pm** 6:36 pm

12 SUNDAY
♀ ⚺ ♅ **3:12 am** 12:12 am
☉ △ ♆ **2:43 pm** 11:43 am
☽ ⚺ ♆ **7:06 pm** 4:06 pm
☽ □ ☉ **7:29 pm** 4:29 pm
☽ □ ♃ **10:25 pm** 7:25 pm
☽ □ ♇ 10:03 pm

13 MONDAY
☽ □ ♇ **1:03 am**
☽ □ ♄ **11:54 am** 8:54 am
☽ ⚹ ☿ 9:56 pm

14 TUESDAY
☽ ⚹ ☿ **12:56 am**
☉ ☍ ♃ **3:58 am** 12:58 am
☽ ⚺ ♂ **8:43 am** 5:43 am
☽ ☌ ♅ **10:14 am** 7:14 am
☽ ⚺ ♀ **12:47 pm** 9:47 am

15 WEDNESDAY
☽ ⚹ ♆ **7:16 am** 4:16 am
☽ △ ♃ **9:56 am** 6:56 am
☽ ⚹ ☉ **12:50 pm** 9:50 am
☽ △ ♇ **1:01 pm** 10:01 am
☉ ☍ ♇ **3:13 pm** 12:13 pm
♂ ⚺ ♅ **7:55 pm** 4:55 pm
☽ △ ♄ **11:21 pm** 8:21 pm

16 THURSDAY
☽ ⚺ ☿ **1:40 pm** 10:40 am
☽ ⚺ ♅ **9:21 pm** 6:21 pm
☽ ⚹ ♂ **10:26 pm** 7:26 pm
☽ ☌ ♀ 11:40 pm

17 FRIDAY
☽ ☌ ♀ **2:40 am**
☽ □ ♆ **5:14 pm** 2:14 pm
☽ ⚻ ♃ **7:15 pm** 4:15 pm
☽ ⚻ ♇ **10:39 pm** 7:39 pm

18 SATURDAY
☽ ⚺ ☉ **3:13 am** 12:13 am
☽ ⚻ ♄ **8:13 am** 5:13 am
☽ ☌ ☿ 9:19 pm

19 SUNDAY
☽ ☌ ☿ **12:19 am**
☽ ⚹ ♅ **5:24 am** 2:24 am
☽ □ ♂ **8:38 am** 5:38 am
☽ ⚺ ♀ **1:12 pm** 10:12 am
☽ △ ♆ 9:01 pm
☽ ☍ ♃ 10:27 pm

20 MONDAY
☽ △ ♆ **12:01 am**
☽ ☍ ♃ **1:27 am**
☽ ☍ ♇ **5:04 am** 2:04 am
☽ ☌ ☉ **1:33 pm** 10:33 am
☽ ☍ ♄ **1:55 pm** 10:55 am
☉ ☍ ♄ **6:28 pm** 3:28 pm

21 TUESDAY
☽ ⚺ ☿ **8:22 am** 5:22 am
☽ □ ♅ **10:22 am** 7:22 am
☽ △ ♂ **3:23 pm** 12:23 pm
☽ ⚹ ♀ **8:27 pm** 5:27 pm

22 WEDNESDAY
☽ ⚻ ♆ **3:59 am** 12:59 am
☽ ⚻ ♃ **4:57 am** 1:57 am
☽ ⚻ ♇ **8:48 am** 5:48 am
☿ ⚹ ♅ **4:25 pm** 1:25 pm
☽ ⚻ ♄ **5:08 pm** 2:08 pm
☽ ⚺ ☉ **8:45 pm** 5:45 pm

23 THURSDAY
☽ △ ♅ **1:16 pm** 10:16 am
☽ ⚹ ☿ **2:47 pm** 11:47 am
☽ ⚻ ♂ **7:55 pm** 4:55 pm
☽ □ ♀ 10:46 pm

24 FRIDAY
☽ □ ♀ **1:46 am**
☽ ☍ ♆ **6:23 am** 3:23 am
☽ △ ♃ **6:57 am** 3:57 am
☽ △ ♇ **11:05 am** 8:05 am
☽ △ ♄ **7:08 pm** 4:08 pm
☽ ⚹ ☉ 11:33 pm

25 SATURDAY
☽ ⚹ ☉ **2:33 am**
☽ ⚻ ♅ **3:28 pm** 12:28 pm

☽ □ ☿ **9:11 pm** 6:11 pm
☽ ☍ ♂ **11:50 pm** 8:50 pm

26 SUNDAY
☽ △ ♀ **6:45 am** 3:45 am
☽ ⚻ ♆ **8:29 am** 5:29 am
☽ □ ♃ **8:41 am** 5:41 am
☽ □ ♇ **1:12 pm** 10:12 am
☽ □ ♄ **9:09 pm** 6:09 pm

27 MONDAY
☽ □ ☉ **8:33 am** 5:33 am
♃ ⚹ ♆ **12:07 pm** 9:07 am
♀ ⚻ ♃ **1:36 pm** 10:36 am
♀ □ ♆ **1:48 pm** 10:48 am
☿ □ ♂ **5:46 pm** 2:46 pm
☽ ☍ ♅ **6:04 pm** 3:04 pm

28 TUESDAY
☽ ⚻ ♂ **4:18 am** 1:18 am
☽ △ ☿ **5:04 am** 2:04 am
☽ ⚹ ♃ **11:08 am** 8:08 am
☽ △ ♆ **11:18 am** 8:18 am
☽ ⚻ ♀ **12:38 pm** 9:38 am
☽ ⚹ ♇ **4:05 pm** 1:05 pm
☽ ⚹ ♄ 9:01 pm

29 WEDNESDAY
☽ ⚹ ♄ **12:01 am**
☽ △ ☉ **3:47 pm** 12:47 pm
☽ ⚻ ♅ **9:47 pm** 6:47 pm

30 THURSDAY
☽ △ ♂ **10:02 am** 7:02 am
☿ ☍ ♃ **10:17 am** 7:17 am
☿ △ ♆ **2:45 pm** 11:45 am
☽ ⚺ ♃ **2:47 pm** 11:47 am
☽ □ ♆ **3:20 pm** 12:20 pm
☽ ⚻ ☿ **3:25 pm** 12:25 pm
☽ ☍ ♀ **8:08 pm** 5:08 pm
☽ ⚺ ♇ **8:14 pm** 5:14 pm
♀ ⚻ ♇ **9:51 pm** 6:51 pm

31 FRIDAY
☽ ⚺ ♄ **4:12 am** 1:12 am
☽ ⚻ ☉ 9:46 pm
☽ △ ♅ 11:56 pm

Eastern time in bold type
Pacific time in medium type

JULY 2020

DATE	SID.TIME	SUN	MOON	NODE	MERCURY	VENUS	MARS	JUPITER	SATURN	URANUS	NEPTUNE	PLUTO	CERES	PALLAS	JUNO	VESTA	CHIRON
1 W	18 38 1	9♋37 46	14♏59	29♊06	9♋49℞	5♊56	1♈46	24♑01℞	0♒04℞	9♉52	20♓57℞	24♑05℞	12♓43	24♑27℞	8♎49	11♋49	9♈23
2 Th	18 41 58	10 34 57	29 12	29 07	9 13	6 10	2 21	23 54	0 00	9 54	20 56	24 04	12 45	24 11	8 59	12 16	9 24
3 F	18 45 54	11 32 08	13♐18	29 08	8 38	6 25	2 57	23 46	29♑56	9 56	20 56	24 03	12 46	23 55	9 09	12 42	9 24
4 Sa	18 49 51	12 29 19	27 14	29 08℞	8 04	6 43	3 32	23 39	29 52	9 58	20 56	24 01	12 48	23 39	9 19	13 08	9 25
5 Su	18 53 47	13 26 30	10♑57	29 08	7 33	7 02	4 08	23 32	29 48	10 00	20 55	24 00	12 49	23 23	9 29	13 34	9 25
6 M	18 57 44	14 23 41	24 24	29 07	7 04	7 23	4 42	23 24	29 43	10 02	20 55	23 58	12 49	23 07	9 40	14 01	9 25
7 T	19 1 41	15 20 52	7♒34	29 05	6 38	7 46	5 17	23 17	29 39	10 04	20 55	23 57	12 49℞	22 50	9 51	14 27	9 26
8 W	19 5 37	16 18 03	20 26	29 03	6 16	8 10	5 52	23 09	29 35	10 06	20 54	23 56	12 49	22 34	10 02	14 53	9 26
9 Th	19 9 34	17 15 15	3♓01	29 00	5 57	8 36	6 26	23 01	29 31	10 07	20 54	23 54	12 49	22 17	10 13	15 20	9 26
10 F	19 13 30	18 12 26	15 20	28 58	5 43	9 04	7 00	22 54	29 27	10 09	20 53	23 53	12 48	22 01	10 24	15 46	9 26
11 Sa	19 17 27	19 09 38	27 27	28 55	5 34	9 33	7 34	22 46	29 22	10 11	20 53	23 51	12 47	21 44	10 36	16 12	9 26℞
12 Su	19 21 23	20 06 51	9♈25	28 54	5 30D	10 03	8 07	22 38	29 18	10 12	20 52	23 50	12 45	21 27	10 48	16 38	9 26
13 M	19 25 20	21 04 03	21 18	28 54 D	5 31	10 35	8 41	22 31	29 13	10 14	20 51	23 48	12 43	21 11	11 00	17 05	9 26
14 T	19 29 16	22 01 17	3♉12	28 54	5 37	11 09	9 14	22 23	29 09	10 16	20 51	23 47	12 41	20 54	11 12	17 31	9 26
15 W	19 33 13	22 58 31	15 10	28 55	5 48	11 43	9 46	22 15	29 05	10 17	20 50	23 45	12 38	20 38	11 24	17 57	9 26
16 Th	19 37 10	23 55 46	27 17	28 57	6 05	12 19	10 19	22 07	29 00	10 19	20 49	23 44	12 36	20 21	11 36	18 24	9 26
17 F	19 41 6	24 53 01	9♊38	28 58	6 27	12 56	10 51	22 00	28 56	10 20	20 49	23 43	12 32	20 05	11 49	18 50	9 26
18 Sa	19 45 3	25 50 17	22 16	28 59℞	6 55	13 35	11 23	21 52	28 51	10 22	20 48	23 41	12 28	19 49	12 02	19 17	9 25
19 Su	19 48 59	26 47 33	5♋13	29 00	7 28	14 14	11 54	21 44	28 47	10 23	20 47	23 40	12 24	19 32	12 15	19 43	9 25
20 M	19 52 56	27 44 50	18 31	28 58	8 07	14 54	12 26	21 37	28 43	10 24	20 46	23 38	12 20	19 16	12 28	20 09	9 25
21 T	19 56 52	28 42 08	2♌08	28 56	8 52	15 36	12 57	21 29	28 38	10 25	20 45	23 37	12 15	19 00	12 41	20 36	9 24
22 W	20 0 49	29 39 26	16 03	28 52	9 41	16 18	13 27	21 21	28 34	10 27	20 45	23 35	12 10	18 45	12 55	21 02	9 24
23 Th	20 4 45	0♌36 44	0♍12	28 47	10 36	17 02	13 57	21 14	28 29	10 28	20 44	23 34	12 05	18 29	13 08	21 28	9 23
24 F	20 8 42	1 34 03	14 30	28 43	11 36	17 46	14 27	21 06	28 25	10 29	20 43	23 32	11 59	18 14	13 22	21 55	9 22
25 Sa	20 12 39	2 31 22	28 52	28 38	12 42	18 31	14 57	20 59	28 20	10 30	20 42	23 31	11 53	17 58	13 36	22 21	9 22
26 Su	20 16 35	3 28 42	13♎13	28 35	13 52	19 17	15 26	20 51	28 16	10 31	20 41	23 30	11 46	17 43	13 50	22 47	9 21
27 M	20 20 32	4 26 02	27 31	28 34D	15 08	20 04	15 55	20 44	28 12	10 32	20 40	23 28	11 39	17 29	14 04	23 14	9 20
28 T	20 24 28	5 23 22	11♏41	28 34	16 28	20 51	16 23	20 37	28 07	10 33	20 39	23 27	11 32	17 14	14 19	23 40	9 20
29 W	20 28 25	6 20 43	25 42	28 35	17 53	21 40	16 51	20 30	28 03	10 34	20 38	23 25	11 25	17 00	14 33	24 06	9 19
30 Th	20 32 21	7 18 05	9♐34	28 36	19 23	22 29	17 19	20 22	27 58	10 35	20 37	23 24	11 17	16 46	14 48	24 33	9 18
31 F	20 36 18	8 15 26	23 15	28 37℞	20 57	23 19	17 46	20 15	27 54	10 36	20 36	23 23	11 09	16 32	15 03	24 59	9 17

EPHEMERIS CALCULATED FOR 12 MIDNIGHT GREENWICH MEAN TIME. ALL OTHER DATA AND FACING ASPECTARIAN PAGE IN **EASTERN TIME (BOLD)** AND PACIFIC TIME (REGULAR).

AUGUST 2020

☽ Last Aspect day	ET / hr:mn / PT	asp	☽ Ingress sign day	ET / hr:mn / PT
2	**9:59 am** 6:59 am	☌ ♄	♒ 2	**2:11 pm** 11:11 am
4	**5:45 pm** 2:45 pm	△ ♀	♓ 4	**10:28 pm** 7:28 pm
7	**8:53 am** 5:53 am	□ ♀	♈ 7	**9:05 am** 6:05 am
9	**3:50 pm** 12:50 pm	□ ♄	♉ 9	**9:28 pm** 6:28 pm
12	**3:55 am** 12:55 am	△ ♄	♊ 12	**9:46 am** 6:46 am
14	**7:19 am** 4:19 am	⚹ ♂	♋ 14	**7:35 pm** 4:35 pm
16	**7:59 pm** 4:59 pm	☍ ♄	♌ 16	10:38 pm
16	**7:59 pm** 4:59 pm	☍ ♄	♌ 17	**1:38 am**
18	10:38 pm	☌ ☿	♍ 19	**4:20 am** 1:20 am
19	**1:38 am**	☌ ☿	♍ 19	**4:20 am** 1:20 am

☽ Last Aspect day	ET / hr:mn / PT	asp	☽ Ingress sign day	ET / hr:mn / PT
20	**11:37 pm** 8:37 pm	△ ♄	♎ 21	**5:16 am** 2:16 am
22	9:20 pm	□ ♄	♏ 23	**6:16 am** 3:16 am
23	**12:20 am**	□ ♄	♏ 23	**6:16 am** 3:16 am
24	11:27 pm	⚹ ♄	♐ 25	**8:49 am** 5:49 am
25	**2:27 am**	⚹ ♄	♐ 25	**8:49 am** 5:49 am
27	**8:00 am** 5:00 am	△ ♂	♑ 27	**1:37 pm** 10:37 am
29	**3:31 pm** 12:31 pm	□ ♂	♒ 29	**8:37 pm** 5:37 pm
31	9:56 pm	⚹ ♂	♓ 9/1	**5:34 am** 2:34 am

☽ Phases & Eclipses phase	day	ET / hr:mn / PT
Full Moon	3	**11:59 am** 8:59 am
4th Quarter	11	**12:45 pm** 9:45 am
New Moon	18	**10:42 pm** 7:42 pm
2nd Quarter	25	**1:58 pm** 10:58 am

Planet Ingress	day	ET / hr:mn / PT
☿ ♌	4	**11:32 pm** 8:32 pm
♀ ♋	7	**11:21 am** 8:21 am
⚴ ♌	11	**7:17 am** 4:17 am
☿ ♍	19	**9:30 pm** 6:30 pm
⊙ ♍	22	**11:45 am** 8:45 am

Planetary Motion	day	ET / hr:mn / PT
♅ ℞	15	**10:25 am** 7:25 am

1 SATURDAY
☽ ⚻ ⊙ **12:46 am**
☽ △ ♅ **2:56 am**
☿ ☍ ♇ **6:52 am** 3:52 am
☽ □ ♂ **5:23 pm** 2:23 pm
☽ ☌ ♃ **7:57 pm** 4:57 pm
☽ ⚹ ♆ **8:55 pm** 5:55 pm
☽ ☌ ♇ 10:57 pm

2 SUNDAY
☽ ☌ ♇ **1:57 am**
☽ ☍ ☿ **4:53 am** 1:53 am
☽ ⚻ ♀ **5:39 am** 2:39 am
⊙ □ ♅ **7:19 am** 4:19 am
☽ ☌ ♄ **9:59 am** 6:59 am
☿ ⚺ ♀ **3:26 pm** 12:26 pm

3 MONDAY
☽ □ ♅ **9:52 am** 6:52 am
☽ ☍ ⊙ **11:59 am** 8:59 am
☿ ☍ ♄ **5:00 pm** 2:00 pm
☽ ⚹ ♂ 11:45 pm

4 TUESDAY
☽ ⚹ ♂ **2:45 am**
☽ ⚺ ♃ **3:01 am** 12:01 am
☽ ⚺ ♆ **4:24 am** 1:24 am
♂ □ ♃ **9:07 am** 6:07 am
☽ ⚺ ♇ **9:38 am** 6:38 am
☽ △ ♀ **5:45 pm** 2:45 pm
☽ ⚺ ♄ **5:47 pm** 2:47 pm
♀ ⚻ ♄ **6:07 pm** 3:07 pm

☽ ⚻ ☿ **10:16 pm** 7:16 pm

5 WEDNESDAY
☽ ⚹ ♅ **7:01 pm** 4:01 pm
☽ ⚻ ⊙ 11:00 pm

6 THURSDAY
☽ ⚻ ⊙ **2:00 am**
♂ ⚺ ♆ **3:30 am** 12:30 am
☽ ⚹ ♃ **12:20 pm** 9:20 am
☽ ☌ ♆ **2:12 pm** 11:12 am
☽ ⚺ ♂ **2:35 pm** 11:35 am
☽ ⚹ ♇ **7:38 pm** 4:38 pm

7 FRIDAY
☽ ⚹ ♄ **3:53 am** 12:53 am
☽ □ ♀ **8:53 am** 5:53 am
☽ △ ☿ **8:12 pm** 5:12 pm

8 SATURDAY
☽ ⚺ ♅ **6:25 am** 3:25 am
☽ △ ⊙ **6:49 pm** 3:49 pm
☽ □ ♃ **11:44 pm** 8:44 pm
☽ ⚺ ♆ 11:03 pm

9 SUNDAY
☽ ⚺ ♆ **2:03 am**
☽ ☌ ♂ **4:35 am** 1:35 am
☽ □ ♇ **7:38 am** 4:38 am
☽ □ ♄ **3:50 pm** 12:50 pm
☽ ⚹ ♀ 11:23 pm

10 MONDAY
☽ ⚹ ♀ **2:23 am**

☿ □ ♅ **8:52 am** 5:52 am
☽ ☌ ♅ **7:05 pm** 4:05 pm
☽ □ ☿ **9:12 pm** 6:12 pm
⊙ ⚻ ♃ 11:35 pm

11 TUESDAY
⊙ ⚻ ♃ **2:35 am**
☽ △ ♃ **11:51 am** 8:51 am
☽ □ ⊙ **12:45 pm** 9:45 am
☽ ⚹ ♆ **2:32 pm** 11:32 am
☽ ⚺ ♂ **7:04 pm** 4:04 pm
☽ △ ♇ **8:03 pm** 5:03 pm

12 WEDNESDAY
☽ △ ♄ **3:55 am** 12:55 am
⊙ ⚻ ♆ **10:32 am** 7:32 am
☽ ⚺ ♀ **7:37 pm** 4:37 pm

13 THURSDAY
♂ □ ♇ **3:14 am** 12:14 am
☽ ⚺ ♅ **6:45 am** 3:45 am
☽ ⚹ ☿ **8:33 pm** 5:33 pm
☽ ⚻ ♃ **10:24 pm** 7:24 pm
☽ □ ♆ 10:16 pm

14 FRIDAY
☽ □ ♆ **1:16 am**
☽ ⚹ ⊙ **4:32 am** 1:32 am
☽ ⚻ ♇ **6:32 am** 3:32 am
☽ ⚹ ♂ **7:19 am** 4:19 am
☿ ⚻ ♃ **7:28 am** 4:28 am
☽ ⚻ ♄ **1:47 pm** 10:47 am
☿ ⚻ ♆ 10:13 pm

15 SATURDAY
☿ ⚻ ♆ **1:13 am**
⊙ ⚻ ♇ **6:13 am** 3:13 am
☽ ☌ ♀ **9:26 am** 6:26 am
☽ ⚹ ♅ **3:18 pm** 12:18 pm

16 SUNDAY
☽ ☍ ♃ **5:33 am** 2:33 am
☽ △ ♆ **8:28 am** 5:28 am
☿ ⚻ ♇ **9:38 am** 6:38 am
⊙ △ ♂ **10:02 am** 7:02 am
☽ ☍ ♇ **1:24 pm** 10:24 am
☽ ⚺ ☿ **2:03 pm** 11:03 am
☽ □ ♂ **3:32 pm** 12:32 pm
☽ ⚺ ⊙ **3:49 pm** 12:49 pm
☽ ☍ ♄ **7:59 pm** 4:59 pm
☿ △ ♂ 10:29 pm

17 MONDAY
☿ △ ♂ **1:29 am**
⊙ ☌ ☿ **11:07 am** 8:07 am
☽ ⚺ ♀ **6:33 pm** 3:33 pm
☽ □ ♅ **8:01 pm** 5:01 pm

18 TUESDAY
☿ ⚻ ♄ **5:17 am** 2:17 am
☽ ⚻ ♃ **9:05 am** 6:05 am
☽ ⚻ ♆ **12:02 pm** 9:02 am
♀ ⚹ ♅ **3:28 pm** 12:28 pm
☽ ⚻ ♇ **4:41 pm** 1:41 pm
☽ △ ♂ **7:51 pm** 4:51 pm
☽ ☌ ⊙ **10:42 pm** 7:42 pm
☽ ⚻ ♄ **10:46 pm** 7:46 pm
⊙ ⚻ ♄ **11:48 pm** 8:48 pm

☽ ☌ ☿ 10:38 pm

19 WEDNESDAY
☽ ☌ ☿ **1:38 am**
☽ △ ♅ **9:52 pm** 6:52 pm
☽ ⚹ ♀ 9:05 pm

20 THURSDAY
☽ ⚹ ♀ **12:05 am**
☽ △ ♃ **10:13 am** 7:13 am
☽ ☍ ♆ **1:15 pm** 10:15 am
☽ △ ♇ **5:48 pm** 2:48 pm
☽ ⚻ ♂ **9:52 pm** 6:52 pm
☽ △ ♄ **11:37 pm** 8:37 pm

21 FRIDAY
☽ ⚺ ⊙ **3:08 am** 12:08 am
☽ ⚺ ☿ **10:06 am** 7:06 am
☽ ⚻ ♅ **10:36 pm** 7:36 pm

22 SATURDAY
☽ □ ♀ **4:25 am** 1:25 am
☽ □ ♃ **10:45 am** 7:45 am
☽ ⚻ ♆ **1:58 pm** 10:58 am
☽ □ ♇ **6:34 pm** 3:34 pm
☽ ☍ ♂ **11:35 pm** 8:35 pm
☽ □ ♄ 9:20 pm

23 SUNDAY
☽ □ ♄ **12:20 am**
☽ ⚹ ⊙ **7:35 am** 4:35 am
☽ ⚹ ☿ **6:42 pm** 3:42 pm
☽ ☍ ♅ 9:00 pm

24 MONDAY
☽ ☍ ♅ **12:00 am**

☽ △ ♀ **9:51 am** 6:51 am
☽ ⚹ ♃ **12:21 pm** 9:21 am
♂ □ ♄ **2:19 pm** 11:19 am
☽ △ ♆ **3:47 pm** 12:47 pm
☽ ⚹ ♇ **8:36 pm** 5:36 pm
☽ ⚹ ♄ 11:27 pm
☽ ⚻ ♂ 11:41 pm

25 TUESDAY
☽ ⚹ ♄ **2:27 am**
☽ ⚻ ♂ **2:41 am**
☿ △ ♅ **11:18 am** 8:18 am
☽ □ ⊙ **1:58 pm** 10:58 am
♀ ☍ ♃ **6:26 pm** 3:26 pm

26 WEDNESDAY
☽ ⚻ ♅ **3:17 am** 12:17 am
☽ □ ☿ **5:47 am** 2:47 am
☽ ⚺ ♃ **4:00 pm** 1:00 pm
☽ ⚻ ♀ **5:53 pm** 2:53 pm
☽ □ ♆ **7:43 pm** 4:43 pm
☽ ⚺ ♇ 9:46 pm

27 THURSDAY
☽ ⚺ ♇ **12:46 am**
☽ ⚺ ♄ **6:46 am** 3:46 am
☽ △ ♂ **8:00 am** 5:00 am
♀ △ ♆ **5:13 pm** 2:13 pm
☽ △ ⊙ **11:09 pm** 8:09 pm

28 FRIDAY
☽ △ ♅ **8:51 am** 5:51 am
☽ △ ☿ **8:04 pm** 5:04 pm
☽ ☌ ♃ **9:56 pm** 6:56 pm
☽ ⚹ ♆ 10:54 pm

29 SATURDAY
☽ ⚹ ♆ **1:54 am**
☽ ☍ ♀ **4:51 am** 1:51 am
☽ ☌ ♇ **7:12 am** 4:12 am
☿ △ ♃ **9:28 am** 6:28 am
☽ ☌ ♄ **1:18 pm** 10:18 am
☽ □ ♂ **3:31 pm** 12:31 pm

30 SUNDAY
♀ ☍ ♇ **9:31 am** 6:31 am
☽ ⚻ ⊙ **11:03 am** 8:03 am
☿ ☍ ♆ **2:44 pm** 11:44 am
☽ □ ♅ **4:31 pm** 1:31 pm

31 MONDAY
☽ ⚺ ♃ **5:55 am** 2:55 am
☽ ⚺ ♆ **10:06 am** 7:06 am
☽ ⚻ ☿ **1:14 pm** 10:14 am
☽ ⚺ ♇ **3:38 pm** 12:38 pm
☽ ⚻ ♀ **6:28 pm** 3:28 pm
☽ ⚺ ♄ **9:49 pm** 6:49 pm
☽ ⚹ ♂ 9:56 pm

Eastern time in bold type
Pacific time in medium type

AUGUST 2020

DATE	SID.TIME	SUN	MOON	NODE	MERCURY	VENUS	MARS	JUPITER	SATURN	URANUS	NEPTUNE	PLUTO	CERES	PALLAS	JUNO	VESTA	CHIRON
1 Sa	20 40 14	9♌12 49	6♑45	28♊37℞	22♋35	24♊09	18♈13	20♑08℞	27♑50℞	10♉36	20♓34℞	23♑21℞	11♓00℞	16♑19℞	15♎18	25♋25	9♈16℞
2 Su	20 44 11	10 10 12	20 03	28 35	24 17	25 00	18 39	20 02	27 46	10 37	20 33	23 20	10 52	16 06	15 33	25 51	9 15
3 M	20 48 8	11 07 36	3♒09	28 31	26 02	25 52	19 05	19 55	27 41	10 38	20 32	23 18	10 42	15 53	15 48	26 18	9 14
4 T	20 52 4	12 05 01	16 03	28 26	27 51	26 44	19 31	19 48	27 37	10 38	20 31	23 17	10 33	15 40	16 03	26 44	9 13
5 W	20 56 1	13 02 27	28 43	28 18	29 43	27 37	19 56	19 42	27 33	10 39	20 30	23 16	10 23	15 28	16 19	27 10	9 11
6 Th	20 59 57	13 59 54	11♓10	28 10	1♌38	28 31	20 21	19 35	27 29	10 39	20 29	23 14	10 14	15 16	16 34	27 37	9 10
7 F	21 3 54	14 57 22	23 24	28 02	3 35	29 25	20 45	19 29	27 25	10 40	20 27	23 13	10 03	15 05	16 50	28 03	9 09
8 Sa	21 7 50	15 54 51	5♈28	27 55	5 34	0♋20	21 08	19 23	27 20	10 40	20 26	23 12	9 53	14 53	17 05	28 29	9 08
9 Su	21 11 47	16 52 21	17 25	27 49	7 34	1 15	21 31	19 17	27 16	10 40	20 25	23 10	9 42	14 43	17 21	28 55	9 06
10 M	21 15 43	17 49 52	29 17	27 45	9 35	2 11	21 54	19 11	27 12	10 41	20 23	23 09	9 31	14 32	17 37	29 21	9 05
11 T	21 19 40	18 47 25	11♉08	27 43 D	11 38	3 07	22 16	19 05	27 08	10 41	20 22	23 08	9 20	14 22	17 53	29 48	9 03
12 W	21 23 37	19 45 00	23 05	27 43	13 41	4 04	22 38	18 59	27 04	10 41	20 21	23 07	9 09	14 12	18 10	0♌14	9 02
13 Th	21 27 33	20 42 36	5♊11	27 44	15 44	5 01	22 59	18 54	27 01	10 41	20 19	23 05	8 57	14 03	18 26	0 40	9 00
14 F	21 31 30	21 40 13	17 32	27 45℞	17 47	5 58	23 19	18 48	26 57	10 41	20 18	23 04	8 45	13 54	18 42	1 06	8 59
15 Sa	21 35 26	22 37 52	0♋13	27 45	19 50	6 56	23 39	18 43	26 53	10 42℞	20 17	23 03	8 33	13 45	18 59	1 32	8 57
16 Su	21 39 23	23 35 32	13 17	27 44	21 52	7 55	23 58	18 38	26 49	10 42	20 15	23 02	8 21	13 37	19 16	1 59	8 55
17 M	21 43 19	24 33 14	26 46	27 40	23 53	8 54	24 17	18 33	26 46	10 41	20 14	23 01	8 09	13 29	19 32	2 25	8 54
18 T	21 47 16	25 30 57	10♌41	27 35	25 54	9 53	24 35	18 28	26 42	10 41	20 12	22 59	7 56	13 21	19 49	2 51	8 52
19 W	21 51 12	26 28 42	24 58	27 27	27 54	10 53	24 52	18 23	26 38	10 41	20 11	22 58	7 44	13 14	20 06	3 17	8 50
20 Th	21 55 9	27 26 28	9♍32	27 18	29 53	11 53	25 09	18 19	26 35	10 41	20 09	22 57	7 31	13 07	20 23	3 43	8 48
21 F	21 59 6	28 24 15	24 17	27 09	1♍50	12 53	25 25	18 14	26 31	10 41	20 08	22 56	7 18	13 01	20 40	4 09	8 46
22 Sa	22 3 2	29 22 03	9♎05	27 00	3 47	13 54	25 40	18 10	26 28	10 40	20 06	22 55	7 05	12 55	20 58	4 35	8 44
23 Su	22 6 59	0♍19 53	23 46	26 54	5 42	14 55	25 55	18 06	26 25	10 40	20 05	22 54	6 52	12 50	21 15	5 01	8 42
24 M	22 10 55	1 17 44	8♏16	26 50	7 35	15 56	26 09	18 02	26 22	10 40	20 03	22 53	6 38	12 44	21 32	5 27	8 40
25 T	22 14 52	2 15 36	22 31	26 48 D	9 28	16 58	26 22	17 59	26 18	10 39	20 02	22 52	6 25	12 40	21 50	5 53	8 38
26 W	22 18 48	3 13 29	6♐28	26 47	11 19	18 00	26 35	17 55	26 15	10 39	20 00	22 51	6 12	12 35	22 07	6 19	8 36
27 Th	22 22 45	4 11 24	20 08	26 48℞	13 09	19 02	26 47	17 52	26 12	10 38	19 59	22 50	5 59	12 31	22 25	6 45	8 34
28 F	22 26 41	5 09 19	3♑33	26 48	14 58	20 04	26 58	17 49	26 09	10 38	19 57	22 49	5 45	12 28	22 43	7 11	8 32
29 Sa	22 30 38	6 07 17	16 43	26 46	16 45	21 07	27 08	17 46	26 06	10 37	19 55	22 48	5 32	12 24	23 01	7 37	8 30
30 Su	22 34 35	7 05 15	29 40	26 42	18 31	22 10	27 17	17 43	26 04	10 36	19 54	22 47	5 19	12 22	23 19	8 03	8 28
31 M	22 38 31	8 03 15	12♒26	26 35	20 15	23 14	27 26	17 41	26 01	10 36	19 52	22 46	5 05	12 19	23 37	8 29	8 26

EPHEMERIS CALCULATED FOR 12 MIDNIGHT GREENWICH MEAN TIME. ALL OTHER DATA AND FACING ASPECTARIAN PAGE IN **EASTERN TIME (BOLD)** AND PACIFIC TIME (REGULAR).

SEPTEMBER 2020

☽ Last Aspect day	ET / hr:mn / PT		asp	☽ Ingress sign	day	ET / hr:mn / PT	
1	**12:56 am**		✶ ♂	♓	1	**5:34 am**	2:34 am
3	**10:34 am**	7:34 am	△ ♀	♈	3	**4:22 pm**	1:22 pm
5		9:45 pm	☌ ♂	♉	6	**4:43 am**	1:43 am
6	**12:45 am**		☌ ♂	♉	6	**4:43 am**	1:43 am
8	**8:47 am**	5:47 am	△ ♄	♊	8	**5:28 pm**	2:28 pm
10		9:48 pm	✶ ♂	♋	11	**4:23 am**	1:23 am
11	**12:48 am**		✶ ♂	♋	11	**4:23 am**	1:23 am
13	**8:05 am**	5:05 am	□ ♂	♌	13	**11:32 am**	8:32 am
15	**11:09 am**	8:09 am	△ ♂	♍	15	**2:37 pm**	11:37 am
17	**7:42 am**	4:42 am	△ ♄	♎	17	**2:56 pm**	11:56 am
19	**10:29 am**	7:29 am	☍ ♂	♏	19	**2:33 pm**	11:33 am
21	**2:13 pm**	11:13 am	✶ ☉	♐	21	**3:32 pm**	12:32 pm
23	**1:31 pm**	10:31 am	△ ♂	♑	23	**7:16 pm**	4:16 pm
25	**11:36 pm**	8:36 pm	□ ☿	♒	25		11:08 pm
25	**11:36 pm**	8:36 pm	□ ☿	♒	26	**12:08 am**	
28	**3:18 am**	12:18 am	✶ ♂	♓	28	**11:34 am**	8:34 am
30	**1:30 pm**	10:30 am	✶ ♄	♈	30	**10:47 pm**	7:47 pm

☽ Phases & Eclipses phase	day	ET / hr:mn / PT	
Full Moon	1		10:22 pm
Full Moon	2	**1:22 am**	
4th Quarter	10	**5:26 am**	2:26 am
New Moon	17	**7:00 am**	4:00 am
2nd Quarter	23	**9:55 pm**	6:55 pm

Planet Ingress		day	ET / hr:mn / PT	
☿	♎	5	**3:46 pm**	12:46 pm
♀	♌	6	**3:22 am**	12:22 am
⚵	♏	20	**7:19 am**	4:19 am
☉	♎	22	**9:31 am**	6:31 am
⚳	♒	27	**3:08 am**	12:08 am
☿	♏	27	**3:41 am**	12:41 am

Planetary Motion		day	ET / hr:mn / PT	
♇	D	5	**9:06 pm**	6:06 pm
♂	R	9	**6:22 pm**	3:22 pm
♃	D	12	**8:41 pm**	5:41 pm
♄	D	28		10:11 pm
♄	D	29	**1:11 am**	

1 TUESDAY
☽ ✶ ♂ **12:56 am**
☿ △ ♇ **6:42 am** 3:42 am
☽ ☍ ☉ 10:22 pm
☽ ✶ ♅ 11:04 pm

2 WEDNESDAY
☽ ☍ ☉ **1:22 am**
☽ ✶ ♅ **2:04 am**
♀ ☍ ♄ **8:18 am** 5:18 am
☉ △ ♅ **10:09 am** 7:09 am
☽ ✶ ♃ **3:48 pm** 12:48 pm
☽ ☌ ♆ **8:09 pm** 5:09 pm
☽ ✶ ♇ 10:55 pm

3 THURSDAY
☽ ✶ ♇ **1:55 am**
☿ △ ♄ **3:23 am** 12:23 am
☽ ✶ ♄ **8:10 am** 5:10 am
☽ ☍ ☿ **8:56 am** 5:56 am
☽ △ ♀ **10:34 am** 7:34 am
☽ ⚺ ♂ **12:07 pm** 9:07 am

4 FRIDAY
♀ □ ♂ **5:12 am** 2:12 am
☿ ⚻ ♂ **9:15 am** 6:15 am
☽ ⚺ ♅ **1:24 pm** 10:24 am
☿ ✶ ♀ **4:32 pm** 1:32 pm
☽ ⚻ ☉ **6:00 pm** 3:00 pm

5 SATURDAY
☽ □ ♃ **3:26 am** 12:26 am
☽ ⚺ ♆ **7:55 am** 4:55 am
☽ □ ♇ **1:54 pm** 10:54 am
☽ □ ♄ **8:09 pm** 5:09 pm
☽ ☌ ♂ 9:45 pm

6 SUNDAY
☽ ☌ ♂ **12:45 am**
☽ □ ♀ **4:52 am** 1:52 am
☽ ⚻ ☿ **6:46 am** 3:46 am
☽ ☌ ♅ 11:00 pm

7 MONDAY
☽ ☌ ♅ **2:00 am**
☽ △ ☉ **12:09 pm** 9:09 am
☽ △ ♃ **4:08 pm** 1:08 pm
☽ ✶ ♆ **8:35 pm** 5:35 pm
☽ △ ♇ 11:39 pm

8 TUESDAY
☽ △ ♇ **2:39 am**
☽ △ ♄ **8:47 am** 5:47 am
☽ ⚺ ♂ **1:42 pm** 10:42 am
☽ ✶ ♀ **11:41 pm** 8:41 pm

9 WEDNESDAY
☽ △ ☿ **4:38 am** 1:38 am
☉ △ ♃ **12:04 pm** 9:04 am
☽ ⚺ ♅ **2:17 pm** 11:17 am

10 THURSDAY
☽ ⚻ ♃ **4:02 am** 1:02 am
☽ □ ☉ **5:26 am** 2:26 am
☽ □ ♆ **8:16 am** 5:16 am
☽ ⚻ ♇ **2:11 pm** 11:11 am
☽ ⚻ ♄ **7:57 pm** 4:57 pm
☽ ✶ ♂ 9:48 pm

11 FRIDAY
☽ ✶ ♂ **12:48 am**
☽ ⚺ ♀ **3:51 pm** 12:51 pm
☉ ☍ ♆ **4:26 pm** 1:26 pm
☽ □ ☿ **10:49 pm** 7:49 pm
☽ ✶ ♅ **11:57 pm** 8:57 pm

12 SATURDAY
☿ ⚻ ♅ **8:35 am** 5:35 am
☽ ☍ ♃ **12:54 pm** 9:54 am
☽ △ ♆ **4:45 pm** 1:45 pm
☽ ✶ ☉ **6:44 pm** 3:44 pm
☽ ☍ ♇ **10:19 pm** 7:19 pm

13 SUNDAY
☽ ☍ ♄ **3:37 am** 12:37 am
☽ □ ♂ **8:05 am** 5:05 am
☽ ☌ ♀ 11:53 pm

14 MONDAY
☽ ☌ ♀ **2:53 am**
☽ □ ♅ **5:33 am** 2:33 am
☽ ✶ ☿ **10:53 am** 7:53 am
☽ ⚻ ♃ **5:38 pm** 2:38 pm
☉ △ ♇ **7:09 pm** 4:09 pm
☽ ⚻ ♆ **9:05 pm** 6:05 pm
☽ ⚻ ♇ 11:18 pm
☽ ⚺ ☉ 11:50 pm

15 TUESDAY
☽ ⚻ ♇ **2:18 am**
☽ ⚺ ☉ **2:50 am**
☽ ⚻ ♄ **7:10 am** 4:10 am
☽ △ ♂ **11:09 am** 8:09 am
♀ □ ♅ **11:29 am** 8:29 am

16 WEDNESDAY
☽ △ ♅ **7:24 am** 4:24 am
☽ ⚺ ♀ **9:04 am** 6:04 am
☽ ⚺ ☿ **5:43 pm** 2:43 pm
☽ △ ♃ **6:54 pm** 3:54 pm
☽ ☍ ♆ **10:03 pm** 7:03 pm

17 THURSDAY
☽ △ ♇ **3:06 am** 12:06 am
☿ □ ♃ **6:34 am** 3:34 am
☽ ☌ ☉ **7:00 am** 4:00 am
☽ △ ♄ **7:42 am** 4:42 am
☽ ⚻ ♂ **11:17 am** 8:17 am
☉ △ ♄ **5:36 pm** 2:36 pm

18 FRIDAY
☽ ⚻ ♅ **7:09 am** 4:09 am
☽ ✶ ♀ **12:41 pm** 9:41 am
☿ ⚻ ♆ **4:05 pm** 1:05 pm
☽ □ ♃ **6:36 pm** 3:36 pm
☽ ⚻ ♆ **9:35 pm** 6:35 pm
☽ ☌ ☿ **10:08 pm** 7:08 pm
☽ □ ♇ 11:39 pm

19 SATURDAY
☽ □ ♇ **2:39 am**
☽ □ ♄ **7:14 am** 4:14 am
☽ ⚺ ☉ **9:53 am** 6:53 am
☽ ☍ ♂ **10:29 am** 7:29 am
☉ ⚻ ♂ **5:55 pm** 2:55 pm

20 SUNDAY
☽ ☍ ♅ **6:56 am** 3:56 am
☽ □ ♀ **4:42 pm** 1:42 pm
☽ ✶ ♃ **6:51 pm** 3:51 pm
☽ △ ♆ **9:47 pm** 6:47 pm
☿ □ ♇ 10:21 pm

21 MONDAY
☿ □ ♇ **1:21 am**
☽ ✶ ♇ **3:07 am** 12:07 am
☽ ⚺ ☿ **3:17 am** 12:17 am
☽ ✶ ♄ **7:50 am** 4:50 am
☽ ⚻ ♂ **10:45 am** 7:45 am
☽ ✶ ☉ **2:13 pm** 11:13 am
♀ ⚻ ♃ **9:12 pm** 6:12 pm

22 TUESDAY
☽ ⚻ ♅ **8:38 am** 5:38 am
☽ ⚺ ♃ **9:27 pm** 6:27 pm
☽ △ ♀ **11:34 pm** 8:34 pm
☽ □ ♆ 9:20 pm

23 WEDNESDAY
☽ □ ♆ **12:20 am**
☽ ⚺ ♇ **6:04 am** 3:04 am
☿ □ ♄ **6:38 am** 3:38 am
♀ ⚻ ♆ **8:45 am** 5:45 am
☽ ⚺ ♄ **11:04 am** 8:04 am
☽ ✶ ☿ **11:31 am** 8:31 am
☽ △ ♂ **1:31 pm** 10:31 am
☽ □ ☉ **9:55 pm** 6:55 pm

24 THURSDAY
☿ ☍ ♂ **6:53 am** 3:53 am
☽ △ ♅ **1:20 pm** 10:20 am

25 FRIDAY
☽ ☌ ♃ **3:11 am** 12:11 am
☽ ✶ ♆ **6:00 am** 3:00 am
☽ ⚻ ♀ **10:29 am** 7:29 am
☽ ☌ ♇ **12:09 pm** 9:09 am
☽ ☌ ♄ **5:26 pm** 2:26 pm
☽ □ ♂ **7:12 pm** 4:12 pm
☽ □ ☿ **11:36 pm** 8:36 pm

26 SATURDAY
♀ ⚻ ♇ **5:22 am** 2:22 am
☽ △ ☉ **9:30 am** 6:30 am
☽ □ ♅ **9:01 pm** 6:01 pm

27 SUNDAY
☽ ⚺ ♃ **11:51 am** 8:51 am
☽ ⚺ ♆ **2:29 pm** 11:29 am
☽ ⚺ ♇ **9:00 pm** 6:00 pm
☽ ☍ ♀ 10:04 pm
☽ ⚺ ♄ 11:30 pm

28 MONDAY
☽ ☍ ♀ **1:04 am**
☽ ⚺ ♄ **2:30 am**
☽ ✶ ♂ **3:18 am** 12:18 am
☽ △ ☿ **2:44 pm** 11:44 am
♀ ⚻ ♄ **4:23 pm** 1:23 pm
♀ △ ♂ **9:01 pm** 6:01 pm
☽ ⚻ ☉ 9:14 pm

29 TUESDAY
☽ ⚻ ☉ **12:14 am**
☽ ✶ ♅ **6:58 am** 3:58 am
♂ □ ♄ **5:50 pm** 2:50 pm
☽ ✶ ♃ **10:40 pm** 7:40 pm
☽ ☌ ♆ 10:00 pm

30 WEDNESDAY
☽ ☌ ♆ **1:00 am**
☽ ✶ ♇ **7:50 am** 4:50 am
☽ ⚺ ♂ **1:04 pm** 10:04 am
☽ ✶ ♄ **1:30 pm** 10:30 am
☽ ⚻ ♀ **6:17 pm** 3:17 pm

Eastern time in bold type
Pacific time in medium type

SEPTEMBER 2020

DATE	SID.TIME	SUN	MOON	NODE	MERCURY	VENUS	MARS	JUPITER	SATURN	URANUS	NEPTUNE	PLUTO	CERES	PALLAS	JUNO	VESTA	CHIRON
1 T	22 42 28	9♍01 16	25♒02	26♊26℞	21♍59	24♋18	27♈34	17♑38℞	25♑58℞	10♉35℞	19♓51℞	22♑45℞	4♓52℞	12♑17℞	23♎55	8♌54	8♈23℞
2 W	22 46 24	9 59 19	7♓27	26 14	23 41	25 22	27 41	17 36	25 56	10 34	19 49	22 44	4 39	12 15	24 13	9 20	8 21
3 Th	22 50 21	10 57 23	19 43	26 01	25 22	26 26	27 48	17 34	25 53	10 33	19 47	22 43	4 26	12 14	24 31	9 46	8 19
4 F	22 54 17	11 55 29	1♈50	25 48	27 01	27 30	27 53	17 32	25 51	10 32	19 46	22 42	4 13	12 13	24 49	10 12	8 16
5 Sa	22 58 14	12 53 37	13 49	25 36	28 40	28 35	27 58	17 31	25 49	10 31	19 44	22 41	4 00	12 13	25 08	10 37	8 14
6 Su	23 2 10	13 51 47	25 42	25 26	0♎17	29 40	28 02	17 29	25 46	10 30	19 42	22 41	3 47	12 12D	25 26	11 03	8 12
7 M	23 6 7	14 49 58	7♉32	25 18	1 53	0♌45	28 05	17 28	25 44	10 29	19 41	22 40	3 34	12 13	25 45	11 29	8 09
8 T	23 10 4	15 48 12	19 22	25 13	3 28	1 51	28 07	17 27	25 42	10 28	19 39	22 39	3 21	12 13	26 03	11 54	8 07
9 W	23 14 0	16 46 28	1♊16	25 10	5 02	2 56	28 08℞	17 26	25 40	10 27	19 37	22 38	3 09	12 14	26 22	12 20	8 04
10 Th	23 17 57	17 44 45	13 20	25 10	6 34	4 02	28 09	17 25	25 38	10 26	19 36	22 38	2 57	12 15	26 41	12 45	8 02
11 F	23 21 53	18 43 05	25 38	25 10	8 06	5 08	28 08	17 25	25 36	10 25	19 34	22 37	2 44	12 17	26 59	13 11	7 59
12 Sa	23 25 50	19 41 27	8♋16	25 09	9 36	6 15	28 07	17 24	25 35	10 23	19 33	22 36	2 32	12 19	27 18	13 36	7 57
13 Su	23 29 46	20 39 51	21 19	25 07	11 05	7 21	28 04	17 24D	25 33	10 22	19 31	22 36	2 21	12 21	27 37	14 02	7 54
14 M	23 33 43	21 38 18	4♌49	25 03	12 33	8 28	28 01	17 24	25 32	10 21	19 29	22 35	2 09	12 24	27 56	14 27	7 52
15 T	23 37 39	22 36 46	18 49	24 56	14 00	9 35	27 57	17 25	25 30	10 19	19 28	22 35	1 58	12 27	28 15	14 53	7 49
16 W	23 41 36	23 35 16	3♍17	24 47	15 25	10 42	27 52	17 25	25 29	10 18	19 26	22 34	1 47	12 30	28 34	15 18	7 47
17 Th	23 45 33	24 33 48	18 07	24 36	16 49	11 50	27 46	17 26	25 28	10 16	19 24	22 34	1 36	12 34	28 53	15 43	7 44
18 F	23 49 29	25 32 22	3♎12	24 25	18 13	12 57	27 40	17 27	25 26	10 15	19 23	22 33	1 25	12 37	29 12	16 08	7 41
19 Sa	23 53 26	26 30 58	18 21	24 14	19 34	14 05	27 32	17 28	25 25	10 13	19 21	22 33	1 15	12 42	29 32	16 34	7 39
20 Su	23 57 22	27 29 36	3♏24	24 06	20 55	15 13	27 24	17 29	25 24	10 12	19 19	22 32	1 05	12 46	29 51	16 59	7 36
21 M	0 1 19	28 28 16	18 12	24 00	22 14	16 21	27 15	17 31	25 24	10 10	19 18	22 32	0 55	12 51	0♏10	17 24	7 33
22 T	0 5 15	29 26 57	2♐40	23 57	23 32	17 29	27 05	17 32	25 23	10 08	19 16	22 31	0 45	12 56	0 30	17 49	7 31
23 W	0 9 12	0♎25 40	16 44	23 56D	24 49	18 37	26 54	17 34	25 22	10 07	19 14	22 31	0 36	13 02	0 49	18 14	7 28
24 Th	0 13 8	1 24 25	0♑25	23 55℞	26 03	19 46	26 42	17 36	25 22	10 05	19 13	22 31	0 27	13 08	1 09	18 39	7 25
25 F	0 17 5	2 23 11	13 43	23 55	27 17	20 54	26 30	17 38	25 21	10 03	19 11	22 31	0 19	13 14	1 28	19 04	7 23
26 Sa	0 21 1	3 21 59	26 43	23 53	28 28	22 03	26 17	17 41	25 21	10 01	19 10	22 30	0 10	13 20	1 48	19 29	7 20
27 Su	0 24 58	4 20 49	9♒27	23 49	29 38	23 12	26 03	17 43	25 20	10 00	19 08	22 30	0 02	13 27	2 07	19 54	7 17
28 M	0 28 55	5 19 41	21 59	23 42	0♏46	24 21	25 49	17 46	25 20	9 58	19 06	22 30	29♒55	13 34	2 27	20 18	7 15
29 T	0 32 51	6 18 34	4♓19	23 32	1 52	25 31	25 34	17 49	25 20D	9 56	19 05	22 30	29 47	13 41	2 47	20 43	7 12
30 W	0 36 48	7 17 29	16 31	23 20	2 56	26 40	25 19	17 52	25 20	9 54	19 03	22 30	29 40	13 49	3 06	21 08	7 09

EPHEMERIS CALCULATED FOR 12 MIDNIGHT GREENWICH MEAN TIME. ALL OTHER DATA AND FACING ASPECTARIAN PAGE IN **EASTERN TIME (BOLD)** AND PACIFIC TIME (REGULAR).

OCTOBER 2020

☽ Last Aspect day	ET / hr:mn / PT	asp	☽ Ingress sign day	ET / hr:mn / PT
2	10:47 pm	□♄	♉ 3	**11:12 am** 8:12 am
3	**1:47 am**	□♄	♉ 3	**11:12 am** 8:12 am
5	**2:41 pm** 11:41 am	△♄	♊ 5	9:03 pm
5	**2:41 pm** 11:41 am	△♄	♊ 6	**12:03 am**
7	**9:57 pm** 6:57 pm	✶♂	♋ 8	**11:45 am** 8:45 am
10	**12:04 pm** 9:04 am	☍♄	♌ 10	**8:24 pm** 5:24 pm
12	**10:29 am** 7:29 am	△♂	♍ 12	9:56 pm
12	**10:29 am** 7:29 am	△♂	♍ 13	**12:56 am**
14	**6:47 pm** 3:47 pm	△♄	♎ 14	10:54 pm
14	**6:47 pm** 3:47 pm	△♄	♎ 15	**1:54 am**
16	**6:11 pm** 3:11 pm	□♄	♏ 16	10:05 pm

☽ Last Aspect day	ET / hr:mn / PT	asp	☽ Ingress sign day	ET / hr:mn / PT
16	**6:11 pm** 3:11 pm	□♄	♏ 17	**1:05 am**
18	**5:43 pm** 2:43 pm	✶♄	♐ 18	9:43 pm
18	**5:43 pm** 2:43 pm	✶♄	♐ 19	**12:43 am**
20	**11:38 pm** 8:38 pm	✶☉	♑ 20	11:44 pm
20	**11:38 pm** 8:38 pm	✶☉	♑ 21	**2:44 am**
22	9:35 pm	☌♄	♒ 23	**8:17 am** 5:17 am
23	**12:35 am**	☌♄	♒ 23	**8:17 am** 5:17 am
24	**5:54 pm** 2:54 pm	✶♂	♓ 25	**5:18 pm** 2:18 pm
27	**8:46 pm** 5:46 pm	✶♄	♈ 28	**4:45 am** 1:45 am
30	**12:12 pm** 9:12 am	☍☿	♉ 30	**5:19 pm** 2:19 pm

☽ Phases & Eclipses phase	day	ET / hr:mn / PT
Full Moon	1	**5:05 pm** 2:05 pm
4th Quarter	9	**8:40 pm** 5:40 pm
New Moon	16	**3:31 pm** 12:31 pm
2nd Quarter	23	**9:23 am** 6:23 am
Full Moon	31	**10:49 am** 7:49 am

Planet Ingress	day	ET / hr:mn / PT
♀ ♍	2	**4:48 pm** 1:48 pm
⚳ ♍	22	**3:38 am** 12:38 am
☉ ♏	22	**7:00 pm** 4:00 pm
☿ ♎	27	**9:33 pm** 6:33 pm
♀ ♎	27	**9:41 pm** 6:41 pm

Planetary Motion	day	ET / hr:mn / PT
♇ D	4	**9:32 am** 6:32 am
☿ ℞	13	**9:05 pm** 6:05 pm
⚳ D	18	**12:59 pm** 9:59 pm

1 THURSDAY
☽ ⚻ ☿ **7:39 am** 4:39 am
☽ ☍ ☉ **5:05 pm** 2:05 pm
☽ ⚺ ♅ **6:29 pm** 3:29 pm

2 FRIDAY
☉ ⚻ ♅ **9:31 am** 6:31 am
☽ □ ♃ **10:58 am** 7:58 am
☽ ⚺ ♆ **12:55 pm** 9:55 am
☽ □ ♇ **8:00 pm** 5:00 pm
☽ ☌ ♂ **11:57 pm** 8:57 pm
☽ □ ♄ 10:47 pm

3 SATURDAY
☽ □ ♄ **1:47 am**
☽ △ ♀ **1:13 pm** 10:13 am
☽ ☍ ☿ 10:17 pm

4 SUNDAY
☽ ☍ ☿ **1:17 am**
☽ ☌ ♅ **6:59 am** 3:59 am
☽ ⚻ ☉ **11:15 am** 8:15 am
☽ △ ♃ 9:07 pm
☽ ✶ ♆ 10:37 pm

5 MONDAY
☽ △ ♃ **12:07 am**
☽ ✶ ♆ **1:37 am**
☽ △ ♇ **8:50 am** 5:50 am
☽ ⚺ ♂ **11:19 am** 8:19 am
☽ △ ♄ **2:41 pm** 11:41 am

6 TUESDAY
☽ □ ♀ **8:41 am** 5:41 am
☽ ⚻ ☿ **6:11 pm** 3:11 pm
☽ ⚺ ♅ **7:29 pm** 4:29 pm

7 WEDNESDAY
☽ △ ☉ **5:18 am** 2:18 am
☽ ⚻ ♃ **12:53 pm** 9:53 am
☽ □ ♆ **1:51 pm** 10:51 am
☿ ☍ ♅ **4:55 pm** 1:55 pm
☽ ⚻ ♇ **9:01 pm** 6:01 pm
☽ ✶ ♂ **9:57 pm** 6:57 pm
☽ ⚻ ♄ 11:46 pm

8 THURSDAY
☽ ⚻ ♄ **2:46 am**
☽ ✶ ♀ 11:16 pm

9 FRIDAY
☽ ✶ ♀ **2:16 am**
☽ ✶ ♅ **6:14 am** 3:14 am
☽ △ ☿ **8:03 am** 5:03 am
♂ □ ♇ **9:09 am** 6:09 am
☽ □ ☉ **8:40 pm** 5:40 pm
☽ ☍ ♃ **11:17 pm** 8:17 pm
☽ △ ♆ **11:44 pm** 8:44 pm

10 SATURDAY
☽ □ ♂ **6:05 am** 3:05 am
☽ ☍ ♇ **6:36 am** 3:36 am
☽ ☍ ♄ **12:04 pm** 9:04 am
♀ △ ♅ **7:08 pm** 4:08 pm

11 SUNDAY
☉ □ ♃ **9:34 am** 6:34 am
☉ ⚻ ♆ **11:31 am** 8:31 am
☽ □ ♅ **1:27 pm** 10:27 am
☽ ⚺ ♀ **3:16 pm** 12:16 pm
☽ □ ☿ **4:50 pm** 1:50 pm

12 MONDAY
♃ ✶ ♆ **3:06 am** 12:06 am
☽ ⚻ ♆ **5:43 am** 2:43 am
☽ ⚻ ♃ **5:44 am** 2:44 am
☽ ✶ ☉ **7:09 am** 4:09 am
☽ △ ♂ **10:29 am** 7:29 am
☽ ⚻ ♇ **12:11 pm** 9:11 am
☿ ✶ ♀ **12:39 pm** 9:39 am
☽ ⚻ ♄ **5:18 pm** 2:18 pm

13 TUESDAY
☽ △ ♅ **4:35 pm** 1:35 pm
☉ ☍ ♂ **7:26 pm** 4:26 pm
☽ ✶ ☿ **8:19 pm** 5:19 pm
☽ ☌ ♀ **10:55 pm** 7:55 pm

14 WEDNESDAY
☽ ☍ ♆ **7:47 am** 4:47 am
☽ △ ♃ **8:12 am** 5:12 am
☽ ⚻ ♂ **11:16 am** 8:16 am
☽ ⚺ ☉ **12:46 pm** 9:46 am
☽ △ ♇ **1:55 pm** 10:55 am
☽ △ ♄ **6:47 pm** 3:47 pm

15 THURSDAY
☉ □ ♇ **6:15 am** 3:15 am
☽ ⚻ ♅ **4:39 pm** 1:39 pm

☽ ⚺ ☿ **7:57 pm** 4:57 pm
☽ ⚺ ♀ 11:53 pm

16 FRIDAY
☽ ⚺ ♀ **2:53 am**
☽ ⚻ ♆ **7:20 am** 4:20 am
☽ □ ♃ **8:06 am** 5:06 am
☽ ☍ ♂ **9:49 am** 6:49 am
☽ □ ♇ **1:22 pm** 10:22 am
☽ ☌ ☉ **3:31 pm** 12:31 pm
☽ □ ♄ **6:11 pm** 3:11 pm

17 SATURDAY
☽ ☍ ♅ **3:37 pm** 12:37 pm
☽ ☌ ☿ **5:52 pm** 2:52 pm

18 SUNDAY
☽ ✶ ♀ **6:05 am** 3:05 am
☽ △ ♆ **6:28 am** 3:28 am
☽ ✶ ♃ **7:39 am** 4:39 am
☽ ⚻ ♂ **8:08 am** 5:08 am
☉ □ ♄ **9:58 am** 6:58 am
♀ ☍ ♆ **10:49 am** 7:49 am
☽ ✶ ♇ **12:43 pm** 9:43 am
☽ ✶ ♄ **5:43 pm** 2:43 pm
☽ ⚺ ☉ **6:15 pm** 3:15 pm
♂ □ ♃ 10:38 pm

19 MONDAY
♂ □ ♃ **1:38 am**
♀ ⚻ ♂ **3:03 am** 12:03 am
♀ △ ♃ **3:35 am** 12:35 am
☽ ⚻ ♅ **3:40 pm** 12:40 pm
☽ ⚺ ☿ **4:02 pm** 1:02 pm
☿ ☍ ♅ **10:53 pm** 7:53 pm

20 TUESDAY
☽ □ ♆ **7:19 am** 4:19 am
☽ △ ♂ **8:08 am** 5:08 am
☽ ⚺ ♃ **9:01 am** 6:01 am
☽ □ ♀ **11:28 am** 8:28 am
☽ ⚺ ♇ **2:00 pm** 11:00 am
☽ ⚺ ♄ **7:24 pm** 4:24 pm
☽ ✶ ☉ **11:38 pm** 8:38 pm

21 WEDNESDAY
☽ ✶ ☿ **3:49 pm** 12:49 pm
♀ △ ♇ **5:42 pm** 2:42 pm
☽ △ ♅ **6:33 pm** 3:33 pm

22 THURSDAY
♂ ⚺ ♆ **5:10 am** 2:10 am
☽ □ ♂ **11:16 am** 8:16 am
☽ ✶ ♆ **11:23 am** 8:23 am
☽ ☌ ♃ **1:44 pm** 10:44 am
☽ ☌ ♇ **6:40 pm** 3:40 pm
☽ △ ♀ **9:09 pm** 6:09 pm
☽ ☌ ♄ 9:35 pm

23 FRIDAY
☽ ☌ ♄ **12:35 am**
☽ □ ☉ **9:23 am** 6:23 am
☽ □ ☿ **5:49 pm** 2:49 pm
☽ □ ♅ 10:02 pm

24 SATURDAY
☽ □ ♅ **1:02 am**
♀ △ ♄ **11:41 am** 8:41 am
☽ ✶ ♂ **5:54 pm** 2:54 pm
☽ ⚺ ♆ **7:05 pm** 4:05 pm

☽ ⚺ ♃ **10:13 pm** 7:13 pm
☽ ⚺ ♇ 11:57 pm

25 SUNDAY
☽ ⚺ ♇ **2:57 am**
☽ ⚺ ♄ **9:21 am** 6:21 am
☽ ⚻ ♀ **11:37 am** 8:37 am
☉ ☌ ☿ **2:23 pm** 11:23 am
☽ △ ☿ **9:59 pm** 6:59 pm
☽ △ ☉ **11:31 pm** 8:31 pm

26 MONDAY
☽ ✶ ♅ **10:44 am** 7:44 am

27 TUESDAY
☽ ⚺ ♂ **3:23 am** 12:23 am
☽ ☌ ♆ **5:40 am** 2:40 am
☽ ✶ ♃ **9:38 am** 6:38 am
☽ ✶ ♇ **1:58 pm** 10:58 am
☽ ✶ ♄ **8:46 pm** 5:46 pm
☿ ⚺ ♀ **9:37 pm** 6:37 pm

28 WEDNESDAY
☽ ⚻ ☿ **4:08 am** 1:08 am
☽ ☍ ♀ **5:32 am** 2:32 am
☽ ⚻ ☉ **4:34 pm** 1:34 pm
☽ ⚺ ♅ **10:25 pm** 7:25 pm

29 THURSDAY
☽ ☌ ♂ **2:33 pm** 11:33 am
☽ ⚺ ♆ **5:51 pm** 2:51 pm
☽ □ ♃ **10:39 pm** 7:39 pm
☽ □ ♇ 11:26 pm

30 FRIDAY
☽ □ ♇ **2:26 am**
☽ □ ♄ **9:30 am** 6:30 am
☽ ☍ ☿ **12:12 pm** 9:12 am
☽ ⚻ ♀ 10:02 pm

31 SATURDAY
☽ ⚻ ♀ **1:02 am**
☽ ☍ ☉ **10:49 am** 7:49 am
☽ ☌ ♅ **10:55 am** 7:55 am
☉ ☍ ♅ **11:53 am** 8:53 am
☽ ⚺ ♂ 11:22 pm

Eastern time in bold type
Pacific time in medium type

OCTOBER 2020

DATE	SID.TIME	SUN	MOON	NODE	MERCURY	VENUS	MARS	JUPITER	SATURN	URANUS	NEPTUNE	PLUTO	CERES	PALLAS	JUNO	VESTA	CHIRON
1 Th	0 40 44	8♎16 26	28♓36	23♊07℞	3♏57	27♌50	25♈03℞	17♑55	25♑20	9♉52℞	19♓02℞	22♑29℞	29♒34℞	13♑57	3♏26	21♌32	7♈06℞
2 F	0 44 41	9 15 25	10♈35	22 53	4 56	28 59	24 46	17 59	25 21	9 50	19 00	22 29	29 27	14 05	3 46	21 57	7 04
3 Sa	0 48 37	10 14 26	22 29	22 41	5 52	0♍09	24 29	18 03	25 21	9 48	18 59	22 29	29 22	14 13	4 06	22 21	7 01
4 Su	0 52 34	11 13 29	4♉20	22 30	6 45	1 19	24 12	18 06	25 21	9 46	18 57	22 29D	29 16	14 21	4 26	22 46	6 58
5 M	0 56 30	12 12 34	16 09	22 22	7 35	2 29	23 54	18 11	25 22	9 44	18 56	22 29	29 11	14 30	4 46	23 10	6 56
6 T	1 0 27	13 11 42	28 00	22 17	8 21	3 40	23 36	18 15	25 23	9 41	18 54	22 29	29 06	14 39	5 06	23 34	6 53
7 W	1 4 24	14 10 52	9♊55	22 14	9 04	4 50	23 18	18 19	25 23	9 39	18 53	22 29	29 01	14 49	5 26	23 58	6 50
8 Th	1 8 20	15 10 04	21 58	22 13D	9 42	6 01	22 59	18 24	25 24	9 37	18 51	22 29	28 57	14 58	5 46	24 23	6 48
9 F	1 12 17	16 09 18	4♋15	22 13	10 16	7 11	22 40	18 28	25 25	9 35	18 50	22 29	28 54	15 08	6 06	24 47	6 45
10 Sa	1 16 13	17 08 35	16 49	22 14℞	10 45	8 22	22 21	18 33	25 26	9 33	18 49	22 30	28 50	15 18	6 26	25 11	6 42
11 Su	1 20 10	18 07 54	29 47	22 13	11 08	9 33	22 02	18 39	25 27	9 31	18 47	22 30	28 47	15 28	6 46	25 35	6 40
12 M	1 24 6	19 07 16	13♌11	22 11	11 25	10 44	21 43	18 44	25 28	9 28	18 46	22 30	28 44	15 39	7 06	25 59	6 37
13 T	1 28 3	20 06 39	27 05	22 06	11 36	11 55	21 23	18 49	25 30	9 26	18 44	22 30	28 42	15 50	7 26	26 22	6 34
14 W	1 31 59	21 06 05	11♍28	21 59	11 40℞	13 07	21 04	18 55	25 31	9 24	18 43	22 31	28 40	16 00	7 46	26 46	6 32
15 Th	1 35 56	22 05 33	26 18	21 50	11 37	14 18	20 45	19 01	25 33	9 21	18 42	22 31	28 39	16 12	8 07	27 10	6 29
16 F	1 39 53	23 05 03	11♎27	21 41	11 25	15 30	20 26	19 07	25 34	9 19	18 40	22 31	28 37	16 23	8 27	27 33	6 27
17 Sa	1 43 49	24 04 36	26 45	21 32	11 06	16 41	20 08	19 13	25 36	9 17	18 39	22 31	28 37	16 35	8 47	27 57	6 24
18 Su	1 47 46	25 04 10	12♏01	21 25	10 38	17 53	19 49	19 19	25 38	9 14	18 38	22 32	28 36D	16 46	9 07	28 20	6 21
19 M	1 51 42	26 03 47	27 05	21 20	10 01	19 05	19 31	19 25	25 40	9 12	18 37	22 32	28 36	16 58	9 28	28 43	6 19
20 T	1 55 39	27 03 25	11♐48	21 18D	9 15	20 17	19 13	19 32	25 42	9 10	18 35	22 33	28 36	17 10	9 48	29 07	6 16
21 W	1 59 35	28 03 05	26 05	21 18	8 22	21 29	18 56	19 39	25 44	9 07	18 34	22 33	28 37	17 23	10 08	29 30	6 14
22 Th	2 3 32	29 02 47	9♑55	21 19	7 21	22 41	18 39	19 45	25 46	9 05	18 33	22 34	28 38	17 35	10 29	29 53	6 11
23 F	2 7 28	0♏02 31	23 18	21 20℞	6 13	23 53	18 23	19 53	25 48	9 02	18 32	22 34	28 39	17 48	10 49	0♍16	6 09
24 Sa	2 11 25	1 02 16	6♒18	21 20	5 01	25 05	18 07	20 00	25 51	9 00	18 31	22 35	28 41	18 01	11 10	0 38	6 07
25 Su	2 15 22	2 02 03	18 59	21 18	3 46	26 17	17 51	20 07	25 53	8 57	18 30	22 35	28 43	18 14	11 30	1 01	6 04
26 M	2 19 18	3 01 51	1♓23	21 14	2 30	27 30	17 37	20 15	25 56	8 55	18 29	22 36	28 46	18 28	11 50	1 24	6 02
27 T	2 23 15	4 01 41	13 35	21 09	1 15	28 42	17 22	20 22	25 58	8 53	18 28	22 37	28 49	18 41	12 11	1 46	6 00
28 W	2 27 11	5 01 33	25 38	21 01	0 04	29 55	17 09	20 30	26 01	8 50	18 27	22 37	28 52	18 55	12 31	2 09	5 57
29 Th	2 31 8	6 01 27	7♈35	20 52	28♎59	1♎08	16 56	20 38	26 04	8 48	18 26	22 38	28 55	19 09	12 52	2 31	5 55
30 F	2 35 4	7 01 22	19 28	20 44	28 02	2 20	16 44	20 46	26 07	8 45	18 25	22 39	28 59	19 23	13 12	2 53	5 53
31 Sa	2 39 1	8 01 20	1♉20	20 35	27 14	3 33	16 33	20 54	26 10	8 43	18 24	22 40	29 03	19 37	13 33	3 15	5 51

EPHEMERIS CALCULATED FOR 12 MIDNIGHT GREENWICH MEAN TIME. ALL OTHER DATA AND FACING ASPECTARIAN PAGE IN **EASTERN TIME (BOLD)** AND PACIFIC TIME (REGULAR).

NOVEMBER 2020

☽ Last Aspect				☽ Ingress			
day	ET / hr:mn / PT		asp	sign	day	ET / hr:mn / PT	
1	**9:29 pm**	6:29 pm	△♄	♊	2	**5:00 am**	2:00 am
4	**8:49 am**	5:49 am	△☿	♋	4	**4:45 pm**	1:45 pm
6	**8:27 pm**	5:27 pm	□☿	♌	6		11:18 pm
6	**8:27 pm**	5:27 pm	□☿	♌	7	**2:18 am**	
9	**6:05 am**	3:05 am	⚹☿	♍	9	**8:30 am**	5:30 am
11	**5:58 am**	2:58 am	△♄	♎	11	**11:09 am**	8:09 am
13	**6:32 am**	3:32 am	□♄	♏	13	**11:19 am**	8:19 am
15	**6:13 am**	3:13 am	⚹♄	♐	15	**10:47 am**	7:47 am
16		11:55 pm	⚹♀	♑	17	**11:35 am**	8:35 am
17	**2:55 am**		⚹♀	♑	17	**11:35 am**	8:35 am
19	**11:30 am**	8:30 am	⚹☉	♒	19	**3:25 pm**	12:25 pm
20	**7:49 pm**	4:49 pm	⚹♂	♓	21	**11:06 pm**	8:06 pm
24	**5:44 am**	2:44 am	⚹♄	♈	24	**10:05 am**	7:05 am
26	**6:46 pm**	3:46 pm	□♄	♉	26	**10:43 pm**	7:43 pm
29	**7:48 am**	4:48 am	△♄	♊	29	**11:16 am**	8:16 am
30	**11:22 pm**	8:22 pm	□♆	♋	12/1	**10:33 pm**	7:33 pm

☽ Phases & Eclipses			
phase	day	ET / hr:mn / PT	
4th Quarter	8	**8:46 am**	5:46 am
New Moon	14		9:07 pm
New Moon	15	**12:07 am**	
2nd Quarter	21	**11:45 pm**	8:45 pm
Full Moon	30	**4:30 am**	1:30 am
●	30	8 ° ♊ 38	

Planet Ingress			
	day	ET / hr:mn / PT	
⚳ ♓	9	**9:48 am**	6:48 am
☿ ♏	10	**4:55 pm**	1:55 pm
♀ ♏	21	**8:22 am**	5:22 am
☉ ♐	21	**3:40 pm**	12:40 pm

Planetary Motion				
		day	ET / hr:mn / PT	
☿	D	3	**12:50 pm**	9:50 am
♂	D	13	**7:36 pm**	4:36 pm
♆	D	28	**7:36 pm**	4:36 pm

1 SUNDAY
- ☽⚺♂ **1:22 am**
- ☽⚹♆ **5:31 am** 2:31 am
- ☽△♃ **11:07 am** 8:07 am
- ☿□♄ **2:06 pm** 11:06 am
- ☽△♇ **2:14 pm** 11:14 am
- ☽⚻☿ **9:15 pm** 6:15 pm
- ☽△♄ **9:29 pm** 6:29 pm

2 MONDAY
- ☽△♀ **7:31 pm** 4:31 pm
- ☽⚺♅ **10:14 pm** 7:14 pm

3 TUESDAY
- ☽⚻☉ **3:52 am** 12:52 am
- ☽⚹♂ **12:57 pm** 9:57 am
- ☽□♆ **5:43 pm** 2:43 pm
- ♀⚻♅ **9:22 pm** 6:22 pm
- ☽⚻♃ 9:00 pm
- ☽⚻♇ 11:24 pm

4 WEDNESDAY
- ☽⚻♃ **12:00 am**
- ☽⚻♇ **2:24 am**
- ☽△☿ **8:49 am** 5:49 am
- ☽⚻♄ **9:43 am** 6:43 am

5 THURSDAY
- ☽⚹♅ **9:19 am** 6:19 am
- ☽□♀ **1:22 pm** 10:22 am
- ☽△☉ **8:07 pm** 5:07 pm
- ☽□♂ **11:08 pm** 8:08 pm

6 FRIDAY
- ☿□♄ **4:12 am** 1:12 am
- ☽△♆ **4:13 am** 1:13 am
- ☽☍♃ **11:01 am** 8:01 am
- ☽☍♇ **12:41 pm** 9:41 am
- ☽☍♄ **7:52 pm** 4:52 pm
- ☽□☿ **8:27 pm** 5:27 pm

7 SATURDAY
- ☉⚻♂ **6:41 am** 3:41 am
- ☽□♅ **5:49 pm** 2:49 pm

8 SUNDAY
- ☽⚹♀ **3:36 am** 12:36 am
- ☽△♂ **6:39 am** 3:39 am
- ☽□☉ **8:46 am** 5:46 am
- ☽⚻♆ **11:46 am** 8:46 am
- ☽⚻♃ **6:49 pm** 3:49 pm
- ☽⚻♇ **7:49 pm** 4:49 pm
- ☽⚻♄ 11:44 pm

9 MONDAY
- ☽⚻♄ **2:44 am**
- ☽⚹☿ **6:05 am** 3:05 am
- ♀☍♂ **11:08 am** 8:08 am
- ☽△♅ **10:50 pm** 7:50 pm
- ☉△♆ 9:11 pm

10 TUESDAY
- ☉△♆ **12:11 am**
- ☽⚻♂ **10:45 am** 7:45 am
- ☽⚺♀ **1:04 pm** 10:04 am
- ☽☍♆ **3:42 pm** 12:42 pm
- ☽⚹☉ **4:53 pm** 1:53 pm
- ☽△♃ **10:55 pm** 7:55 pm
- ☽△♇ **11:20 pm** 8:20 pm

11 WEDNESDAY
- ☽△♄ **5:58 am** 2:58 am
- ☽⚺☿ **12:35 pm** 9:35 am
- ♀⚻♆ **7:31 pm** 4:31 pm
- ☽⚻♅ 9:31 pm

12 THURSDAY
- ☽⚻♅ **12:31 am**
- ☽☍♂ **11:50 am** 8:50 am
- ☽⚻♆ **4:37 pm** 1:37 pm
- ♃☌♇ **4:39 pm** 1:39 pm
- ☽☌♀ **6:31 pm** 3:31 pm
- ☽⚺☉ **9:17 pm** 6:17 pm
- ☽□♇ 9:00 pm
- ☽□♃ 9:05 pm

13 FRIDAY
- ☽□♇ **12:00 am**
- ☽□♃ **12:05 am**
- ☽□♄ **6:32 am** 3:32 am
- ☽☌☿ **4:44 pm** 1:44 pm
- ☽☍♅ 9:10 pm

14 SATURDAY
- ☽☍♅ **12:10 am**
- ☽⚻♂ **11:23 am** 8:23 am
- ☉⚹♇ **2:48 pm** 11:48 am
- ☽△♆ **4:05 pm** 1:05 pm
- ☽⚺♀ **10:11 pm** 7:11 pm
- ☉⚹♃ **10:57 pm** 7:57 pm
- ☽⚹♇ **11:31 pm** 8:31 pm
- ☽⚹♃ 9:03 pm
- ☽☌☉ 9:07 pm

15 SUNDAY
- ☽⚹♃ **12:03 am**
- ☽☌☉ **12:07 am**
- ☽⚹♄ **6:13 am** 3:13 am
- ♀□♇ **2:43 pm** 11:43 am
- ☽⚺☿ **8:48 pm** 5:48 pm
- ☽⚻♅ **11:40 pm** 8:40 pm
- ♀□♃ 9:33 pm

16 MONDAY
- ♀□♃ **12:33 am**
- ☽△♂ **11:21 am** 8:21 am
- ☽□♆ **4:07 pm** 1:07 pm
- ☽⚺♇ **11:53 pm** 8:53 pm
- ☽⚺♃ 9:58 pm
- ☽⚹♀ 11:55 pm

17 TUESDAY
- ☽⚺♃ **12:58 am**
- ☽⚹♀ **2:55 am**
- ☿☍♅ **3:07 am** 12:07 am
- ☽⚺☉ **4:03 am** 1:03 am
- ☽⚺♄ **7:03 am** 4:03 am
- ☽△♅ 10:00 pm

18 WEDNESDAY
- ☽△♅ **1:00 am**
- ☽⚹☿ **3:32 am** 12:32 am
- ☽□♂ **1:42 pm** 10:42 am
- ☽⚹♆ **6:34 pm** 3:34 pm
- ☉⚹♄ 11:18 pm
- ☽☌♇ 11:58 pm

19 THURSDAY
- ☉⚹♄ **2:18 am**
- ☽☌♇ **2:58 am**
- ☽☌♃ **4:43 am** 1:43 am
- ♀□♇ **6:29 am** 3:29 am
- ☽☌♄ **10:51 am** 7:51 am
- ☽□♀ **11:16 am** 8:16 am
- ☽⚹☉ **11:30 am** 8:30 am
- ☉⚺♀ **11:45 pm** 8:45 pm

20 FRIDAY
- ☽□♅ **5:41 am** 2:41 am
- ☽□☿ **3:15 pm** 12:15 pm
- ☽⚹♂ **7:49 pm** 4:49 pm
- ☽⚺♆ 9:42 pm

21 SATURDAY
- ☽⚺♆ **12:42 am**
- ☽⚺♇ **9:51 am** 6:51 am
- ☽⚺♃ **12:25 pm** 9:25 am
- ☽⚺♄ **6:34 pm** 3:34 pm
- ☽□☉ **11:45 pm** 8:45 pm
- ☽△♀ 9:43 pm

22 SUNDAY
- ☽△♀ **12:43 am**
- ☿⚻♂ **9:00 am** 6:00 am
- ☽⚹♅ **2:11 pm** 11:11 am

23 MONDAY
- ☽⚺♂ **5:52 am** 2:52 am
- ☽△☿ **8:37 am** 5:37 am
- ☽☌♆ **10:31 am** 7:31 am
- ☽⚹♇ **8:18 pm** 5:18 pm
- ☿△♆ **11:40 pm** 8:40 pm
- ☽⚹♃ **11:47 pm** 8:47 pm

24 TUESDAY
- ☽⚹♄ **5:44 am** 2:44 am
- ☽△☉ **4:13 pm** 1:13 pm
- ☽⚻♀ **6:36 pm** 3:36 pm
- ☽⚺♅ 10:35 pm

25 WEDNESDAY
- ☽⚺♅ **1:35 am**
- ☽☌♂ **6:39 pm** 3:39 pm
- ☽⚺♆ **10:43 pm** 7:43 pm

26 THURSDAY
- ☽⚻☿ **5:46 am** 2:46 am
- ☽□♇ **8:50 am** 5:50 am
- ☽□♃ **1:15 pm** 10:15 am
- ☽□♄ **6:46 pm** 3:46 pm

27 FRIDAY
- ☿⚹♇ **5:38 am** 2:38 am
- ☽⚻☉ **10:35 am** 7:35 am
- ♀☍♅ **12:11 pm** 9:11 am
- ☽☌♅ **2:10 pm** 11:10 am
- ☽☍♀ **2:25 pm** 11:25 am

28 SATURDAY
- ☽⚺♂ **8:17 am** 5:17 am
- ☽⚹♆ **11:29 am** 8:29 am
- ☽△♇ **9:40 pm** 6:40 pm
- ☿⚹♃ **9:51 pm** 6:51 pm
- ☽△♃ 11:53 pm

29 SUNDAY
- ☽△♃ **2:53 am**
- ☉⚻♅ **3:20 am** 12:20 am
- ☽☍☿ **3:33 am** 12:33 am
- ☽△♄ **7:48 am** 4:48 am
- ☽⚺♅ 11:19 pm

30 MONDAY
- ☽⚺♅ **2:19 am**
- ☽☍☉ **4:30 am** 1:30 am
- ☽⚻♀ **9:38 am** 6:38 am
- ☿⚹♄ **2:01 pm** 11:01 am
- ☽⚹♂ **9:13 pm** 6:13 pm
- ☽□♆ **11:22 pm** 8:22 pm

Eastern time in bold type
Pacific time in medium type

NOVEMBER 2020

DATE	SID.TIME	SUN	MOON	NODE	MERCURY	VENUS	MARS	JUPITER	SATURN	URANUS	NEPTUNE	PLUTO	CERES	PALLAS	JUNO	VESTA	CHIRON
1 Su	2 42 57	9 ♏ 01 19	13 ♉ 10	20 ♊ 29℞	26 ♎ 37℞	4 ♎ 46	16 ♈ 22℞	21 ♑ 03	26 ♑ 13	8 ♉ 40℞	18 ♓ 23℞	22 ♑ 40	29 ♒ 08	19 ♑ 51	13 ♏ 53	3 ♍ 37	5 ♈ 48℞
2 M	2 46 54	10 01 20	25 03	20 23	26 11	5 59	16 12	21 11	26 16	8 38	18 22	22 41	29 13	20 05	14 14	3 59	5 46
3 T	2 50 50	11 01 23	6 ♊ 58	20 21	25 57 D	7 12	16 03	21 20	26 20	8 35	18 21	22 42	29 18	20 20	14 34	4 21	5 44
4 W	2 54 47	12 01 28	18 59	20 19 D	25 54	8 25	15 54	21 28	26 23	8 33	18 20	22 43	29 23	20 35	14 55	4 42	5 42
5 Th	2 58 44	13 01 35	1 ♋ 09	20 20	26 03	9 39	15 47	21 37	26 26	8 30	18 19	22 44	29 29	20 50	15 15	5 04	5 40
6 F	3 2 40	14 01 44	13 30	20 21	26 21	10 52	15 40	21 46	26 30	8 28	18 19	22 45	29 35	21 05	15 36	5 25	5 38
7 Sa	3 6 37	15 01 56	26 06	20 23	26 50	12 05	15 34	21 55	26 34	8 25	18 18	22 46	29 42	21 20	15 56	5 47	5 36
8 Su	3 10 33	16 02 09	9 ♌ 02	20 24℞	27 28	13 19	15 29	22 05	26 37	8 23	18 17	22 47	29 48	21 35	16 17	6 08	5 34
9 M	3 14 30	17 02 24	22 20	20 24	28 13	14 32	15 24	22 14	26 41	8 21	18 17	22 48	29 55	21 51	16 37	6 29	5 32
10 T	3 18 26	18 02 41	6 ♍ 04	20 23	29 06	15 46	15 21	22 24	26 45	8 18	18 16	22 49	0 ♓ 03	22 06	16 58	6 50	5 31
11 W	3 22 23	19 03 01	20 14	20 20	0 ♏ 05	16 59	15 18	22 33	26 49	8 16	18 15	22 50	0 11	22 22	17 18	7 10	5 29
12 Th	3 26 20	20 03 22	4 ♎ 48	20 17	1 10	18 13	15 16	22 43	26 53	8 13	18 15	22 51	0 19	22 38	17 39	7 31	5 27
13 F	3 30 16	21 03 45	19 44	20 12	2 19	19 27	15 14	22 53	26 57	8 11	18 14	22 52	0 27	22 54	17 59	7 51	5 25
14 Sa	3 34 13	22 04 10	4 ♏ 52	20 08	3 33	20 41	15 14 D	23 03	27 01	8 08	18 14	22 53	0 35	23 10	18 20	8 11	5 24
15 Su	3 38 9	23 04 37	20 04	20 05	4 50	21 55	15 14	23 13	27 06	8 06	18 13	22 54	0 44	23 26	18 40	8 32	5 22
16 M	3 42 6	24 05 05	5 ♐ 09	20 03	6 10	23 08	15 16	23 23	27 10	8 04	18 13	22 55	0 53	23 43	19 01	8 51	5 20
17 T	3 46 2	25 05 35	19 58	20 02 D	7 32	24 22	15 18	23 33	27 15	8 01	18 12	22 57	1 03	23 59	19 21	9 11	5 19
18 W	3 49 59	26 06 07	4 ♑ 26	20 03	8 57	25 36	15 20	23 44	27 19	7 59	18 12	22 58	1 13	24 16	19 42	9 31	5 17
19 Th	3 53 55	27 06 40	18 26	20 04	10 23	26 50	15 24	23 54	27 24	7 57	18 11	22 59	1 23	24 33	20 02	9 50	5 16
20 F	3 57 52	28 07 14	2 ♒ 00	20 05	11 51	28 05	15 28	24 05	27 28	7 55	18 11	23 00	1 33	24 49	20 23	10 10	5 15
21 Sa	4 1 49	29 07 49	15 07	20 07	13 20	29 19	15 33	24 16	27 33	7 52	18 11	23 02	1 43	25 06	20 43	10 29	5 13
22 Su	4 5 45	0 ♐ 08 26	27 52	20 07℞	14 50	0 ♏ 33	15 39	24 27	27 38	7 50	18 11	23 03	1 54	25 23	21 04	10 48	5 12
23 M	4 9 42	1 09 03	10 ♓ 17	20 07	16 21	1 47	15 46	24 38	27 43	7 48	18 10	23 04	2 05	25 41	21 24	11 06	5 11
24 T	4 13 38	2 09 42	22 27	20 06	17 52	3 01	15 53	24 49	27 48	7 46	18 10	23 06	2 16	25 58	21 45	11 25	5 10
25 W	4 17 35	3 10 22	4 ♈ 27	20 04	19 24	4 16	16 01	25 00	27 53	7 43	18 10	23 07	2 28	26 15	22 05	11 43	5 08
26 Th	4 21 31	4 11 03	16 20	20 02	20 57	5 30	16 10	25 11	27 58	7 41	18 10	23 09	2 40	26 33	22 25	12 01	5 07
27 F	4 25 28	5 11 45	28 10	19 59	22 30	6 44	16 19	25 23	28 03	7 39	18 10	23 10	2 52	26 50	22 46	12 19	5 06
28 Sa	4 29 24	6 12 28	10 ♉ 00	19 57	24 03	7 59	16 29	25 34	28 08	7 37	18 10	23 12	3 04	27 08	23 06	12 37	5 05
29 Su	4 33 21	7 13 13	21 54	19 55	25 36	9 13	16 40	25 45	28 14	7 35	18 10 D	23 13	3 16	27 26	23 26	12 55	5 04
30 M	4 37 18	8 13 59	3 ♊ 52	19 54	27 09	10 28	16 51	25 57	28 19	7 33	18 10	23 15	3 29	27 43	23 46	13 12	5 03

EPHEMERIS CALCULATED FOR 12 MIDNIGHT GREENWICH MEAN TIME. ALL OTHER DATA AND FACING ASPECTARIAN PAGE IN **EASTERN TIME (BOLD)** AND PACIFIC TIME (REGULAR).

DECEMBER 2020

☽ Last Aspect day	ET / hr:mn / PT	asp	☽ Ingress sign day	ET / hr:mn / PT
11/30	**11:22 pm** 8:22 pm	□♆	♋ 1	**10:33 pm** 7:33 pm
4	**5:29 am** 2:29 am	☍♄	♌ 4	**7:53 am** 4:53 am
5	**5:28 pm** 2:28 pm	△♂	♍ 6	**2:46 pm** 11:46 am
8	**5:35 pm** 2:35 pm	△♄	♎ 8	**7:01 pm** 4:01 pm
10	**7:56 pm** 4:56 pm	□♄	♏ 10	**8:59 pm** 5:59 pm
12	**8:58 pm** 5:58 pm	⚹♄	♐ 12	**9:39 pm** 6:39 pm
14	**11:17 am** 8:17 am	☌☉	♑ 14	**10:35 pm** 7:35 pm
16	9:34 pm	☌♃	♒ 16	10:27 pm
17	**12:34 am**	☌♃	♒ 17	**1:27 am**
19	3:45 am **12:45 am**	⚹☉	♓ 19	**7:39 am** 4:39 am
21	**5:25 am** 2:25 am	⚹♇	♈ 21	**5:32 pm** 2:32 pm
23	**5:51 pm** 2:51 pm	☌♂	♉ 24	**5:55 am** 2:55 am
26	**6:32 am** 3:32 am	△♇	♊ 26	**6:33 pm** 3:33 pm
28	**10:01 pm** 7:01 pm	⚹♂	♋ 29	**5:28 am** 2:28 am
31	**8:45 am** 5:45 am	□♂	♌ 31	**1:58 pm** 10:58 am

☽ Phases & Eclipses phase	day	ET / hr:mn / PT
4th Quarter	7	**7:37 pm** 4:37 pm
New Moon	14	**11:17 am** 8:17 am
●	14	23° ♐ 08′
2nd Quarter	21	**6:41 pm** 3:41 pm
Full Moon	29	**10:28 pm** 7:28 pm

Planet Ingress	day	ET / hr:mn / PT
☿ ♐	1	**2:51 pm** 11:51 am
♀ ♒	7	**7:14 am** 4:14 am
♀ ♐	15	**11:21 am** 8:21 am
♄ ♒	16	9:04 pm
♄ ♒	17	**12:04am**
⚳ ♐	18	**12:25 pm** 9:25 am
♃ ♒	19	**8:07 am** 5:07 am
☿ ♑	20	**6:07 pm** 3:07 pm
☉ ♑	21	**5:02 am** 2:02 am

Planetary Motion		day	ET / hr:mn / PT
⚷	D	15	**5:17 pm** 2:17 pm

1 TUESDAY
☽ ⚻ ♇ **9:26 am** 6:26 am
☽ ⚻ ♃ **3:22 pm** 12:22 pm
☽ ⚻ ♄ **7:38 pm** 4:38 pm
☽ ⚻ ☿ **11:40 pm** 8:40 pm

2 WEDNESDAY
☽ ⚹ ♅ **1:00 pm** 10:00 am
☽ ⚻ ☉ **8:28 pm** 5:28 pm
☽ △ ♀ 11:43 pm

3 THURSDAY
☽ △ ♀ **2:43 am**
☽ □ ♂ **8:28 am** 5:28 am
☽ △ ♆ **9:32 am** 6:32 am
☽ ☍ ♇ **7:22 pm** 4:22 pm
☽ ☍ ♃ 10:52 pm

4 FRIDAY
☽ ☍ ♃ **1:52 am**
☽ ☍ ♄ **5:29 am** 2:29 am
☽ △ ☿ **4:52 pm** 1:52 pm
☽ □ ♅ **9:38 pm** 6:38 pm

5 SATURDAY
☽ △ ☉ **9:41 am** 6:41 am
♂ ⚺ ♆ **4:44 pm** 1:44 pm
☽ □ ♀ **4:47 pm** 1:47 pm
☽ ⚻ ♆ **5:27 pm** 2:27 pm
☽ △ ♂ **5:28 pm** 2:28 pm
♀ △ ♆ **11:53 pm** 8:53 pm
♀ ⚻ ♂ 10:41 pm
☽ ⚻ ♇ 11:56 pm

Eastern time in bold type
Pacific time in medium type

6 SUNDAY
♀ ⚻ ♂ **1:41 am**
☽ ⚻ ♇ **2:56 am**
☿ ⚻ ♅ **7:43 am** 4:43 am
☽ ⚻ ♃ **9:53 am** 6:53 am
☽ ⚻ ♄ **12:53 pm** 9:53 am

7 MONDAY
☽ △ ♅ **3:45 am** 12:45 am
☽ □ ☿ **6:24 am** 3:24 am
☽ □ ☉ **7:37 pm** 4:37 pm
☽ ☍ ♆ **10:45 pm** 7:45 pm
☽ ⚻ ♂ **11:47 pm** 8:47 pm

8 TUESDAY
☽ ⚹ ♀ **3:21 am** 12:21 am
☽ △ ♇ **7:52 am** 4:52 am
☽ △ ♃ **3:09 pm** 12:09 pm
☽ △ ♄ **5:35 pm** 2:35 pm

9 WEDNESDAY
☽ ⚻ ♅ **7:17 am** 4:17 am
☉ □ ♆ **2:41 pm** 11:41 am
☽ ⚹ ☿ **4:13 pm** 1:13 pm
☽ ⚻ ♆ 10:33 pm
☽ ⚹ ☉ 11:22 pm

10 THURSDAY
☽ ⚻ ♆ **1:33 am**
☽ ⚹ ☉ **2:22 am**
☽ ☍ ♂ **3:31 am** 12:31 am
♀ ⚹ ♇ **6:52 am** 3:52 am
☽ □ ♇ **10:21 am** 7:21 am
☽ ⚺ ♀ **10:40 am** 7:40 am
☽ □ ♃ **5:58 pm** 2:58 pm
☽ □ ♄ **7:56 pm** 4:56 pm
☉ △ ♂ 10:01 pm

11 FRIDAY
☉ △ ♂ **1:01 am**
☽ ☍ ♅ **8:43 am** 5:43 am
☽ ⚺ ☿ **11:18 pm** 8:18 pm
☽ △ ♆ 11:35 pm

12 SATURDAY
☽ △ ♆ **2:35 am**
☽ ⚻ ♂ **5:30 am** 2:30 am
☽ ⚺ ☉ **6:58 am** 3:58 am
☽ ⚹ ♇ **11:17 am** 8:17 am
☽ ☌ ♀ **3:59 pm** 12:59 pm
☽ ⚹ ♃ **7:23 pm** 4:23 pm
☽ ⚹ ♄ **8:58 pm** 5:58 pm

13 SUNDAY
☿ □ ♆ **6:38 am** 3:38 am
☽ ⚻ ♅ **9:13 am** 6:13 am

14 MONDAY
☽ □ ♆ **3:15 am** 12:15 am
☽ ☌ ☿ **5:42 am** 2:42 am
☽ △ ♂ **7:14 am** 4:14 am
☽ ☌ ☉ **11:17 am** 8:17 am
☽ ⚺ ♇ **12:07 pm** 9:07 am
♀ ⚹ ♃ **3:58 pm** 12:58 pm
☽ ⚺ ♃ **8:59 pm** 5:59 pm
☽ ⚺ ♀ **9:23 pm** 6:23 pm
☽ ⚺ ♄ **10:13 pm** 7:13 pm
☿ △ ♂ **11:24 pm** 8:24 pm
☉ ⚺ ♇ **11:39 pm** 8:39 pm

15 TUESDAY
♀ ⚹ ♄ **8:00 am** 5:00 am
☽ △ ♅ **10:22 am** 7:22 am

16 WEDNESDAY
☽ ⚹ ♆ **5:12 am** 2:12 am
☽ □ ♂ **10:32 am** 7:32 am
☽ ⚺ ☿ **2:03 pm** 11:03 am
☽ ☌ ♇ **2:33 pm** 11:33 am
☽ ⚺ ☉ **5:32 pm** 2:32 pm
☿ ⚺ ♇ **6:35 pm** 3:35 pm
☽ ☌ ♃ 9:34 pm
☽ ☌ ♄ 10:28 pm

17 THURSDAY
☽ ☌ ♃ **12:34 am**
☽ ☌ ♄ **1:28 am**
☽ ⚹ ♀ **5:16 am** 2:16 am
☽ □ ♅ **1:50 pm** 10:50 am

18 FRIDAY
☽ ⚺ ♆ **10:01 am** 7:01 am
☽ ⚹ ♂ **5:08 pm** 2:08 pm
☽ ⚺ ♇ **8:06 pm** 5:06 pm
☽ ⚹ ☿ 11:49 pm

19 SATURDAY
☽ ⚹ ☿ **2:49 am**
☽ ⚹ ☉ **3:45 am** 12:45 am
☽ ⚺ ♃ **7:38 am** 4:38 am
☽ ⚺ ♄ **8:07 am** 5:07 am
☽ □ ♀ **5:40 pm** 2:40 pm
☽ ⚹ ♅ **8:50 pm** 5:50 pm
☉ ☌ ☿ **10:26 pm** 7:26 pm

20 SUNDAY
☽ ☌ ♆ **6:34 pm** 3:34 pm
☿ ⚺ ♃ **11:34 pm** 8:34 pm
☿ ⚺ ♄ 9:37 pm
♀ ⚻ ♅ 10:12 pm

21 MONDAY
☿ ⚺ ♄ **12:37 am**
♀ ⚻ ♅ **1:12 am**
☽ ⚺ ♂ **3:52 am** 12:52 am
☽ ⚹ ♇ **5:25 am** 2:25 am
♃ ☌ ♄ **1:21 pm** 10:21 am
☉ ⚺ ♄ **4:52 pm** 1:52 pm
☉ ⚺ ♃ **5:22 pm** 2:22 pm
☽ ⚹ ♄ **6:33 pm** 3:33 pm
☽ ⚹ ♃ **6:36 pm** 3:36 pm
☽ □ ☉ **6:41 pm** 3:41 pm
☽ □ ☿ **9:04 pm** 6:04 pm

22 TUESDAY
☽ ⚺ ♅ **7:22 am** 4:22 am
☽ △ ♀ **10:56 am** 7:56 am

23 WEDNESDAY
☽ ⚺ ♆ **6:17 am** 3:17 am
♂ □ ♇ **9:53 am** 6:53 am
☽ □ ♇ **5:37 pm** 2:37 pm
☽ ☌ ♂ **5:51 pm** 2:51 pm

24 THURSDAY
☽ □ ♄ **7:31 am** 4:31 am
☽ □ ♃ **8:10 am** 5:10 am
☽ △ ☉ **12:48 pm** 9:48 am
☽ △ ☿ **6:57 pm** 3:57 pm
☽ ☌ ♅ **7:56 pm** 4:56 pm
☿ △ ♅ 11:05 pm

25 FRIDAY
☿ △ ♅ **2:05 am**
☽ ⚻ ♀ **6:49 am** 3:49 am
☽ ⚹ ♆ **7:10 pm** 4:10 pm

26 SATURDAY
☽ △ ♇ **6:32 am** 3:32 am
☽ ⚺ ♂ **8:42 am** 5:42 am
☽ △ ♄ **8:41 pm** 5:41 pm
☽ △ ♃ **9:54 pm** 6:54 pm

27 SUNDAY
☽ ⚻ ☉ **6:53 am** 3:53 am
☽ ⚺ ♅ **8:13 am** 5:13 am
☽ ⚻ ☿ **4:33 pm** 1:33 pm
☉ △ ♅ **10:25 pm** 7:25 pm
☽ ☍ ♀ 10:47 pm

28 MONDAY
☽ ☍ ♀ **1:47 am**
☽ □ ♆ **6:59 am** 3:59 am
☽ ⚻ ♇ **6:03 pm** 3:03 pm
☽ ⚹ ♂ **10:01 pm** 7:01 pm

29 TUESDAY
☽ ⚻ ♄ **8:04 am** 5:04 am
☽ ⚻ ♃ **9:47 am** 6:47 am
☽ ⚹ ♅ **6:32 pm** 3:32 pm
☽ ☍ ☉ **10:28 pm** 7:28 pm

30 WEDNESDAY
♀ □ ♆ **5:19 am** 2:19 am
☽ ☍ ☿ **11:04 am** 8:04 am
☽ △ ♆ **4:31 pm** 1:31 pm
☽ ⚻ ♀ **5:42 pm** 2:42 pm

31 THURSDAY
☽ ☍ ♇ **3:10 am** 12:10 am
☽ □ ♂ **8:45 am** 5:45 am
☽ ☍ ♄ **4:56 pm** 1:56 pm
☽ ☍ ♃ **7:05 pm** 4:05 pm
☽ □ ♅ 11:26 pm

DECEMBER 2020

DATE	SID.TIME	SUN	MOON	NODE	MERCURY	VENUS	MARS	JUPITER	SATURN	URANUS	NEPTUNE	PLUTO	CERES	PALLAS	JUNO	VESTA	CHIRON
1 T	4 41 14	9 ♐ 14 46	15 ♊ 57	19 ♊ 53 D	28 ♏ 43	11 ♏ 42	17 ♈ 03	26 ♑ 09	28 ♑ 24	7 ♉ 31 ℞	18 ♓ 10	23 ♑ 16	3 ♓ 42	28 ♑ 01	24 ♏ 07	13 ♍ 29	5 ♈ 03 ℞
2 W	4 45 11	10 15 34	28 11	19 53	0 ♐ 16	12 57	17 16	26 21	28 30	7 29	18 10	23 18	3 55	28 19	24 27	13 46	5 02
3 Th	4 49 7	11 16 24	10 ♋ 34	19 54	1 50	14 11	17 29	26 32	28 35	7 27	18 10	23 19	4 09	28 37	24 47	14 03	5 01
4 F	4 53 4	12 17 14	23 09	19 55	3 23	15 26	17 43	26 44	28 41	7 25	18 10	23 21	4 22	28 56	25 07	14 19	5 00
5 Sa	4 57 0	13 18 06	5 ♌ 58	19 55	4 57	16 41	17 57	26 56	28 47	7 23	18 10	23 22	4 36	29 14	25 27	14 35	5 00
6 Su	5 0 57	14 19 00	19 02	19 56	6 31	17 55	18 12	27 09	28 52	7 21	18 11	23 24	4 50	29 32	25 47	14 51	4 59
7 M	5 4 53	15 19 54	2 ♍ 22	19 56	8 05	19 10	18 27	27 21	28 58	7 20	18 11	23 26	5 04	29 51	26 07	15 07	4 59
8 T	5 8 50	16 20 50	16 01	19 56 ℞	9 38	20 25	18 43	27 33	29 04	7 18	18 11	23 27	5 19	0 ♒ 09	26 27	15 23	4 58
9 W	5 12 47	17 21 47	29 59	19 56	11 12	21 40	19 00	27 45	29 10	7 16	18 11	23 29	5 34	0 28	26 47	15 38	4 58
10 Th	5 16 43	18 22 45	14 ♎ 15	19 56	12 46	22 55	19 17	27 58	29 16	7 14	18 12	23 31	5 48	0 46	27 07	15 53	4 57
11 F	5 20 40	19 23 45	28 48	19 56D	14 20	24 09	19 35	28 10	29 22	7 13	18 12	23 32	6 03	1 05	27 27	16 08	4 57
12 Sa	5 24 36	20 24 46	13 ♏ 32	19 56	15 54	25 24	19 53	28 23	29 28	7 11	18 13	23 34	6 19	1 24	27 47	16 22	4 57
13 Su	5 28 33	21 25 47	28 22	19 56	17 28	26 39	20 11	28 36	29 34	7 10	18 13	23 36	6 34	1 43	28 07	16 37	4 57
14 M	5 32 29	22 26 50	13 ♐ 10	19 56 ℞	19 02	27 54	20 30	28 48	29 40	7 08	18 14	23 38	6 50	2 01	28 27	16 51	4 57
15 T	5 36 26	23 27 54	27 50	19 56	20 36	29 09	20 50	29 01	29 46	7 07	18 14	23 39	7 06	2 20	28 47	17 04	4 56D
16 W	5 40 22	24 28 58	12 ♑ 14	19 56	22 10	0 ♐ 24	21 10	29 14	29 52	7 05	18 15	23 41	7 22	2 39	29 06	17 18	4 56
17 Th	5 44 19	25 30 03	26 17	19 56	23 45	1 39	21 30	29 27	29 59	7 04	18 15	23 43	7 38	2 59	29 26	17 31	4 56
18 F	5 48 16	26 31 08	9 ♒ 57	19 55	25 19	2 54	21 51	29 40	0 ♒ 05	7 02	18 16	23 45	7 54	3 18	29 46	17 44	4 57
19 Sa	5 52 12	27 32 14	23 11	19 54	26 54	4 09	22 12	29 53	0 11	7 01	18 17	23 47	8 11	3 37	0 ♐ 05	17 56	4 57
20 Su	5 56 9	28 33 20	6 ♓ 02	19 53	28 29	5 24	22 34	0 ♒ 06	0 18	7 00	18 17	23 48	8 27	3 56	0 25	18 08	4 57
21 M	6 0 5	29 34 26	18 31	19 52 D	0 ♑ 03	6 39	22 56	0 19	0 24	6 58	18 18	23 50	8 44	4 16	0 44	18 20	4 57
22 T	6 4 2	0 ♑ 35 33	0 ♈ 44	19 52	1 39	7 54	23 18	0 32	0 31	6 57	18 19	23 52	9 01	4 35	1 04	18 32	4 57
23 W	6 7 58	1 36 40	12 44	19 52	3 14	9 09	23 41	0 46	0 37	6 56	18 20	23 54	9 18	4 54	1 23	18 43	4 58
24 Th	6 11 55	2 37 46	24 37	19 53	4 50	10 24	24 04	0 59	0 44	6 55	18 21	23 56	9 36	5 14	1 43	18 54	4 58
25 F	6 15 51	3 38 53	6 ♉ 26	19 54	6 25	11 39	24 28	1 12	0 50	6 54	18 21	23 58	9 53	5 33	2 02	19 04	4 59
26 Sa	6 19 48	4 40 01	18 17	19 56	8 01	12 54	24 51	1 26	0 57	6 53	18 22	24 00	10 11	5 53	2 21	19 15	4 59
27 Su	6 23 45	5 41 08	0 ♊ 14	19 57	9 38	14 09	25 16	1 39	1 04	6 52	18 23	24 02	10 29	6 12	2 40	19 24	5 00
28 M	6 27 41	6 42 16	12 19	19 58 ℞	11 14	15 24	25 40	1 53	1 10	6 51	18 24	24 04	10 46	6 32	2 59	19 34	5 00
29 T	6 31 38	7 43 23	24 35	19 58	12 51	16 39	26 05	2 06	1 17	6 50	18 25	24 05	11 05	6 52	3 18	19 43	5 01
30 W	6 35 34	8 44 31	7 ♋ 04	19 57	14 28	17 54	26 30	2 20	1 24	6 49	18 26	24 07	11 23	7 12	3 37	19 52	5 02
31 Th	6 39 31	9 45 39	19 47	19 55	16 05	19 10	26 56	2 33	1 31	6 49	18 27	24 09	11 41	7 31	3 56	20 00	5 03

EPHEMERIS CALCULATED FOR 12 MIDNIGHT GREENWICH MEAN TIME. ALL OTHER DATA AND FACING ASPECTARIAN PAGE IN **EASTERN TIME (BOLD)** AND PACIFIC TIME (REGULAR).

Notes

Notes

Notes